W9-CYF-931

Daily Reflections for 2021:

Exploring the Message of Our Lady of La Salette

Edited by Fr. Ron Gagné, M.S.

Missionaries of La Salette Corporation
915 Maple Avenue
Hartford, CT 06114-2330, USA

website: www.lasalette.org

First edition (1990s): ISBN 0-9663546-1-3 (pbk), edited by Fr. Roger Plante M.S.

Third Edition (expanded edition): Copyright © September 19, 2020 by Missionaries of Our Lady of La Salette, Province of Mary, Mother of the Americas, 915 Maple Avenue, Hartford, CT, 06106-2330, USA

Imprimi Potest: Rev. Fr. Rene J. Butler, M.S., Provincial Superior Missionaries of Our Lady of La Salette, Province of Mary, Mother of the Americas, 915 Maple Avenue Hartford, CT 06106-2330, USA

All rights reserved. No part of this book may be reproduced, stored in a retrieval system, or transmitted, in any form or by any means, electronic, mechanical, photocopying, recording or otherwise, without the written permission of La Salette Communications Center Publications, 947 Park Street, Attleboro, MA 02703 USA

Scripture texts in this work, unless otherwise indicated, are tak- en from the New Jerusalem Bible and are used by permission of the copyright owner, Catholic Online. (catholic.org). All Rights Re- served. No part of the New Jerusalem Bible may be reproduced in any form without permission in writing from the copyright owner.

Editor: Fr. Ron Gagné, M.S.

Booklet Design & Digital Formatting: Jack Battersby and Fr. Ron Gagné, M.S.

This and other La Salette titles are available in paper, e-book and audiobook formats at: www.Amazon.com, itunes.Apple.com, and www.lasalette.org

Note: Please refer to the Appendix for the La Salette Anniversary Novena, 11th-19th.

ISBN: 978-1-946956-66-8

Introduction

An Expanded Edition

This book is an expanded edition of *Great News: Reflections on the weekday Gospels and the La Salette message*, edited by Fr. Roger Plante, M.S. in the late 1990s. We have added reflections for all Sundays and Feasts of the year. This edition is intended for use in the year 2021 with its day-by-day reflections and their daily lectionary numbers for your reference.

Our Authors, Past and Present

All our authors are connected to La Salette and come from all parts of the United States, Canada and, in a few cases, from other parts of the English-speaking world. They have participated in a variety of ministries in the La Salette Congregation and in the Church: parish ministry, retreat and parish missions, missions abroad, education and religious formation, as well as community administration.

They are a great mix of brothers, priests and laity, yet they have one thing in common: a love of the La Salette Event. They were asked to "sit with the mystery " of Mary's Apparition at La Salette which happened in 1846. In these daily Gospel Meditations, they share their personal sensitivity to the Lord's call, "Come, follow me," and his Mother's plea at La Salette, "Make this known to all my people."

Our La Salette Anniversary Year

From September 19th, 2020 to September 19th, 2021, the La Salette Missionaries worldwide are celebrating the 175th Anniversary of the La Salette Apparition with all those who have devotion to Our Weeping Mother. We invite you, in using this book for your reflection, to avail yourself of the special La Salette Anniversary Novena included in our Appendix at the end of this book. From the 11th to the 19th of each month your will be invited to pray this Novena of nine days for any personal intention. May Mary guide you and God bless you!

Fr. Ron Gagné, M.S., editor

Our Authors

Sundays of the Year: Wayne Vanasse and Rev. Fr. René Butler, M.S., Provincial; Feast Days of the Year: Fr. Ronald G. Gagné, M.S.

Advent - Christmas

Advent weeks 1-2: Fr. Camille J. Doucet, M.S.

Advent week 3: Fr. Gilles M. Genest, M.S.

December 17-24: Fr. Donald L. Paradis, M.S.

Christmas and January 2-7: Fr. Edward J. Richard, M.S.

Epiphany: Bro. Robert J. Belliveau, M.S.

Lent – Easter

Ash Wednesday and Week 1 of Lent: Fr. Richard W. Lavoie, M.S.

Weeks 2 and 3 of Lent: Fr. Robert J. Campbell, M.S.

Weeks 4 and 5 of Lent: Fr. George B. Brennan

Holy Week and Easter Octave: Fr. Eugene G. Barrette, M.S.

Weeks 2 and 3 of Easter: Fr. Donald L. Paradis, M.S.

Weeks 4 and 5 of Lent: Fr. John R. Nuelle, M.S.

Weeks 6 and 7 of Easter: Daniel P. Bradley

Ordinary Time

Weeks 1 and 2 in Ordinary Time: Fr. William Kaliyadan, M.S.

Week 3 in Ordinary Time: Fr. Terry E. Niziolek, M.S.

Week 4 in Ordinary Time: Fr. Fernand Cassista, M.S.

Weeks 5 and 6 in Ordinary Time: Fr. Manuel C. Pereira, M.S.

Weeks 7 and 8 in Ordinary Time: Fr. Terry E. Niziolek, M.S.

Weeks 9 and 10 in Ordinary Time: Fr. John F. Gabriel, M.S.

Weeks 11 and 12 in Ordinary Time: Fr. Leo C. Holleran, M.S.

Weeks 13 and 14 in Ordinary Time: Fr. Joseph P. Gosselin, M.S.

Weeks 15 and 16 in Ordinary Time: Fr. Joseph M. O'Neil, M.S.

Prologue:

The Story of the La Salette Apparition

On Saturday, September 19, 1846, a "Beautiful Lady" appeared to two children, both from Corps, in France Alps: Maximin Giraud, eleven-year-old, and Mélanie Calvat, almost fifteen, who were watching their herds on the slope of Mont Planeau, approximately 6,000 feet in altitude, not far from the village of La Salette. In a little hollow, they suddenly noticed a globe of fire – "as though the sun had fallen on the spot." Within the dazzling light they gradually perceived a woman, seated, her elbows resting on her knees and her face buried in her hands.

The Beautiful Lady rose, and said to the children in French:

Come closer, my children; don't be afraid. I am here to tell you great news.

She took a few steps towards them. Maximin and Mélanie, reassured, ran down to her and stood very close to her.

The Beautiful Lady wept all the time she spoke. She was tall, and everything about her radiated light. She wore the typical garb of the women of the area: a long dress, and apron around her waist, a shawl crossed over her breast and tied behind her back, and a close-fitting

3

Discovery of the Weeping
Mother

bonnet. Along the hem of her shawl she wore a broad, flat chain, and from a smaller chain around her neck there hung a large crucifix.

Under the arms of the cross there were, to the left of the figure of Christ, a hammer, and, to the right, pincers. The radiance of the en- tire apparition seemed to emanate from this crucifix, and shone like a brilliant crown upon the Beautiful Lady's head. She wore garlands of roses on her head, around the edge of her shawl and around her feet.

The Beautiful Lady spoke to the two shepherds. first in French, in these words:

If my people refuse to submit, I will be forced to let go the arm of my Son. It is so strong and so heavy, I can no longer hold it back.

How long a time I have suffered for you! If I want my Son not to abandon you, I am obliged to plead with him constantly. And as for you, you pay no heed!

However much you pray, however much you do, you will never be able to recom- pense the pains I have taken for you.

I gave you six days to work; I kept the seventh for myself, and no one will give it to me. This is what makes the arm of my Son so heavy. And then, those who drive the carts cannot swear without throwing in my Son's name. These are the two things that make the arm of my Son so heavy.

If the harvest is ruined, it is only on account of yourselves. I warned you last year with the potatoes. You paid no heed. Instead, when you found the potatoes spoiled, you swore, and threw in my Son's name. They are going to continue to spoil, and by Christmas this year there will be none left.

Mélanie was intrigued by the expression, pommes de terre. In the local dialect, potatoes were called las truffas. She looked inquiringly

4

at Maximin, but the Beautiful Lady anticipated her question.

Don't you understand, my children? Let me find another way to say it.

Using the local dialect, she repeated what she had said about the harvest, and then went on:

If you have wheat, you must not sow it. Anything you sow the vermin will eat, and whatever does grow will fall into dust when you thresh it.

A great famine is coming. Before the famine comes, children under seven will be seized with trembling and die in the arms of the persons who hold them. The rest will do penance through the famine. The walnuts will become worm-eat- en; the grapes will rot.

At this point the Beautiful Lady confided a secret to Maximin, and then to Mélanie. then she went on:

If they are converted, rocks and stones will turn into heaps of wheat, and potatoes will be self- sown in the fields.

Do you say your prayers well, my children?

"Hardly ever, Madam," the two shepherds answered candidly.

Ah, my children, you should say them well, at night and in the morning, even if you say only an Our Father and a Hail Mary when you can't do better. When you can do better, say more.

In the summer, only a few elderly women go to Mass. The rest work on Sundays all summer long. In the winter, when they don't know what to do, they go to Mass just to make fun of religion. In Lent they go to the butcher shops like dogs.

Have you never seen wheat gone bad, my children?

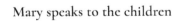

Mary speaks to the children

They answered, "No, Madam."

The Beautiful Lady then spoke to Maximin.

But you, my child, surely you must have seen some once, at Coin, with

5

your father. The owner of the field told your father to go and see his spoiled wheat. And then you went, and you took two or three ears of wheat in your hands, you rubbed them together, and it all crumbled into dust. While you were on your way back and you were no more than a half hour away from Corps, your father gave you a piece of bread and said to you: "Here, my child, eat some bread while we still have it this year; because I don't know who will eat any next year if the wheat keeps up like that."

"Oh, yes," answered Maximin, "Now I remember. Just then, I didn't remember it."

The Beautiful Lady then concluded, not in dialect but in French:

Well, my children you will make this known to all my people.

Then she moved forward, stepped over the stream, and without turning back she gave the injunction.

Very well, my children make this known to all my people.

The vision climbed the steep path which wound its way towards the Collet (little neck). Then she rose into the air as the children caught up to her. She looked up at the sky, then down to the earth. Facing southeast, "she melted into light." The light itself then disappeared.

On September 19, 1851, after "a precise and rigorous investigation" of the event, the witnesses, the content of the message, and its repercussions, Philibert de Bruillard, Bishop of Grenoble, pronounced his judgment in a pastoral letter of instruction. He declared that "the apparition of the Blessed Virgin to two shepherds, September 19, 1846, on a mountain in the Alps, located in the parish of La Salette,... bears within itself all the characteristics of truth and that the faithful have grounds for believing it to be indubitable and certain."

In another pastoral letter, dated May 1, 1852, the Bishop of Grenoble announced the construction of a Shrine on the mountain of the apparition, and went on to add:

"However important the erection of a Shrine may be there is something still more important, namely the ministers of religion destined to look after it, to receive the pious pilgrims, to preach the word of God to them, to exercise towards them the ministry of reconciliation, to administer the Holy Sacrament of the altar, and to be, to all, the faithful dispensers of the mysteries of God and the spiritual treasures of the Church.

"These priests shall be called the Missionaries of Our Lady of La Salette; their institution and existence shall be, like the Shrine itself, and eternal monument, a perpetual remembrance, of Mary's merciful apparition."

The first priests imbued with the spirit of the Apparition and who devoted themselves to the service of the pilgrims, felt from the beginning the call to and the need for religious life. Six of them pronounced their first vows on February 2, 1858, in accordance with their provisional Constitutions, adapted in 1862 to include Brothers. From that time, Fathers and Brothers have constituted one religious family.

Mary's apparition at La Salette is a modern-day reminder of an ancient truth: that Mary constantly intercedes for us before God; that she is the Reconciler of Sinners, calling us back to the message and way of her Son, Jesus.

Mary melted into light

Reflection Questions:

- What quality do you most admire about Mary's appearance at La Salette?
- When and where did you first hear the message of Our Lady of La Salette?

Prayer:

Mary, Humble Maiden, your message and witness on the Mountain of La Salette is that of a true reconciler. You invite us to draw near, you speak to our hearts and then you send us off to spread your message of faith, forgiveness and good news to all your people.

As Mother of the Church, you are concerned about our daily life with its challenges and blessings. In your goodness, assist us in our journey of faith; guide us with your loving presence and assure us of your Son's grace as we make our way together, back to the Father.

We ask this through your intercession, and in the name of your Son, Jesus, who lives with the Father and the Holy Spirit, one God, fore ever and ever. **Amen.**

La Salette Invocation:

Our Lady of La Salette, Reconciler of Sinners, pray without ceasing for us who have recourse to you.

Friday, January 1 (#018)
Feast of Mary, Mother of God

Luke 2:16-21: *"As for Mary, she treasured all these things and pondered them in her heart."*

Reflection:

A woman tells of her 105 year old grandmother, Edna. From the time Edna turned 90 her quality of life took a significant turn. Her body ached all over. She couldn't see well enough to read, write, crochet, or even watch TV. She couldn't hear well enough to carry a conversation. Edna spent much of the last 15 years of her life in her recliner, sitting in silence staring out the window at birds she couldn't see. What a way to live! And yet, Edna never grew despondent. She always seemed content and happy. She was never one to complain. One day, her daughter asked, "Mama, tell me, what do you think about all day long?" "O honey," Edna responded, "I've got enough memories to last a lifetime."

The Madonna of the Book **by Sandro Botticelli (1445-1510)**

What is the job description of the Mother of God? I imagine it might say, "First: do what all mothers do – love them always; be a good example to them; respond to their needs; correct them when it's needed. And when they grow up, accept them as they are. Second: treasure your memories. On this feast of Mary, the Mother of God, we hear in the gospel that she began treasuring her memories of Jesus from his very birth. And fortunately she is our mother from the time when Jesus gave her to us, the members of the Church, on the cross at Calvary.

IF THERE IS ANY QUALITY WHICH MARY SHOWED AT LA SALETTE with the two children it was her mothering of them: *"Come near, my children, do not be afraid... See, let me tell it to you another way..."* Mary was a "mother personified" in her solicitous attention, her love and compassion and even her direction to make her message known. She wanted the children to become loving and faithful members of the Church, true evangelizers of her only Son.

Reflection Questions:

- Can you remember an event or quality which you cherish about your own mother?
- What would Mary say to you about your own life as an active Catholic, as a follower of her Son?

Saturday, January 2 (#205)

John 1:19-28: *"So (John the Baptist) said, 'I am, as Isaiah prophesied: A voice of one that cries in the desert: Prepare a way for the Lord. Make his paths straight!'"*

Meditation:

When John the Baptizer comes proclaiming the Messiah, his role is something like a parent's when he or she introduces the child to a Christian way of life. Like John who prepares the way for the reception of Jesus and points him out when he arrives, parents are the ones who will introduce the child to Jesus. John describes his own identity as "a voice of one that cries in the desert." This is his response to the question, *"Who are you?"* His answer tells us that John's identity cannot be fully known without Jesus. Christian parents also find the fullness of their personalities in the living witness they give to their children about the life and teachings of Jesus. Jesus Christ reveals to us the truth about ourselves.

THE TRUTH ABOUT THE PARENTAL ROLE and the meaning of one's personal identity in Jesus is once again portrayed when Our Lady comes to La Salette to herald the Good News. It is clearly Mary's desire to open up the hearts of the children to receive her Son. As always in authentic Catholic practice, we rightly think of Mary and her role in salvation as being inseparable from Jesus himself. And so it is with

Christian parents. The truth about the role of parents in relationship to their children, even their own identity, is discovered and fully understood in relationship to Jesus as one who wants their children to know him.

Reflection Questions:

- Who am I? Is my relationship with Jesus the most important aspect of my personality?
- What does it mean to be a father or mother according to the Gospel?

Sunday, January 3 (#020_02)
The Epiphany of the Lord

(Isaiah 60:1-6; Ephesians 3:2-6; Matthew 2:1-12)

Meditation: *Epiphanies*

Adoration of the Magi by **Raphael** (1483 - 15200)

For Christians, the word Epiphany has a limited, specific meaning. If you look it up in a dictionary of Ancient Greek, you might be surprised to see how many meanings it has. Examples include: what something looks like; when something or someone comes into view; what is visible on the surface; the sensation created by someone. In short, something or someone is seen or noticed.

The Magi created a sensation when they arrived in Jerusalem. Before that, they saw a star come into view. They received an epiphany and

11

then became one themselves when they appeared on the scene.

Another translation of the Greek word is simply Appearance, interchangeable with Apparition.

AT LA SALETTE, the bright globe of light the children first noticed revealed within itself a woman seated, her face in her hands, weeping. Thus begins the story of her epiphany, her Apparition. Mélanie and Maximin described what they saw. This created a sensation. We could paraphrase the words of the Gospel and say: The mayor was greatly troubled, and all the region around La Salette with him. And, like Herod, local authorities tried to hush everything up.

Epiphanies are not restricted to visual phenomena, however. Just as we say, "I see," meaning "I understand," there is more to an epiphany than meets the eye.

This is why we devote more attention to the message of the Beautiful Lady than to her appearance; why we study the history of the event, before and after September 19, 1846; why the lives of the two children matter; and why the Apparition is still an epiphany today.

Isaiah, as a prophet, experienced many epiphanies. St. Paul experienced one, on the Road to Damascus. As a result, both proclaimed the inclusion of the Gentiles in God's plan of salvation: "Nations shall walk by your light;" "The Gentiles are coheirs... copartners in the promise in Christ Jesus."

The Magi represented the Nations. They walked by the light of a star which changed their lives.

As long as La Salette remains an epiphany, it will have the power to change lives.

Monday, January 4, (#212)
Monday After Epiphany

Matthew 4:12-17,23-25: *"The people that lived in darkness have seen a great light."*

Meditation:

Jesus traveled to Capernaum so that what Isaiah had prophesied might be fulfilled. His disciples are called one by one to follow him. As for them, on being called they left what they were doing, in fact leaving everything behind. In following Jesus they experienced first-hand, so to speak, his ministry, his proclamation of the Good News, his healing of the sick, the lame and the blind. Their eyes, too, were opened and they became Christ's first and most dedicated followers.

WE, TOO, ARE CALLED BY MARY at La Salette to follow Jesus, her Son. She came in radiant light and in tears to remind us of Jesus' love for us all. How do we respond to her message? *"Do not be afraid,"* were the words she spoke to nudge us that we might listen to and proclaim the Good News of her Son in and through our own life. Let us respond as well as we can to her message of reconciliation by truly being her "children" and followers of Christ, her Son.

Reflection Questions:

- How can I share the word of Christ with those I meet today?
- Who were the first people to share their faith with me in my youth?

Tuesday, January 5, (#213)
Tuesday After Epiphany

Mark 6:34-44: *"Give them something to eat yourselves."*

Meditation:

On seeing the crowd Jesus *"took pity on them."* He saw – perhaps felt is the better word – their hunger. And so he told his disciples to feed them. Not mentioned, but most probably on his mind, was a deeper and more significant hunger, a spiritual hunger. The crowd was there primarily to hear Jesus' words, his message of love, concern and compassion. So, the gospel tells us, *"he set himself to teach them at some length."*

MARY AT LA SALETTE does the same for Maximin and Melanie, the two witnesses. She too pitied "her people." She taught them, gave them a message, and spoke to them of God's hunger. How often do we pass by the hungry without even a glance in their direction – not to mention stopping to feed them spiritually, with a kind word or a moment's attention? The apparition at La Salette did not last very long, but its message and impact have proven timeless.

Reflection Questions:

- What can I do to relieve the hunger of those I meet?
- When has someone fed me by their presence, their witness, their words of comfort or inspiration?

Wednesday, January 6, (#214)
Wednesday After Epiphany

Mark 6:45-52: *"Courage! It's me! Don't be afraid."*

Meditation:

Fear! What a big part of life it can be. In the city at night, one senses how fearful the people can be who must walk alone to their cars or the bus stop after work. Apartment dwellers too are often apprehensive in their neighborhood. A change of work, of ministry, an entirely new situation can often make our stomach fluttery and result in sleepless nights. We are afraid of what an unknown situation may demand of us. We are fearful when the future looks rather uncertain or our job security is shaken. Some of our fears are an appropriate and necessary response to perilous prospects; these fears can help prepare us to adapt to new circumstances, provided we do not allow them to paralyze us. One of the goals of the Christian life should be to live in confidence and trust, free of useless fears. The Lord is with us on the stormy sea. He reassures us not to be afraid.

MARY ADDRESSES OUR FEAR AS WELL. She tells us: *"Come near, my children; do not be afraid."* She bids us draw close to her and to her Son. She came in tears, but not in fear. She also came in love and with much compassion for us, her people, to console us in our anxieties and confusion, just as Jesus did in behalf of his disciples.

Reflection Questions:

- What fears do I bring to my daily encounters?
- What events has frightened me in the past?

Thursday, January 7, (#215)
Thursday After Epiphany

Luke 4:14-22a: *"The Spirit of the Lord is on me."*

Meditation:

And then Jesus adds, still quoting Isaiah, *"to proclaim a year of favor from the Lord."* We know from subsequent happenings that the Lord did not simply announce a year of favor but centuries and lifetimes of God's favor, the Good News we call the Gospel. We, among many others, have been blessed by it. A single term which sums up what we've been given is faith. Our parents and godparents were asked at our Baptism what they were asking in our behalf; their response was faith. With the help of parents, under the influence of teachers and mentors, that faith has grown. Faith primarily means trust and confidence in God through Christ. It reassures us that our life and the world are in God's hands. Beyond this, faith means a way of seeing the world and life itself.

Faith conquers the world because it gives us assurance about important things relative to life and this world which mere human eyesight or insight could never detect. And so it is that by faith we know that – despite devastating illnesses, tragic accidents, crimes and war – life, joy and peace will have the final say. "Your world," it tells us, "is a world God has loved and will go on loving forever."

MARY ANNOUNCED this same message of life, joy and peace in Christ, her Son. Her words brought tidings of gospel gladness. They reminded us that God continues to break into our world with the joy of salvation, as sin is forgiven, death is destroyed, and broken hearts are healed.

Reflection Questions:

• How faithful am I in sharing this Good News with those I meet?
• How often have I stopped in prayer to thank God for God's many gifts, especially those people I truly treasure?

Friday, January 8, (#216)
Friday After Epiphany

Luke 5:12-16: *"Sir, if you are willing you can cleanse me."*

Meditation:

In spite of our faith, despite the fact that we have been baptized, in spite of all our good works, daily Masses and thousands of communions, we still might have those days when we wonder if we are going to heaven or not. Will God really forgive me my sins, especially the real terrible ones? For gossiping, for my unkindnesses, my lies, my insults? There are so many skeletons in our soul's closet that we might well worry from time to time whether or not we have really been forgiven? From experience we have all discovered that once a thing is done, there is no going back and undoing it. Yes, we can surely make a mess of our lives.

Though I most certainly do not advocate wrongdoing, I recognize that if it were not for the sins we have already committed, especially the most grievous, would we be going to Mass every Sunday, even daily? Would we have made Christ so central to our lives? Would we have returned to him again and again, confessed our sorrow to him, and relied so desperately on his love and forgiveness? A question we could ask about the leper in Luke's gospel story: Would he have gone to Jesus if he hadn't been suffering from leprosy? Jesus cured the man's body. He cures our souls. All we need do is ask, and choose to believe.

BY HER INVITATION that we *"Come near"*, Mary asks that we too draw near to her Son, the Christ. She invites us to come to him that we may find relief from our burdens and refreshment for our spirits. This desire of the Lord is Mary's as well, that her children, meaning ourselves, should feel welcomed, loved and forgiven.

Reflection Questions:

- What makes me hesitate to come to Jesus for help?
- Who has helped me in the past? Who would unhesitatingly respond to my needs?

Saturday, January 9, (#217)
Saturday After Epiphany

John 3:22-30: *"He must grow greater, I must grow less."*

Meditation:

Probably all of us at one time or another have wished that we could be President of the United States, at least for a day. We think of all the things we would do. Imagine being the chief resident of the White House for four or eight years. One could do so much good for so many people, not to mention the fabulous parties one would be invited to attend. But what happens when it is all over? And someone else takes your place? I would think it would be a big comedown – to be number one no longer.

Corporation presidents must step down, store managers, pastors, religious superiors, assembly-line workers must all move on to make space for others. Even parents must let their grown children be. Others must come to center stage while we step to one side. The same holds true of our decision-making. Christians are to live according to God's will, not their own. We are to do God's thing, not our own thing. Are we willing to do that – only if we are willing to decrease and let Christ increase in our lives.

OUR LADY OF LA SALETTE chose two simple children to be her messengers. They certainly could not have been lower in social standing – simple, poor, uneducated shepherds. But they were chosen above all others. Isn't that what we see ourselves as – Mary's chosen sons and daughters, being able to let go of our positions, whatever they may be? We are called to follow the Lord in humble service, living up to what Mary and her Son ask of us.

Reflection Questions:

• How willing am I to "let go and let Jesus" take over every aspect of my life?
• How trusting am I of even my closest friends, allowing them to help me when I need them the most?

Sunday, January 10 (#021B)
The Baptism of the Lord

(Isaiah 55:1-11; Acts 10:34-38; Mark 1:7-11)

Meditation: *Acceptable*

The Baptism of Christ
by Hans Brosamer (1495-1554)

St. Peter says to Cornelius, "In every nation whoever fears God and acts uprightly is acceptable to him." This seems hardly a lavish endorsement. Imagine telling your acquaintances that they are "acceptable"!

For St. Peter, however, being acceptable to God is a wonderful thing. It is very nearly the same as saying that God is "pleased," with us, as he is with the Suffering Servant in Isaiah. That idea is expanded in today's Gospel, to include also the notion of "beloved."

The opposite of "acceptable" is "unacceptable." At La Salette Mary came to say that her People's attitude and behavior were unacceptable to her Son—inconsistent, incompatible and incongruous with the baptism they had received.

UNACCEPTABLE AS WE MAY BE, we nevertheless remain beloved, for God is love and cannot not love. All the more reason, then, for us to want to please him.

Jonathan Edwards, a preacher in colonial New England, gave a famous sermon in 1741 which bears the title, "Sinners in the Hands of an Angry God." For many decades after the Apparition of La Salette, Mary's message was usually interpreted in that very spirit. In fact, as I have had occasion to note before, the first Memorare to Our Lady of La Salette refers to the pains she has taken to "shield me from the justice of God."

St. Peter's comment about "whoever fears God" must not be taken in that light. "Fear of the Lord," a Gift of the Spirit, has nothing to do with dread, but with deep, abiding respect for all that pertains to God (his Name, his Day, etc.)

We can try to please others for two reasons: 1) we stand to gain by it, or 2) we do so simply out of love. It's a little like "imperfect and perfect contrition" (Catechism of the Catholic Church, nos. 1451-1453 and 1492). Both are good, but one it so much better than the other.

There is no question about how Mary wishes us to please God. She knows we are his beloved children. Responding to that love would make us so much more than acceptable.

Monday, January 11, (#305)
First Week in Ordinary Time

Note: Today you may wish to begin the First Day of the Novena to Our Lady of La Salette, in the appendix of this book.

Mark 1:14-20: *"And at once (the disciples) left their nets and followed (Jesus)."*

Meditation:

The gospel reading tells us about Christ calling some fishermen to share with him the responsibility of gathering God's family and proclaiming the Good News of salvation. Soon after he had begun his public life Jesus wanted to lay a solid foundation for the continuation of his mission. Although he was not as popular at this early stage of his ministry as his miracles and acts of mercy would later make him, Jesus succeeded with his plan to build up his staff. His presence and words must have been tremendously powerful and marvelously inviting. As both God's message and messenger, he is the cornerstone of the Kingdom. He must gather to himself a small band of kindred spirits to whom he can unburden his own heart and upon whose hearts he may write his message. Christ approaches these men in their own life situation, as they were carrying out their daily chores. In response to the call, the fishermen left behind their precious nets and began to walk the dusty roads of Palestine with Jesus.

At La Salette Mary spoke the words of her Son, *"Come near, my children...."* God's invitation is continuously extended through Mary. She comes to us with a plea that we abandon our sinful ways and turn back to Christ. She calls us near him, because as a person she knew the pain of being in this world of alienation and suffering. She is truly our mother whose heart yearns to help us find lasting refuge in Jesus, the Savior. Her entire conversation focused on him. He comes to us, as he did to his first recruits, in our daily struggles and tasks.

Reflection Questions:

- Like Mary should we not center our focus on Christ?
- What holds us back from abandoning our nets and favorite shores?

Tuesday, January 12, (#306)
First Week in Ordinary Time

Mark 1:21-28: *"What do you want with us, Jesus of Nazareth?"*

Meditation:

Jesus began his preaching in the synagogue, primarily an institution of learning. In tone and method, his teaching struck his listeners as a new revelation. He did not teach like the scribes, the experts in the Law. He was a man with a message. He spoke that message with authority and power. He himself was the new Torah, the supreme rule of faith and life. Such authority astonished his audience and the evil powers. "What have you to do with us? Mind your business. Go away. Go anywhere so long as you don't interfere with our ways." The powers wished to go on exploiting men, women, youth, and children, wanted to keep them addicted, bound by hatred and jealousy, burdened by inhuman abuse and cruelty. To this cry of the evil spirit, Jesus answered, *"Be quiet! Come out of him."* He makes the same answer today. He is concerned with every burden that weighs heavily on human shoulders.

At La Salette Our Lady brought a message of freedom to her people. A freedom that requires complete trust in God and obedience to his will. *"If my people will not submit, I shall be forced to let fall the arm of my Son."* Mary's words were spoken from her heart. They were not meant to alarm us with the fear of punishment but to sharpen our concern about our personal relationship with Jesus. She urges us to cultivate that relationship so that he might become more transparent in our lives as we grow more confident in his power. His power can and must own and possess us.

Reflection Questions:

- We all need to be owned and possessed. By whom shall I be possessed?
- Have I allowed Jesus to manifest his authority over my whole life?

Wednesday, January 13, (#307)
First Week in Ordinary Time

Mark 1:29-39: *"(Jesus) went in to her, took her by the hand and helped her up."*

Meditation:

Peter's mother-in-law was ill; the simple household was upset. And for the disciples the most natural thing in the world was to tell Jesus about it. After the exhausting experience of the synagogue service, Jesus could have claimed the right to rest. But once again nothing could keep him from doing good. The need of others took precedence over his desire for rest. He could feel the anxiety and concern of his disciples. He did not wait for an audience in order to exercise his healing power. He was there to heal Peter's mother-in-law. That world is our world, a world full of men and women haunted by fear, burdened with worry. This world seeks a healer. Personal fatigue could not keep Jesus from performing an act of kindness and healing. We must learn to look at people with compassion, to feel their anguish of heart. We are never blessed for ourselves alone, but for *others*.

THE APPARITION AT LA SALETTE is rooted in the vision our Mother has of us, her needy, poor, sinful and wretched children. Her never-tiring and endless love finds expression in the tears she shed at La Salette. There she opened her heart and spoke to Maximin and Melanie in a soft and tender voice. Through them, she was speaking to us as well. Like that of Jesus, Mary's compassion overflowed in tears. We are eternally grateful to God for giving us such a mother. She appears to us in our daily lives with a helping hand. Since we long for healing, she will certainly lead us to Christ, her Son.

Reflection Questions:

- Isn't it true that tiredness is often used as an excuse for not doing good?
- *"And let us never slacken in doing good"* (Galatians 6:9) How can I put this sound advice of the apostle Paul into practice?

Thursday, January 14, (#308)
First Week in Ordinary Time

Mark 1:40-45: *"Feeling sorry for him, Jesus stretched out his hand, touched him."*

Meditation:

The psychologist Erich Fromm wrote: "Alienation as we find it in modern society is almost total; it pervades the relationship of man to his work, to the things he consumes, to the State, to his fellowmen and to himself." Today's gospel speaks about this sort of alienation. In the New Testament no disease terrified people nor moved them to pity more than leprosy. The leper's fate was indeed hard. Ritually unclean, the leper was to remain segregated from the community, avoid all contact with others. Though he had no right to approach or to speak to him, the leper sensed that Jesus' compassion was his only recourse. Upon receiving his healing the man could not contain his inner joy. His heart overflowed with boundless gratitude. The Lord could have cured him from a distance, but chose to do so by touching him. We, too, must help others; but we must be ready to touch one another's lives. We must make sure that our care, our concern and our love touch those who need our help.

"SHE WEPT ALL THE WHILE SHE SPOKE TO US," the children of La Salette reported. Mary's tears spoke more loudly of her inner beauty, one of her most attractive characteristics as a woman. Mary was present, as always, to bring life, to give care, to show love. It is a wonderfully feminine virtue to be there with passion for those one loves, especially in moments of affliction and distress. She was there in tears on the mountain with Maximin and Melanie, representatives both of our broken world.

Reflection Questions:

- Can we see Our Lady's tears as a reflection of the sorrow and pity of the Son as he looks upon an ailing and wounded world?
- What attitude of mine might repel those in my life circle?

Friday, January 15, (#309)
First Week in Ordinary Time

Mark 2:1-12: *"... some people came bringing him a paralytic carried by four men."*

Meditation:

The crowd had jammed the pavement around the door to listen to Jesus. Into this crowd came four men bearing on a stretcher a friend who was paralyzed. We are not told his name nor the names of those who brought him to Jesus. They are referred to simply as "four men." Where would this world be without such people? They were the first of an endless company of those who have made it possible for others to reach the healing hands of Christ, anonymous apostles doing good quietly, unselfishly and without fanfare. People whose names never make the headlines. When he saw the faith of these four men Jesus must have smiled an understanding and affirming smile. In his sight, this was a loud proclamation of living faith. In what was perhaps one of the most joyous moments in his ministry, he looked at the man, and said, *"My child, your sins are forgiven."* Healer of soul and body, Jesus is truly Lord of life.

MARY'S WORDS AT LA SALETTE reiterate the baptismal call of every believer. She appeared not to add fame or glory to her credit but to bring us her Son's healing touch. Her persistent and enduring love compels her to intercede for us and to carry us to Jesus. Probably that is why her appearance and intercession are known in every corner of the world. Her message is a worldwide call to rediscover Jesus as Savior; it breaks down our self-erected barriers that we might immerse our paralyzed selves in Christ's healing love.

Reflection Questions:

- What hinders me from going out of my way to help others?
- Where should I look for the motivation to deal with pockets of inertia in my own Christian life?

Saturday, January 16, (#310)
First Week in Ordinary Time

Mark 2:13-17: *"(Jesus) said to him, 'Follow me.'"*

Meditation:

Jesus was walking by the lakeside, teaching like any rabbi of his day. He must have stopped when he saw Matthew, a tax collector in his booth. Tax collectors extracted from people as much as they possibly could and filled their own pockets with the surplus once the law's requirements had been met. Matthew was, therefore, thoroughly hated. He was sitting in his office, sitting in his sins, in his own world of alienation and public scorn.

But he had the will to respond to the entirely unexpected call of Jesus, *"Follow me."* He had probably heard about Jesus; he might have listened on the fringes of crowds to his message, and some-thing must have stirred in his heart at Jesus' words. He sprang to his feet, followed Jesus and spent his life in the service of the one who lifted him out of his emptiness and sin. Matthew manifested his gratitude by hosting a banquet, a tangible expression of reconciliation with God. A meal shared is, in fact, a life shared.

WE LEARN ABOUT PERSONAL INVOLVEMENT from the children of La Salette. They were called to proclaim their Beautiful Lady's good news. Her apparition blessed and marked their lives. Every blessing comes with a corresponding duty, a responsibility they did not shirk. Before and after the apparition, we see in them an amazing willing-ness to move freely with the Spirit. Leaving their beloved mountains and their untroubled way of life behind, they lent their words, their hearts and their sufferings to this stirring message. Discipleship in-volves extra sacrifice and a life-long commitment.

Reflection Questions:

- How does the Eucharist, the meal I share with my Lord, affect my personal conversion?

•When counting my blessings, do I give a thought to the responsibility each of them entails?

Sunday, January 17 (#065)
Second Sunday in Ordinary Time

(1 Samuel 3:3-19; 1 Corinthians 6:13-20; John 1:35-42)

Meditation: *Translation*

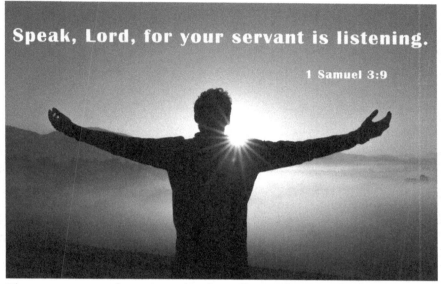

Speak, Lord, for your servant is listening.

1 Samuel 3:9

Three times in today's Gospel, John tells us what a Hebrew word means. We can conclude, therefore, that his audience was not familiar with them, and that he considered it important or, at least, useful to know and understand them. There are many similar cases in the New Testament, most notably the cry of Jesus on the Cross: *Eli, Eli, lama sabachthani (My God, my God, why have you forsaken me).*

Our Lady of La Salette, observing that at one point the children appeared confused, said, "Don't you understand, my children? Let me find another way to say it." Then she translated the previous sentence or two into their dialect, and continued speaking that way almost to the very end of her message. She, too, knew the importance of understanding.

In the first reading, old Eli explained to young Samuel the nature of the voice he was hearing, and the importance of listening to it. After that, the boy went on to become one of the greatest of God's spokespersons, discerning and interpreting God's will for the people and their rulers.

St. Paul, without using the word, deals with a different kind of translation, not from one language to another, but from theory to practice or, better, from faith to life. He reminds the Corinthians that they have become temples of the Holy Spirit, and must act accordingly. Elsewhere he writes that because of that same Spirit we can call God Abba. Even in modern Hebrew, that is the name by which children call their father.

AT LA SALETTE, THE BEAUTIFUL LADY LAMENTS that her people have failed to translate their Christian heritage into a Christian way of life, that life which is sometimes called simply 'the Way' in the Acts of the Apostles.

This reflection gives me the opportunity to thank three men in a special way. Brother Moisés Rueda, M.S., and Mr. Paul Dion, have been faithfully translating these reflections every week, respectively into Spanish and French; and Fr. Henryk Przeździecki, M.S., publishes them on the Internet. Together they make these reflections accessible to so many whom I cannot reach.

But you don't really need to be a linguist to translate the message of La Salette. Just live it!

Monday, January 18, (#311)
Second Week in Ordinary Time

Mark 2:18-22: *"As long as they have the bridegroom with them, they cannot fast."*

Meditation:

In the Jewish faith fasting was mandatory only one day in the entire year, and that was the Day of Atonement. Stricter Jews fasted two days each week. Jesus did not oppose fasting as such. It could help people learn to appreciate and value God's gifts, gain spiritual strength against evil and focus entirely on God. He faulted the Pharisees for making their fasting a way of drawing attention to their own righteousness, rather than a genuine expression of devotion to God. Fasting accompanied the rites of mourning in Israel. Jesus was with his disciples still; so there was no need to fast. It was time to celebrate and feast with him at table. We touch here the interplay between Advent and Christmas, between Good Friday and Easter. Our entire life in Christ is interplay between fasting and feasting. The Lord is truly present to us, yet we await his coming in glory. We receive the Lord in our hearts in the Eucharist, but that presence will not be complete until he comes again.

WHEN SHE HELPED HIM RECALL the day he saw the fragile wheat at Coin with his father, Mary at La Salette reminded Maximin that God's care is constant. Eucharist is an everlasting reminder of God's love for us. Our attitude, experience, understanding, and our voice are all-important to our appreciation of God's coming to us in the Eucharist. Each moment of our lives must be a crystal clear reflection of the Lord who comes to us through bread, broken and shared. Our abstinence and our sacrifice will enable us to savor the Eucharistic mystery and center our lives on the Lord's table.

Reflection Questions:

• *"As long as they have the bridegroom with them, they cannot fast."* Have we lost this joy?
• Have we lost the sense of the Lord's presence in our midst whether we are at home, at Mass or elsewhere?

Tuesday, January 19, (#312)
Second Week in Ordinary Time

Mark 2:23-28: *"The Son of man is master even of the Sabbath."*

Meditation:

In their deep reverence for God's command that the Lord's Day be kept holy, the Pharisees elaborated some thirty-nine rules governing its proper observance; they ranged from a prohibition against harvesting grain to a ban on carrying heavy loads. What made their attitude devious was their use of God's command to impose burdens on people, thereby complicating their lives. "What is the purpose of the law?" is a question we should often ask ourselves. Blind obedience to law, whether civil, moral or spiritual, is never enough. This can make narrow-minded or scrupulous Christians of us. We need to educate ourselves to each law's intent, the reason behind God's inspiration of that particular precept. Does our fondness for gossip reveal a hidden desire to appear wiser and holier than others? The Pharisee in us often talks louder than Jesus in us.

WHEN THE BEAUTIFUL LADY APPEARED AT LA SALETTE she said to the children, *"The seventh day I have kept for myself."* In doing so she revealed the deep-seated reason for the Sabbath. The Lord loves us so much, she reminded us, that he wants us to spend this special day in his company. Sunday worship cannot be a mere matter of fulfilling an obligation. It should be the joyful act of a grateful heart. Mary wishes us to grow in gratitude, to journey in faith, not alone but in the big family of believers. She wants us to don the garment of integrity and sincerity as we take our place at table with Jesus.

Reflection Questions:

- Is the Pharisee or Jesus my standard of behavior?
- Am I overly narrow-minded in my Sunday observance?

Wednesday, January 20, (#313)
Second Week in Ordinary Time

Mark 3:1-6: *"Is it permitted on the Sabbath day to do good, or to do evil; to save life, or to kill?"*

Meditation:

Jesus takes time off from his lakeside preaching and healing. Once again he enters the synagogue on the Sabbath. The leading Jews and members of the Sanhedrin were there to scrutinize hi every move. They wanted no unlawful act from him that might mislead the people and entice them from the right way. It was the Sabbath; all work was forbidden. Had he been a fearful prophet, Jesus would have managed not to see the sick man. He well knew that to see him was to heal him, and to heal him could only mean trouble. *"Is it lawful on the Sabbath day,"* Jesus asks, *"to save life, or to kill?"* He thus discloses the priority God assigns to compassion in all his dealings with humanity. The law was meant to enhance the community's sense of human

dignity. How can healing the paralytic jeopardize this intent? It can't. Jesus was frustrated with the Pharisees, not because they observed the Law, but because they were narrow-minded and burdened others in its application.

MARY'S APPEARANCE and intervention at La Salette was rather necessary and most timely in a world become licentious and self-centered. More than an appeal, her message carried transforming power and served as a salutary reminder that evil is to be rejected energetically, that God is to be embraced enthusiastically. Mary stands at La Salette as our spiritual mother and a woman, committed and faithful, dedicated with all her feminine heart to what is good and right. The voice she raised at La Salette needs to be heard even today.

Reflection Questions:

- How do I utilize God-given opportunities to do acts of mercy?
- What might I learn if I write a list of God's commands and their underlying intent?

Thursday, January 21, (#314)
Second Week in Ordinary Time

Mark 3:7-12: *"great numbers… heard of all that (Jesus) was doing."*

Meditation:

The synagogue authorities and the community elders were set for a conflict with Jesus over the good works he did on the Sabbath. Jesus discreetly avoids the situation, however, and keeps the focus on his mission. Leaving the synagogue, he went out to the lakeside and the open sky. It was not that he withdrew through fear, but that his hour had not yet come and that he had much more to do. Undaunted by the controversy, the crowd fearlessly followed Jesus. *"(They) heard of all that (Jesus) was doing."* Reports of his deeds, his assistance to all in need, served as a magnet that drew them. Most were drawn to Christ by an inner desire to taste and see divine acts. The region was electrified. Everyone wants to see a miracle at least once in a lifetime! Miracles in themselves do not sustain faith. For the believer, no miracle is necessary; for the unbeliever, no miracle is possible. What we need most is the courage and strength to decide resolutely for Jesus in the

difficult moments of our lives.

THE LA SALETTE MESSAGE focuses on people's refusal to give God the time he re-quests, their disrespect for his name, and the hardness of their hearts. It was addressed to people who refused to welcome the word of God into their lives. Maximin and Melanie were so very blessed to hear Mary's comforting and energizing words. They were set free from fear and anxiety. The miracle of the apparition did not come in answer to any desire of theirs, it simply dawned in their lives. They afterwards gave their whole lives to make the Lady's message known to all. Having freely received, they freely gave.

Reflection Questions:

- How fearless a follower of Christ can I truthfully say I am?
- What is it about Jesus and his teaching that excites me?

Friday, January 22, (#315)
Second Week in Ordinary Time

Mark 3:13-19: *"(Jesus) appointed twelve; they were to be his companions and to be sent out to proclaim the message, with power to drive out devils."*

Meditation:

Jesus takes one more step forward in carrying out his mission. He had articulated his message; he had selected his method; he had shown his divine authority over evil spirits and illness. He had seen large crowds following him, eager to taste divine love. He had felt this flock's inner thirst. Now he had to find an effective way to make his message a lasting one, one that would extend beyond Galilee. To further his mission he chose ordinary men who were willing to give their lives for the sake of God's Kingdom. He called them *to be his companions and to be sent out to proclaim the message, with power to drive out devils.* These three charges are essential components of the disciple's calling: to be with Jesus, to understand him, to capture his spirit, to share his trust in God, to go out and preach the Word of life, the Word made flesh, to heal the world of all evil spirits. Each of these blessings carries with it a responsibility. To love God is to love his works and his children beyond measure.

At La Salette Mary is indeed sent by God and speaks the words of God. She unabashedly refers to her two most precious possessions: her Son and her people. Her pleading in behalf of her children was ongoing, and sinners were drawn to her Son that they might find in him forgiveness, healing and reconciliation. In a world broken and divided, the La Salette message remains relevant. To take the Word of God, called to our attention by Mary, to the ends of the world is our primary baptismal responsibility. Jesus' death and resurrection have earned us heavenly citizenship. Mary's apparition reminds us that sacred duties and responsibilities accompany blessings such as this.

Reflection Questions:

• As a disciple of Christ do I recognize the responsibilities my discipleship entails?
• Do I act accordingly?

Saturday, January 23 (#316)
Second Week in Ordinary Time

Mark 3:20-21: *"They said, '(Jesus) is out of his mind.'"*

Meditation:

The crowd follows Jesus with great affection and excitement. They have seen him performing miracles and have heard his powerful words. Still we see them thirsting for more of his wisdom and miracles. Certainly a good number of them believed in him and their hearts were yearning to be formed in the ways of God. All these things sounded so bizarre and strange to his own family, who then decided that the time had come to take him home. They perhaps feared the consequences of such acts and preferred not to be condemned by the Jewish leaders. The language of Mark's Gospel here offers a dramatic picture of Jesus' humanness: his reaction and the wide range of emotions he displays are so much like our own. He was pained when people disappointed him. For the good things he was doing, he was anything but appreciated by those closest to him. His own relatives said, "He is out of his mind." We sometimes do good and are suspected of having ulterior motives.

THE LA SALETTE EVENT INVITES US TO LOOK AT THE EVENTS OF OUR LIVES and our world with the eyes of faith. Whatever causes pain in our relationships must be viewed from a faith perspective. It was the absence of a faith perspective that made Mary's presence at La Salette so necessary. Her single-minded focus on her Son should be ours as well. Our modern world and self-congratulatory attitude have created blind spots and denials that challenge us to stand up for Jesus with integrity and proclaim his word with unflagging enthusiasm.

Some Reflection Questions:

- How do you react when your loved ones do not appreciate you?
- Why does affirmation by those closest to you perhaps mean so much to you?

Sunday, January 24 (#068)
Third Sunday in Ordinary Time

(Jonah 3:1-10; 1 Corinthians 7:29-31; Mark 1-14-20)

Meditation: *Urgent Message*

Over the centuries, well over a hundred dates have been predicted for the end of the world, by an interesting variety of persons: St. Martin of Tours, Pope Sylvester II, the artist Sandro Botticelli, Martin Luther, Christopher Columbus, and a host of other famous or unknown prognosticators. Not one of those prophecies has been fulfilled. The most recent date predicted was just four months ago!

Jonah enters into that category. He was a true prophet, sent by God, to proclaim to the Ninevites that their time was up. But in Chapter 4 of the Book of Jonah, the prophet

The Calling of Saint Peter and Saint Andrew **by James Tisson (1836-1902)**

blames God for sending him on a fool's errand. He knew all along, he claims, that he would fail and God would relent of the punishment he had threatened.

St. Paul writes that time is running out. Mary at La Salette says: "If my people refuse to submit, I will be forced to let go the arm of my Son. It is so strong and so heavy, I can no longer hold it back." Both seem to speak with a certain threatening urgency.

We can say that Mary at La Salette was hoping for the same sort of failure that Jonah suffered. She did not want her predictions of famine and the death of children to be fulfilled. She offered an alternative. It is never too late! Transformation is always possible.

Jesus begins his public ministry by proclaiming a time of fulfillment and calling people to repentance. There is nothing threatening about this. Still, Jesus is announcing the end of the world—as we know it! A time of transformation lies ahead. This is what St. Paul means when he writes that "the world in its present form is passing away."

We have no way of knowing just why Simon, Andrew, James and John left everything to follow Jesus. One thing is certain: it was the end of their world as they had known it. Becoming disciples of Jesus dramatically changed them in every way imaginable.

For us, as for them, the encounter with Christ inevitably changes us, and not just once, but over and over. But sometimes we resist that change and need to be called or challenged yet again. That's where the message of La Salette finds its place. It takes a Beautiful Lady, or someone who loves her, to make it known.

Monday, January 25, (#519)
The Conversion of Saint Paul

Mark 16:15-18: *"Jesus... said to them: 'Go out to the whole world; proclaim the gospel to all creation.'"*

Meditation:

There is a contradiction in the life of Saul of Tarsus that seems to be an impediment to his becoming Saint Paul, the apostle to the Gentiles. It is his fierce faith, his devotion to God. After all he is a learned

Jew who eats and drinks the Word of God and waits for the all-powerful Messiah who was, in the common view of the Jewish nation, to overcome their enemies and make the Jewish people powerful in the eyes of all the world. Instead Saul realizes, once he meets Jesus "on the road", that his kingdom is not of this world and that his hopes for secular power for his nation are now turned into a life of sacrifice and humble service to Jesus of Nazareth, a carpenter's son. Yet by the grace of God, the conversion makes this staunch Jew into an apostle of Jesus to the gentiles – who could have believed it could come to this!

MARY'S APPEARANCE AT LA SALETTE is also rife with contradictions. She chooses to appear in a most remote place to two seemingly insignificant children instead of in a public place, witnessed by a cast of thousands, addressing a Bishop or other Church notable. Yet her choice miraculously was the right one! The two children received from her a mandate similar to that which Jesus gave to his own disciples: "Go out to the whole world (all my people)" and make the message known. Yet by the grace of God, her words and their effect have truly been miraculous – first, in the life of Maximin's father who came back to the sacraments, and then thereafter to countless pilgrims whose faith was renewed and strengthened by Mary's message of respect for the name of her Son, the importance of daily prayer, Sunday worship and a responsibility to share her message with others.

Reflection Questions:

- How have you acted like Saint Paul, encouraging people to believe, reaching out to others in their need?
- What particular words or actions of Mary at La Salette touched your heart?

Tuesday, January 26, (#318)
Third Week in Ordinary Time

Mark 3:31-35: *"Here are my mother and my brothers. Anyone who does the will of God, that person is my brother and sister and mother."*

Meditation:

Someone once observed that Catholics have a penchant for putting

the cart before the horse when they think that their goodness produces heaven when, in truth, it is heaven that is the source of all goodness. When Jesus speaks of family, all manner of questions arise about his relatives, about the meaning of brothers and sisters. Or are they cousins? But Jesus is on another page. More than his closeness to us, to his followers, then and now, to his mother, to all his brothers and sisters, Jesus is one with his heavenly Father. His primary relationship is with his Father. He invites us into that relationship by asking us to do the will of the Father. The reign of God, for Jesus, rests in the personal communion of men and women who do the will of God. Loving the unlovable, the outcast, the enemy requires a love thicker than blood. The question we ought to be asking ourselves is "who isn't my brother or sister or mother?"

NOT ONLY DOES MOTHER MARY come to us speaking words of wisdom, "Let it be," she knows the full meaning of that response to God. To say "yes" to God is to give life to love, to hope, to peace, to the presence of God among us. Mother Mary says, "Let it be done to *you* according to God's will." Is it any wonder that Jesus prays in a like manner and teaches us to pray *"thy will be done."* Mother Mary comes to us at La Salette speaking words of wisdom, saying "let me do again for you what I was always meant to do. Let me bring Brother Jesus to all of you who have forgotten that he is your brother."

Reflection Questions:

- What is the will of God asking of me today?
- Whom do I know who tries to act according to God's will?

Wednesday, January 27, (#319)
Third Week in Ordinary Time

Mark 4:1-20: *"Listen! Imagine a sower going out to sow."*

Meditation:

The people to whom Jesus speaks are being encouraged to be good soil, to be good listeners. Jesus isn't simply asking that his words be given a hearing, but that they be cultivated and allowed to produce an abundance of meaning. The measure that they produced, whether thirty, fifty or a hundred percent according to their abilities, wasn't

what concerned Jesus. What he demanded of his hearers was that his words receive a response, that they make a difference. At his word, people are healed, forgiven, saved. He speaks not merely to enlighten our minds but to touch our hearts. To hear with our hearts is to put faith in him, to believe. Without faith the words can be confusing: *"Love your enemies," "The last shall be first." "Happy are those who mourn."* In *The Little Prince*, we are told that what is essential is invisible to the eye and that it is only with the heart that one sees rightly. And so it is that only with the heart can one hear rightly. The heart is the core of hearing and seeing. We can see and hear in those who are in good soil the power of an abundant response to the word of God. We can hear and see gentleness and generosity and undying hope. An abundant harvest is unmistakable.

"Come near, my children, do not be afraid. I am here to tell you great news." Like the words of the Gospel, the words of La Salette are meant to be heard again and again. They weren't addressed only to those who heard them the first time. They were meant for a wider audience, for repeated proclamation. *"Make this known to all my people."* They have a claim upon us because they speak to our deepest yearnings for meaning and healing, for an abundance of life and love.

Reflection Questions:

- Who, in my life, speaks gentleness, generosity and undying hope?
- Whom do I know who has been most generous to me?

Thursday, January 28, (#320)
Third Week in Ordinary Time

Mark 4:21-25: *"Take notice of what you are hearing. The standard you use will be used for you -- and you will receive more besides."*

Meditation:

Listen carefully! To whom do we listen? Do we listen only to the loudest, the most articulate, the most pleasant? Do we listen with the Lord to the cries of the poor, the inarticulate, the lonely? Do we listen to people or just to words? Do we listen for new ideas, for gossip, for the sensational? Do we listen to the Good News? Henri Nouwen spoke of "learning about God as the very opposite of piling up ideas."

To truly listen is to embrace the silence that allows us to hear others speak to us about God.

If we listen carefully, "God can be listened out of people." Whose love, whose welcome, whose compassion reflects the love, the welcome and the compassion of our God? From whose life do we receive the Word of God? There is a full measure of revelation awaiting those who have ears to hear. The power of God's word is not confined to our limited hierarchical and holy expectations. The alien, the outcast, the sinner spoke to Jesus of God and so he listened. "Real learning" said Nouwen, "in a spiritual sense, is a growing willingness to listen."

WHEN MOTHER MARY says to Melanie and Maximin, *"I am here to tell you great news,"* she asks for a hearing from her children. She asks for a hearing of her suffering and pain on our behalf. She asks us to listen to the meanings of the signs of the times. She asks to hear our prayers. She asks for our voices to tell the world the Good News of God's reconciling love.

Reflection Questions:

- Where and when and by whom does God surprise you with his revelation?
- When have you felt inspired when you someone doing something good?

Friday, January 29, (#321)
Third Week in Ordinary Time

Mark 4:26-34: *"The reign of God... is like a mustard seed... the smallest of all the seeds on earth...it grows into the biggest shrub of them all."*

Meditation:

Expect the kingdom to happen in small ways. The kingdom is like the innocent heart of a small child eager to love and to learn. It is like the smallest gift of the widow who gives all that she had. It is like the tiniest of seeds that produces the largest of plants. The smallest of beginnings can have great results. God works his wonders among us in very subtle almost unnoticeable ways ac-cording to his own timetable and manner.

The kingdom grows unnoticed while we go about our lives as usual. It happens constantly, mysteriously. The message of the mustard seed encouraged us to face the world with our small resources and trust that God will accomplish great things through them. If God can take the smallest of seeds to produce the largest of shrubs, how much more can he do with our lives. The images of the reign of God are hidden in the obvious, waiting for the recognition of those who have faith to believe, eyes to see and ears to hear.

If the kingdom can be seen in the gospel images of a child's innocence, in the generosity of a widow and in the beauty of creation then it can also be seen in the love of someone who quietly enlarges our life and time and world. There are always some people in whom the seed takes root and flourishes. God is never without kingdom people. They touch our lives with little acts of kindness and love which by the world's standards seem insignificant. But the unfolding mystery is in plain sight for those who have faith to see.

THE KINGDOM OF GOD IS LIKE A MOTHER who gave her all when she gave the world her son. He grew in grace and love, offering himself for the salvation of the world. But it is a story that is all too often ignored, denied, rejected and opposed. So the story needs to be told again and again. La Salette is an invitation to faith, the planting anew of the seeds of hope and the cultivating of the kingdom of reconciling love.

Reflection Questions:

- Where do you see the kingdom taking root and flourishing?
- When have you been touched by the reconciling love of God in another person?

Saturday, January 30, (#322)
Third Week in Ordinary Time

Mark 4:35-41: *"Master, do you not care? We are lost!...Then (Jesus) said to them, 'Why are you so frightened? Have you still no faith?'"*

Meditation:

Jesus reassures the apostles that when he is with them they have nothing to fear. He also reassures them his own serenity comes from

trusting in the Father who is always with him. That false sense of isolation that exists in our imagination, that sense of separateness is usually at the bottom of all our fears. St. Augustine once said: "The tragedy of human life is that so many of us walk through life side by side thinking no one else has a problem like ours and all the way to the grave the people at our side were experiencing the same things."

The popularity of support groups and Twelve Step programs today, however, suggests that drowning people are calling out for help. When we cry out in our panic, like Peter, we have to believe that it does matter to God and that he does send help to quiet the storms. There is no disgrace in calling out for help as Peter does. Jesus may not solve the problem or change the situation but he will change us and give us peace, which in reality does calm the storm. Being in the boat with Jesus doesn't mean that there won't be any storms. It does mean that we won't have to face them alone. It just takes a little faith and some capacity for surprise.

MOTHER MARY'S FIRST WORDS AT LA SALETTE to Melanie and Maximin were, *"Come near, my children, do not be afraid."* She does this while sharing a worried mother's concern for her children. She came to encourage her children to put aside their fears, to be reconciled to God's loving, merciful presence in their lives. Mary's words at La Salette echo across the years and miles to all her children, *"Come near, do not be afraid."*

Reflection Questions:

- Where in your life do you hear the Lord saying to you, "Why are you so terrified? Why are you lacking faith? Be still!"
- In what situation did you feel the peace of the Lord in your life?

Sunday, January 31 (#071)
Fourth Sunday in Ordinary Time

(Deuteronomy 18:15-20; 1 Corinthians 7:32-35; Mark 1:21-28)

Meditation: *New and Old*

Jesus was, to say the least, an interesting personality, a phenomenon. People were amazed at his power and the authority with which he presented a new teaching.

In our second reading, we find a specific new teaching, a novel idea put forward by St. Paul. He thought that it was better not to marry, so as to devote oneself more to pleasing God than to pleasing a wife or husband.

That was nearly 2000 years ago. While most of St. Paul's writings are normative for Christian faith, his idea about marriage never really caught on. The teachings of Jesus have, of course, been around for a very long time. In a sense, the Good News isn't news any more.

Jesus healing in Gennesaret
by **Gustave Dore (1832-1883)**

When Mary told Maximin and Mélanie, "I am here to tell you great news," she really did not have anything new to say, but what she had to say was vitally important, nonetheless. Her message echoes the Good News, as well as the Old Testament. But she did not just repeat Bible teachings; she had to get us to hear them in a new way. That is the prophetic approach.

If you read Isaiah, Jeremiah, and Ezekiel, you will find very similar messages, but the language and the personality of each individual prophet is different. How true this is of the Beautiful Lady as well!

We may reasonably expect some similarity between her words and the Lamentations of Jeremiah, and indeed the tragic image of dying children recurs there quite often. In Jeremiah 14:17 we read, "Let my eyes stream with tears, day and night, without rest." This evokes for us not only Mary's weeping, but also her praying for us without ceasing.

Still, certain dimensions of the Apparition are unique: the unusual elements of Mary's costume, her choice of witnesses. The newness of her message lies in the direct application to current events. Critics say that potatoes are not a suitable topic for the Blessed Virgin to address. True enough in the abstract, perhaps, but potatoes and wheat represented life to her people, and so constituted an effective way to get their attention.

The 'new teaching' of Jesus is ancient, but not old, never passé. La Salette reminds us of the importance of finding new, more effective ways to announce it.

Monday, February 1 (#323)
Fourth Week in Ordinary Time

Mark 5:1-20: *"Then (Jesus) asked, 'What is your name?' He answered, 'My name is Legion...'"*

Meditation:

We, like the man in the Gospel, sometimes find ourselves in the grip of things and habits that are not life-giving and keep us restrained or prevent us from growing as persons. Jesus found it important to ask the name of the spirit in this man. Once he was able to name the demon, he had power over it and could cast it out. The same is true for us. We can grow only if we call our demons and fears by their names, and, "they are many," both personal and communal. Only in acknowledging or naming these weaknesses can we begin to allow God to help us change our destructive habits. Only when we have done so, when we've allowed God to help us see rightly, can we progressively change and be renewed. Then, like the man in the Gospel who is healed, we are better able to proclaim the news that God has been powerful in our life, and that God can give us a new heart, if we allow him to do so.

At La Salette Mary urges us to do the same. She calls us to a change of heart. She names some of the demons of the time, which still apply today: indifference to prayer, to the Eucharist, to respect of the Lord's Day and the Lord's Name. Mary tells us that God cares, as she does. God desires to be the true God in our life. She reminds us to what great extent God has gone to reveal the mystery of divine love in Jesus. Mary in tears urges us to return to her Son, with our whole heart.

Reflection Questions:

- Are you able and willing to name your "demons"?
- Which of these is the greatest obstacle to your spiritual growth and relationship with Jesus?

Tuesday, February 2, (#524)
The Presentation of the Lord

(Malachi 3:1-4; Hebrews 2:14-18; Luke 2:22-40)

Meditation: *The Lord in his Temple*

The presentation of Christ in the Temple
By Hans Holbein the Elder (1465–1524)

Malachi has a vision in which *"the Lord whom you seek will come suddenly to his temple,"* and who will purify the Levites, ministers of the temple. Only then will their sacrifices be pleasing to God, *"as in the days of old, as in years gone by."*

Purification is a painful process. The "refiner's fire" conjures up the image of gold or silver being melted over an intense heat so that the impurities will float to the surface and can be skimmed off. The "fuller's lye" was a caustic substance used to clean and whiten woolen cloth before it was made into garments, especially for worship.

At La Salette there is a like kind of purification. When Mary says, *"If the harvest is ruined, it is only on account of yourselves"* and catalogues the disasters that have been visited upon her people, she is using images not unlike those used by Malachi. The purpose is not to impose a burden of guilt, much less cause suffering. On the contrary, it is to restore us, to show us where and how we need to be purified. Whatever the pain, sorrow or shame Our Lady's words and tears may cause us, we must not lose sight of the love behind them.

In the Gospel scene of the presentation of Jesus in the temple—a fulfillment of Malachi's prophecy—Simeon says to Mary, *"Look ... a sword will pierce your soul (heart) too."* The image of our Weeping Mother seems to be part of the fulfillment of that prophecy.

In 1 Corinthians 3:16, St. Paul reminds us that we are God's temple. Just as we would expect a physical temple to be as splendid and spotless as possible, so also we ought to be concerned for our inner splendor and integrity, worthy of our indwelling Lord.

Our Lady of La Salette appeared in splendor. Even her radiance is a call, an invitation to be aware of what we might be, if only we would submit simply and humbly to God's will. We are the temple. Let the Lord enter!

Wednesday, February 3, (#325)
Fourth Week in Ordinary Time

Mark 6:1-6: *"With the coming of the Sabbath he began teaching in the synagogue, and most of them were astonished."*

Meditation:

The Gospel tells us that as a faithful Jew, Jesus observed Sabbath. He understood not only the law of the Sabbath but also the deeper meaning of the law. Jesus observed many weekly Sabbath moments when he retired to pray in the silence of the night, by the sea, on the mountains, in moments of contemplation of God's wondrous and beautiful creation. The birds of the air and the flowers of the field were contemplated as signs of God's love.

These Sabbath experiences allowed him to see God present to him and to hear God speak of the harmony of life. As a consequence of his listening and hearing, Jesus grew in his knowledge of God and God's will. He could then speak and teach about God to any and all who desired to hear. Those who were caught in webs of legalism, conservatism and tradition did not understand or refused to understand. Attentiveness could have helped them answer their own question. "Where did he get all this?" In his prayer and communication with God.

At La Salette, Mary urges us to remember the sacredness of the Sabbath, the Lord's Day. Mary, like Jesus, knows that the Sabbath rest is not only a way of taking time to worship our loving God, but it is also a gift to us, a way and a day to allow ourselves to be re-created, to be renewed in body and spirit. It is a time to pause and reflect on the true meaning of our lives, our work, our priorities and especially on the truth that only God is God. All else in life is secondary. When we observe Sabbath, the Lord's Day or mini-Sabbath experiences, we become aware of who we are and who God is. Then our preaching and teaching, both in word and deed, will tend to be filled with gratitude, joy and a faithful reflection of God.

Reflection Questions:

• How do I observe the Sabbath?
• Do the Sabbath experiences of my life help make me more aware of God's love, or are they days of more busyness and distractions which draw me away from my true self?

Thursday, February 4, (#326) Fourth Week in Ordinary Time

Mark 6:7-13: *"(Jesus) instructed them to take nothing on the journey."*

Meditation:

It has been said that in Palestine in the time of Jesus, the natives had five articles of clothing: a long inner tunic, an outer cloak, a belt, sandals and the oriental headdress. Travelers carried a bag for food. In sending the disciples forth to preach and teach, Jesus recommends that they take only the bare essentials: clothing and a traveling stick for support and protection. No food, no extras. But they were to take the Word – the good news, the message of freedom and liberation. How challenging for the disciples and for us. No extras! No cumbersome distractions and burdens! An invitation to trust in the power given them by Jesus, the power of the Word. Their mission is accomplished. Their joy and amazement are profound!

On the Holy Mountain of La Salette, Mary sends the visionaries forth with nothing but their innocence and simplicity and their experience of the Mountain Vision. It is the Beautiful Lady herself and what she said, and the dazzling crucifix on her breast that would sustain them. She sends them forth as they are, innocent and undeserving visionaries who have been blessed with a transforming experience. *"Well, my children, make this known to all my people."* The tenderness, the warmth and intimacy of this experience are enough to convince her people and lead them to a change of heart. The people will know that the message and meaning here are more than these ignorant and innocent children could fabricate. Her people were converted, then and ever since.

Reflection Questions:

•As a disciple of Jesus and a son/daughter of Our Lady of La Salette, have I been "touched" by my experience of Jesus and Mary at La Salette?

•Are there any "extras" that I probably carry along to fill in the gaps, lack of experience or lack of trust in the power of the Word?

Friday, February 5, (#327)
Fourth Week in Ordinary Time

Mark 6:14-29: *"When (Herod) heard John (the Baptist) speak he was greatly perplexed, and yet he liked to listen to him."*

Meditation:

This gospel scene is a flashback interjected in the middle of the story of the mission of the disciples and their return to Jesus. The flashback serves to give us an insight into what Herod thought of Jesus. The scriptures say, *"King Herod has heard about (Jesus), since by now his name was well known."* Mark takes the occasion to remind his readers that it was this Herod who had John the Baptist beheaded. The flashback also tells us of Herod's weakness, Herodias' grudge against John and Salome's famous dance and her being manipulated into requesting the head of the Baptist as a reward for pleasing Herod. In addition to telling us about these people, the flashback serves to not only dredge up painful and sorrowful events of the past but to bring forth, as well, happy memories of blessings received.

AT LA SALETTE, Mary reminds people of things they have done and are doing. Her message includes flashbacks which most people find to be disturbing reminders of our human weakness and sinfulness. But the apparition also includes two very positive flashbacks. The first is the reminder of Jesus' crucifixion and death which is the sign that "God loved the world so much," as John the Evangelist tells us. The crucifix on Mary's breast is the blinding reminder. The second is the famous reminder of the episode in the field of Coin where Mary reminds Maximin and us that, in her motherly love and concern, she is present to us in the details of our life. How wonderful to be reminded!

Reflection Questions:

- What recent flashbacks in my own life and prayer have helped to make me more grateful for God's love and presence in my life?
- When have I been reminded of a good experience which I had forgotten?

Saturday, February 6, (#328)
Fourth Week in Ordinary Time

Mark 6:30-34: *"Come... and rest for a while."*

Meditation:

In this Gospel scene, Jesus is revealed as the "Divine Psychologist" and the "Man with a Heart." The disciples return from their mission excited and happy with the success of their work but exhausted by its demands. Jesus encourages them to get some rest, to balance their work with leisure and prayer. He invites them to enjoy a mini-Sabbath experience. He knows that one cannot be whole nor even survive long without the necessary physical rest and relaxation. He has seen to this balance in his own life. Here he reveals his loving concern for the disciples, for their wholeness and well-being. Later he is touched with pity for the crowds who were *"like sheep without a shepherd."* He teaches them and leads them to "green pastures," to "still waters" where he refreshes their souls.

Our Lady of La Salette appears in the desert highlands of the Alps. Her very presence there is an invitation for us and for all pilgrims to "come away and rest a while." She invites all her children to enter into that mountain retreat in order to be quiet, to rest, to reflect and to be refreshed by the good news of God's love that she brings.

"Come," she says, *"be not afraid. I have come to tell you great news."*

Reflection Questions:

- How often do I allow myself to go into that sacred place of retreat, to hear Mary's motherly message and call to repentance, conversion and reconciliation?
- What is a favorite place which reminds you of the joy of the simple pleasures of life?

Sunday, February 7 (#074)
Fifth Sunday in Ordinary Time

(Job 7:1-7; 1 Corinthians 9:16-23; Mark 1:29-39)

Meditation: *Purpose in Life*

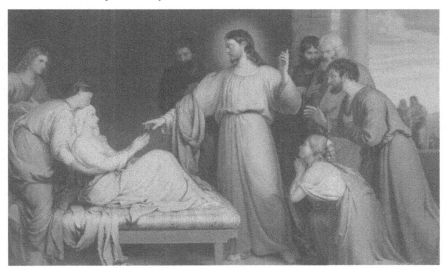

Christ Healing the Mother of Simon Peter's Wife **by John Bridges (1818–1854)**

"Woe to me," writes St. Paul, "if I do not preach the Gospel." He is not complaining, just stating the fact that this responsibility, laid on him without his being consulted, had become the all-consuming purpose of his existence.

Jesus says something similar: "For this purpose I have come," namely his preaching.

Job takes us to the other extreme. His life has become a drudgery, and he finds no purpose in it. He expects that he will never know happiness again.

The tears of Mary at La Salette, such a beautiful and powerful image, are troubling in a way. They can make us repent our sins; that is good. But some wonder how Mary, in heaven, can experience unhappiness.

And yet she talks about the trouble her people's infidelity have caused her personally: "How long a time I have suffered for you! ... You pay no heed... You will never be able to recompense the pains I have taken for you." More than a sign of unhappiness, her tears are a sign of her compassion, which she cannot possibly have set aside in heaven.

Peter's mother-in-law can help us understand the situation. Once healed, what does she do? She waits on Jesus and his companions. In her illness she was, so to speak, enslaved and without purpose. The Lord restored her to her dignity as the lady of the house. Her honor lay in honoring her guests. The same could probably be said of all the persons Jesus cured that day, especially those he delivered from demons.

The purpose of the Beautiful Lady is the same: to restore us to our dignity as Christians. She came to speak to those who were Catholics in name only—including Mélanie and Maximin. Were they even aware of the promises made on their behalf at baptism?

We might paraphrase St. Paul and the message of La Salette together by saying, "Woe to me if I do not live the Gospel." Mary lists her people's woes, the consequence of their religious indifference.

In 1980, St. Pope John Paul II issued a challenge to the Christians of France: "France, eldest daughter of the Church, are you faithful to your baptismal promises?"

Monday, February 8, (#329)
Fifth Week in Ordinary Time

Mark 6:53-56: *"And all who touched (Jesus) were saved."*

Meditation:

This final verse of Mark 6 reinforces a theme that is of special significance to the evangelist and to us who make our pilgrim way to the Father's house. The theme of healing. We are all in need of healing, whether physical or spiritual. We seek a confessor, a doctor, or a therapist that we may find the healing we need. Jesus said, *"It is not the healthy who need the doctor, but the sick."* (Mark 2:17). All four gospels attest to the fact that, in the power of the Spirit, Jesus ministered God's healing to all who were in need of it. In response to people's faith, healing poured forth from Jesus, like a never-ending flow of living water. Thus were fulfilled the words of the prophet: *"He who pities them ... will guide them to springs of water"* (Isaiah 49:10b). The wholeness Jesus brings is healing at its deepest level. God's love, incarnate in him, gushes forth as a saving fountain, curing body, mind, spirit. Its power pulsated in the very "tassel of his cloak."

To the bewilderment of her two chosen witnesses, Mary showed herself at La Salette in tears. Her tears bring to mind the healing water flowing from Christ's pierced side (John 19:34). *"The thirsty land,"* Isaiah had prophesied, will become *"springs of water"* (Isaiah 35:7a). The frequency of the word sin in the Bible and its almost total absence from contemporary talk point to a contemporary "thirsty ground." The recognition that human life is infected by sin is, one would think, an essential part of any realistic description of the human condition. How well-inspired those peasant villagers were who, from the beginning, invoked their heavenly Visitor as Our Lady of La Salette, Reconciler of *sinners*!

Reflection Questions:

- Do I find it easy or difficult to admit that I am in need of healing?
- Can I imagine what it might be like to feel the healing touch of Jesus?

49

Tuesday, February 9, (#330)
Fifth Week in Ordinary Time

Mark 7:1-13: *"In this way you make God's word ineffective."*

Meditation:

One of the controversial things Jesus did in the course of his ministry was to redefine the proper application of Jewish ritual purity laws. By no means was he opposed to the Torah. He had little tolerance, though, for what he considered to be abuses of religious authority inflicted on the little people by the so-called spiritual leaders. We know that many struggle with God's will as stated in divine law and the observance of certain customs and practices that nullify and make a mockery of God's Word.

How often are we ourselves torn between the law of God and man-made laws? The Pharisees in our gospel passage accuse Jesus and his disciples of eating with defiled hands. In reply Jesus unambiguously states that what matters is our inner life with our God and not its outward trappings. What comes from within – a pure heart and a well-formed conscience – interests him a great deal. Cleanse your hearts, put your faith in me, he tells us, and keep from performing empty rituals for others to see.

THE DUTY OF OBEYING GOD'S law goes largely ignored in our secular world. Mary at La Salette underscores her children's disrespectful attitude toward commandments that spell out the duties of humble gratitude and service we owe to our Creator: *"If my people will not submit, I shall be forced to let fall the arm of my Son."* The initiative she showed that September day at La Salette means, essentially, that even in glory the Queen of heaven is ever engaged in the reconciliation of her people on earth.

Reflection Questions:

- Do I set time aside each day to go within and allow Jesus to speak to my heart?
- Is it true that laws make good servants but poor masters?

Wednesday, February 10, (#331)
Fifth Week in Ordinary Time

Mark 7:14-23: *"For it is from within, from the heart, that evil intentions emerge."*

Meditation:

We choose to hear only what we want to hear, or we interpret teachings so that they will fit into our own self-serving scheme of things. Jesus was a fine teacher. He taught with wisdom and clarity. His message provides no loopholes, it leaves no room for excuses or false interpretations. He always speaks the truth clearly and further illustrates it with concrete examples. He tells us today that high ideals are not to replace our heart's need of God. It is not through the perfect observance of dietary laws, Jesus points out, that we are saved. We must rather pay attention to the inner designs and movements of our own heart and respond heartily to God and to our neighbor. He cautions that our ideals can become our idols! Real defilement dwells in the inner person. Jesus calls not so much for a change of outward behavior but for a change of heart.

OUR LADY OF LA SALETTE speaks of inner change, of spiritual transformation in the most dramatic of terms: *"If they are converted, rocks and stones will be changed into mounds of wheat and potatoes will be self-sown in the fields."* Jesus the Savior, she reminds us, came to change the world – from the inside out. Yes, he chose to bring that radical transformation about by changing human hearts, one by one.

Reflection Questions:

- Does my need to be perfect keep me from seeing where my heart is truly centered?
- How conscious an effort have I invested in the cultivation of my inner world?

Thursday, February 11, (#332)
Fifth Week in Ordinary Time

Note: Today you may wish to begin the First Day of the Novena to Our Lady of La Salette, in the appendix of this book.

Mark 7:24-30: *"But she spoke up, 'Ah yes, sir,' she replied, 'but little dogs under the table eat the scraps from the children.'"*

Meditation:

We have all heard the saying: Good news travels fast. St. Mark stresses that Jesus "could not escape notice." Jesus' fame had spread far and wide, even into Gentile territory. So it is that we meet a Syro-Phoenician woman, the mother of a sick child, who beseeches him to drive out the demon besieging her daughter. Jesus tells her that God must look after his own first and that his healing power must first benefit the members of his chosen family.

He puts her faith to the test and, surprisingly, really tries her composure and self-control: *"It is not right to take the food of the children,"* he tells her, *"and throw it to the dogs."* Hers was a deep and strong faith; it passed Jesus' test with flying colors. She gave as good as she got: *"Please, Lord,"* she insisted, *"even the dogs under the table eat the family's leavings."* The refreshing resourcefulness of faith!

THE FINAL NEW TESTAMENT REFERENCE to Our Lady presents her as calling the early church community to prayer, *"They devoted themselves with one accord to prayer, together with some women, and Mary the Mother of Jesus"* (Acts 1:14). In her apparition at La Salette, the Mother of the Lord calls our attention to the need to pray well and unceasingly: *"Do you pray well, my children? ... If I want my Son not to abandon you I must plead with him without ceasing."* Personal and communal needs and problems challenge us to claim prayer's unique power: *"Will not God secure the rights of his chosen ones? Will he be slow to answer them? I tell you he will see that justice is done for them speedily"* (Luke 18:7-8).

Reflection Questions:

- How willing am I to accept and love all persons – including "outsiders" – as Jesus did?
- Does the resourcefulness of faith show itself in my prayer?

Friday, February 12, (#333)
Fifth Week in Ordinary Time

Mark 7:31-37: *"Everything he does is good, he makes the deaf hear and the dumb speak."*

Meditation:

The hymn says, "Jesus, you are wonderful!" I love to sing this song over and over again. It soothes my soul and helps me give glory to God the Father for the gift of his Son to me, to us all. In the exercise of my healing ministry I have been given many opportunities to sing the wonders of the Lord. It is perhaps because his love and mercy endure forever, that he is so full of surprises. The cure of the deaf man is a classical gospel miracle story. A person in need of healing is brought to Jesus. By deed and word Jesus restores wholeness. People's utter amazement and exuberant praise attest to, and validate, the wonderful deed. Such works manifest Jesus as the agent of the Father who is *"rich in faithful love"* (Ephesians 2:4) and *"generous to all, his tenderness embraces all his creatures."* (Psalm 145:9). The man's ears were opened, he heard God's saving word; he believed in its transforming power, his tongue was unleashed; joyful praise gushed forth from a heart as thankful as it was astounded.

AT LA SALETTE Mary invites her children to set fear aside and draw near in their brokenness. She bids them approach Christ, the wounded healer, whose crucified image she wore on her breast. Familiar with human need and mindful of the first of Jesus' signs given *"at Cana in Galilee,"* Mary repeats the advice she offered then: *"Do whatever he tells you"* (John 2:5). Appropriate and wise counsel for today's disciples as well.

Reflection Questions:

- Can I hear the voice of Christ through the deafening distractions of life around me?
- How much enthusiasm do I bring to my praise of the Savior?

Saturday, February 13, (#334)
Fifth Week in Ordinary Time

Mark 8:1-10: *"(Jesus) took the seven loaves, and after giving thanks he broke them and began handing them to his disciples to distribute; and they distributed them among the crowd."*

Meditation:

Mark sets a crowd scene before our eyes. A multitude of people. A hungry multitude. Jesus performs a miracle of striking compassion; he feeds them all. When all have had their fill, plenty of loaves and fishes remain. This miraculous feeding obviously looked back to the feeding of the Israelites with manna in the wilderness; it also pointed to our own communal celebrations of the Eucharist. *"(Jesus) took the seven loaves, and after giving thanks he broke them and began handing them to his disciples to distribute; and they distributed them among the crowd."*

God's good creation faithfully and humbly provides for us all each year. But earth's crops are, for better or for worse, in our hands. We hold God's bounty and lavish gifts in trust. We must share them. Our world is not without its own multitudes of homeless, naked and hungry people. Hungry not only for bread, but for love. Naked not only for clothing, but for human dignity and respect. Homeless not only for want of a brick shelter, but because of indifference and rejection.

IT IS WITH THE DEEPEST SORROW, we are entitled to believe, that Mary spoke these words at La Salette: *"A great famine is coming."* She well knew that some of her children would suffer from famine brought on by natural causes; that many others would suffer from famines of human making, she was also painfully aware. The psalmist offers an encouraging promise: *"Yahweh will himself give prosperity, and our soil will yield its harvest."* (Psalm 85:12). The land's increase, however, remains in human hands.

Reflection Questions:

- Am I aware that pity without service to others is mere sentimentality?
- Am I convinced that God's gifts are to be shared, that love must be put into action?

Sunday, February 14 (#077)
Sixth Sunday in Ordinary Time
(Leviticus 13:1-2 and 44-46; 1 Corinthians 10:31-11:1; Mark 1:40-45)

Meditation: *A Reconciling Touch*

St. Paul may appear to be vain when he writes, "Be imitators of me, as I am of Christ." But he was, in fact, a good model of discipleship, and all of us are called, likewise, to be imitators of Christ, doing everything for the glory of God.

Very recently I met a woman who had a wooden sculpture, a gift from a missionary Sister. It was carved by a leper, who gave it to the Sister to acknowledge his special gratitude, because she was the only person who had ever touched him. She was an imitator of Christ as we see him in today's Gospel.

His touch produced more than the physical healing. It was surely unexpected, perhaps even shocking, and, therefore, a very powerful sign, an example to follow. It was a healing and reconciling touch.

Christ Healing the Leper, from
The Story of Christ by
Georg Pencz (1500–1550)

Normally we think of reconciliation as the restoration of a relationship between persons separated by some deep offense. It is, as you know, a key word in the vocabulary of La Salette Missionaries, Sisters, and Laity, who desire all to be reconciled to God and fully incorporated into the Mystical Body of Christ.

How does this apply to leprosy? Apart from two clear examples (Miriam in Numbers 12, and Gehazi in 2 Kings 5), there was no offense associated with the disease.

The fact remains that, by law, as we read in Leviticus, lepers lived in a state of alienation. Unclean, they could have no association with others, and anyone who had contact with them became unclean as well, though only for a short time. That situation was here reversed. By a touch the leper was restored to health and to a normal life. He could once again enter the temple. His alienation was over. This was an act of reconciliation.

In the 1960's the Missionaries of Our Lady of La Salette founded a leprosarium in Burma. Fr. William Doherty wrote: "We established a leprosarium for the many people afflicted by this dread disease—people until that time unwanted and uncared for." This was perfectly in keeping with our mission of reconciliation. These persons, unfortunately, could not be restored to their families. But their total alienation was ended.

Not only sin committed or offense given, but any form of alienation, calls for a reconciling touch.

Monday, February 15, (#335)
Sixth Week in Ordinary Time

Mark 8:11-13: *"And with a profound sigh (Jesus) said, 'Why does this generation seek a sign?'"*

Meditation: This Markan passage strikes a sharp note of taunting and testing. The Pharisees argue with Jesus, hoping to discredit or entrap him. They insist that he guarantee through "some heavenly sign" the authority he claims. Such profound misunderstanding on their part disturbs Jesus deeply. He himself is the "heavenly sign," a powerful sign. A sign that stands every human notion of power on its head, however. He bans anger and name-calling (Matthew 5:22), he teaches non-resistance to evil (Matthew 5:39), he preaches love of enemies (Matthew 5:44), he will wash the disciples' feet (John 13:3-11), and the humiliation of the cross will be his exaltation (John 19:32). Seeking a sign is natural enough. Have we not at times thought, "If only I were given a sign, my faith would grow stronger"? "Open your eyes, remove your blinders," the Lord says. "Signs of my loving presence surround you." How much smaller, how much more hidden could he have made himself than a bit of bread? Who but God Almighty would come to

us in such self-emptying?

"If the harvest is ruined, it is only on account of yourselves," Our Lady admonishes in her apparition at La Salette. *"I warned you last year with the potatoes. You paid no heed."* She rests her reasoning on a cause-and-effect inevitability. To do the same things over and over again, expecting better, different and new results is tantamount to folly. *"I gave you a warning sign last year. You paid it no mind."*

Reflection Questions:

- Does my faith allow me to put my complete trust in the Lord's word?
- Do I go on trusting the Lord even in the absence of clear signs?

Tuesday, February 16, (#336)
Sixth Week in Ordinary Time

Mark 8:14-21: *"Do you still not understand, still not realize? Are your minds closed?"*

Meditation:

His disciples were very close to Jesus. They ate, shared shelter and traveled with the Master. They saw him interact with the blind, the deaf, the lame and had a hand in two amazing multiplications. His patience sorely tried, he plies them with rapid-fire questions: "Do you have eyes and not see? Do you remember when I broke the five loaves for the 5000? The seven loaves for the 4000? How many baskets of leftovers did you collect? Do you still not understand?" What is it they failed to grasp?

They should not have seen Jesus as the *wonder worker* walking across the water but as the *unifier* who calmed the storm in order to secure passage to the Gentile side of the lake. They had missed the point of the lesson. Two feedings had taken place, one on each side of the lake. A first benefited a Jewish population; a second, Gentiles. In showing them how to feed God's flock, Jesus had taught them to be bridge-builders. 12 baskets left over, Israel's 12 tribes, Jewish Christians; seven baskets left over, seven deacons, Greek Christians. So much to learn, so much to let go of?

IN CONTRAST TO LOURDES AND FATIMA, for example, Mary at La Salette did not directly indicate who she was. Her opening statement, however, made her identity quite clear: *"If my people will not submit, I shall be forced to let fall the arm of my Son."* Sharing deeply in the mediating ministry of Christ, "the one loaf," she reminds us that she stands between the Bread of Life and those he wishes to feed. Our Lady further challenges us to claim our role as bridge-builders between peoples and races.

Reflection Questions:

- Am I convinced that the same loving hand that created me created all those who are outwardly so different from me?
- Have I drawn the logical conclusion that we are all God's children, brothers and sisters one and all?

Wednesday, February 17 (#219-02)
Ash Wednesday

Matthew 6:1-6, 16-18: *"...when you give alms, your left hand must not know what your right is doing."*

Meditation:

Jesus warns us that we should avoid doing "what the hypocrites do in the synagogues and in the streets to win human admiration." The words "hypocrite" meant an "actor"; in other words, actions were done primarily to be seen by others. Of course our good and generous actions should not have as their main motivation the praise of others. We should be doing good things literally just for the love of it!

MARY AT LA SALETTE CAME OUT OF LOVE FOR HER PEOPLE. Her visit in tears was her special gift to us. It certainly wasn't an opportunity to scold us from her anger but rather to urge us out of her motherly concern to follow the ways and message of her Son. During this Lenten season, when the Church calls us to somehow make this

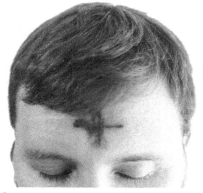

season special, we should grasp this opportunity to reflect, pray and act to make this season one of grace and mercy, doing those things that will remind us of the special love Jesus and his Tearful Mother have for each of us.

Some Reflection Questions:

- What way can you give alms during this Lenten season?
- Is there a person or particular family that might benefit from your generosity. Respecting Jesus' words in the gospel for today, your alms could even be done in secret.

Thursday, February 18, (#220)
Thursday After Ash Wednesday

Luke 9:22-25: *"What benefit is it to anyone to win the whole world and forfeit or lose his very self?"*

Meditation:

That's the bottom line?" This is a question often asked when people face an undertaking. There is more than a bottom line to look at. What's beyond the bottom line? How does our activity affect our health, our relationships with family members, community or friends? The bottom line may indicate a profit, but at what cost? The gospel tells us that the ultimate bottom line is salvation. That's the reality lens through which we should look at our lives. That lens is not rose-colored. Jesus makes it very clear. *"If anyone wants to be my follower, he must renounce himself and take up his cross every day and follow me."* The bottom line here is salvation attained through the victory of the cross.

MARY LIVED THE GOSPEL FULLY at La Salette. She reminds us, *"However much you pray, however much you do, you will never be able to repay the pains I have taken for you."* Mary carried her cross. She asks us to do the same.

Reflection Questions:

- Can I look beyond the bottom line and carry my cross daily?
- What people do I know that carry their crosses, their burdens with much faith?

Friday, February 19, (#221)
Friday After Ash Wednesday

Matthew 9:14-15: *"... when the bridegroom is taken away from them, and then they will fast."*

Meditation:

Fasting isn't what it used to be. I remember my grandmother weighing out on a postal scale the exact amount of meat allowed back then – a long way from the modest fasting rules for today. Fasting is ordinarily thought of in terms of reducing food consumption. Fasting can, however, be applied to other areas of our lives as well. We can fast from television viewing and instead engage in a real conversation with others in the household.

We can fast from music or news in order to allow ourselves, in the ensuing quiet, to get in touch with what is going on inside ourselves. We can fast from our opinions – this, admittedly, is a tough one – to put aside our view of things, our way of doing things, our way of praying and allow another to touch our mind, our heart, and even our soul.

MARY, AT LA SALETTE, reminds us to fast. *"During Lent they go to the meat markets like dogs."* Fasting is not strictly a Lenten practice. As we abstain, we simply make room for God in our lives. That should be a daily practice.

Reflection Questions:

- How am I called to fast? What should I be fasting from?
- With whom do I need to be more positive in my attitude toward them?

Saturday, February 20, (#222)
Saturday After Ash Wednesday

Luke 5:27-32: *"I have come to call not the upright but sinners to repentance."*

Meditation:

Myopia, Webster's dictionary says, is a "deficiency of foresight or discernment." So myopia is not only a matter of our eyes; our minds can be myopic as well. Lack of discernment makes it difficult to see ourselves as we really are. Somehow we overlook our shortcomings, our character blemishes, our sins. Yet only when we see ourselves as we really are can we respond to Jesus' invitation to a change of heart, to conversion.

If we see ourselves as healthy, we don't go to a doctor even though we may need care. If we see ourselves as spiritually healthy, we don't go to Jesus for a change of heart. No matter where we may be on our spiritual journey, there is always room for change, for conversion. Jesus called Levi to a change of heart. He is calling us also.

At La Salette Mary came to call us to a change of heart, for the purpose of focusing our entire life on her Son. She assures us of our abundant harvest – *"if they are converted."*

Reflection Questions:

• Can I hear and respond to Jesus' call no matter what my myopic vision sees in me?
• Do I look at myself and accept myself as I truly am? Do I do that for others as well?

Sunday, February 21 (#023)
First Sunday of Lent

... he was in the wilderness forty days, being tempted by Satan
Mark 1:13

(Genesis 9:8-15; 1 Peter 3:18-22; Mark 1:12-15)

Meditation: *Peace with God*

The noun "bow" occurs 77 times in the Hebrew text of the Old Testament. It always refers to a weapon of war, even in today's first reading. But God says he will set his bow in the clouds as a reminder of the covenant between himself and humanity, a covenant of peace.

After the flood, God had made a resolution: "Never again will I strike down every living being as I have done." He was now renouncing forever the violence with which he had wiped out all but eight persons on the earth.

This explains why this passage from Genesis is the first reading at the Mass for the Feast of Our Lady of La Salette. One might even wonder whether Bishop de Bruillard had this same text in mind when he wrote of the Missionaries of Our Lady of La Salette: "Their institution and existence shall be, like the Shrine itself, an eternal monument, a perpetual remembrance, of Mary's merciful apparition."

There are many Scripture passages after the story of Noah, in which God fights with the armies of his people, and Psalm 24 says that God is "mighty in war;" but Psalm 46 presents a different image. God "stops wars to the ends of the earth, breaks the bow, splinters the spear... [saying,] 'Be still and know that I am God.'"

'Be still' can be variously translated as let go, stop, desist. It is not so much an invitation to be quiet as a call to refrain from acts of war and violence.

"Know that I am God" means acknowledging and, above all, respecting God. This is an important element in the Beautiful Lady's words. She twice laments the abuse of her Son's name and the failure to give God the worship and honor that is his due.

Today, Mark's Gospel gives no details about the tempting of Jesus in the desert, but we know them through Matthew and Luke; there we find that Jesus holds fast to the importance of worshiping God alone.

There is always the temptation to forget who God is and who we are. This does not mean we are unimportant. On the contrary, God tells us, "I, the Lord, am your God, ... you are precious in my eyes" (Isaiah 43:3-4). We are meant to be at peace with God. That is the message at the heart of the message of La Salette.

Monday, February 22, (#535)
The Chair of St. Peter the Apostle

Matthew 16:13-19: *"You are Peter and on this rock I will build my community."*

Meditation:

We all need heroes or examples of good qualities to encourage us on the road of life. Jesus sees in Simon Peter and his faith-filled response – "You are the Christ, the Son of the living God" – a man worthy of the position of leadership. He professed a faith that only the Spirit could give him. He was, in a sense, speaking for all the disciples present. From this moment on, Jesus would no longer call him Simon-bar-Jonah but rather Peter, meaning *rock* (Greek *petros*).

With this change of name, Jesus was also commissioning him to be the solid foundation upon which Jesus would build the Christian community, the Church. Peter became the speaker and the example of faith in Jesus. Yet later even though Peter would deny Jesus during Christ's passion, his life powerfully reminds us that we must always remember our innate need for Jesus and his strength that will help us persevere in our mission or vocation in life. We cannot live our Christian life without the center of our faith, Jesus Christ.

MARY AT LA SALETTE emphasizes constantly the centrality of Jesus for our life of faith. She stresses the importance of weekly Eucharist, of reverence for Jesus' name, daily prayer, respect for the Lord's Day, and Lenten habits of faith such as (fasting and) abstinence. All these can strengthen our faith in the Lord from which marvelous blessings will flow. Peter, in his strength as well as his weakness, shows us how faith can triumph over our weakness and failures. God will lift us up through the power of his love and mercy.

Reflection Questions:

•Who first taught you about faith and prayer, about Jesus' love and forgiveness?
•Who for you is an example of strong faith? How does Mary inspire you in your faith?

Tuesday, February 23, (#225)
First Week of Lent

Matthew 6:7-15: *"So you should pray like this..."*

Meditation:

What was one of the first prayers your parents taught you? Chances are that What the sign of the cross it was the *Our Father*. That prayer, said more or less accurately, was the launching pad of our communication with God. Prayer has since taken on many shapes and forms – vocal prayer, quiet prayer, sitting and thinking about God, conversation with God, letting our being be awed by the beauty of creation. No matter how we now choose to pray, the fundamental element in all forms of prayer is that God is God and that we are not. Prayer is the creature standing before the Creator with open hands ready to receive, ready to surrender all. In the *Our Father* Jesus put our relationship to God into words.

AT LA SALETTE Mary speaks of her own prayer. *"I am compelled to pray to (my on) without ceasing."* She also invites Maximin and Melanie to prayer, *"You must say your prayers well in the evening and in the morning, even if you say only an Our Father and a Hail Mary when you can't do more. When you can do better, say more."*

Reflection Questions:

- How well do I pray? How much time do I give to prayer?
- What forms of prayer do I most enjoy?

Wednesday, February 24, (#226)
First Week of Lent

Luke 11:29-32: *"The only sign (this generation) will be given is the sign of Jonah."*

Meditation:

Jonah spoke God's word; the Ninevites changed. The name of this change is conversion. Conversion is not only for bad people; we are all called to conversion. Conversion is that change of heart which makes us see things differently and adjust our lives accordingly. Every time we experience Jesus at a new and deeper level, we are called to conversion. It's our response to Jesus' invitation to know him and love him more intimately. Conversion is not exclusively our doing. It is our response to Jesus' intrusion in our lives, our response to grace. The invitation to conversion may come in any form – a book, a sermon, a word spoken by a friend, even a child's question. We respond only to the degree that we are aware of Jesus' invitation. Our "yes" opens the door to a new relationship with him.

At La Salette Mary invites the shepherds to *"come nearer,"* an invitation to conversion. Her presence, her words, her whole being pleads with us to respond "yes" to her Son, Jesus.

Reflection Questions:

- Have I become so entrenched in my relationship with Jesus that I no longer hear his invitation to deeper conversion?
- Who is a good example to me of openness to growth in faith?

Thursday, February 25, (#227) First Week of Lent

Matthew 7:7-12: *"'Everyone who asks receives."*

Meditation:

"How come I've been praying for a special grace for a long time and I haven't received it yet?" We've all made a similar statement at one time or another. But are we putting the cart before the horse? Before storming heaven for our special grace, did we ask God if we really needed that grace? Often what we need is evident to us, after all, it's what we need. But do we see with God's vision; do we really know what is best for us? Praying to be enlightened to our need is the first step, then with God's answer in mind we ask and we will receive. Jesus did everything in the will of the Father, for the Father's glory. Jesus gave us the example of perfect prayer; we do well to imitate him.

At La Salette Mary promised *"rocks and stones will be changed into mounds of wheat and potatoes will be self-sown in the fields."* Her promise is preceded by *"If they are converted,"* which means, if they are conformed to the Father's will.

Reflection Questions:

- As we pray, are we one with the Father and his will for us?
- When we ask for forgiveness from the Father, do we also promise to "forgive those who trespass against us"?

Friday, February 26, (#228)
First Week of Lent

Matthew 5:20-26: *"... leave your offering there before the altar, go and be reconciled with your brother first."*

Meditation:

Forgiveness is the decision of one person. We decide to forgive and it is done. Reconciliation requires two people, one to forgive and one to accept the forgiveness. Jesus asks us to go one step beyond forgiveness to reconciliation and reach out to the one who has offended us. Jesus challenges us to seek out not only the one we have offended, but the one who has offended us. We wouldn't think of going to a wedding without getting ready and bringing a gift. Jesus invites us to the altar to share his Body and his Blood with one another. He also tells us to get ready to do this by seeking forgiveness and by bringing a gift, reconciliation with our sister or brother. Together then we may approach the altar.

AT LA SALETTE Mary leaves the altar of Jesus' presence to invite us to reconciliation. Her Son forgives; she wants us to accept that wonderful gift.

Reflection Questions:

- Can we respond to Mary's call? Can we be reconciled with her Son, and with each other?
- Whom do you know is a good example to you of active forgives?

Saturday, February 27, (#229)
First Week of Lent

Matthew 5:43-48: *"Be perfect, just as your heavenly Father is perfect."*

Meditation:

Impossible. We cannot be as perfect as the Father! What does that sentence in Matthew really mean? William Barclay tells us, "A thing is perfect if it realizes the purpose for which it was planned, human beings are perfect if they realize the purpose for which they were created and sent into the world." We are created in the image of God. God is love and love knows no bounds. God reaches out to everyone. Our perfection then consists in loving others and reaching out to them no matter who they are. We cannot love to the degree God loves. We can love to the fullest degree possible for us. The U.S. Army recruiting poster says it very well, "Be all you can be." Therein lies our perfection.

AT LA SALETTE Mary lives her perfection. Her love for us calls us to full and utter reconciliation with her Son. She is all she can be – a mother concerned for all her children.

Reflection Questions:

- Can I ask God to make me "all that I can be"?
- Where in my life is reconciliation still needed?

Sunday, February 28 (#026)
Second Sunday of Lent

(Genesis 22:1-18; Romans 8:31-34; Mark 9:2-10)

Meditation: *The Son*

At the conclusion of the dramatic story of what transpired on a mountain in the land of Moriah, Isaac's life is spared, a substitute is found for the holocaust, and Abraham, who was willing to offer up his beloved son at God's command, is rewarded for his unstinting faith. In Old Testament and New Testament times, the place

Transfiguration
by Raphael (1483–1520)

where it was believed Abraham went to sacrifice his son continued to be venerated. The Temple of Jerusalem was built there.

In our second reading, St. Paul alludes indirectly to another small mount within easy walking distance of the Temple. The evangelists call it Golgotha.

And on an unnamed mountain, somewhere in Galilee, Jesus appeared in his glory, along with Moses and Elijah.

These various elements all find a resonance at yet another mountain, in the French alps, called La Salette.

In remembrance of the Passion of Jesus, the Beautiful Lady wears a large crucifix on her breast. It is the brightest point in the Apparition, the source of its light. The hammer and pincers, instruments of the Passion, draw attention to it in a unique way.

Reminding us of the covenant proclaimed through Moses, and calling us to the steadfast commitment of Elijah, she speaks in the manner of the prophets. (It is interesting to note that in 2 Peter 1:18, the place of the Transfiguration is referred to as 'the holy mountain.' We use the same phrase when we speak of La Salette.)

Finally, like God speaking to Abraham, Mary also makes a grand promise of hope and prosperity to those who will live by faith.

More important than any of these similarities, however, is the word Son. "Take your only son, whom you love, and offer him up as a holocaust;" "God did not spare his own Son, but handed him over for us all;" "This is my beloved Son."

When Our Lady of La Salette speaks of her Son, it is to reproach her people for their ingratitude to him and their disrespect for his Name. We must never allow ourselves to forget that her Son is God's beloved Son, handed over for us.

As he is at the heart of Scripture, he must be at the heart of our faith, of our way of life. Lent is a good time to ask ourselves if this is really the case.

Monday, March 1, (#230)
Second Week of Lent

Luke 6:36-38: *"The standard you use will be the standard used for you."*

Meditation:

Jesus has given us a model. The measure we measure with will be given back to us. Mercy and compassion must be the yardstick we use in measuring our daily behavior. What obligation do others have to be merciful, forgiving and compassionate with us if we are unwilling to practice these virtues in their regard? Jesus puts his teaching plainly in today's gospel. *"Do not judge and you will not be judged."* Just as we expect our merciful God to look upon us with forgiving kindness, so should we treat others in the same way. We cannot claim to love God and yet refuse to love others. We are encouraged to be people who make it possible for God to reach out to others through us and bring into their lives the compassion and understanding they need. The better we become, the more of God's goodness will others receive. And in this way we become special vessels, carriers of God's love to others.

MARY AT LA SALETTE was the carrier of good news. She was the messenger sent by God to exhort his children to take heed. She came to make us aware that prayer, penance and reconciliation must remain an integral part of our everyday lives. Our Lady highlighted the mission confided to Maximin and Melanie when she repeated these words: *"Well, my children, you will make this known to all my people."* And as a result, many men and women all over the world have found the message of La Salette to be a vessel of conversion, an opportunity for renewed commitment to Christ and to the service of his people.

Reflection Questions:

- How have I become an instrument for the good?
- Have I generously allowed God to use me as his vehicle in giving of my time, my talent, and my presence for the sake of others?

Tuesday, March 2, (#231)
Second Week Of Lent

Matthew 23:1-12: *"Anyone who raises himself up will be humbled, and anyone who humbles himself will be raised up."*

Meditation:

Quite clearly, Jesus teaches us to reject the ways of those who make a show of their status. Listen to sound teachings, but don't follow the path of the hypocrite. Jesus preaches a humble way. And the humble way can be described in one word: truth. The core of humility is a real awareness of who we are as God's creatures. We must not lose sight of this most basic truth about ourselves. God is our Creator and our loving Father. Every gift and talent we have comes to us from God. Humility does not require that we deny our talents but that we acknowledge their source. We do not, therefore, need to put on airs, belittle others, nor should we lord it over them. We do not have to do this. We know the truth, and *"the truth will set you free"* (John 8:32).

During Jesus' public life Mary remained in the background. Very few of the words she spoke have been recorded in the Gospels. Those that have come down to us, however, are filled with meaning and sum up essential aspects of her personality. Faithful obedience: *"Let it happen to me as you have said"* (Luke 1:38). Joy and praise: *"My soul proclaims the greatness of the Lord"* (Luke 1:46). Tenderness and charity: *"They have no wine"* (John 2:3). Faith and humility: *"Do whatever (Jesus) tells you"* (John 2:5).

At La Salette ministries around the world, today more than ever, the Mother of Jesus, attentive to all her people, draws to her Son all who see God's love reflected in her tears. She comes to a people who refuse to submit. And how long will she be able to withhold the strong and heavy arm of her Son? She can only repeat the words she spoke to the waiters at Cana: *"Do whatever he tells you"* (John 2:5).

Reflection Questions:

• Today will I acknowledge with gratitude and honesty a certain gift (name it here) with which the Lord has blessed me?
• Do I acknowledge very often the source of my abilities and talents?

Wednesday, March 3, (#232)
Second Week of Lent

Matthew 20:17-28: *"... anyone who wants to become great among you must be your servant,n and anyone who wants to be first among you must be your slave."*

Meditation:

The hour of Jesus was drawing near. *"Jesus was going up to Jerusalem, and on the road he took the Twelve aside by themselves and said to them, 'Look, we are going up to Jerusalem, and the Son of man is about to be handed over to the chief priests and scribes. They will condemn him to death..."*

Yet, even at this late hour, Zebedee's sons and the other apostles as well, failed to understand fully what was about to happen. James and John, their mother speaking in their behalf, wanted ringside seats at the Messiah's triumph. What they did not understand is that the promise of a place in Jesus' Kingdom can be fulfilled only in the life to come, *not* in this one. Once more Jesus had to repeat a fundamental theme of his teaching. Like the master, the disciple is not to *"lord it over others, but serve the needs of all."* Service is what counts with Jesus: a nurse's service to patients, a pastor's service to parishioners, a parent's service to children. *"... anyone who wants to become great among you must be your servant."*

"I am the servant of the Lord," were Mary's words when asked by the angel Gabriel to become the Mother of God. Her calling, her vocation, was summed up in those words. Her dialogue with the angel and her response place her in the line of those whom God calls to a specific mission. This response indicated free and full acceptance of the vocation made known to her.

At La Salette Mary continues to be the Lord's servant and the servant of her children. Her sensitivity, her concern for us all is a clear manifestation of that. *"Come near, my children; don't be afraid ... If my people refuse to submit ... if they are converted... ."* Her maternal solicitude covers every detail and event of our lives. How can we resist her tears and fail to heed this loving messenger of her Son?

Reflection Questions:

- Whether I hold a position of authority or not, do I ever lord it over others?
- Today how can I exercise whatever authority is mine in a true Christian spirit of service?

Thursday, March 4, (#233)
Second Week of Lent

Luke 16:19-31: *"There was a rich man ... ."*

Meditation:

The rich man in today's gospel enjoyed the pleasures of life and seemed to have no need for God. After his death, he experiences the torture that comes from life without God. Lazarus, on the other hand, spent his life in misery but was at peace in his heart because his life was deeply rooted in faith. It is important for us to note what the rich man's sin was as the parable describes it. It is not that he calls the police to have Lazarus removed from his door. It is not that he objects to giving Lazarus scraps from his table. It is not that he abuses Lazarus each time he passes him.

The rich man's sin is that he ignores Lazarus. He doesn't lift a finger to help him. He even closes his eyes to the fact that Lazarus exists. His sin is not what he *does* to Lazarus. Rather it is what he *doesn't do* for him. We all know many "Lazaruses" in the world. Through no fault of their own, many go without food, medical attention, jobs and, of course, basic opportunities. Television news has often zeroed in on their plight. While we enjoy our privacy and security, they remain outside our gates. How long can we go on ignoring them? Even the dog in the story Jesus told did something. He licked Lazarus's sores.

DURING HER SHORT VISIT AT LA SALETTE, Mary showed us an ailing and suffering world. She spoke of a people *"who cannot swear without bringing in the name of her Son."* She spoke of many who will not observe the Sabbath. *"During Lent they go to the meat markets like dogs,"* she commented. *"A great famine is coming. Before the famine comes, children under seven will be seized with trembling and die in the arms of those holding them. The rest will do penance through the famine."* Those who are rich can be saved if they, like the poor, acknowledge their dependence upon God.

Reflection Questions:

- How sensitive am I to the pain that so many in the world are suffering? Am I listening well to those I meet when they share their painful experiences with me?
- How often do I merely pass by a person asking for help? How often do I pray for them?

Friday March 5, (#234)
Second Week of Lent

Matthew 21:33-43,45-46: *"The stone which the builders rejected has become the cornerstone."*

Meditation:

People in general do not like to rub elbows with excellence. It is much easier to live with mediocrity and the status quo. Alongside an outstanding example of heroic caring and loving, the rest of the community is made to feel that it is far from living up to its potential. So they can begin to feel inadequate. Those who stand head and shoulders above the crowd, in fact, are most often persecuted.

Martin Luther King, Jr., who was assassinated; Nelson Mandela, who was jailed. Both were Nobel Peace Prize winners and yet were mocked and ridiculed for their peacemaking efforts. Ironically, it is these very ones who end up saving the rest of society from its own worst enemy – itself! Today's parable illustrates Jesus' plight. The Father, the owner of the vineyard, has provided his people's livelihood, but they resent his servants and even kill his son. They fail to see that they are killing the one who alone can ensure their salvation. Yet the death of Jesus will still save that society from itself. *"The stone which the builders rejected has become the cornerstone."*

During this season of Lent we must ask ourselves where we stand on that hill of crucifixion. Are we with Mary entering into her Son's agony by our active and compassionate presence? Or could it be that we are part of the mob crucifying the Son of Man again? His mother shared Jesus' suffering not only on Calvary but all through his life. Each mystery of her life is faithfully marked by her loving relationship with God, and with God's Son and hers.

HER MESSAGE AT LA SALETTE bids us share in the sufferings of her children all over the world. The crucifix with hammer and pincers she wears upon her heart makes her call to conversion resonate. It was fitting that the brightness in which she and the children stood should emanate from that crucifix. Jesus is the pivotal point of wisdom, goodness and generosity for all who come to know him. He is in fact the cornerstone of their life.

Reflection Questions:

- Will I pray to the Lord to help me identify a rough edge in my own life today?
- Is Jesus the true cornerstone of my life and future? How does that show in my life and actions?

Saturday, March 6, (#235)
Second Week of Lent

Luke 15:1-3,11-32: *"But it was only right we should celebrate and rejoice, because your brother here was dead and has come to life; he was lost and is found."*

Meditation:

Can you imagine yourself doing what the father of this prodigal boy did? Your son goes off and engages in all sorts of immoral and maybe illegal things, and all of it with your funds. He then returns home, not because he loves you, but because he's broke and wants to use your goodness further. More likely than not you'd take him to task in these or similar terms: "What are you crawling back to me for? Because my money is gone now? You'd better shape up and get serious, you good-for-nothing, before you land in jail! You've got your nerve coming back here." And yet, maybe you would say no such thing. Neither did the father of the prodigal. He gave his son an exultant homecoming. Despite all the sinning we have done, despite our misuse of his gifts, nothing can keep our loving and merciful God from wanting to hug us and shower us with gifts and celebrations to remember.

Most of us can identify with the prodigal son. At times, however, we act like the elder son and get angry when we feel we have been taken for granted or slighted. Perhaps we are tempted to pout, sulk and refuse to rejoice when the lost have been found. All we need do is recall that we have all been prodigals in need of a warm welcome back home.

THE HEART OF THE LA SALETTE MESSAGE is that of conversion. It is a return to the Father that will mean an unforgettable celebration. *"If they are converted,"* Mary said, *"rocks and stones will be changed into mounds of wheat and potatoes will be self-sown in the fields."* Mary's words call us back to the realities of life and the demands of our faith. If this wonder is to come about, we must return to the Father with all our whole heart.

Reflection Questions:

• What words do I hear the Father speak to the prodigal on his return home? Can I act in that manner as well when someone asks for my forgiveness?

• What words do I hear him speak to the older son as he vented the disappointment he felt at his brother's reception? Can I empathize with the hurting viewpoint of the old son and truly understand his feelings?

Sunday, March 7 (#028)
Third Sunday of Lent

(Exodus 20:1-17; 1 Corinthians 1:22-25; John 2:23-25)

Meditation: *Hallowed be...*

Every time we recite the Lord's Prayer, we say, Hallowed be thy name. This is raised as a concern by Our Lady of La Salette, in two distinct contexts. First she expresses her sadness at the abuse of her Son's name. Later, she encourages the children to say at least an Our Father and a Hail Mary in their night and morning prayers.

This is also her way of reminding us of the Commandment: You shall not take the name of the Lord, your God, in vain.

Interestingly, the notion of "hallow" occurs in the next commandment: Remember to keep holy the Sabbath day. Our Lady reminds us of this commandment as well. 'Hallow' and 'holy' are what linguists call cognate words. Like 'strengthen' and 'strong,' one is a verb and the other an adjective to express the same idea.

In the Gospel, Jesus was angry that the Temple, his Father's house, was being turned into a marketplace. The very place that contained the Holy of Holies was not being kept holy. The sellers of sacrificial animals had forgotten God's word to Solomon: "I have consecrated this house which you have built and I set my name there forever; my eyes and my heart shall be there always" (1 Kings 9:3).

The reading from St. Paul is from the first chapter of First Corinthians. The letter opens with Paul addressing "the church of God that is in Corinth, to you who have been sanctified in Christ Jesus, called to be holy." Coming so early in the letter, it states the theme of much that is to follow. Later In the same letter he writes: "The temple of God, which you are, is holy."

Without using those words, Mary surely has that same notion in mind when she speaks of "my people." There can be no doubt that she means the people ransomed by her Son, called to be "a chosen race, a royal priesthood, a holy nation, a people of his own" (1 Peter 2:9).

Jesus taught us to pray, "Hallowed be thy name." This is a promise on our part to hallow it. In that same spirit of commitment we might add:

Hallowed be thy day;
Hallowed be thy house;
Hallowed be thy people.

Monday, March 8, (#237)
Third Week of Lent

Luke 4:24-30: *"No prophet is ever accepted in his own country."*

Meditation:

Jesus is in his hometown. He is among his friends and family – his own people! Yet they hate him enough to try to take him to the top of a hill and hurl him off. Those townsfolk really didn't want to hear anything that might disturb their way of thinking and living. They seemed to have gone to the synagogue only to be comforted, to hear how good they were and how special they were to God. That, however, didn't seem to be what Jesus had in mind. He wanted to make them aware of their faults and invite them to shape up. They were far from believing this, and didn't want to hear anything about it.

It must have pained Jesus very much that the people of Nazareth, where he had been raised, put no faith in him. Likewise, members of our families, parishes and communities often go unheard when they offer observations or recommendations that challenge what we find customary and comfortable. We prefer to bring in outside facilitators, consultants and counselors. We give far more credence to speakers from afar than to the folks with the familiar faces. What we have yet to learn is how powerfully God's truth can be present in our everyday life.

JESUS SENDS HIS WEEPING MOTHER TO LA SALETTE. People have not fully accepted her Son and his message. Will they give his mother a warmer welcome? Following Mary's invitation to *"come near, don't be afraid,"* Maximin and Melanie are reassured that the Lady had come *"to tell us great news."* She comes as an ambassador of peace and reconciliation. Mary helps us to recall those means that have been given to help us return to her Son. Her mission was entrusted to her on Calvary. She now passes it on to us through the two children who saw her at La Salette. We in turn must *"make it known to all (her) people,"* the people of God.

Reflection Questions:

• Can you recall a time when you were slighted or scorned by a family member or a dear friend? Have you forgiven this offense? •Have you ever had to ask forgiveness of another when you were wrong or acted inappropriately?

Tuesday, March 9, (#238)
Third Week of Lent

Matthew 18:21-35: *"Were you not bound, then, to have pity on your fellow-servant just as I had pity on you?"*

Meditation:

There is something more to the gift of forgiveness we receive from God; it is meant to be accepted but also shared. The merciless official in today's parable pleaded for mercy and received it. *"... the servant's master felt so sorry for him that he let him go and cancelled the debt."* But when that same official was approached by one who owed him, he refused to hear the plea for mercy and demanded what was owed. This official was given a reality check when the master told him: *"Were you not bound, then, to have pity on your fellow-servant just as I had pity on you?"* You must forgive if you want to be forgiven.

The forgiveness we receive must extend to others. To forgive is the greatest gift we can give to others and to ourselves. True, at times, we might be obsessed with feelings of anger or revenge. But forgiveness is given from our will. If we sincerely will to forgive, want to forgive, then we are forgiving. Bad feelings may remain. We may have to struggle to rid ourselves of them but they are not what Jesus is talking about. Let's forgive and get on with our friendship; get on with our good relationship. As the African proverb has it, "The one who forgives ends the quarrel."

THE MESSAGE OF THE BLESSED VIRGIN MARY at La Salette is a renewal of the message we find in Scripture. It speaks to us from the perspective of the cross and exhorts us to conversion and reconciliation. *"If they are converted"*... all will be forgiven... *"for nothing is impossible with God."* The father of the prodigal is forever watching and waiting for his son to return. His only intent is to forgive completely. Mary reassures us that Jesus will do likewise for all his repentant children.

Reflection Questions:

- Do I accept forgiveness from others but fail to forgive them?
- Having received God's forgiveness, do I still find it hard to forgive myself?

Wednesday, March 10, (#239)
Third Week of Lent

Matthew 5:17-19: *"Do not imagine that I have come to abolish the Law or the Prophets. I have come not to abolish but to complete them."*

Meditation:

When Jesus talks about keeping the law he is not talking about a legalistic approach, a literal keeping of the law. He is speaking about the spirit of the law. He came not to abolish laws but to open eyes to the real meaning contained in all that God has ever commanded his people. Jesus found himself in conflict with many of the religious people of his day. A number of them accused him of trying to destroy the old customs and beliefs of their religious heritage. Jesus reassures them that it is not his intent to destroy teachings handed down by the prophets. He has instead come to fulfill them.

We should always remember Jesus' own sense that law is fulfilled in *love* – wholehearted love of God and compassionate love of neighbor. Our problem is that we tend to "abolish the law," indeed to abolish love as soon as we encounter conflict, disappointment or disagreement. If we are honest, we discover that where we most need conversion to the love Jesus requires is in the rather ordinary situations of our everyday life – in our telephone conversations, in our dealings with authority, in our attitude and behavior in traffic, and in our homes.

WE ARE VERY FORTUNATE that Mary appears at La Salette to remind us that God has given us basic laws to follow if we wish to live happily now and with him forever. As a concerned mother, she warns us of the consequences that will follow, if we fail to take heed. In her conversation with the two witnesses, Our Lady does mention specific commandments. She speaks of our lack of submission to God's will, our irreverence toward the name of her Son, our disregard of the seventh-day rest, our need to pray daily, our obligation to participate in weekly Eucharist, and follow the laws of Lenten observance.

Reflection Questions:

- In my view, what of God's laws a blessing or a burden? In what sense?
- How faithfully do I follow Mary's various reminders?

Thursday, March 11 (#240)
Third Week of Lent

Note: Today you may wish to begin the First Day of the Novena to Our Lady of La Salette, in the appendix of this book.

Luke 11:14-23: *"Anyone who is not with me is against me."*

For Your Reflection:

People often like to hang quotes on their wall to remind themselves of some important lesson they have learned. Now and then we read one that really makes us think. The one which comes to my mind could make me uncomfortable. It reads, "If you are not part of the solution, you are part of the problem." Suddenly, letting others worry about the homeless makes me part of the cause of homelessness. Not raising my voice against drug abuse, racism, makes me part of those problems. At the close of the gospel passage Jesus offers a similar mind teaser, "Whoever is not with me is against me." As God's people, the members of his audience were invited to join him and enter the Kingdom of God. They refused to do so. Jesus tells them they are part of the problem. They stand against him and are scattering while he tries to gather. Jesus offers us the same choice. By its very nature this choice is not one that should be put off. Lent is a perfect time to become part of the solution.

MARY HAS LEFT MANY TANGIBLE SIGNS IN TESTIMONY TO HER APPEARANCE AT LA SALETTE. She chose shepherd children because her message was a crucial one. She knew the children would share it candidly, truthfully and completely. She wore a crucifix, placing her crucified Son before our eyes. She came not to focus attention on herself, but rather on the Crucified and Risen Lord. The miraculous spring, that has not stopped flowing since the time of the apparition, serves as a perpetual sign of her visit. A large basilica stands at that remote Alpine site.

The La Salette religious community of brothers, priests and sisters, now serving in over twenty countries, was founded to proclaim the Beautiful Lady's message and attest to its enduring timeliness.

Reflection Questions:

- Do you seek signs of God's love in the world? Where should you look?
- What signs of God's peace can you find in your own immediate surroundings?

Friday, March 12, (#241)
Third Week of Lent

Mark 12:28b-34: *"There is no commandment greater than these."*

Meditation:

The scribe in today's gospel wanted Jesus to cite the most important of all the commandments. Jesus quotes the command to love God wholeheartedly and neighbor as oneself. In doing so he was presenting the Christian mission statement. No other words could better capture the spirit and goals of Christian living. But imagine having to be commanded to love. Can anyone be ordered to love? Love must be freely given or it isn't true love. Genuine concern and care for others must result from personal choice.

Why then does Jesus say the first of all the commandments is to love God with our entire being and that the second is to love our neighbors as ourselves? Could it be that he wished to impress this essential commandment upon us? I believe so. Because we are created in God's image and because God is love, love is absolutely vital to our existence. Jesus then goes on to congratulate the scribe. Practice this and live it. Only then will you reign with God.

"I saw her tears flow, how they flowed and flowed, and halfway to the ground, melted into the light." It is in these terms that Melanie described Mary's tears at La Salette. Mary's crucifix and the tears she shed there are undoubtedly eloquent symbols of the immense love that Jesus and Mary have for us. During her visit at La Salette, Mary expressed her own undivided love: *"How long a time I have suffered for you!"*

Reflection Questions:

- Does God occupy a central place in my life? How does that show in my daily life?
- Do I forget to thank God before I ask for a favor?

Saturday, March 13, (#242)
Third Week of Lent

Luke 18:9-14: *"For everyone who raises himself up will be humbled, but anyone who humbles himself will be raised up."*

Meditation:

We learn from the tax collector what it means to love. Most tax collectors in his day were accused of being unfair in their dealings with their own people. This tax collector, however, wished to be right with God. His sacrifice was acknowledging that he was a sinner and in need of God's help. He did not raise his eyes nor lift his hands towards heaven. Instead he struck his breast and, confessing the sins in his heart, he implored God's mercy. At the point of realizing that he couldn't pick himself up, pull himself together, set things right, he appealed to God for mercy.

Though he was apparently trying to live according to God's law, the Pharisee boasted of his virtue and looked down on everyone else. It is never tolerable, however, to knock someone else down in order to build oneself up. That is where the Pharisee made his mistake. If we are self-centered and self-seeking, we become too proud and self-righteous. God asks that we be humble enough to admit our sinfulness, our true dependence upon him alone. Facing the truth about oneself is not a pleasant enterprise but face that reality we must!

THE APPEARANCE OF MARY AT LA SALETTE on September 19, 1846, was a major Marian apparition, an exciting intervention by God in Christian history. Saints, pastors and writers – St. John Bosco, the holy Curé of Ars, St. Peter Julian Eymard, Leon Bloy, Paul Claudel, Raïssa and Jacques Maritain, to name but a few – have been profoundly influenced and marked by the gift of La Salette. What influence can it be as we all take up the challenges of our third Christian millennium?

Reflection Questions:

- Can my criticism of others' weaknesses, however true my remarks may be, make me look like a better person?
- What changes do I need to make in my own life as I prepare for Holy Week and Easter?

Sunday, March 14 (#032)
Fourth Sunday of Lent

(2 Chronicles 36: 14-23; Ephesians 2:4-10; John 3:14-21)

Meditation: *Saved by Grace*

Growing up in Nazareth, the Blessed Virgin must have learned the history of her people, the people of God. Remembering what had happened to them because of their infidelity, she came to La Salette to warn her other people, given to her at the foot of the cross, of what was about to happen to them, and for the same reason.

God had compassion on his people, but they ignored his kindness and suffered the consequences. Even then, he did not abandon them altogether. After 70 years of exile, he brought them back to their homeland.

From this point on, they took God's law very seriously. Although eventually this led to the legalism that we associate with the Scribes and Pharisees, it was nevertheless better than the situation that is described in the first part of today's reading from 2 Chronicles.

John's Gospel says that God showed his love for the world by sending Jesus, so that we might have eternal life. This dovetails perfectly with Paul's words

Moses Pointing to a Great Snake: Illustration from the 1897 *Bible Pictures and What They Teach Us*

about the richness of God's mercy and the free gift of salvation.

It also dovetails with the La Salette event. Mary's words and gentle demeanor, the light that surrounds her, her proximity to the children—everything reflects what John says: "God did not send his Son into the world to condemn the world, but that world might be saved through him."

Even her language about the strong, heavy arm of her Son does not contradict this merciful attitude. Why would she speak in this way, if not to set us on the right path and spare us the punishment we deserve, to shield us from the justice of God? As St. Paul says, even when we were dead in our transgressions, God still had great love for us.

He asks only that we love him back and live accordingly. This is a form of submission—to authority, certainly but, at a deeper level, to grace. Think of the scene of the Annunciation, where Mary, full of grace, says: "Behold the handmaid of the Lord, be it done to me according to your word." The desire to do God's will makes it easy to submit to it.

This is perhaps what St. Paul means by saying we are created for the good works that God has prepared in advance, that we should live in them.

Monday, March 15, (#244)
Fourth Week of Lent

John 4:43-54: *"The (royal official) believed what Jesus said to him and went on his way home."*

Meditation:

The royal official had much political authority and power, but now he was facing his own powerlessness. He could not save his dying son. Most people in his situation panic when they feel so needy, because it is difficult to know whom to trust at a time like that. Maybe his initial request was not an act of trust; maybe it was panic that became trust when Jesus did not respond in the anticipated way. Instead of traveling to the official's house, Jesus makes a promise and does not explain how it will be fulfilled. *"Your son will live,"* he said. We don't know what enabled the official to trust that promise, but we do know that experiencing God required that he trust.

WHEN THE CHILDREN AT LA SALETTE encountered the one they called the Beautiful Lady, they did not know that she was the Mother of God, but they did trust that their story was meant to be retold. How interesting that Grandma Pra was so quick to trust that this was the Mother of God speaking to the two children! The people of that area were perhaps feeling a vulnerability like that of the royal official. There was something about the words they heard that evoked a trusting response in the children. Vulnerable moments do not have to lead to panic; they can be invitations and opportunities to trust.

Reflection Questions:

- Do I find it hard to trust God?
- I believe that he preserved the life of the official's son and continually revives people spiritually. Why should I think God will treat me any differently than he treated them?

Tuesday, March 16, (#245)
Fourth Week of Lent

John 5:1-3,5-16: They harassed Jesus because he healed the man on the Sabbath.

Meditation:

How wonderful that someone who had been sick for such a long time was finally well again! How unfortunate that some eyewitnesses were unable to share in the joy of the moment – all because they were rigid in their religious beliefs. So concerned were they about their own actions that they were unable to see what God was doing. They had lost the Sabbath spirit, a willingness to rest, and allow God to speak to our stillness and change our hearts.

At La Salette Mary voiced concern about people's failure to observe the Sabbath spirit properly. Her concern was not limited to what people did on the Sabbath day. She noted that their actions on the Sabbath revealed that something was amiss in their relationship with

God on the other days of the week as well. They lacked the Sabbath spirit. They had become so taken with business matters that they were scarcely aware of God. Similarly we can become preoccupied with schedules, future planning, and even church-related activities and still be lacking a genuine Sabbath spirit. Making time for God is a challenge because it means more than simply squeezing a bit more prayer into an already hectic schedule. True Sabbath time is what is needed.

Reflection Questions:

- Do I distort the spirit of the Sabbath by hanging on to certain ideas about God?
- Do I distort the spirit of the Sabbath by maintaining a hectic lifestyle?

Wednesday, March 17 (#246)
Fourth Week of Lent

John 5:17-30: *"(Jesus) spoke of God as his own Father."*

Meditation:

To speak of God as his own Father was one more way in which Jesus challenged people's assumptions about their relationship with God. His concern was not to define God's gender, however, but to invite people to a closer relationship with God. He wanted people to know that God was more concerned about them and more approachable than they had ever thought possible. Nonetheless, some who heard were more concerned about maintaining their assumptions about God than they were about hearing this Good News.

MARY SPOKE OF A GOD WHO DESIRES TO BE INTIMATELY INVOLVED IN OUR LIVES. She herself was so concerned about us that she wept. She too wanted people to know that God is deeply concerned about them and approachable. Mary's tears and Jesus' use of the familiar term Abba spoke a similar message. God is more concerned about us than we realize. Most people find it difficult to relate to others in an "up-close-and-personal" manner. The experience is all the more challenging when God is involved. We find it difficult to believe that God, or any power greater than ourselves, wishes to bring out the best in us.

Individual and corporate lives, as a result, are marked by selfishness, greed and illusions of security. We lower our expectations and eventually stop expecting much of anything from God.

Some Reflection Questions:

- Are you convinced that your God wishes to be close to you?
- Are you ready to take your own first step toward greater intimacy with God?

Thursday, March 18, (#247)
Fourth Week of Lent

John 5:31-47: *"Come to me to receive life!"*

Meditation:

Jesus' words and works did not make sense unless they were understood as part of a divine plan that began with the creation of the world. That plan is an ongoing story of people and events, reminding us that God is faithful, even when we are unfaithful. It also teaches us that the faithful God wants to share life with us. As we respond to the people and events of salvation history, we learn more and more about God, we possess more and more of that life and live our lives much differently.

LA SALETTE IS ALSO AN ONGOING STORY. It is a story about God's people being reminded again and again of the faithful God who calls his own people to possess more of that life that only he can give. For Maximin and Melanie it was a reminder that their failure to pray was preventing them from possessing God's life. Over the years the ongoing understanding of the La Salette story has helped us to see that it is not our personal failures alone that prevent us from possessing God's life. Social systems also can prevent us from experiencing the fullness of God's life. Becoming more aware of God's life begins with personal change but it goes beyond that and must lead to social change.

Reflection Questions:

- Why are you so slow to possess more of God's life?
- Is it because you realize how frightening the prospect of change can be?

Friday, March 19, (#543)
St. Joseph, Spouse of
the Blessed Virgin Mary

Matthew 1:16, 18-21, 24a: *"When Joseph woke up, he did what the angel of the Lord had told him to do."*

Meditation:

As the Second Vatican Council reminded us, each of us has a vocation – not just priests and religious. All are called by God. As we can see in this passage, the evangelist Matthew sees Joseph as central to the beginning of Christ's life. In this passage we sense Joseph's anguish at learning that Mary is with child. And we hear of his dream in which an angel speaks to him to guide his decision. When Joseph hears that Mary "has conceived what is in her by the Holy Spirit", he listens and responds to the angel, seen by Israel as a messenger from God. Joseph lives out his call very well and responds in other situations to the voice of God.

MARY AT LA SALETTE could nothing other than bring the message of her Son to the two children standing before her. Their initial fear of this Beautiful Lady, weeping before them, encircled in a globe of light was natural. But Mary managed to invite them forward to converse with her and their fear melted away. Mary's call was to bring her Son's message to those children and ultimately to all God's people. She acted as God's messenger for these children, welcoming them, warning them and sending them forth with good news for all to hear. We learn both from Joseph and from Mary appearing at La Salette that sometimes we are asked by God to do difficult things – always supported by God's grace, wisdom and strength.

Reflection Questions:

• When have you felt God's support in making an important decision in your life?
• Whom do you know who has acted with courage that you judge can only come from God?

Saturday, March 20, (#249)
Fourth Week of Lent

John 7:40-53: *"Would the Christ come from Galilee?"*

Meditation:

Galilee was the geographic place that symbolized acceptance of the Gospel. In keeping with their tradition, the people of Jesus' day had assumptions and expectations about how the saving power of God would become visible in the world. Those assumptions limited their ability to understand what God was promising them. That is why God has often been called a God of Surprises. God reveals to us not only that he is faithful but also that our expectations of him are too low.

No ONE EXPECTED that a place as isolated and unpretentious as the hamlet of La Salette in France would be the site from which God would call his people back to himself; neither did they expect that the call would be spoken by the Mother of God. For that reason, some did not believe the message. Others paid attention to what had happened there by invoking the Visitor as Our Lady of La Salette. Over time, spiritual healings linked to La Salette have by far exceeded people's expectations.

Reflection Questions:

- Are you afraid to expect too much from God?
- Are you reluctant to believe in a God of Surprises?

Sunday, March 21 (#035)
Fifth Sunday of Lent

(Jeremiah 31:31-34; Hebrews 5:7-9; John 12:20-33)

Meditation: *God Speaks to the Sinner*

My child, you have no idea how important it is to me that you allow me to forgive you. Please don't put it off. Now is the acceptable time.

Is there something from the distant past that you have

89

never been able to confess? Now is the acceptable time.

Come now, let us set things right. Though your sins be like scarlet, they may become white as snow. They will be totally washed away in the blood of my only Son, who willingly offered himself up for you. Through his suffering, through his obedience, he has paid the full price of your redemption.

He is like the grain of wheat. When he died, he brought forth abundant fruit, to be shared by all. The free banquet of grace awaits you.

I would like nothing better than to place my Law within you and write it on your heart. Just think! It would then be the most natural thing in the world for you to live in my love and to please me.

With age-old love I have loved you; so I have kept my mercy toward you. With your permission and humble cooperation, I will remove your sins from you as far as the East is from the West. Or, if you prefer, I will cast them into the depths of the sea. Surely you must understand the delight it gives me to do so.

Remember what my Son said: "There will be more joy in heaven over one sinner who repents than over ninety-nine righteous people who have no need of repentance." That individual glorious source of joy— that could be you!

Lifted up on the cross, my Son became the source of eternal salvation for all who obey him. He can sympathize with your weakness, because he has been tested in every way, yet without sin. Let him draw you to himself.

Standing near his cross you will find his Mother, Mary. She is your Mother, too. You might know her as the Beautiful Lady. She will help you see what you must do.

Please, please, my child, hand your sins over to me. Then they will be no longer yours, but mine, and I will throw them away. I will cast them behind my back, and I will never look back at them again. Never.

Monday, March 22, (#251)
Fifth Week of Lent

John 8:1-11: *"Neither do I condemn you."*

Meditation:

The Mosaic Law condemned the woman. The crowd condemned her too. But Jesus had a different response. He did not condemn her; he reacted to those who did the condemning. Those who wanted to throw stones were preoccupied with other people's sins and were paying no attention to their own. Perhaps they were unable to show compassion toward others because they had forgotten about God's compassion towards them. Jesus did not interrogate the woman about the accusations; he did not even lecture her about the why and how of God's compassion. He showed compassion by his initial silence and this simple statement: *"Neither do I condemn you."*

AT LA SALETTE MARY SPOKE TO THE CHILDREN about the sins of the world, but she did not condemn. She did not give a lengthy explanation of why her Son was compassionate. Like that of Jesus, her gesture of compassion was a simple one; she wept. Since that time many people have been freed from the burden of past guilt because they were touched by her tears.

Reflection Questions:

•What are the gestures in your life that speak to others of a compassionate God?
•Are you willing to acknowledge your sin that you may be more compassionate towards others?

Tuesday, March 23, (#252)
Fifth Week of Lent

John 8:21-30: *"They did not recognize that (Jesus) was talking to them about the Father."*

Meditation:

Jesus spoke to people about a God who loved them in a way that went beyond their usual understanding of love. In order to understand the meaning of this newly revealed love they would have to look beyond their usual experience. *"You are from below; I am from above."* When people are confused and do not understand a new experience they are inclined to get frustrated and give up. However, people who were persistent in their attempt to understand the newness of Jesus' message came to believe in him. They wrestled with God (and with themselves) in order to discover the life that he was offering.

AT LA SALETTE the children initially did not understand initially what the Beautiful Lady was saying. It is not just that she spoke a different language than they did; she spoke about problems that were beyond their grasp. Nonetheless, they knew that something important was being said and they shared their story with others at home. Their willingness to share their confusion was their way of wrestling with God. Because they did not give up when they were confused, they (and others) came to a new understanding of God's love.

Reflection Questions:

• Is it difficult to believe that God will guide you through life's confusing experiences?
• Are you willing to wrestle with God in order to discover God in new ways?

Wednesday, March 24, (#253) Fifth Week of Lent

John 8:31-42: *"... the truth will set you free."*

Meditation:

The words of Jesus promising freedom are directed at people who had not realized how enslaved they were. They were the ones who paid so much attention to the details of the Law that they could not appreciate its spirit. They were well intentioned, but they had a shallow understanding of what it means to believe. That kind of belief is itself enslaving.

AT LA SALETTE Mary encouraged people to avoid shallowness in their faith. She asked: *"Do you pray well?"* Praying well was not simply a matter of saying more prayers. It meant that their fidelity to prayer would help them to be honest with themselves and open them to that truth which would set them free.

Reflection Questions:

- If Jesus could accept society's outcasts, do you find it hard to accept them?
- Do you find it difficult to accept the truth about yourself? Are you afraid to be truly free?

Thursday March 25, (#545)
The Annunciation of the Lord

Luke 1: 26-38: *"The angel said to her, 'Mary, do not be afraid.'"*

Meditation:

Since the earliest days of the Church, Mary was seen as the first disciple of Jesus. Her vocation, like our own from our Baptism, was to accept God's will and live out our common mission to spread the good news of the Gospel every moment of every day. However in the midst of the various events and preoccupations of our daily lives, we humans can forget that mission. We may lose focus on being children of God and instead concentrate too much on our own will.

AT LA SALETTE, Mary continues to carry out that common mission. In fact, she echoes the words of the angel at her Annunciation by greeting the two children at La Salette with: *"Come near my children, do not be afraid."* She had experienced fear when the angel appeared and she identified with the children who were afraid of her sudden appearance within a brilliant globe of light. Her words and attitude during the apparition were a mixture of warnings and promises, reminders and encouragement.

Mary's concern for the daily lives of these two children even extended to the family of Maximin, whose father was seriously concerned whether he could continue to feed his poor family. Her final words to the two children which actually are extended to all those who hear her message were: *"Make this message known to all my people."* She reminds us of the basics of our Baptismal call; namely, daily prayer, the important place of Eucharist in our life, reverence for God's name, a call to constant conversion, the proper place of Lenten customs of faith, and evangelizing others, reminding them of God's love and forgiveness. This is our call as "her children", the children of her loving Son.

Reflection Questions:

- How are you opening your life to God through prayer, the Eucharist, faith practices and spreading the Good News of her Son?
- Where can you do better?

Friday, April March 26, (#255)
Fifth Week of Lent

John 10:31-42: *"... even if you refuse to believe in me, at least believe in the work I do."*

Meditation:

It troubled some people to think that this man, Jesus, could also be God. Jesus had taught them a new kind of love that included forgiveness and unconditional acceptance. Some thought that kind of love could only be accomplished by God. To believe that Jesus' kind of loving was the same as God's meant that we were being challenged to love as God himself loves. Those outcasts who had been recipients of Jesus' new kind of love, on the other hand, were more than willing to take up that challenge.

WHEN MARY TOLD MELANIE AND MAXIMIN, *"My children, make this known to all my people,"* she challenged them (and us) to be as compassionate as Jesus is. We should not expect God to love, forgive and accept us unconditionally if we ourselves are unwilling to do the same.

Reflection Questions:

- Are you willing to forgive as God forgives?
- What might help you accept others unconditionally?

Saturday, March 27, (#256)
Fifth Week of Lent

John 11:45-56: *"If we let him go on in this way everybody will believe in him."*

Meditation:

Those who did not understand, feared that unless they took steps to control Jesus' popularity, they might lose the very things that insured their security – their sanctuary and their nation. They feared that the whole world would change entirely and affect the personal security they enjoyed. It never occurred to them that a world transformed by God's love might be a desirable place, not only for themselves but for everyone. It seemed to them too good to be true.

JUST AS THE GOSPEL IS MEANT FOR ALL PEOPLE, the story of La Salette is a story that is meant for the whole world to hear. People who understand that God's compassion is more powerful (and important) than our sinning, realize that they have shared in something that must be passed on – a spirit of reconciliation.

Reflection Questions:

- Do you have a desire to control people and situations, thus preventing others from experiencing God's love?
- Do you feel a need to cling to a false sense of security?

Sunday, March 28, (#038B long form) Palm Sunday

(Mark 11:1-10; Isaiah 50:4-7; Philippians 2:6-11; Mark 14:1—15:47)

Meditation: *Paradoxical*

The readings for Palm Sunday create unexpected pairings. In the first Gospel passage, Jesus is recognized by the crowd as the one who comes in the name of the Lord, before whom they shout 'Hosanna.' Later the crowd clamors for his crucifixion. On Calvary, the Roman centurion supervising the crucifixion of Jesus comes to believe that Jesus is the Son of God.

The Psalm, which begins with a famous cry of despair, ends on a note of exultation. God's servant described by Isaiah is treated shamefully, yet firmly believes he will not be put to shame. And St. Paul portrays Jesus as emptying and humbling himself, obedient to the point of death, but also as exalted, given a name above all other names—Lord.

It ought not to surprise us to find similar pairings at La Salette. Mary

Christ and disciples at table in the house of Simon the leper, with Mary Magdalene and Martha serving

appears in heavenly light, but she weeps. She speaks of the dire consequences of lost faith, and yet does so with infinite gentleness. She gives an important mission to two children who can scarcely make sense of what she has said to them.

When we look at the Church, we find much the same. The brilliant English author G.K. Chesterton (1874-1936) pointed out many paradoxes which one finds in the Church: variously criticized as "the enemy of women, and their foolish refuge;" a "solemn pessimist and a silly optimist," who produced "fierce crusaders and meek saints;" the list goes on at some length. He sums up his thoughts with the central paradox of Christian theology: "Christ was not a being apart from God and man, like an elf, nor yet a being half human and half not, like a centaur, but both things at once and both things thoroughly, very man and very God."

This pairing of "true man and true God" is indeed at the very center of our faith. Hard as it is to understand, we proclaim it in our creed.

These are not simply theological musings. They say a lot about us as well. As Christians we are a paradox; we are aware of the contradictions within ourselves, sinners and saints that we are, individually and as Church. The La Salette call to conversion must be taken seriously, but we will never be able to say: Now I am holy. And yet we do not despair of reaching that goal under the watchful eye of the Beautiful Lady.

Monday, March 29, (#257)
Holy Week

John 12:1-11: *"You have the poor with you always, you will not always have me."*

Meditation:

There is something disturbing about the scene. Mary's profound gratitude to Jesus for what he had done in her life led her to be extravagant. Deep and true love does not count the cost. As the odor of the precious ointment filled the house, so did a sense of awe at this bold act of love. But a voice pierced this atmosphere and declared this a shocking waste that the money could have been used for the poor. (The value of the ointment, made in India, amounted to an ordinary worker's yearly wage, commentators say.) Perhaps we ourselves silently agree? But Jesus did not agree. He reveals what is really happening. This anointing prepares his body for the death and burial he will soon be facing. The poor will always be with us, and when he is gone, they will be a privileged place for ministering to Jesus himself. There is also a place for devotion, love, reverence, and worship. Our challenge is to discern what, here and now, is the most appropriate response to those myriad ways in which Jesus remains present to us.

At La Salette Mary wore peasant garb. She spoke to two children from very poor families. The words she spoke were jolting and disturbing yet she was vested with dazzling radiance and glory. The light surrounding her served to identify the Beautiful Lady. Its rare brilliance awakened in Maximin an impulse to reach out and grasp some of this beauty.

Reflection Questions:

• Has your faith ever found inspiration in a magnificent church building or religious work of art?
• Are you able to see and help others see the faith reality and appropriateness behind this kind of "extravagance"?

Tuesday, March 30, (#258)
Holy Week

John 13:21-33,36-38: *"At that instant, after Judas had taken the bread, Satan entered him... It was night."*

The scene is the Last Supper. Judas leaves to tell the officials where they can find and arrest Jesus. Step by step, Judas has been walking the cold, calculated path of betrayal. He deliberately leaves the glow of the light and plunges into the night. Jesus tells the disciples that he must leave them now but that they cannot follow him. Blustering, impetuous Peter immediately leaps into the conversation: *"Lord, why can I not follow you now? I will lay down my life for you."* One can almost see Jesus sadly shaking his head and telling Peter – or is he chiding him? – that before the cock crows he will have betrayed him three times. And so it happened. But Peter's heart, overflowing with love for the Lord, was not a place where Satan might find a welcome. Jesus could see the depths of Peter's heart and the love within it. It is this love that enabled Peter to emerge from that night and confidently claim Jesus' loving forgiveness.

MARY'S RECITATION OF HER PEOPLE'S SINS and neglect of God can at times seem to be a path into darkness. As she breaks open the political reality France was then experiencing and its consequences, we may be tempted to block our ears and run away. That is why the light radiating from her and the crucifix on her breast is what dispels the darkness. From the heart of darkness, the suffering and death of Jesus shines as the light that will transform the night forever.

Reflection Questions:

• Do you make an about-face when your choices make you dim the guiding lights on your path of life?
• What can help you turn what is often a "long day's journey into the night" into a "long day's journey into the light"?

Wednesday, March 31, (#259)
Holy Week

Matthew 26:14-25: *"Better for that man (Judas) if he had never been born!"*

Meditation:

It is not uncommon to be bewildered by Judas. (The film, *Jesus Christ Super Star*, includes a scene of Judas running in the desert, huge tanks pursuing him – powerful images of his fate, his destiny, about to destroy him.) In the divine plan, someone was to betray Jesus. It could have been someone who did not know Jesus personally, a Roman soldier, a member of the Sanhedrin. However it ended up being a trusted friend. And yet Jesus had chosen Judas.

He had given him a position of confidence in the group. Jesus did not shut Judas out. Even on the night of the betrayal, he let Judas know that he was aware of what was going on. Jesus exerted no power to stop Judas. The only power he used was the heartfelt appeal that Judas remain a faithful disciple, a faithful friend but to no avail.

Did Judas die in despair, believing he could never be forgiven? Was his vision so desperately closed in on himself that he neither saw nor entirely understood the extent of Christ's mercy and compassion? Ours is a God of second and seemingly infinite chances! Simply by asking, Judas could have been reborn in Christ's unconditional love. We have no idea what happened during those seconds between the hanging and actual death (Matthew 27:5). Judas may have whispered, "I'm sorry. Please forgive me."

AT LA SALETTE Mary's message gives us the promise that can break the chain of sin and the consequent sufferings and dyings. "*If* my people are converted..." *If* is the hinge word. *If* smashes "fated" or "destined" punishment. *If* is a precious reminder of our continued second chances. If takes us beyond.

Reflection Questions:

- How have you experienced the Lord's powerful forgiveness?
- How do you convey to others this core truth of your faith in Jesus?

Thursday, April 1, (#039)
Holy Thursday

John 13:1-15: "*If I therefore ... have washed your feet, you must wash each other 's feet ... so that you may copy what I have done to you.*"

Meditation:

On this day celebrating the institution of the Eucharist, it is surprising that the familiar words transforming bread and wine into the body and blood of Jesus, as recorded in the Gospels of Mark, Matthew and Luke, are not found in the gospel for the Mass of the Lord's Supper. In John's account, Jesus provides instead a different way of remembering him and making him present to one another. It is the remembrance and presence of loving service.

In washing the feet, Jesus turns our understanding of authority and power upside down. The Lord who holds all power and authority manifests himself as servant. His act is an example that we are challenged to imitate and repeat in our own culture and society, so taken with control, force, might and power. Jesus invites us to believe in the counter-cultural power of humble, loving service.

AT LA SALETTE Mary shows the power of a weeping mother. Her apparition manifests a *kenosis* (Philippians 2:7) or *self-emptying*, all its own. She has bent over her children just as Jesus bent over the feet of his disciples. She does not stand aloof, but comes near. She wants our hearts to be washed with her tears of love. And as she came to call us to conversion; she confers that same task on us. As she has done, so should we do.

Reflection Questions:

- How do I make Jesus present to others?
- How frequently do I engage in "bending down" in service to others?

Friday, April 2, (#040)
Good Friday

John 18:1 –to 19:42: *"I was born for this, I came into the world for this, to bear witness to the truth; and all who are on the side of truth listen to my voice."*

Meditation:

The truth of Good Friday shone in the glory of Jesus' suffering and death. No, we have not yet reached the Easter moment. We are at the foot of the cross. In the words, *"It is finished,"* Jesus declares the astounding truth that all that has happened is part of the Father's plan. "It," the plan, has been brought to its fulfillment, although not in the manner messianic hopes had imagined. In God's plan, Jesus had to undergo such pain, such vulnerability, such darkness, such near despair. This is the truth this day challenges us to walk in and remain in for a while. Jesus has made all of our sufferings, and even our death, his own. All suffering and dying itself have, therefore, been infused with meaning beyond what we can comprehend. This is the truth that Easter has guaranteed us forever.

But let us not move too quickly to Easter. Let us stay with this day's pain and overwhelming truth. All this suffering, and dying, "for love of me … for love of us." There is always the strong temptation to avoid "Good Friday moments" at all cost. It is all part and parcel of *"If anyone wants to be a follower of mine, let him renounce himself and take up his cross and follow me"* (Mark 8:34). It is an intricate part of what we sometimes glibly call the Paschal Mystery. Good Friday's "truth" is that the "no" of death is not the last word; its "truth" is that life ultimately conquers death; its "truth," by now almost a cliché, that there can be no Easter unless there is a Good Friday.

AT LA SALETTE Mary helped us to see the "truth" underlying the events of those crucial days. Like the prophets, she sliced open the reality and allowed us to see an even deeper reality beneath it. Prophets help us see the layers of truth in the world. Mary's tears and the brilliant light surrounding this Queen of Prophets invited us to look and see with the eyes of our hearts. The truth of love comes to hearts alert and open.

Reflection Questions:

- How well do I recognize my Good Friday experiences and my Easter experiences? Can I name some of them?
- What impresses me most about Jesus on this Good Friday?

Saturday, April 3 (#041B)
Holy Saturday

Mark 16:1-8: *"And the women came out and ran away from the tomb because they were frightened out of their wits; and they said nothing to anyone, for they were afraid."*

Meditation:

As baptized followers of Jesus, we have some responsibilities – to live as his followers (be active Christians), reach out to others with love and understanding (love our neighbors and help the needy), and share the message (be evangelizers in his Name). Many of us unhesitatingly respond to the first two parts but are uncomfortable with the last being evangelizers. Yet in 1974, Pope Paul VI explained that evangelization is not an optional part but a permanent and constitutive necessity of the Church. "The Church exists to evangelize!" The Church on earth is missionary by her very nature!

In Pope Francis' Apostolic Exhortation, "*Evangelii Gaudium* (The Joy of the Gospel)" he begins by placing Mary in the midst of her people, present among the disciples in the upper room when the Holy Spirit came upon them (Acts 1:14). In fact, he says: "She is the Mother of the Church which evangelizes, and without her we could never truly understand the spirit of the new evangelization."

We could well take as a good example how Pope Francis personally evangelizes. Cardinal Renato Martino explained: "The Holy Father instructs with his words, but effectively teaches through his actions.. This is his uniqueness and his magnetism" (*L'Osservatore Romano*, Dec. 13, 2013, p. 7).

MARY AT LA SALETTE IS HERSELF A GREAT EVANGELIZER. As Pope Francis shares: "There is a Marian 'style' to the Church's work of evangelization. Whenever we look to Mary, we come to believe once again in the revolutionary nature of love and tenderness. In her we see that humility and tenderness are not virtues of the weak but of the strong who need not treat others poorly in order to feel important themselves... She is the woman of prayer and work in Nazareth, and she is also Our Lady of Help, who sets out from her town 'with haste' (Luke 1:39) to be of service to others."

Some Reflection Questions:

•Whom are some people you know who encourage others to believe— through their words and example?
•Whom have you (or someone you know) encouraged another to become more active in their faith?

Sunday, April 4 (#042)
Easter Sunday

(Acts 10:34-43; Colossians 3:1-4; John 20:1-9. Other options possible.)

Meditation: *Witnesses*

In the first reading, Peter states that he and his companions were witnesses to three distinct realities: 1) Jesus' public ministry; 2) the risen Christ; and 3) that Jesus has been appointed judge of the living and the dead.

Paul, in the second reading, bears witness to the resurrection of Jesus and, in a particular way, to its meaning for our Christian life.

Mary Magdalen, Peter and the disciple whom Jesus loved also were witnesses, in the account we

Jesus resurrected meets
Mary Magdalene

read today from John's gospel. Witness to what, exactly? To nothing, to absence, to emptiness—or, more accurately, to mystery.

The mystery of Jesus' resurrection is so fundamental that it is not easy to express in words what it means to us. In 1972, Easter fell on April 2. That day, the truth of Easter struck me in a way I cannot adequately describe. I can say, however, that it was the most life-changing spiritual experience of my life.

The beloved disciple, John, entered the tomb, saw, and believed. In that emptiness he experienced the deepest possible faith. His goal from then on was to help others to experience the same. Near the end of his Gospel, he writes: "These [signs] are written that you may believe that Jesus is the Messiah, the Son of God, and that through this belief you may have life in his name."

"Life in his name"—Mary at La Salette does not use those words, but that is the meaning of her message. Like Moses in Deuteronomy, she places before us life and death, and begs us to choose life. Those who do so become witnesses to the transforming mystery of what St. Paul calls a life "hidden with Christ in God."

Not knowing, not understanding, is not necessarily a bad thing. Mélanie and Maximin did not know who was speaking to them, nor did they understand everything they heard; but at the Beautiful Lady's invitation, they entered into that mystery, into what a 14th century spiritual classic calls the Cloud of Unknowing.

In telling others, like Peter, what they had seen and heard, the children were actually witnessing to what they did not know. They drew others into the mystery of Mary's love, revealing the fathomless depths of God's mercy, of which we too can be witnesses.

Monday, April 5, (#261)
Easter Monday

Matthew 28:8-15: *"Do not be afraid; go and tell my brothers that they must leave for Galilee."*

Meditation:

What an extraordinary gift it is to have the Lord's peace that can take away our fears. The Lord often prefaces his appearances to the disciples with the greeting that grants this peace. Ultimately, this peace is a fruit of the Holy Spirit and it is very much needed because fear prevents us in many ways from being fully present and attentive. Fear can have us cringe, squint and look away, thus severely limiting our capacity to see and take in the whole picture. Fear can set our heart and mind racing, searching for a defense, looking for an escape. Fear can cause the fight or flight mechanism to kick in. Fear can cause us to run and not stop to look and listen to what is truly happening. This is especially true when we are dealing with a powerful spiritual experience. And fear can be so totally absorbing that it can make us forget.

Good Friday had been so overwhelming that the women and the disciples forgot what Jesus had said about his dying and rising. The encounter at the empty tomb left them "half-overjoyed and half-fearful." Did they dare hope and believe that Jesus was risen? And into this excitement the risen Lord appears. Jesus takes their dramatically renewed energy and sends them off to bring the good news to the others.

AT LA SALETTE Our Lady follows the same pattern. She invites the children to come near and not to be afraid. Her message, however, certainly could raise fear in their hearts and leave them filled with anxiety. Along with her command to *"make this known"* it would seem that Our Lady gave her confidants a special strength allowing them to hold steadfast to their story, even when threatened by authorities.

Reflection Questions:

- What fears at times prevent me from living and sharing the Lord's gift of peace?
- Are there fears that hold me back from witnessing to the Risen Lord?

Tuesday, April 6, (#262)
Easter Tuesday

John 20:11-18: *"(The angels) said to (Mary Magdalene): 'Woman, why are you weeping?'"*

Meditation:

A heavy cloak of sadness is Mary Magdalene's attire this morning. Her grieving heart has tunneled her vision into a single thought, "He is gone. He is dead. All my hopes, all that had helped me make sense out of life, all were dashed on that horrid day. There is nothing I can do now but give final anointing to his dead body. There is nothing else."

It is into this brokenhearted experience that Jesus appears. Just as it is in the confusion and disappointment of the disciples going to Emmaus that Jesus appears. Just as it is into the fear of the disciples barricaded behind locked doors that Jesus appears. Yes, we find and experience Jesus in moments of joy, of love, of celebration. But often Jesus breaks into the weeping moments of our lives – times of painful failure, unfulfilled hopes, broken plans, unattained goals and disappointed hopes. At times Jesus breaks into the hurting fragments of our broken commitments that can appear irreparable, irretrievable. Times and places such as these seem to be favorite entries for Jesus.

AT LA SALETTE no one asked Mary why she was weeping. The children thought at first that she was a mother from the area and that her children had beaten her. But her message soon put the reason for her tears beyond speculation – her children were suffering. Hers were tears of love – love so strong that it breaks into her "beatific state of being" and causes anguish and pain. What makes no sense to the theologian's mind makes eminent sense to the loving heart.

Reflection Questions:

- Have I allowed myself to touch the roots of some of the sadness in my life?
- If the Lord were to ask me "why are you weeping," how would I answer?

Wednesday, April 7, (#263)
Easter Wednesday

Luke 24:13-35: "... *how our chief priests and our leaders handed him over to be sentenced to death and had him crucified.*"

Meditation:

Our text is found in the account given by the Emmaus disciples of what had recently happened in Jerusalem. Is it farfetched to imagine that part of their pain came from a deep sense that they had been betrayed by their religious leaders? These disciples do not refer to "*the* chief priests and leaders" but to "*our* chief priests and leaders." How could it all have gone so wrong? How could the One who seemed to fulfill their messianic hopes and dreams be destroyed by the very guardians and teachers of their faith, including faith in the expected Christ?

The two disciples welcomed a stranger into their fear, doubts and disillusionment. Jesus the Stranger reviews the Scripture passages relating to the Messiah and helps them to see how the events of recent days fulfilled the predictions of the prophets. What is more, he set their hearts on fire. They understood the deeper meaning of those events. Their hope reborn, they rushed back to Jerusalem to share their experience with the other disciples. Easter's living light had now pierced the darkness of their despondent feelings of betrayal.

THE LA SALETTE EVENT, like other officially recognized apparitions, knew stormy beginnings. But even before canonical approval had been given, thousands flocked to the favored mountain and felt their hearts catch fire as the words Mary had spoken there helped them understand the "meaning" of contemporary events and their link to the providence of God. Many hurried down from the mountain and shared their experience with others.

Reflection Questions:

- What or who has contributed most to my own search for meaning?
- Has my heart ever been "set on fire"?

Thursday, April 8, (#264) Easter Thursday

Luke 24:35-48: *"Why are you so agitated... See by my hands and my feet that it is really I myself.. Touch me and see for yourselves; a ghost has no flesh and bones as you can see I have."*

Meditation:

The Incarnation has a unique continuance after the Lord has been raised from the dead. In speaking of the post-Resurrection Christ, we stress that we are dealing with his glorified body. That is true. But we must avoid the danger of spiritualizing too much. At the heart of our faith is Jesus' bodily resurrection. In his Easter and post-Easter appearances to the disciples, Jesus went out of his way to have them recognize that he was no phantom or hallucination. He invites them to look at his hands and feet. They are signed with the wounds he suffered for love of us and in obedience to the Father. In these appearances Jesus shows that his glory and the cross must always remain together. We are *incarnational* people. Our faith, our religion, is *incarnational*. Our sacraments offer visible, tangible signs of God's grace and presence. It's not wrong to expect or seek moments of encounter with the Lord that will touch and move us.

AT LA SALETTE the brilliant light surrounding Our Lady, and then embracing the children, was truly a sign of glory. As the two herders observed, this light seemed to emanate from the crucified Christ on the cross that Mary wore on her breast. That dark, dark moment of Good Friday is here revealed in its ultimate reality: Glory.

Reflection Questions:

- How do I respond to Christ's invitation to relate to him in the humanity he shares in with me?
- How do I find and relate to him in the wounds his people bear?

Friday, April 9, (#265)
Easter Friday

John 21:1-14: *"Simon Peter said (to the disciples), 'I'm going fishing.' They replied, 'We'll come with you.'"*

Meditation:

This gospel passage recounts Jesus' third appearance to the disciples. As they had been instructed, they were waiting for the Lord in Galilee. Peter decides to go fishing. The others join him. Fishermen by trade, they returned to what they knew best, giving us a life-goes-on feeling. After an unsuccessful night of fishing, a man walking along the shore tells them they should cast their nets once again. They do so and a tremendous catch of fish results, bringing vividly to mind their very first encounter with Jesus: *"Come after me and I will make you fishers of people"* (Matthew 4:19). John is the first to recognize him. *"It is the Lord!"* he says.

There is something evocative about the scene. The disciples labor in vain. When the as yet unrecognized Lord offered direction they might have been tempted to tell him they were seasoned at their trade, had been fishing all night, and that if there were fish to be caught they would have caught them. As members of our "instant everything" culture, we are quick to toss off one single failed attempt and move on to a new try. "Been there, done that" is a mantra of our age. Yet we often row to shore, nets empty and spirits drooping. Perhaps our attempts need only one more try. The grace moment may be the very next one. And when success does come, do we exclaim: *"It is the Lord!"*?

AT THE TIME OF THE APPARITION AT LA SALETTE, it took a grandmother to realize that the Beautiful Lady was in fact the Blessed Mother. There is much "waiting" in the hearts of our elderly. And it is in that patient waiting that an understanding and recognition of spiritual realities become clearer. The timeless "light on the mountain" reveals the divine presence in the events of our time.

Reflection Questions:

- Can I identify times when the Lord has transformed my seemingly fruitless efforts into blessings?
- Is this patient attitude of "waiting for something" a part of my faith life and Christian ministry?

Saturday, April 10, (#266)
Easter Saturday

Mark 16:9-15: *"(Jesus) showed himself (to the two disciples) under another form."*

Meditation:

The Easter Week gospels have dealt with the post-Resurrection appearances of Jesus. Jesus shows his wounds, invites the disciples to touch him, breaks bread, cooks fish and eats with them. He is not a ghost; he is really present. But he is also able to walk through closed doors, appear and disappear at will, and presents a changed appearance. Sightings and encounters with him were first reported to the apostles by some of the women and two of the disciples. Most of the apostles did not believe them. When Jesus did appear to them by the lake, he reprimanded them for their disbelief and the stubbornness they showed in not putting faith in these witnesses.

We are people called to believe in Jesus as a living presence, but he is very much the Jesus of a changed appearance. Mark, Matthew and Luke identify his presence in the bread and wine consecrated in his memory. For John, it is a presence hidden in humble, loving service to others and the indwelling of the Holy Spirit. The invitation to believe and experience Jesus' presence turns the popular saying upside down. "I'll believe it when I see it" becomes "I'll see it when I believe it."

MARY'S MESSAGE AT LA SALETTE invites us to recognize the presence of God in our everyday lives. The passage about the wheat field at Coin reveals God's ear close to earth, hearing Mr. Giraud's expression of care and concern for his son, Maximin, if the wheat crop continues to fail. The connectedness between the here and the hereafter can be seen, if we believe.

Reflection Questions:

- How often have I recognized Jesus in the unexpected events of my life or that of others?
- How much faith and confidence do I put in the faith experience of others?

Sunday, April 11 (#044)
Second Sunday of Easter
(Divine Mercy Sunday)

Note: Today you may wish to begin the First Day of the Novena to Our Lady of La Salette, in the appendix of this book.

(Acts 4:32-35; 1 John 5:1-6; John 20:19-31)

Meditation: *Imperfect Faith*

The end of Chapter 4 of the Acts of the Apostles paints a picture of the first Christians as a perfect society. Chapter 5, however begins with the story of a couple who tried to perpetrate a fraud on the community, and Chapter 6 describes quarrels over the distribution of the donations brought to the apostles.

And in the Gospel, we find Thomas refusing to trust the other apostles.

This is not so surprising. Even today there are strong differences of opinions, and sometimes conflicts, among Christians. These have led to tragic divisions.

We are divided among ourselves because we are divided within ourselves. In other words, all of us are—and each of us is—always in need of conversion and reconciliation. None of us will ever be able to say, Now I'm perfect. But help is always available.

The Christian community in Acts received the grace it needed to overcome situations dangerous to their unity. Thomas received from Jesus himself the help he needed in his moment of crisis.

The first major divisions in the Church had begun in the fourth century, over matters of doctrine. Was Jesus really God? What does the Church believe about the Holy Spirit? The Nicene Creed goes back to those times.

Fast-forward to 1846. The grace of La Salette was given to the Church in response to a new danger, worse even than doctrinal differences. People had stopped caring about such things. They had become indifferent to doctrine, to the commandments, and to the practice of their faith. Either they had rejected these things outright, or they had simply drifted away from them.

Mary was rightly concerned about the impact of all this on her people. They could not afford to sever their relationship with her Son, their Savior.

At Mass, before the sign of peace, we pray, "Look not on our sins but on the faith of your Church." Our sins and the faith of your Church refer to the same group of people. We are sinners, we are Church. These are not mutually exclusive.

Imperfect and weak our faith may be, but it is real and can grow if we will let it. That is the Beautiful Lady's hope—and ours—as she calls us to reconciliation.

Monday, April 12, (#267)
Second Week of Easter

John 3:1-8: *"Nicodemus said to (Jesus), 'How can anyone who is already old be born? Is it possible to go back into the womb again and be born?'"*

Meditation:

Embracing Jesus as the Christ means becoming an entirely new person. Such a prospect alarms Nicodemus, the captivated yet cautious night-caller. He stammers this question, "Do you mean I must re-enter my mother's womb?" Slow-witted? Literal-minded? Not likely. This is rather an instance of radical resistance to the drastic change Jesus' words imply. New birth always follows upon a death of sorts. Birth pangs in one form or another. Under these circumstances who would not try to buy a little time?

"If the harvest is ruined," Mary said at La Salette, *"it is only on account of yourselves. I warned you last year. You paid no heed."* Paying heed can be a tricky affair. Promptings toward conversion can be shrugged off or they can be put on hold. However, "later on" can come much sooner than we think. Just as the gentle, mysterious breeze unexpectedly parts our hair and strokes our face, may God's Spirit stir mightily in us and help us claim the stirring.

Reflection Questions:

- In my life when has my hesitation been a grace for me?
- On the contrary, when is my hesitation a sign of timid shirking or a refusal to see?

Tuesday, April 13, (#268) Second Week of Easter

John 3:7-15: *"'How is that possible?' asked Nicodemus."*

Meditation:

Trustee of the past, heir to a rich legacy, Nicodemus comes forward, willing and wanting at least to learn about the new. That he is sincere, we discover from the progression in his questions about the reality, the how, and the when of this birth from above. The questions he puts to Jesus, his surprise at the answers he gets, suggest that, although he is thoroughly schooled in the sacred writings and culture of his people, he has not yet discovered what it really means to be lost or saved, to be dead or alive. The questions we puzzle over can take us to the innermost boundaries of our yearning, to the outermost reaches of our desire.

IN LIVING HER GRACED LIFE and in fulfilling her exalted calling, Mary asked few questions. She pondered in her heart the words and deeds of the Lord. How to love to the point of laying down one's life, she learned, is the answer to the most basic of life's questions. Knowing only Christ and Christ crucified, she appears on the mountain of La Salette wearing his crucifix upon her heart. "Loveliest of all," as Melanie and Maximin later delighted to repeat, "was the Lady's cross, the source of the light that enveloped her entirely."

Reflection Questions:

- What questions do I raise in my intimate encounters with Jesus?
- What do these questions say about the boundaries of my own yearning?

Wednesday, April 14, (#269) Second Week of Easter

John 3:16-21: "... whoever does the truth comes into the light."

Meditation:

A familiar, if not universally welcome, sight is that of the fellow brandishing the John 3:16 placard before the television cameras in sports arenas and stadiums. If a few people pause a moment and think to themselves: "This is really what it all comes down to"; if several more say to themselves: "This is truly good news"; if yet others flirt with the idea of acting on this reassuring word, our man will have proved to be a clever publicist and an effective evangelist.

JUST AS GOD HAD REFUSED to surrender the first human couple to their fear and shame, but came looking for them, so too did the risen Jesus seek the very ones who had deserted him and fled into the dark night. Our Lady's appearance at La Salette in a globe of resplendent brightness, inviting the children to step into her very light, tells us that our salvation is nothing less than God's relentless effort to find us and lure us out of hiding – from God and from ourselves – in order to strip us of the evasions, pretenses and rationalizations with which we have clothed our shame.

Reflection Questions:

- Am I conscious of any locked, dark rooms in my spiritual house?

• "Fortunately, it is in the nature of cover-ups to be uncovered," William Safire once wrote. How wholeheartedly do I agree with him?

Thursday, April 15, (#270)
Second Week of Easter

John 3:31-36: *"The Father loves the Son and has entrusted everything to his hands."*

Meditation:

Today's gospel reading calls for probing and penetrating reflection as it puts before us such profound realities as discipleship, the community of life and the communion of love. Jesus discloses to us here the decisive underlying pattern of our whole life in him. The love of the Father for the Son, a love that the Son returns in obedience, establishes a community of life between the Father and the Son and this shared life manifests itself when the Son speaks the Father's words and does the Father's works. The love of Jesus for the disciples, a love the disciples return in obedience, establishes a community of love between Jesus and them, and this shared life manifests itself whenever the disciples proclaim his words and carry out his works. The key word here – some would call it the problem word – is obedience.

THE OPENING WORDS SPOKEN AT LA SALETTE by the Mother of the Lord, who herself accepted with loving submission her place and part in God's plan, keynote the entire discourse she delivered there: *"If my people refuse to submit, I will be forced to let go the arm of my Son."* This stark statement of fact contrasts sharply with her own wholehearted commitment as the first among the disciples. The large chain embracing her shoulders tells us we are all interlocking links in a chain of divine life. "All things are yours," she seems to say, "and you are Christ's, and Christ, of course, is God's" (see 1 Corinthians 3:21,23).

Reflection Questions:

• Do I balk inside at the mere mention of obedience?
• In what specific ways will submission to my Lord set me free? What concerns or situations can I let go of when God is in charge?

Friday, April 16, (#271)
Second Week of Easter

John 6:1-15: *"Where can we buy some bread for these people to eat?"*

Meditation:

There can be no doubt that the early church was rather partial to the multiplication story. We find it in all four gospels: twice in Mark, twice in Matthew, once each in Luke and John. It focuses on a most basic and shared human reality – the need to eat. In his gift of bread, Jesus gives himself entirely, feeding our bodies and satisfying the many hungers of the human heart. A bit of bread and a bit of fish wondrously became a lot of bread and a lot of fish. Every year through the good earth, the Creator makes a little barley and a little wheat into much barley and much wheat – enough to feed a world. In the feeding of the multitude, God incarnate does up close, on a smaller scale and at an accelerated pace, in hands just like ours, what he has always done.

With touching sadness Mary cautions at La Salette that the wheat will become scarce and that hunger will surely follow: *"If you have wheat you must not sow it. Anything you sow the insects will eat, and whatever does come up will fall into dust when you thresh it."* To bring her poignant message home to us more vividly, she echoes the distress and powerlessness of a father before his child's hunger: *"Child, eat some bread… I don't know who will eat any next year if the wheat continues this way."* How are we to deal with humanity's growing needs? One lad's provision for a day out is where one should begin. The need will never be too great for our resources, if we share them as the Lord bids us do.

Reflection Questions:

- What are some of the deepest hungers of the human spirit?
- How concerned am I about world hunger? What have I done to "feed the hungry"?

Saturday, April 17 (#272)
Second Week of Easter

John 6:16-21: *"The disciples saw Jesus walking on the sea."*

Meditation:

From our vantage point in time we realize that as Jesus came walking toward them on the sea, the disciples were witnessing a miracle of the new creation. That brief glimpse was, so to speak, a crocus miracle. Crocuses, to our delight, break through the earth's winter crust and snow. They signal that a crucial corner has been turned.

In the walking on the waves we see the relations between spirit and nature changed to the point where nature can be made to do whatever the spirit pleases. This new obedience of nature cannot, of course, be separated from the obedience of the human spirit to the Creator.

"IF MY PEOPLE ARE CONVERTED," the Mother of the risen Christ promised at La Salette, "rocks and stones will be changed into mounds of wheat and potatoes will be self-sown in the fields." She well knew that hope must always describe a future that few think possible or even imaginable. Queen of Prophets, she reminds us that language about "what will be later" must necessarily contradict language about "what is now."

Some Reflection Questions:

- Can you honestly say that hope is a favorite virtue of yours?
- How do optimism and hope differ?

Sunday, April 18 (#047)
Third Sunday of Easter

(Acts 3:13-19; 1 John 2:1-5; Luke 24:35-48)

Meditation: *Facts of Life*

St. Peter takes a conciliatory approach in addressing those who crucified Jesus: "You acted out of ignorance." And he offers them the prospect of having their sins wiped away.

St. John writes something similar to his Christian community. He takes for granted that they will commit sin, and assures them that they have an advocate, Jesus, who will not only plead their cause but is himself expiation for their sins.

Neither Peter nor John is remotely suggesting that it is all right to sin. That would be like saying it is all right to drink poison as long as you have the antidote.

Continuing the health analogy, it is a fact of life that people do eat things that are bad for them, or neglect things that are good for them. Diabetics can find it hard to resist sweets;

Jesus appears to the disciples
by William Hole (1846–1917)

overweight persons may be unwilling to exercise. So, too, a "besetting sin" can have tremendous power over us.

Peter and John were realists. They understood human nature and recognized that sin is a fact of life. They also realized that sin should not lead to despair. Peter knew this from personal experience. He denied Jesus. Afterward he proclaimed him to any who would listen.

Ignorance and doubt are also a fact of life. In Luke's Gospel, Jesus' has trouble convincing the disciples that it really is he standing there, and finally he proves it by eating baked fish. At the same time he, too, points to the gift of repentance for the forgiveness of sins.

At La Salette, Mary is painfully aware of the reality of sin. Her list of offences is not exhaustive, but enough to indicate the nature of the sins that cause her the deepest concern. Here, too, there is no need to despair. "If they are converted," is a turning point in her discourse.

In all of the above, the promise is based on the Passion and Resurrection of Christ. That is why Jesus draws attention to his hands and feet, rather than his face, to verify his identity. That is why the Beautiful Lady wears a large crucifix. He who conquered death can surely conquer sin.

Yes, sin is a fact of life. But thanks to Peter and John and Luke, and Our Lady of La Salette, we are reminded of another fact of life, which we call hope.

Monday, April 19, (#273)
Third Week of Easter

John 6:22-29: *"Do not work for food that goes bad, but work for food that endures for eternal life."*

Meditation:

Food drive sponsors are careful to indicate whether perishable as well as nonperishable items are acceptable. If nature abhors a vacuum, human nature deplores waste. The ongoing project of this world's creation claims from each of us major contributions of effort, energy and work. But our life's work must leave room for us to become more and more the person God is calling us to be. Six days a week we seek to master the world. On the seventh day we try to master ourselves. The world has our hands but our hearts belong to the Creator of the world.

FROM HER MOUNTAINTOP and with the deepest concern, Our Lady of La Salette observes her children trudging their way over life's pathways, toiling for their livelihood. *"I gave you six days to work,"* she says, speaking as prophets do in God's very name, *"I have kept the seventh for myself."* Six days we are to work at the creation of the world, on the seventh we are to enjoy the world of creation. The Lord's day calls us to marvel, to praise, to wonder. "Gather together," it invites us, "eat and drink. Sit comfortably and relax. Rest and be restored. The feast is prepared and ready. It awaits you: body, spirit and soul."

Reflection Questions:

• One year from now which of my currently pressing concerns will I even remember?
• How can what I do benefit me, if I neglect who I am? How am I taking care of myself?

Tuesday, April 20, (#274)
Third Week of Easter

John 6:30-35: *"Jesus answered them, 'I am the bread of life. No one who comes to me will ever hunger.'"*

Meditation:

Combative voices in the crowd put this snide question to Jesus: "What is the work you do?" The answer to this question, however, can only benefit those who follow Christ. He could well have replied: "The work I do? I do the will of the Father to whom I am totally dedicated. I make known the God no one has ever seen. I proclaim good news to the poor and the dispossessed. I allay every human fear. I bear witness to the truth, the truth that sets hearts free. I speak words of pardon and peace. I bring healing and wholeness to body, mind and spirit. I restore God's distorted image in his rebellious children. I seek out all who have strayed. I lay down my own life for love of my friends. I consecrate myself as a sacrifice of praise and reconciliation. In dying I destroy death, your death."

All this Jesus admirably summed up in the hopeful words of this day's gospel: *"I am the bread of life. No one who comes to me will ever hunger."*

AS HER APPARITION AT LA SALETTE TEACHES US, the Mother of Jesus and our Mother, places herself "in the middle"; that is, she draws the attention of her Son to our needs and hungers, as she draws our attention to the deep need of our hearts for her Son: *"If my people will not submit, I will be forced to let go the arm of my Son."* She bids us ponder his actions, savor his words, commune with his silences and remain expectant before his loving gaze.

Reflection Questions:

- Is the overriding ambition of my life to be "someone," or to follow Christ faithfully?
- Can I say that Christ is enough for me? What else do I need?

Wednesday, April 21, (#275)
Third Week of Easter

John 6:35-40: *"I will certainly not reject anyone who comes to me."*

Meditation:

Listing the striking qualities of the love Jesus gave to his own requires no effort at all. His love for those first disciples was affirming, compassionate, constant, forgiving, gentle, loyal, patient, trusting, and unfailing. That same love for his own in the world now goes on giving courage and strength; it continues to show endless patience and understanding. Despite our slowness to believe, our lack of spiritual understanding, our less than prompt response, this loving Savior assures us that we are not a burden, but rather a gift to him from the Father, whose will it is that "Jesus should lose none of those given to him."

SEEING HIS MOTHER IN TEARS on the mountain of La Salette, how could we not recall the stirring scene of Jesus weeping over Jerusalem? In each instance a hearty and timely response to the invitation of grace is at issue. *"How long a time I have suffered for you!"* Do we not too often keep the Lord waiting? Our impulsive pride, capricious love and inordinate self-absorption put all but ourselves and our preoccupations on hold. And the Lord does wait. *"I will certainly not reject anyone who comes to me."* He bides his time and will patiently tell us tomorrow what we refuse to hear today.

Reflection Questions:

- Is Christ really my closest friend, sharing in all I do and experience?
- Have I thanked the Lord lately for the privilege of being "one of his own"?

Thursday, April 22, (#276)
Third Week of Easter

John 6:44-51: *"... the bread that I shall give is my flesh, for the life of the world."*

Meditation:

This promise was fulfilled at the Last Supper, itself the anticipation of Calvary. Now and then the words, "This is my body" take you by surprise, seeping quietly into that void you had forgotten was there. You live a timeless moment as you receive that flesh given for you and feel inwardly linked with the divine, certain that you are looked upon with mercy and love. The person behind you steps up to your place to receive this bread. And it's not just that one person, there are two long lines of them. And over and over again "The Body of Christ. This is my body given for you," until the words mean more than you. Before you and behind you others reach out, having brought there their flushes of fervor, their pulses of doubt, their dearest dreams and their unspoken hopes. We are many and we are one. We are happy and we hurt. We are much in need of grace and we hunger to hear "This is my flesh for you, for the life of the world."

To preserve for the Lord a people he may continue to call his own is the purpose of Mary's ministry at La Salette: *In the summer only a few somewhat aged women go to Mass. The rest work on Sunday all summer long.* Once and for all God's love has been given and received. The covenant has been sealed once and for all. The church is the community sealed by this definitive gift of God to us in Jesus Christ. When Christians gather in remembrance of their Lord and celebrate his death until he comes again, they actualize and express their God-given identity and fulfill their God-given mission. If their Scriptures and consecrated signs bear fruit in humanizing love, then the world for whose sake they witness and worship will find them eloquent indeed.

Reflection Questions:

- Is the Eucharist the center of my life?
- At Eucharist do I look to the Word and Body of Christ to transform me?

Friday, April 23, (#277)
Third Week of Easter
(St. Joseph the Worker)

John 6:52-59: *"The Jews started arguing among themselves, 'How can this man give us his flesh to eat?'"*

Meditation:

The devil offered Jesus all the kingdoms of the world. He rejected the offer. The tempter suggested that he change stones into bread and satisfy his hunger. Jesus refused to do so. Earlier in this chapter of John's Gospel the enthusiastic crowd wanted to make Jesus king. He fled. Some Pharisees warned him at some point: "Herod wants to kill you. Leave here." That time he did not go away. *"How can this man give us his flesh to eat?"* many ask here in angry disgust. Rather than dilute his statement, as we might advise him to do, Jesus enlarged upon it: *"If you do not eat the flesh of the Son of man and drink his blood, you have no life in you."* How little inclined the Lord was to conform to our standards of accommodation, moderation and reasonableness! The quarreling goes on.

"IN THE WINTER WHEN THEY DON'T KNOW WHAT TO DO," the Mother of Christ noted, her cheeks wet with tears, *"they go to Mass just to make fun of religion."* How easily we can forget that worship is the joyous acknowledgment that we did not make ourselves but are dependent on the One who must not be made into a guarantor of reality as we would like it to be. A truth tailored to our own measure would be a pitifully partial truth. A God entirely of our own making would be a God far too small.

Reflection Questions:

• How sincerely do I invite the Lord to open my understanding to his Word?
• Do I usually look to Scripture for confirmation of what I am already thinking or doing?

Saturday, April 24, (#278)
Third Week of Easter

John 6:60-69: *"Then Jesus said to the Twelve, 'What about you, do you want to go away too?'"*

Meditation:

Pollsters report the results of their surveys under three headings: agree, disagree, no opinion. In times of crisis, when trying to reach

a decision, we usually consider three possibilities: for, against, undecided. God never put three choices before the people of Israel. The alternatives were always these: *"I put before you a blessing and a curse. I set before you life and prosperity, death and doom"* (Deuteronomy 11:16; 30:15). The choice is yours. *"Fully aware that his disciples were murmuring at what he said,"* Jesus at this critical point leaves them no middle ground either. He challenges them to decide: *"Do you want to go away too?"* This approach is rooted in our very freedom. Every moment of our life we move either toward or away from our true fulfillment; we must say "yes" or "no" to the reality that we are. There is no way to say "maybe" or "undecided" to existence.

RECOGNIZING IN GABRIEL'S WORDS the will of the Most High, the Virgin of Nazareth entrusted herself fully and freely to the person and work of her Child. The choice she made in freedom on that blessed day, she would freely ratify each day of her faith pilgrimage to the foot of the cross. It is no surprise then that her entire message at La Salette hinges on the classical "ifs" of free choice: **"IF** *my people will not submit,* … **IF** *my people are converted…"*

Reflection Questions:

- How deeply do I share in my Lord's risen life, a life which death can no longer reach?
- Do I choose to yield or to cling? to hurt or to heal?

Sunday, April 25 (#050)
Fourth Sunday of Easter

(Acts 4:8-12; 1 John 3:1-2; John 10:11-18)

Meditation: *Belonging*

This is Good Shepherd Sunday. Each of the three years of the liturgical cycle has—on the fourth Sunday of Easter—we hear a different portion of John 10, where Jesus calls himself Shepherd.

"I know mine and mine know me," Jesus says. This is the basis of trust for those who follow him. They know they are his; he will never abandon them. The Shepherd and his flock belong to each other. How many times God promises, "I will be your God, you will be my people."

In his first letter, St. John uses a different image: "We are God's children now." This, too, is an invitation to trust.

"Come closer, my children, don't be afraid." Our Lady of La Salette claims Maximin and Mélanie as her children and, through them, all of us as well, whom she calls "my people." She belongs to us, we belong to her. After being terrified at first, the children came to her with perfect confidence. Even though much of what she said was unpleasant to hear, she did not inspire fear.

St. Peter in his discourse powerfully urges his audience to put their trust in Jesus. "There is no salvation through anyone else, nor is there any other name under heaven given to the human race by which we are to be saved."

In the rite of infant baptism, the priest addresses the child with the words, "The Christian community welcomes you with great joy. In its name I claim you for Christ our Savior by the sign of his cross." Child and Savior belong to each other, so too the child and the Christian community. This means that each has a claim on the other.

In the Gospels, Jesus tells us that people of faith should expect God to hear their prayers. In Hebrews 4:16 we read: "Let us confidently approach the throne of grace to receive mercy and to find grace for timely help." (This verse, by the way, used to serve as the Introit for the Mass in honor of Our Lady of La Salette.)

But God has a legitimate claim on us: obedience and respect. This is not burdensome. It is part of the trust that we place in the Good Shepherd.

We belong to Christ's flock, to the family of God's children, to Mary's people. Why would we ever be afraid?

Monday, April 26, (#279)
Fourth Week of Easter

John 10:1-10: *"… one by one he calls his own sheep and leads them out."*

Meditation:

In the Middle East it was the custom of shepherds to bring their flocks together into a secure fold for the night. Here, while their fellow shepherds slept, a chosen few could easily guard many flocks from predators. In the morning each shepherd would enter the fold and call his sheep. They would respond to the familiar voice and confidently follow it – to green pastures; to running water, even through the valley of darkness, on to the fullness of life. In Jesus' time sheep were raised primarily for their wool and milk, not as a source of meat. To the shepherds they were much like domestic animals, even pets. They had names. Shepherds didn't use sheep dogs to nip and snap at the heels of their sheep. Called by name, each of the sheep responded.

ONE OF THE INTRIGUING THINGS about the apparition at La Salette was that the Beautiful Lady never referred to Maximin and Melanie by name. When speaking of prayer she asked: *"Do you say your prayers well, my children?"* When inquiring about spoiled wheat: *"Have you never seen wheat gone bad, my children?"* And when they gave a negative answer, she addressed Maximin: *"But you, my child, surely you have seen some…"* I have often wondered why she didn't use their names, yet she went on to recount a very intimate moment in the life of the lad and his father. Again at the end of the discourse Mary says: *"Well, my children, you will make this known to all my people."*

Reflection Questions:

• Is my God near and supportive, or distant and silent?
• When I think of and pray to God, do I call him by an intimate or more impersonal name?

Tuesday, April 27, (#280)
Fourth Week of Easter

John 10:22-30: *"The sheep that belong to me listen to my voice; I know them and they follow me."*

Meditation:

Words, sounds, voices are such a great part of our lives. From our first conscious moments, they are our major means of expression, of communication. They take on meaning for ourselves and for others, not because they are heard but because they are listened to. Listening requires attention to words and to persons. It involves discernment and leads to choices. How often Jesus felt flustered because people heard without listening, without understanding, without opening their hearts. His teaching was not about dogma but about relationship with a loving God to whom we could cry, *"Abba"* (Galatians 4:6). Rather than listen to his voice, so often we continue to close our ears and cry out, *"Crucify him"* (Mark 15:13).

AT LA SALETTE the children said that once they heard the voice of the Beautiful Lady their fears melted away. They found themselves drawn into her company, standing so close that no one could have passed between them and her. They listened attentively. Enthralled with the person before them, they didn't always understand her words but did grasp the urgency of her message. Their dialogue with her was etched into their memories, into their lives. But it took time to flower, to ripen, to mature into practice. Remember that on the day after the apparition, Maximin didn't even attend Mass after he and Melanie had recounted their story to Father Perrin, the parish priest.

Reflection Questions:

- Where have I matured lately after listening to the gospel message?
- Is my heart afire when a word in Scripture truly challenges me?

Wednesday, April 28, (#281)
Fourth Week of Easter

John 12:44-50: *"... anyone who rejects me and refuses my words has his judge already."*

Meditation:

Coming right before the narration of the Passion, these words reflect how Jesus might have looked at the result of his years of teaching, preaching, working miracles, trying to shed new light on the reality of our world. Was he a success or a failure? Except for a few trusted friends, people didn't perceive him as a shining light. People didn't hear his loving message of forgiveness and conversion. People didn't believe in him but wanted to use him for what they could get out of him. Even Judas thought he could get his thirty pieces of silver and that Jesus would somehow get away. Jesus, however, knew that the end was near –r rather that a new beginning, so far removed from any miracle he had worked till then, was at hand. Yet he had not come to judge or condemn but to save.

AT LA SALETTE Mary tries to help us realize the effects of our actions. *"If the harvest is ruined, it is only on account of yourselves… If they are converted, rocks and stones will turn into mounds of wheat and potatoes will be self-sown in the fields."* Our pernicious choices help create a social structure that brings ruin upon ourselves and upon others, extending over and beyond what we imagine. We might feel distant from those who died in the great famine of 1846, but can we think of ourselves as uninvolved in what is happening in the Balkans today? If we believe we can escape the effects of what is going on, we are deaf to Mary's words: *"It is only on account of yourselves."*

Reflection Questions:

• Do I recognize that what I am, what I believe, and what I do all have repercussions on my life and on that of others?
• What actions should this call me to perform? Where should I get involved?

Thursday, April 29, (#282)
Fourth Week of Easter

John 13:16-20: *"Whoever welcomes the one I send, welcomes me."*

Meditation:

We have all heard stories of a Jesus in disguise coming to visit a household as a beggar, a child, a homeless person. Those who welcomed him were astonished to discover him under the disguise. The stories are touching and the reality is even more so. Jesus comes indirectly to us through those who touch our lives. We shouldn't be surprised when we don't recognize him. Mary Magdalene didn't recognize him until he spoke her name. The apostles recognized him only when they saw his wounds. Though they walked with him for hours, looked into his eyes and heard his voice, the disciples going to Emmaus needed to share the bread of fellowship before they recognized him. Welcoming people means receiving them with pleasure, satisfaction and hospitality. It means sharing what we have. It means caring about those we receive as well as for them.

WHEN MAXIMIN AND MELANIE first saw the globe of dazzling light they were afraid. They would have fled had not the globe parted to reveal the Beautiful Lady. Like her Son, Mary came disguised. Maximin naively thought she had come up there to cry her heart out because her children had struck her. When she stood and invited them to come near, their fears melted. As Mary came toward them, they approached her. Each welcomed the other. She brought Christ into their lives, first through the shining crucifix on her breast and then by the conversion which would gradually take place in their lives. Hospitality is considered one of the chief Christian trademarks. It calls us to welcome disguised saints and sinners into our lives, where Jesus can have the pleasure and satisfaction of encountering them.

Reflection Questions:

• What fears hold me back from welcoming Christ into my life today?
• What fears hold me back from sharing the bread of fellowship with my brothers and sisters?

Friday, April 30, (#283)
Fourth Week of Easter

John 14:1-6: *"I am going now to prepare a place for you."*

Meditation:

Jesus must have experienced a whole range of feelings as he bid farewell to his disciples. Things would never be the same. Their solidarity would be broken. Judas would betray him. Peter would deny him. All would flee. As Son of God, he had come down from heaven. As son of Mary, he would be going home for the first time. What expectation, what joy! But to get home, he would have to suffer and die. What horror, what revulsion! Though he would rise from the dead, he would no longer be with his disciples as before. Is it any wonder that he tried to forestall their fears. *"I am going now to prepare a place for you."*

MANY OF US HAVE EXPERIENCED that place which is special to her Missionaries and to all her devotees - Our Lady's shrine in the French Alps. This conjures up a blend of physical, psychological and spiritual attitudes, feelings, judgments and memories. For some La Salette is a picturesque place of prayer, for others it means a barren wilderness of sorts. Some felt at home, while others have been there and known desolation. For those who minister there week after week, routine can set in; whereas for first-time visitors, feelings of anxiety before the unfamiliar could arise. However we view this mountain sanctuary of La Salette, it is a steppingstone in the spiritual lives of countless pilgrims. After her visit to earth on this mountain, Mary returned to heaven. We can echo Maximin's words: "We should have asked her to take us with her." Hopefully, one day she will.

Reflection Questions:

• What range of feelings surges in me when I think of going home to Jesus?
• Is mine a peaceful confidence that I shall indeed follow where Jesus has gone?

Saturday, May 1, (#284)
Fourth Week of Easter
(Saint Joseph the Worker)

John 14:7-14: *"If you know me, you will know the Father too."*

Meditation:

The word Father appears ten times in this short passage. When I predicate a word, a name, or idea of God my understanding is colored by my own experience. What relationship did I have with my father? What influence did he have in shaping my life? Was he a stem taskmaster, a soft touch, a mentor at play and work, or one who made me feel like a klutz? Did he challenge me, encourage me? Was he present when I needed him or was he always too busy? Or did I completely lack a father figure because of death, divorce, separation, or abandonment? All these shape my understanding of God as Father. Shape it, yes; limit it, no. Jesus, God-become-flesh-for-me, gave me another way of knowing God as Father. His human experience of God has become mine, opening up my heart and soul to this revelation of the heavenly Father.

A FATHER WHO CARES INTENSELY FOR HIS CHILDREN sent Mary to La Salette. My understanding of him through her words will be colored by my human experience and by my life of faith. The incident of Maximin with his father in the field at Coin can surely show how much God the Father cares for me, provides for me. *"Here, my child, eat some bread this year while we still have some. I don't know who will eat any next year if the wheat continues like that."* Mr. Giraud's words bring to mind other words I so often speak to my Father: *"Give us today our daily bread"* (Matthew 6:11). And we recall Jesus' tribute to the concern parents have for their children: *"What father among you, if his son asked for a fish, would hand him a snake?"* (Luke 11:11).

Reflection Questions:

- How do I envisage God as my Father?
- Is there still a shadow of the punitive parent over my personal image of God?

Sunday, May 2 (#053)
Fifth Sunday of Easter

(Acts 9:26-31; 1 John 3:18-24; John 15:1-8)

Meditation: *Ouch!*

After Saul encountered Jesus on the road to Damascus, he remained blind, and had to be led by hand into the city. The Lord sent a certain Ananias to pray over him and restore his sight. Ananias objected, "I have heard from many sources about this man, what evil things he has done to your holy ones;" but Jesus answered, "I will show him what he will have to suffer for my name."

In our first reading we see what Jesus meant. Saul is at first shunned by the Christians of Jerusalem; and even once he is accepted by them, the former persecutor is himself persecuted and must flee.

Saul, later known as Paul, would go on to produce abundant fruits of grace. But, as a new branch on the vine of Christ, he had to be pruned. Ouch! that hurts!

No one can be said to enjoy this part of discipleship, but it is inescapable. In the message of Our Lady of La Salette, her first words after calling the children to her, are, "If my people refuse to submit..." Submit? Ouch! No, thank you.

But when St. John tells us to love in deed and in truth, isn't he saying fundamentally the same thing? It is easy to utter loving words, but putting love into practice puts serious demands on us. We are to love one another as Jesus commanded us.

Jesus presents the same thought in a very different way: "Remain in me as I remain in you... Anyone who does not remain in me will be thrown out like a branch and wither...thrown into a fire." Ouch!

It was clear to Our Lady that her people had not remained in her Son. Like any mother who sees her children not living in harmony, she was pained by the situation, and decided to do something about it, to ease their suffering

In the message of our heavenly Queen, there is much that can cause us pain and remorse. It is meant to be medicinal, its goal is healing.

We are in the Easter season, but did you notice that our responsorial Psalm is the same one as on Palm Sunday? Today we have the joyful conclusion of that Psalm, such a contrast to its opening cry of despair. Another Psalm puts it more concisely: "At nightfall, weeping enters in, but with the dawn, rejoicing."

Monday, May 3 (#561)
Saints Philip and James, Apostles

John 14:6-14: *"(You) will perform even greater works (than I)"*

Meditation:

In looking back over Jesus' choice of his first disciples, we would perhaps have chosen differently. If a "report" had been given beforehand to Jesus concerning his proposed choices by a Jerusalem Management Agency, it might have read: "It is the opinion of our staff that most of your nominees are lacking in background, education and vocational aptitude for your proposed enterprise. They have no team concept. Simon Peter is emotionally unstable and given to fits of temper. Andrew has no qualities for leadership. The two brothers James and John place personal interest above company loyalty. Thomas shows a skeptical attitude that would tend to undermine morale. Matthew has been blacklisted by the Jerusalem Better Business Bureau. James the son of Alphaeus, and Thaddeus, definitely have radical leanings, and registered a high score on the manic-depressive scale. One of the candidates however, shows real potential. He is a man of ability and resourcefulness, meets people well, and has contacts in high places. He is highly motivated, ambitious, and responsible. We recommend Judas Iscariot as your controller and right-hand man." How "God's ways are not our ways"!=

WHEN MARY APPEARED TO THE TWO CHILDREN, Maximin and Melanie, an outsider Management Team would certainly have told Mary that these children were the weakest of applicants for the mission she intended to give them. Yet despite all their faults and lack of personal qualities, their attestation to what they saw and heard was remarkable and unwavering. They simply told people what they witnessed and they were faithful to that mission until their death.

As Jesus reminds us in the gospel for today, "whoever believes in me will perform the same works as I do myself, and will perform *even greater works*." Who would expect that of Jesus' first disciples or of

Maximin and Melanie? Yet as we learn repeatedly in the scriptures, "for God, all things are possible" (Matthew 19:26).

Some Reflection Questions:

- Have you heard about or seen people who are examples of Jesus' words, "whoever believes in me will perform the same works as I do myself, and will perform even greater works"?
- Have some of the saints of the past or present (or even people whom you have known personally) shown what great things God can do with the seemingly weakest of followers?

Tuesday, May 4, (#286)
Fifth Week of Easter

John 14:27-31a: *"Peace I bequeath to you; my own peace I give you."*

Meditation:

The gift of peace is echoed in every Mass yet it so often eludes us. When it is experienced, it exudes wholeness, a reconciliation, a sense of union with all of creation and beyond. Could that be why Jesus left it to us as his farewell gift? He was about to reconcile the world to himself, to join again the created and the Uncreated in a special relationship. The result would be that peace which he alone could give, a joy for which all of creation had been groaning (Romans 8:22). St. Augustine was possibly describing it when he said that a Christian should be alleluia from head to toe. We are an Easter people and, with that farewell gift in our hearts, *alleluia* is our song.

WHEN WE FIRST HEAR OF LA SALETTE, there seems to be no echo of peace and joy. Rather we find a continual flow of tears, we hear of suffering, of God's arm grown heavy, people swearing, human beings behaving like dogs, famine, worm-eaten crops, children dying. Hardly a reason to sing *alleluia*! But as we look deeper into the meaning of the tears and the message we can distinguish the call to conversion, to reconciliation, to joy and peace. We come to understand the meaning of the word *if* that Mary spoke. Christ left us his farewell peace as a gift that must be received, not as something foisted upon us. He said that we have his life in us, that salvation, peace and joy are ours, *"If you love me."* Anyone who has experienced the grace of reconciliation

133

knows the profound peace that comes when the *if* changes to *yes*.

Reflection Questions:

- What would it take for me to experience a deeper sense of Jesus' farewell gift of peace?
- How expectant and trusting is my relationship with him?

Wednesday, May 5, (#287)
Fifth Week of Easter

John 15:1-8: *"Anyone who does not remain in me is thrown away like a branch -- and withers; these branches are collected and thrown on the fire and are burnt."*

Meditation:

Chapter 15 of John's Gospel is a richly constructed monologue in which Jesus goes far beyond a farewell to his disciples. The imagery of the first part is clear – no life in branches separated from the vine, abundant fruit when branches are trimmed. One way or another some part of the vine is going to be trimmed, cut, pruned with branches separated from the stem. These branches will be placed on the vineyard wall to dry, then used for firewood. I remember being in a vineyard once where such precious branches were removed from their drying place and used to make a very hot fire over which to roast our dinner of shellfish. I have also seen them used to kindle a fire in an outdoor oven for baking bread. Even these seemingly no-good twigs are precious and useful.

THE LA SALETTE EVENT often reminds me of these separated branches. When Mary spoke to the children, she was directing her words primarily to people who were like severed twigs – abandoning church, not observing the Lord's Day, swearing, neglecting private and communal prayer. They were surely cut off. Yet there still must have been some life in them. They were precious enough for her to come and plead for their return. A desperate situation surely, but not a hopeless one. It seems that an incision had to be made into the vine so that it might receive as a graft those not completely withered branches.

La Salette, then, is a miracle of hope. Mary was willing to let us see

her sorrow, her tears, her maternal solicitude for us when we stray. Perhaps it is because of her tears falling on us that we retain some spark of life and are kept from withering and dying.

Reflection Questions:

- What have I done lately to thank the Lord for not allowing me to wither and die spiritually?
- To what extent have I made the moral and spiritual values of Christian life inwardly my own?

Thursday, May 6 (#288)
Fifth Week of Easter

John 15:9-11: *"I have kept my Father's commandments and remain in his love."*

Meditation:

Fidelity is not a quality particularly required, sought after or cherished in today's society. This is true in business dealings, in interpersonal relationships, in marriage and in religious life. To Jesus, however, it was essential. He was faithful to his Father, to his mission, to his word, to his disciples and friends. His joy came from being loyal and faithful, in loving and being loved. His obedience was shown in his loyalty to his Father. This same loyalty brought Jesus to his death, yes, even death on the cross. It also paved the way for his resurrection – new life for him and for us. Sharing that joy, sharing that life, sharing that fidelity, will bring us completeness.

WE CAN MARVEL AT THE FAITHFULNESS OF MELANIE AND MAXIMIN to what they witnessed at La Salette. These two uneducated children, Maximin – a scatterbrain, and Melanie – an introvert, had to undergo personal scrutiny, long hours of questioning, buffeting by family and friends, and even scorn from churchmen. Yet they remained faithful. We find Maximin's last testament a marvelous declaration of fidelity. "I firmly believe, even were it to cost the shedding of my blood, in the renowned apparition of the Blessed Virgin on the holy mountain of La Salette, September 19, 1846, the apparition to which I have testified in words, in writings, and in suffering. After my death let no one assert that he has heard me make any retraction concerning the

great event of La Salette, for in lying to the world he would be lying to himself. With these sentiments I give my heart to Our Lady of La Salette."

Some Reflection Questions:

- How have you shown the quality of fidelity in your life?
- To what and to whom do you feel most firmly attached?

Friday, May 7, (#289)
Fifth Week of Easter

John 15:12-17: *"I commissioned you to go out and to bear fruit, fruit that will last."*

Meditation:

Perhaps the word that best describes the thirst of society today is freedom – freedom of assembly, freedom of choice, freedom of speech, freedom from restraints of all kinds, especially authority. Freedom of choice is foremost. It generally implies the liberty to choose whom and what I want, when and how I want it. It is often said that you can't choose family but you do choose friends. In choosing us to be his friends, though, Jesus puts a damper on freedom. *"You are my friends if you do what I command you."* Does the price of friendship mean taking orders? Now that's counter-cultural! The friendship he offers, however, is not based on one-to-one equality. *"It was not you who chose me; I commissioned you to go out and to bear fruit, fruit that will last."*

MAXIMIN AND MELANIE WERE CHOSEN and given a mission. As wonderful as it may have been to be chosen to witness the apparition, they paid a price. Their lives were disrupted. From obscure, uneventful lifestyles they were thrown first into the path of belligerent critics only to become objects of excessive adulation later on. Free-spirited Maximin was hemmed in too quickly by the walls of the seminary classroom when all he desired was the freedom of the mountain slopes. Taciturn, melancholy Melanie was soon caressed by fame and a following; her chances of living a simple, hidden religious life thus permanently damaged.

Reflection Questions:

• How often do I stop and think about the call and mission the Lord has chosen to give me?

• What counter-cultural efforts can I expect to make, if I choose to be Jesus' friend in this day and age?

Saturday, May 8, (#290)
Fifth Week of Easter

John 15:18-21: *"... in my name."*

Meditation:

Every name is sacred, yours and mine included. Shakespeare asked, "What's in a name?" Some names still instill fear, some inspire awe, some foster tenderness, others ooze with hate, some leave us indifferent and unmoved. For most people, God's name, be it Yahweh, Allah, Jesus or Zeus, carries a special reverence. In God's name, people have sacrificed their lives for others just as Jesus did for all humankind. In the name of God, wars were waged; infidels, heretics, and innocent people were tortured and put to death; the gospel was preached far and wide; grace was dispensed; innumerable prayers and sacrifices were offered; saints were canonized. Jesus knew his name would be reverenced, cursed, defiled and invoked as a panacea for every ill, and often by the same person – me.

AT LA SALETTE, Mary underlines the irreverence people have for God's name. It comes in the form of swearing and is also seen in indifference to what God asks through the commandments, the laws of the church, the requirements of sacramental life. That attitude was not limited to 1846. I have only to consider the extent to which I accept and live the reality of the post-Vatican Council II world and church to realize the necessity of voicing my present-day *mea culpa*. But do I? *"And as for you, you pay no heed."* I know my indifference touches Jesus deeply, because Mary accented it as *"one of the two things that make the arm of her Son so heavy."*

Reflection Questions:

• When I pray in the name of the Father, and of the Son, and of the

Holy Spirit, how do I come into the presence of my God?
•Does my prayer continue to have an influence in my life even long after the words have passed my lips?

Sunday, May 9 (#056)
Sixth Sunday of Easter

(Acts 10:25-48; 1 John 4:7-10; John 15:9-17)

Meditation: *Who Started it?*

People in conflict, whether individuals or nations, children or adults, tend to blame each other for starting the quarrel. Even at La Salette, Mary literally tells her people, *"If the harvest is ruined, it is only on account of yourselves."*

This is my command:

Love each other

John 15:17

The same may occur in a positive context. It is gracious to give credit to others for their part in our success. In Acts, the Apostles never take the credit for their accomplishments. As in today's reading, they acknowledge that the Holy Spirit takes the initiative, in spectacular ways and with extraordinary gifts, such as the gift of tongues.

Notice, however, that the new disciples are doing two things: speaking in tongues, and glorifying God. Which of these is more important?

In writing to the Corinthians St. Paul addresses a controversy surrounding the gifts, and famously concludes: "If there are tongues, they will cease... So faith, hope, love remain, these three; but the greatest of these is love."

Which brings us to the Gospel and the second reading, both from John, where love is mentioned a total of eighteen times. We are "beloved," and God is love. John's "Let us love one another," finds even stronger expression in the Gospel: "This I command you: love one another."

The last words of last week's Gospel were, "By this is my Father glorified, that you bear much fruit and become my disciples." The very next verse is the first statement of Jesus today: "As the Father loves me, so I also love you. Remain in my love." There is a connection, then, between glorifying God and abiding in the Lord's love.

Mary appeared at a time of crisis in the life of her people. She chided them—lovingly—and then—lovingly—pointed them to the way of hope and peace. She is in turn much loved, but directs our love to her Son. Her message is echoed in the new translation of the Missal, in one of the forms of dismissal at the end of Mass: "Go in peace, glorifying the Lord by your life."

That includes love. John writes, "In this is love: not that we have loved God, but that he loved us." He sustains our love. He will see it through. Because he started it!

Monday, May 10, (#291)
Sixth Week of Easter

John 15:26 to 16:4: *"... you have been with me from the beginning."*

Meditation:

"Cradle Catholics" often speak of having been "born Catholic." Tertullian, one of the early North African Church Fathers, offered this corrective: "Christians are made, not born." If it is true that we Christians are not born but made, then how is it that we are made? In the same way that Peter, Mary of Bethany, James, Mary Magdalene, John, Martha, Andrew, and the rest were made like Christ: by dwelling with him, by following him. We *become* his disciples, we are not *born* so. It is something we must choose daily. Those of us who have been with him from a time shortly after our birth do sometimes take our Catholic Christian faith for granted. But the Risen Lord comes to stir us out of complacency and into a more mature responsibility for our faith as adults.

BECAUSE OF CHRISTIANITY'S EARLY HISTORY IN FRANCE, the country is sometimes referred to as "the eldest daughter of the Church." Unfortunately today, there is much indifference and some hostility to the

Christian faith in this ancient cradle of Catholicism. Mary, Mother of the Church and Mother of La Salette, went to the people of this eldest daughter in order to rouse them from their sleep, to bring their faith to life again in the name of Jesus her Son. Her words apply still to the Church throughout the world. For the renewal Mary sought to bring to "all her people" to be effective, we must continually grow in our faith, coming to a more mature level of trust in her Son.

Reflection Questions:

- In what ways do I take my faith for granted and fail to truly appreciate this gift of God to me?
- Have I thought to pray for the children and adults who were baptized in my parish this Easter Season?

Tuesday, May 11, (#292)
Sixth Week of Easter

Note: Today you may wish to begin the First Day of the Novena to Our Lady of La Salette, in the appendix of this book.

John 16:5-11: *"And when (the Paraclete) comes, he will show the world how wrong it was, about sin..."*

Meditation:

We don't usually think of advocates as those who tell us what we have done wrong. We think of them as those who stand up for us and fight for us to the last. The Holy Spirit, our promised Paraclete before the Father, shows us the ways in which we have betrayed ourselves, the ways in which we have contradicted our true selves, the ways in which we have done wrong. We, who are flesh and spirit, must learn from the divine Spirit how to be human. It is the Spirit who leads us to recognize how wrong we are about our sins. The Spirit calls us away from both these extremes: our sins either don't matter at all or they are too great to be forgiven. As this Paraclete helps us to see how wrong we have been, he also shows us how right with God, self and others we can be.

MARY'S MESSAGE OFTEN SEEMS STERN TO ME. That sternness is tempered, however, when I recall that it was spoken by a mother. The image I have of a stern mother always includes that of a child who has just done something to hurt a friend, or him- or herself. "Why did you hit Bobby? ... Get away from that stove now! You'll get burned! ... Go to bed. You need your rest." *"If my people will not repent, I will be forced to let go the arm of my Son,"* said Mary at La Salette. Reading between the lines, I am tempted to insert, "I'm warning you. It's for your own good."

Reflection Questions:

- What warnings have I heard that I do not heed?
- Do I take the counsel of others seriously, or am I a spiritual individualist, insisting on learning *only* from my own experience of God, rather than trusting in the experience of others, like the saints, and my brothers and sisters in the Lord?

Wednesday, May 12, (#293)
Sixth Week of Easter

John 16:12-15: *"... the Spirit of truth ... will lead you to the complete truth ... and he will reveal to you the things to come."*

Meditation:

"Apocalyptic things" (revealing the end-of-the-world) are all around us. There is much talk and fascination about the end of the world. In light of this, we might be tempted to think about the end of the world when Jesus tells his disciples that the Spirit will reveal what is to come. When we look for the magic formula that gives us the day on which the world will end and Jesus will come in glory, we risk forgetting to welcome him into our life this very day, this very moment. Perhaps those *"things that are to come"* refer not to the end of the world, but to this world's evolution toward God's Kingdom and the revelation of God's will for us, our calling and direction in life. Some go through life aimlessly wandering, never sure of their steps, yet hoping to stumble into the right direction. With the Spirit as our guide, however, our steps are sure, and we walk the straight and narrow path of Christ (Matthew 7:14), not out of fear, but out of faith.

MARY'S MESSAGE AT LA SALETTE is apocalyptic in the truest sense of the word. Apocalypse means revelation. Mary's message manifested the divine disappointment over the way things had gone (rotting crops) and also the divine hope that things would be much improved (self-sown seeds). Just as the earth sometimes seems to withhold a harvest from us, so too our hearts sometimes withhold justice from each other, obedience and worship from God. At other times, though, our response seems generous, pure, spontaneous, full of good will. At La Salette, Mary calls us to such Spirit-led spontaneity.

Reflection Questions:

- When is it easy for me to bear good fruit in following the Lord? When does it seems more difficult?
- How can I persevere in the hard times, and show my gratitude in the good times?

Thursday, May 13

Note: *On this day, depending on your location and diocese your daily celebration will either be The Ascension of the Lord, or Thursday of the Sixth Week of Easter. Both are provided here.*

(#058B)
The Ascension of the Lord

Mark 16: 15-20: *"Go out to the whole world; proclaim the gospel to all creation."*

Meditation:

MARY'S WORDS SPOKEN IN FORMAL FRENCH ARE PROPHETIC WORDS OF WARNING. She spoke about two refusals of her people: one concerned her people's lack of keeping the Sabbath holy. It is supposed to be a day of repose, a day of prayer and celebration. Their second refusal concerned their irreverent and senseless use of the name of her Son. Their respect for his name was upsetting to her.

Her visit at La Salette was certainly an expression of her humility and tenderness (the way she spoke so directly and compassionately with the two children); a call for her people to attain a balance between their need for prayer (daily and in Sunday worship) and the work responsibilities of their daily life; and finally giving her people a final mandate – not only the two children standing before her but anyone who hears her words –– to "make (her) message known to all (her) people." Essentially her parting words are a call to action, an invitation to share the reconciling message of her Son with everyone we meet, a true call to evangelization. She closely echoes the words of her Son: "Go out to the whole world; proclaim the gospel to all creation" (Mark 16:20).

Reflection Questions:

- When have I been moved to evangelize someone, encouraging them to become more active in their faith?
- Was there an incident in your life when someone expressed their faith or religious motivation to you? How did you respond?

Alternate for May 13
(#294)
Sixth Week of Easter

John 16:16-20: *"What does he mean?"*

Meditation:

Earlier in the Gospel of John it was the Pharisees who failed to understand. Maybe they didn't even want to understand. Now, however, it is Jesus' own disciples, those who welcomed the Kingdom, who fail to understand. Indeed, a few hours after these words are spoken, John tells us these same disciples, who shared in that last supper conversation, will scatter to the four winds for fear of their lives. They will abandon their master. But they will see him again, and the very sight of him will be enough to overcome their fear of the same fate, and the shame of their abandonment. For now, however, they fail to understand this "short time" remaining until he goes away. The Resurrection surprised even those like Peter and John, who had been closest to him. However close to or distant from the Lord we may be, there are parts of our walk as disciples that we do not understand.

PEOPLE WERE NOT QUITE AS PUZZLED BY MARY'S WORDS AT LA SALETTE. To speak of spoiled wheat and rotting potatoes in a time of famine brings immediate recognition of the truth of the message. The famine before their eyes was quite obvious to everyone in 1846. The famine in their hearts was not quite so obvious to them. Often we do not see our own sins. Something needs to happen for the scales to fall from our eyes. The supernatural character of the apparition at La Salette is not attested to so much by crutches left behind as at Lourdes, but by hearts renewed and turned back to God. "Our Lady of La Salette, Reconciler of sinners, pray without ceasing for us who have recourse to you."

Reflection Questions:

•What in Jesus' message do you find difficult to understand and live?

•Would it be appropriate for you to pray that God would remove the scales that blind you to your own sinful ways, and then make a good examination of your conscience?

Friday, May 14 (#564)
St. Matthias, Apostle

John 15:9-17: *"You did not choose me, no, I chose you."*

Meditation:

The sad truth is that, despite these many years after Vatican II, many people still feel that only clergy or religious have "vocations." This, of course, comes from the mindset that all vocations comes from and are based on "the main vocation-sacrament – Holy Orders." However the Fathers of Vatican II first reminded us of the "universal call to holiness," saying: "... all the faithful of Christ of whatever rank or status, are called to the fullness of the Christian life and to the perfection of charity ... The classes and duties of life are many, but holiness is one-that sanctity which is cultivated by all who are moved by the Spirit of God... Every person must walk unhesitatingly according to his own personal gifts and duties in the path of living faith, which arouses hope and works through charity. (*Lumen Gentium*, #40-41)" It is therefore our common Baptism that is the basis from this common call to holiness. As today's scripture reminds us, we all need to remember the words of Jesus: *"You did not choose me, no, I chose you."*

AT LA SALETTE Mary spoke similar words to those of the Fathers at

Vatican II. She did not choose the local Bishop or a priest but rather two unschooled children to *"make (her) message known."* This was certainly a surprising choice of messengers but just shows us how important each baptized member of the Church is! On this feast of St. Matthias, we hear that "we are all chosen" as the scripture reminds us, no matter what our state. We are all chosen to follow Christ and use the gifts he gave us to build the Kingdom of God where we live and work and serve. What a simple, basic and profound view of the importance of every person!

Reflection Questions:

- In your own state in life, where is your Baptismal call the easiest to live?
- Where is your Baptismal the most challenging to live?

Saturday, May 15, (#296)
Sixth Week of Easter

John 16:23b-28: *"Anything you ask from the Father he will grant you in my name."*

Meditation:

To ask or pray in the name of Jesus requires more than simply tacking on "We ask this through Christ our Lord," or "In Jesus' name we pray" at the end of our prayers. The *Constitution on the Sacred Liturgy* of Vatican Council II teaches us that in the liturgy all who are gathered are called to fulfill the priestly office of Jesus Christ (#7). This high calling to pray in Jesus' name and fulfill his priestly office by our own prayer means more than just "name-dropping" at the close of our intercessions.

To be a Christian at prayer is to make Jesus' longing for the Father and the coming of the Reign of God one's very own longing ("Thy kingdom come; thy will be done."). It requires that at Mass, in union with the Risen Lord, we put on the altar alongside the gifts of bread and wine, our own lives, our self-offering to be sustained throughout the rest of the day and week. Yes, praying in Jesus' name is no magic formula; rather it is a way of life, a responsibility all Christians are invited, even commanded, to carry out.

MARY'S COMMAND to pray the *Our Father* and *Hail Mary* (and to pray more when we can) at evening and morning is more than just a good way to start the day off right and end it appropriately. We begin and end by praying as Jesus prayed so that all through the day we will live as he lived (with the aid of his Mother's intercession, of course).

Reflection Questions:

- What are the best times for me to pray? What does it mean to me to pray *well*?
- What keeps me from praying regularly, attentively? Does my prayer help me to walk more faithfully in the ways of the Lord?

Sunday, May 16

Note: *On this day, depending on your location and diocese your daily celebration will either be The Ascension of the Lord, or the seventh Sunday of Easter. Both are provided here.*

(#058B)
The Ascension of the Lord

Mark 16: 15-20: *"Go out to the whole world; proclaim the gospel to all creation."*

Meditation:

MARY'S WORDS SPOKEN IN FORMAL FRENCH ARE PROPHETIC WORDS OF WARNING. She spoke about two refusals of her people: one concerned her people's lack of keeping the Sabbath holy. It is supposed to be a day of repose, a day of prayer and celebration. Their second refusal concerned their irreverent and senseless use of the name of her Son. Their respect for his name was upsetting to her.

Her visit at La Salette was certainly an expression of her humility and tenderness (the way she spoke so directly and compassionately with the two children); a call for her people to attain a balance between their need for prayer (daily and in Sunday worship) and the work responsibilities of their daily life; and finally giving her people a final mandate – not only the two children standing before her but anyone who hears her words –- to "make (her) message known to all (her) people." Essentially her parting words are a call to action, an invitation to share the reconciling message of her Son with everyone we meet, a true call to evangelization. She closely echoes the words of her Son: "Go out to the whole world; proclaim the gospel to all creation" (Mark 16:20).

Ascension
by John Singleton Copley (1738–1815)

Reflection Questions:

• When have I been moved to evangelize someone, encouraging them to become more active in their faith?

• Was there an incident in your life when someone expressed their faith or religious motivation to you? How did you respond?

Alternate for May 16 (#060) Seventh Sunday of Easter

(Acts 1:15-26; 1 John 4:11-16; John 17:11-19)

Meditation: *Why Me?*

Why does God choose a particular person for a particular purpose? The Bible doesn't say that Ruth, or Moses, or David, or even Mary was better than anyone else. They were God's chosen instruments, prepared by him for a special role.

In today's reading from the Acts of the Apostles, we see the same reality of choice, as "the lot fell upon Matthias" to make him a "witness to the resurrection." The time had come to replace Judas. The disciples reduced the number of candidates to two, and then God chose between them.

Maximin and Mélanie were the chosen witnesses of Our Lady of La

Salette. Why them? We can (and do) speculate, but the most honest answer is the simplest: we don't really know. The La Salette Missionaries and the La Salette Sisters, as well as the many lay people devoted to our Weeping Mother are her chosen witnesses today. Why us? Again, we just don't know.

Often the words, "Why me?" are used when something bad happens to us. But we might well ask the same question when something great and wonderful happens, and in particular when we recognize that God is calling us for a special purpose.

Many people can explain what first attracted them to another person, or to a religious order, or to a certain career or ministry. It is a different matter when we look at it from the point of view of being chosen. Why did that person, that vocation, that career or ministry choose me? In other words, what was/is God's purpose for my life?

We do know this much, however. It isn't because we are better than anyone else. Mary's choice, like God's choice, is a mystery—not to be solved, but to be lived.

Jesus had chosen his Apostles, and three years later, at the Last Supper he prayed to his Father to protect them, to "consecrate them in the truth." After all, they were to be his faithful witnesses.

Therein lies the challenge, to live what we are called to be, focused on the what and the how and the where, much more than on the why.

Monday, May 17, (#297)
Seventh Week of Easter

John 16:29-33: *"Do you believe at last?"*

Meditation:

Just when we think we have figured it out, something always seems to come along and cloud our crystal clear understanding. We find ourselves back at square one, trying to make sense of life, faith, loss. We who follow Christ in the third millennium can take comfort in the fact that the gospels all tell us of the confusion the disciples often experienced on hearing him speak or seeing him act. No one has ever been so misunderstood in all of history as Jesus of Nazareth. No one is more misunderstood today as he. I sometimes pretend to know more about Jesus and his ways than I actually do know. It is an occupational hazard. As one who is called upon to preach several times a week, I am "supposed" to know who Christ is, what Christ means. The best response I can offer is the one I some-times gave my father when I was younger: shoulders that shrug, a head and heart that hope to understand more and know better the next time.

"YOU DO NOT UNDERSTAND, MY CHILDREN?" Mary asked and then went from flawless French to a more approachable *patois*, Maximin's and Melanie's local dialect. Communication can be difficult when we aren't speaking the same language, or when we are not interpreting words the same way. Perhaps Our Lady was exercising the gift of tongues she received at Pentecost, showing us how language, so divisive at times, can also unite. Whatever her reason for speaking both French and *patois*, she wanted the children to understand her Good News about Jesus as much as he wanted the disciples to understand his about the Kingdom. Neither did the first disciples nor these humble La Salette visionaries comprehend the fullness of what was entrusted to them. As we hear the Gospel today, we are sure to miss the total picture too – but not entirely.

Reflection Questions:

• What puzzles me about Jesus and the call to be his disciple?
• Am I waiting until I understand more before I make a deeper commitment to Christ, or am I willing to trust and to learn as I follow him day by day?

Tuesday, May 18, (#298)
Seventh Week of Easter

John 17:1-11a: *"Now, Father, glorify me with that glory I had with you before the world existed."*

Meditation:

This is not "good ol' boy" talk about the good ol' days, a lament over things gone downhill since they did that "Eden thing" and everything went sour. This is no lament that Father and Son are sharing. This is the Son's disclosure of his deepest desire for the completion of the work he had begun: not just what we saw at Bethlehem, but what had been prepared from the foundation of the world. While Thomas Aquinas, the Dominican theologian, believed that Christ came among us because we needed to be redeemed from sin, his contemporary, the Franciscan theologian, Duns Scotus, believed that God intended that the eternal Word should become incarnate even if human beings had never sinned. We would have been incomplete, he argued, as long as God had not become one with his creation. In this perspective, the dialogue about the glory between Jesus and his Father is not about good ol' days, but about the days they had always longed and planned for, days when not only Father, Son and Spirit would be one, but all creation would be one with them.

"ONLY A FEW SOMEWHAT AGED WOMEN GO TO MASS!" Between the famine and low church attendance, 1846 certainly was not. Neither would our day qualify. Pope John Paul II's apostolic letter about the centrality of Sunday, a day meant to be the Day of the Lord from start to finish, seems to have fallen on deaf ears, as did Mary's cry. What is this Sunday observance about anyway? Sunday is about celebrating the manifestation of God's glory in human flesh, that of the Risen Jesus, the pledge that we share in unending life and will rest one day from our labors. On Sunday, the day above all other days, we celebrate the promise that God's glory will be ours too.

Reflection Questions:

• When you realize that God is prepared (indeed desperately desires) to share his very life, his glory, with you, how does that make you feel?
• What do you do on Sunday that distracts you from the revelation of God's glory, even in the partial way we experience it in this life?

Wednesday, May 19, (#299)
Seventh Week of Easter

John 17:11b-19: *"They do not belong to this world any more than I belong to the world."*

Meditation:

I once caught myself saying in a homily, "... the Mother Teresas of this world." I don't recall exactly what I was speaking about, but I'm sure it had something to do with her exceptional holiness as an example for us to imitate. Months later this phrase came to mind out of the blue, and I realized the irony of it: Mother Teresa was not "of this world." She was simply in it. It was not the benevolence of the human heart that made her what she was for the creatures of this planet, but the greatness of God's grace that made her so. Like the Christ she so humbly followed, Mother Teresa had set her heart on the will of her heavenly Father. She sought no compensation in this world, but to know she was a beloved daughter of God. She excelled in giving Christian witness, because she belonged first to Christ and only in him did she belong to the world to which he gave her. We may not be so great as she in giving our witness to Christ, but we too are called "out of this world" to live in Christ. But he will likely give us back to the world as witnesses to his love.

"**BEHOLD THE HANDMAID OF THE LORD,** be it done to me according to your word" (Luke 1:38). Mary's *fiat* continued in the apparition and message of La Salette. As she encountered the *no* of the children of God, her *yes* resounded all the louder. Once again, she came to earth to draw us closer to her Son, she brought us the opportunity to be filled with the blessing of the "fruit of her womb." No doubt Mary's yes to Christ echoed in Mother Teresa's life. May it echo in yours and mine as well!

Reflection Questions:

• Do I see myself as one who is "of this world" or "of Christ"?
• Can I see myself as given back to the world by Christ to make it holy by my life of faith, like Mary, Mother Teresa and all the saints?

Thursday, May 20, (#300)
Seventh Week of Easter

John 17:20-26: *"The world will recognize that it was you who sent me and that you loved them as you loved me."*

Meditation:

Jesus clearly turns his attention to the future. He anticipates the success in time of the disciples' mission, praying *"for those who will believe in him through their words"* and foresees their presence in eternity *"with him where he is."* He expresses his Last Will: *"that they may all be one"* and goes on to sketch the essential traits of this ardently desired unity. Its model is the unity of Father and Son. It is a unity in diversity (despite their perfect oneness Father and Son remain distinct persons). This unity must be visible enough to challenge the world, just as he did, to recognize God present and at work in him. The fact that Jesus prays to the Father for this gift tells us that it lies within the sole power of God. It is fitting that this majestic and stirring prayer which concludes the Farewell Dis-course itself closes on the note of the unity of all believers, "the fruit that will remain."

AT LA SALETTE the Mother of Jesus expresses concern about various harvests: grapes, potatoes, walnuts, wheat. She is solicitous of earth's produce in field, garden, orchard and vineyard. In biblical language, such productivity mirrors the fruitfulness of the human spirit as it obediently carries out the Creator's purpose. Mindful of the solemn words her Son spoke at the Last Supper, *"You did not choose me, no, I chose you; and I commissioned you to go out and to bear fruit, fruit that will last"* (John 15:16), she cares deeply about the spiritual fruit human hands and hearts are to bring forth for the life and unity of the world.

Reflection Questions:

• Science and technology in future years will be much improved. Their human manipulators, however, won't be. Am I nonetheless hopeful?
• In light of Jesus' prayer can I imagine a day when human life will have been completely transformed?

Friday, May 21, (#301)
Seventh Week of Easter

John 21:15-19: *"Simon, son of John, do you love me?"*

Meditation:

Sometimes one spouse has trouble saying, "I love you." When the question is raised (usually because "I love you" never gets spoken!)

the response is defensive: "Yes, you know I love you. ... Of course I love you. ... I'm hurt. How could you even ask; you know I love you." People cite the many things they do, the hardships they endure, the many things they have sacrificed, the lengths to which they have gone. There is something about hearing it, however, that seems to make a difference. Showing it is walking the talk, but saying it is still important because mere routine, or who knows what, could be what keeps the relationship going. Sometimes the question is asked even when the answer is known for certain. Jesus, who knows what's on our mind before we say it, still seems to want to hear us say it. Maybe he realizes that it will make a difference to us if we say it, and realize we mean it.

NOT HEARING THAT YOU'RE LOVED can lead to tears and much sadness. Maybe that's what Mary's tears were about? "How could someone who had experienced the glory of God in heaven be sad and cry?" Some wondered when the children reported that the Beautiful Lady wept for the entire duration of the apparition. Maybe she realized how much her children – the children of the Church, the children of God – were missing out on when they failed to practice what they professed, and failed to appreciate what they practiced.

Reflection Questions:

• Whom do you love that you have taken for granted lately?
• How can you show those you love that you love them today – perhaps to strengthen your own awareness as well as theirs?

Saturday, May 22, (#302)
Seventh Week of Easter

John 21:20-25: *"So the word among the brothers that (the disciple that Jesus loved) would not die."*

Meditation:

At a recent gathering of La Salette Missionaries that focused on our Marian roots, we were reminded that apparitions, including that of Our Lady at La Salette, always address "the last things." This doesn't mean that La Salette Missionaries go around predicting a precise day, time or even the extreme nearness of these "last things." Nor does it mean that they are to be dismissed altogether. Talk about the end times in Catholic circles has always intended to bring about repentance here and now and not to cause hysteria or panic. In the midst of our hectic and sometimes reactionary age in which many will vaguely hint or specifically point to Christ's Second Coming, we are to look closely at the signs of the times and recognize that, whether or not his return is imminent, now is always the moment for repentance. Whether they live until Jesus comes or whether generation upon generation will yet follow, Christians know it's never too early to return to their Lord with all their hearts.

THE AUTHORITIES WERE WORRIED that if Mary's dire predictions about the crops were to get out, no one would risk planting anything. Reasons for opposing the La Salette message were not just anti-religious, but very practical. Mary's words expressed concern about the kind of daily bread that would feed spirits, not just stomachs, however important the latter may be. The authorities may have been aware that "people don't live on bread alone," but they also knew that at least a little bread was needed. In the story of Maximin's father offering him a piece of bread on the way home to Corps, we have evidence that Mary is aware of both the bread of this world as well as the bread of the Kingdom to come. She knows the role each of these must play, and is willing to intercede in order that body and soul be kept together and ordered rightly to our ultimate good.

Reflection Questions:

• What am I feeding my body? What am I feeding myself mentally, emotionally, morally, and spiritually? Is it all healthy? Is it what I should be feeding myself? Is it what I need?

• How am I taking care of the physical, emotional and spiritual parts of my life?

Sunday, May 23 (#063B)
Pentecost Sunday

(Acts 2:1-11; Galatians 5:16-25; John 15:26-27, 16:12-15)

Meditation: *All Things to All*

Our title today is taken from 1 Corinthians 9:22, where St. Paul

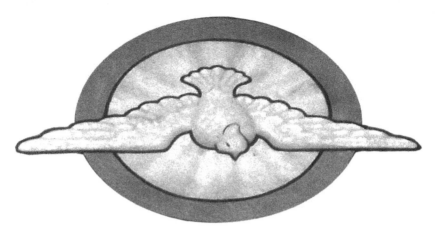

writes, "I have become all things to all, to save at least some." But, compared to the Holy Spirit, St. Paul's claim is empty.

After the second reading there is a 'sequence,' the poem, *Veni Sancte Spiritus*. Here the Spirit is described as "source of all our store," meaning that all spiritual gifts come from him. In one verse, he is "grateful coolness in the heat;" later, we pray that he will "melt the frozen, warm the chill." In other words, the Spirit comes always with the gift that is needed.

In our readings we see this in the multiplicity of languages in Acts, in St. Paul's famous fruits of the Spirit, and in Jesus' promise that the Spirit of truth will guide us to all truth. Truth is unchanging, but its expression needs to correspond to the context in which it is spoken: language, culture, etc. We need the Spirit to accomplish that.

Mary came to La Salette to speak truth. Today I am inclined to think of the brilliant light in which she first appeared—which Maximin and Mélanie compared to the sun—as the fire of the Spirit, preparing her for what she was about to do and say.

Without using St. Paul's words, she spoke, in two languages, of the works of the flesh (many forms of selfishness, distance from God) and demonstrated the fruits of the spirit in her demeanor and speech.

She used the gifts at her disposal: tears, beauty, costume, compassion, pleading (not afraid to describe herself as our advocate), honesty (not hesitating even to inspire feelings of guilt).

All this and more, to all her people, to speak the truth that they need to hear: that they are still loved by the God and Savior whom they have forgotten. Another quotation from St. Paul is appropriate here: "God proves his love for us in that while we were still sinners Christ died for us" (Romans 5:8). This is why Our Lady of La Salette wears the Crucifix prominently on her breast.

Can we be all to all? Like Mary, can we speak the truth to our world? In what language (words and action)? The Spirit places gifts at our disposal. Let's use them!

Monday, May 24 (#744)
Mary, Mother of the Church

John 20: 19-23: *'As the Father sent me, so am I sending you.'*

Meditation:

"Pope Francis has decreed that the ancient devotion to the Blessed Virgin Mary, under the title of Mother of the Church, be inserted into the Roman Calendar. The liturgical celebration... will be celebrated annually as a Memorial on the day after Pentecost. ... the Holy Father wishes to promote this devotion in order to "encourage the growth of the maternal sense of the Church in the pastors, religious and faithful, as well as a growth of genuine Marian piety".

The decree reflects on the history of Marian theology in the Church's liturgical tradition and the writings of the Church Fathers. It says Saint Augustine and Pope Saint Leo the Great both reflected on the Virgin Mary's importance in the mystery of Christ. "In fact the former [St. Augustine] says that Mary is the mother of the members of Christ, because with charity she cooperated in the rebirth of the faithful into the Church, while the latter [St. Leo the Great] says that the birth of the Head is also the birth of the body, thus indicating that Mary is at once Mother of Christ, the Son of God, and mother of the members of his Mystical Body, which is the Church." The decree says these reflections are a result of the "divine motherhood of Mary and from her intimate union in the work of the Redeemer" (Vatican News).

IN 1846 MARY SHOWED THE QUALITIES OF HER MOTHERHOOD by appearing to the two children near the hamlet of La Salette in 1846. She was bringing the merciful message of her Son to France and the world. Pope Paul VI "declared the Blessed Virgin Mary as 'Mother of the Church, that is to say of all Christian people, the faithful as well as the pastors, who call her the most loving Mother' and established that 'the Mother of God should be further honored and invoked by the entire Christian people by this tenderest of titles" (Vatican News). Like her Son, she could well have said, "As the Father sent me, so am I sending you." As Mother of the Church, she truly was sent from God to bring the message of her Son, Jesus, to all her people, her needy children.

Reflection Questions:

• What qualities of your own mother do you see in Our Lady of La Salette?
• Whom have you "mothered" through your tender concern and love for them?

Tuesday, May 25 (#348)
Eighth Week in Ordinary Time

Mark 10:28-31: *"We have left everything and followed you."*

Meditation:

In reaction to the man in yesterday's gospel who felt Jesus had asked for too much, Peter takes credit for having "left everything and followed Jesus," for having given up family and possessions. He now wonders aloud what's in it for him. He has stayed on, he points out, and in doing so has lost everything he was formerly familiar with. He implicitly asks, "What's my reward?" Comparing himself to the man "who went away sad," Peter too claims to know how costly following Jesus can be. So now what can he expect to get in return? Everything! Jesus gives his word. Everything that has been put aside for the sake of the kingdom will be returned a hundredfold. He gives Peter this solid assurance and asks him not to worry because God is generous and never to be outdone in generosity. Why think in terms of personal reward? Why not think in terms of the divine reversal where "the first shall come last and the last shall come first"?

At La Salette the Mother of Jesus asks that we measure all that we are — all that we could hope to be — against all that her Son offers for the building of God's reign and the fulfillment of those chosen. Beyond the undeniable alienation and pain our sinfulness brings, there is the healing and wholeness, pardon and peace God gives. The Gospel promise, dramatically echoed in her apparition, is a pledge of unfailing divine generosity: "If they are converted, rocks and stones will turn into heaps of wheat and potatoes will be self-sown in the fields."

Reflection Questions:

- What have you put aside to follow Jesus?
- What more must you put aside in order to serve him more faithfully?

Wednesday, May 26 (#349)
Eighth Week in Ordinary Time

Mark 10:32-45: *"Can you drink the cup I shall drink?"*

Meditation:

As in all those statements of reversal that keep asking us to see the world as he sees it, Jesus tells us today that real greatness comes at a high cost. He challenges us to turn our keen self-interest into concerned compassion for others. He asks us to pay the price he himself paid. Having come "not to be served but to serve," the Master drinks from the cup of suffering and first serves us — just as "he first loved us" (1 John 4:9, 19). This calls to mind the very first lesson many learned from the Baltimore Catechism: "we were created to know, to love and to serve God..." It is we, however, who are the first to be known, loved and served by our Maker and Savior. So we are not to lord it over others but are rather to be Lorded over by the knowing, loving and serving Son of God "who came to give his life in ransom for the many." His example teaches us that only when joy and sorrow come together in the cup of one's life does it become the cup of salvation.

The La Salette mystery is deeply rooted in the vision our Mother Mary has of us, her lovable yet self-centered, sinful, squabbling children. We should be forever grateful that she chooses to see us through her loving Mother's eyes, that the entire life she placed at her Son's service embraced the unspeakable joys and sorrows of her unique Motherhood. If at times we behave like hurt little ones, competing for her attention, perhaps it's because we know she will hear us and come to our rescue as she did in her apparition.

Reflection Questions:

• "Can you drink the cup I shall drink?" Jesus asks. What answer do I give him?
• What joy and what sorrow come together in the cup of my life today?

Thursday, May 27 (#350)
Eighth Week in Ordinary Time

Mark 10:46-52: *"Rabbuni, let me see again."*

Meditation:

The blind man of Jericho cannot see the face of Jesus but, intuiting in faith, he "sees" that he is the Messiah. Ironically, he sees by faith what the spiritually blind cannot begin to fathom. Believing is seeing, and the blind beggar is the only one here with sharp, penetrating vision. He sees Jesus' identity more clearly in fact than the disciples do. Even more clearly does Jesus see him. Why ask this man what he wanted him to do for him? What else might a blind man want of a miracle worker but to see? There is much more than a physical cure happening here. Though unspoken, themes of identity, faith, and discipleship that Jesus' followers would struggle with in every age are very much at issue here. His physical sight restored, the thankful beggar of Jericho "followed him up the road"! What is it we want Jesus to do for us? With his help do we want to win the lottery? Do we simply want a good day, sun shining and birds singing? Do we want the courage, perseverance and resolve to follow Jesus wherever he leads us?

MORAL BLINDNESS TODAY CALLS FOR HEARTS that can see beyond personal, private concerns. A clear vision of the path human beings are to follow is desperately needed. And so we reflect on the message brought to La Salette by a highly favored and graced woman who surrendered totally to God's will, who pondered his healing word and deeds (Luke 2:19), and who taught her child to cure human short-sightedness. We honor this woman of singular faith by making of our own life a journey of reconciling love with her.

Reflection Questions:

- "What do you want me to do for you?" Jesus asks me. What is my reply?
- Can I identify one of my blind spots?

Friday, May 28 (#351)
Eighth Week in Ordinary Time

Mark 11:11-26: *"My house will be called a house of prayer for all peoples…"*

Meditation:

The two fig tree incidents that frame the temple cleansing underscore its meaning as a dramatic act so typical of prophetic ministry. Jesus is challenging the validity of a corrupted temple system. Having been repudiated by so many who held power and in a life-and-death struggle, he comes to the temple to free it from the powers that be and reclaim it for God, whose house they claim it is. He rejects a temple of politics and privilege and establishes a new order founded on God's non-discriminating will to save. To stand with Jesus is to stand with an indomitable power for good against all that would tear us apart and leave us in hell. A brief examination of our collective conscience will tell us that self-interest carries the day. Abuses of power are rampant and could lead us to overestimate evil's might. That would be to deny the absolute power of good, the power of God.

THE GIFT THAT IS LA SALETTE is none other than the gospel blessing of a new beginning. "For anyone who is in Christ, there is a new creation; the old creation has gone, and now the new one is here. This is all God's doing" (2 Cor 5:17-18). This deed of God empowers all the fallen children of Mother Mary to embrace new life, entertain new hope and to share such great news with any who are willing to submit to the power of God's healing mercy.

Reflection Questions:

- Have I ever experienced powerlessness firsthand?
- Do I feel called to counter the effects of ageism, racism, and sexism in our society?
- How am I a reconciler in my family, at work, with my friends?

Saturday, May 29 (#352)
Eighth Week in Ordinary Time

Mark 11:27-33: *"What authority have you for acting like this?"*

Meditation:

Jesus really had no better credentials other than himself. When the disciples of John the Baptist came to him and asked, "Are you the one who is to come, or should we look for another?" he simply answered, "The blind regain their sight, the lame walk, lepers are cleansed, the deaf hear, and the dead are raised, the poor have the good news proclaimed to them" (Luke 7:20,22). He overturned longstanding expectations and claimed full authority to do so. Challenging all misconceptions, he made God truly known. In word and deed he made it plain that God is supremely free to love unconditionally and forgive universally. Such views were bound to baffle the chief priests, scribes and elders. They believed that only faithful keeping of the law could offer spiritual security and guarantee merciful judgment. In questioning Jesus' authority they revealed more than they perhaps intended about themselves. They cared little about John, less about the baptism he preached. They obviously cared very much about their power over people. They stood face to face before the full authority of God and managed to miss seeing it!

AT JESUS' PRESENTATION IN THE TEMPLE, the aged Simeon spoke an ominous prophecy: "Behold, this child is destined to be a sign that will be contradicted" (Luke 2:34). And so Mary had to be aware of the contempt, distrust, envy, and suspicion her Son would arouse in so many hearts in his lifetime. That was true in his own day, in the turbulent political climate of her appearance at La Salette in 1846, and it remains true to this very day. Witness Our Lady's pleas for our conversion throughout history – pleas so long unheeded.

Reflection Questions:

- Is Jesus mostly a reassuring presence in your spiritual life, or does he present a challenge?
- What particular teaching of Jesus do you view as a stumbling block?

Sunday, May 30 (#165)
The Most Holy Trinity

(Deuteronomy 4:32-40; Romans 8:14-17; Matthew 28:16-20)

Meditation: *Fear of the Lord*

Depiction of the Holy Trinity from
the Open air museum in Sanok

"The eyes of the Lord are upon those who fear him,
upon those who hope for his kindness,
To deliver them from death and preserve them in spite of famine."

If we could imagine the Blessed Virgin in heaven meditating on the Scriptures, we might think that these verses from today's Responsorial Psalm made her decide to come to La Salette. She wanted her people to be preserved from the impending famine and delivered from the death of small children.

But there was a problem: her people were not among those who feared God. "Fear of the Lord," is a recurring theme (about 750 times) in the Bible. It does not mean being afraid of God but being in absolute awe of him. (If you were being introduced to a famous person whom you greatly respected, wouldn't want to avoid anything that might give offense?)

Mary told the children, "Don't be afraid." That did not keep her from trying to restore proper fear of the Lord among her people.

Clearly, like the generations after Moses, they had forgotten all the wonders God worked for them. They were baptized, as Jesus commanded, in the name of the Father and of the Son and of the Holy Spirit, but their adoption as children of God had lost its meaning. It did not make them disciples.

They did not put their trust in God or hope for his kindness. They showed little respect for their Savior, using his name to vent their anger. They rejected the gift of the Sabbath rest. They refused God the worship that was his due. They did not fear him.

Still, they were living in fear, not of God but of a bleak future. The Beautiful Lady even accentuated this by prophesying the failure of the wheat crop, the potatoes, the grapes, even the walnuts.

But she didn't stop there. A brighter future was possible, if only they could understand that the relationship between God and us is essential, not optional.

Her message is like that of Moses: "You must now know, and fix in your heart, that the Lord is God in the heavens above and on earth below, and that there is no other. You must keep his statutes and commandments that I enjoin on you today, that you and your children after you may prosper, and that you may have long life...."

Monday, May 31 (#572)
The Visitation of the Blessed Virgin Mary

Luke 1:39-56: *"Why should I be honored with a visit from the mother of my Lord?"*

Meditation:

Many people can look at the experience of their childhood upbringing and honestly say that they basically remember being loved and nourished in their home. What a gift to be able to say that! Others can remember being loved but they also experienced considerable disruption due to sibling or parents who had difficulty getting along. Whatever the situation, we have all been blessed by some people who loved us. This is the purpose of family: to nurture and love those around us. When Mary went to visit Elizabeth it was an arduous journey but Mary went simply because she loved Elizabeth and wanted to help he in her advanced age.

At La Salette the reason for Mary's visit to the two children was love, plain and simple. Out of loving concern for "her children" she came to remind all her children of the basics of our faith and express God's concern for our struggles and hardships. She did that so well that, as the children readily mentioned, when they first saw her they were afraid. But upon hearing her invitation to "Come near, my children", their fear dissolved and they gladly approached their heavenly visitor.

Some Reflection Questions:

- Who has surprised me with a visit to say hello?
- Whom might I visit or contact to find out how they are doing?
- Do I appreciate that Mary came to La Salette to bring her concerns for us, her children?
- What do her tears mean to me?

Tuesday, June 1, (#354)
Ninth Week in Ordinary Time

Mark 12:13-17: *"Their amazement at him knew no bounds."*

Meditation:

Amazement is one of the gifts of the Holy Spirit that was given to us at our Baptism and ratified at our Confirmation. That gift is commonly known as "fear of the Lord," but amazement seems to give a better sense of the power this gift bestows. Amazement is the awesome realization of and wonder at God's interaction with us. Amazement leads to dumbfounded silence then boundless praise of God's love and mercy. Jesus is the ultimate source of amazement – God loving us so much that he sent his Son into the world. People who experienced Jesus also experienced amazement, like the Pharisees and Herodians did in today's gospel. Their amazement may have left them dumbfounded, but it failed to prompt the praise of God.

At La Salette the two children were entranced by Mary's beauty and awestruck by her message – so much so that they were able to repeat word-for-word what she said to them and, through them, to us and to the whole world. The people who heard these children were likewise amazed that two poor, uneducated herders should be given such a task. Perhaps this gift of amazement needs to be nurtured in today's world where so much is taken for granted and so many wonders often go unnoticed. Only then might we become like innocent children and look at our world with the eyes of childlike faith. We would perhaps then notice God more often! We might even get a taste of what heaven is like! We would be amazed to experience the fullness of God's love.

Reflection Questions:

• What was it that amazed you recently?
• Sit for a while in silent awe, look around you and wonder at God's tremendous love for you.

Wednesday, June 2, (#355)
Ninth Week in Ordinary Time

Mark 12:18-27: *"You understand neither the scriptures nor the power of God."*

Meditation:

It is amazing how an attitude, bias or preconceived idea can distort a teaching and blind us to the saving truth of the gospel. The Sadducees strongly believed that there is absolutely no resurrection from the dead, and that stubborn belief blinded them to the freedom God's plan of salvation enfolds. Their bias and unwillingness to change narrowed their vision to the point where they could not envision the possibility, let alone the reality, of the resurrection of the dead. It is also worth considering that a narrow belief system can generate ridicule and stubbornness when confronted with an alternative vision and truth. The Sadducees concocted the tale about the brother and the seven-times-widowed woman in an attempt to refute Jesus and trivialize his teaching about the resurrection.

AT LA SALETTE Mary said that if we can only see ourselves as God sees us, then *"rocks and stones will turn into heaps of wheat and potatoes will be self-sown in the fields."* But if we continue to see ourselves as sinners, and fail to hope in the salvation of the Cross then, *"the walnuts will* become *worm-eaten and the grapes will rot!*" It is within our power to change our self-image, our image of others and our image of God. In so doing we can unleash the miraculous power of God's loving Spirit. But if we continue to see ourselves merely as sinful, hemmed in and undeserving of God's love, such a vision will affect not only our own future but the future of our world as well. Pray to God that we can truly *"Repent, and believe in the gospel"* (Mark 1:15).

Reflection Questions:

- What are your basic attitudes about yourself? Others? God? What blinds you to God's love?
- What needs to be changed in your life?

Thursday, June 3, (#356)
Ninth Week in Ordinary Time

Mark 12:28-34: *"You are not far from the reign of God."*

Meditation:

In Mark's Gospel the scribe who asked Jesus about the greatest commandment questioned him in a spirit of honest and sincere inquiry. This particular scribe did not appear on the scene to test Jesus or to try to trip him up in some way, as his counterpart does in the retelling of the incident by St. Matthew and St. Luke. Rather he seriously ponders Jesus' words on the commandment of the love of God and neighbor and self and responds thoughtfully and sincerely. In the scribe's own words, *"Yes, to love him with all our heart, with all our thoughts and with all our strength, and to love our neighbor as ourselves is worth more than any burnt offering or sacrifice."* Jesus praises him for this insight and tells him, *"You are not far from the reign of God."*

ON THE MOUNTAIN OF LA SALETTE Mary came to ask us to consider another great gospel truth, namely, the challenge to "turn away from sin and believe in the good news." Mary invites us to *"come near and not be afraid"* as she shares that good news with us. The good news is that Jesus is coming and that his arm is heavy, laden as it is – not with judgment and threats but – with unclaimed blessings, forgiveness, mercy, redemption, in a word, salvation. If we can see and believe in the truth of this message then we ourselves *"are not far from the reign of*

God."

Reflection Questions:

- How would your life be changed if Jesus told you, "You are not far from the reign of God"?
- What would you say to Jesus after he shared that piece of good news with you? Tell him in a prayer of gratitude and praise.

Friday, June 4, (#357)
Ninth Week in Ordinary Time

Mark 12:35-37: *"How can the scribes claim, 'The Messiah is David's son'?"*

Meditation:

We always try to put God into a little box that we might comprehend God within the narrow limits of our human understanding. The scribes of the past and the scribes of today try to explain God by describing what God can and cannot be, what God can and cannot do. The scribes of today warn us that Jesus is coming soon, and that he will be cloaked in a mantle of anger, condemnation, and judgment. When Jesus comes, the world will suffer and we will really pay for our sins, they assure us. Jesus is coming and there is nothing we can do to stop him. We wait in dread, shame and terror for Jesus' return. What today's scribes distort beyond all recognition is the heartfelt and well-founded declaration believers pro-claim every time they celebrate the Eucharist: "We wait in joyful hope for the coming of our Savior, Jesus Christ."

AT LA SALETTE SHRINES WORLDWIDE, Mary is honored as the Reconciler of sinners, a title spontaneously conferred upon her by the earliest pilgrims to her chosen mountain. She appeared there wearing a crucifix with hammer and pincers, encircled by a chain and multicolored roses - eloquent symbols of Jesus' love breaking down all barriers, using our strengths and our weaknesses as he heals and saves us. Both the hammer of our sinfulness and the pincers of our repentance play key roles in Christ's death and resurrection for us. So obscured has our vision become that the abyss of God's generous mercy is beyond what we dare imagine. All we can do is submit to that immense love, believe in the good news and "wait in joyful hope for the coming of our Savior."

Reflection Questions:

- Reflect on the symbols of the hammer and pincers on the crucifix that Mary wore in her apparition. How do they connect her message with that of her Son?
- Reflect on the symbols of the chain and roses that Mary wore in her apparition. How do they connect her message with that of her Son?

Saturday, June 5, (#358)
Ninth Week in Ordinary Time

Mark 12:38-44: *"One poor widow came."*

Meditation:

The widow. She surely knows the keen ache of loss. At the death of her beloved husband, the world she knew and depended upon for support and self-esteem fell apart. She feels the sadness of the void his passing left. She tastes the bitterness of death. And yet – despite her loss, she is generous in giving. *"She gave from her want, all that she had to live on."* The widow encounters death and in that experience comes to know life's real value. She puts into practice what St. Francis preached many centuries later, namely, that *"it is in giving that we receive."* Death and loss teach her well how to be generous in life. She contributes her two cents' worth – and for centuries afterward the world takes a lesson from the generosity of the widow's mite— and her might! She gives until it hurts and manifests the true meaning of dignity and self-respect.

THE WIDOW. THE HOLY WIDOW COMES TO US AGAIN, BROKEN AND IN TEARS. She wears the dress of a peasant woman. The children suspect she is a mother who was beaten by her children and has fled to the mountain to cry in solitude. Such is the ache of loss and desolation. Yet see what wealth this widow shares as she offers her two cents' worth, a basic, down-to-earth message. Heeding her words can mean blessings in abundance, hope rekindled, love both received and returned. She bears on her breast the image of her Beloved, the only Son. In his loss, the loss of his precious life, is our eternal gain. How rich, indeed, this poor widow is. How she wishes to share her riches with us who are poorer than we know.

Reflection Questions:
- Where is your poverty?
- Where are your true and lasting riches?

Sunday, June 6 (#168)
The Most Holy Body and Blood of Christ

(Exodus 24:3-8; Hebrews 9:11-15; Mark 14:12-16, 22-26)

Meditation: *Covenant*

The Institution of the Eucharist by Justus van Gent (1410-1480)

Two words stand out in today's readings: blood and covenant.

A covenant is an agreement or treaty, in which the rights and responsibilities of the parties are stated clearly. It is something like a contract or a business arrangement.

It is much more than a contract, however, precisely because, in the Bible at least, it concerns first and foremost a relationship. The people of Israel understood what that implied, and said, "We will do everything that the Lord has told us." Their relationship with the God who had delivered them from slavery meant everything to them.

The covenant between God and Israel is summed up in the words, "I will be your God and you will be my people."

"My people:" these words occur once at the beginning and twice at the end of Mary's discourse at La Salette. She expresses herself in this way because she has a special place in the covenant, assigned to her at the foot of the cross. The people for whom her Son shed his blood are her people, too.

His covenant-blood is, as the Letter to the Hebrews reminds us, more effective than the blood of any of the prescribed animal sacrifices. It is shed 'for many,' for the multitudes that will come to find salvation in him and celebrate that gift in the Eucharist.

"In the summer, only a few elderly women go to Mass. The rest work on Sundays all summer long." At some point in their history her people had ceased to appreciate the sacrament of Christ's Body and Blood. Instead of being the sign of the Covenant, the Mass had become an unwanted obligation, a burden to be cast off. The gift was no longer being celebrated.

Anyone who thinks that Mary came to La Salette only to demand obedience to obligations is missing the point completely. Her message is aimed at restoring an awareness of the covenant between her Son and her people, and an appreciation of the immense worth of that relationship.

Taking her words to heart, we can pray with the psalmist, "How shall I make a return to the Lord for all the good he has done for me?"

Monday, June 7, (#359)
Tenth Week in Ordinary Time

Matthew 5:1-12: *"Be glad and rejoice, for your reward in heaven is great."*

Meditation:

We seem always to be in search of the elusive reward, those achievements that will bring us applause, honor, and recognition. The reward will tell us that we are better than we thought we were. When we get our reward we will have finally attained our rightful place in this world. No matter how hard we try, how much we achieve, we can never seem to fill that void within that tells us that something, or Someone, is still missing. Not only does it fail to satisfy that inner longing, the reward seems to leave us emptier than ever. Jesus tells us that only the meek, the oppressed, the poor and the persecuted find the truly satisfying reward. They are indeed happy in their discovery that God's love alone can fill the void. The pursuit of possessions, fame and fortune cannot do so. Heartfelt love of God and neighbor for their sakes can.

OUR LADY OF LA SALETTE ASKS US to take a good look at all our possessions and those rewards we prize so highly. Compared to God's love and compassion these possessions of ours will seem like so much "spoiled wheat and rotted potatoes!" Mary asks us to give all these away and acknowledge her Son as the source and summit of our salvation and happiness. Then we will know our true worth. Then we will realize what real gladness and rejoicing mean. The kingdom of heaven will be ours, at least in anticipation.

Reflection Questions:

- What is that void that always needs filling in your life?
- What is it that fills your life with meaning and purpose?

Tuesday, June 8, (#360)
Tenth Week in Ordinary Time

Matthew 5:13-16: *"You are the salt of the earth. You are the light of the world."*

Meditation:

Jesus tells us what he really thinks of us! The judge of all is plainly calling us *"the salt of the earth"* and *"the light of the world."* Normally, we would attribute such titles to Jesus alone, praising him as the light that shines in our darkness, or the living Bread that sustains us. But today Jesus holds us up to view and asks that we look at ourselves as our God in heaven sees us – as gifts to be dearly valued and unsparingly shared with others. *"Your light must shine before others, that they may see your good deeds and glorify your heavenly Father."* Imagine what the world would be like if we lived out the truth of who we are, the image and likeness of God, and the astonishing fact that God saw fit to call the entire creation *"very good"* (Genesis 1:31).

ON THE HOLY MOUNTAIN, Mary appears to Melanie and Maximin in a globe of bright light. She invites them to *"come closer"* and share in that brightness. Echoing her Son, she reminds us that we are the light of the world, and that if we could see ourselves in the light of God's love for us, we would obtain heaven. As she vanishes into the light, she urges us to relay that message to all her people, a reaffirmation of what her Son told us long ago: *"You are the light of the world"*!

Reflection Questions:

- Do you find it easy or difficult to accept the praise Jesus speaks of you in today's gospel?
- Are you sharing God's gifts of "salt" and "light" with others?

Wednesday, June 9, (#361)
Tenth Week in Ordinary Time

Matthew 5:17-19: *"I have not come to abolish, but to fulfill."*

Meditation:

Jesus affirms that what he is about is doing the will of his Father. It is not God's will that the earth should be destroyed, but redeemed. It is not the will of God that we should be cast out of heaven, but that we should draw ever closer to our eternal happiness. *"For God so loved the world that he gave his only Son, so that everyone who believes in him might not perish but might have eternal life. For God did not send his Son into the world to condemn the world, but that the world might be saved through him"* (John 3:16-17). Jesus fulfills the law by restating the greatest commandment, the commandment that sums up the entire law and the prophets: *"You shall love the Lord, your God, with all your heart, with all your soul, and with all your mind... You shall love your neighbor as yourself"* (Matthew 22:37,39).

THE BEAUTIFUL LADY OF LA SALETTE asks us to *"come near and not be afraid."* The question is why are we so terrified of this good news?

172

What is it that holds us back from the saving arm of Mary's Son? Maybe it is that, in order to renew the world of God's creation, we have to give up the world that we ourselves have created and are quite complacent in – even if it is filled with false hopes and empty promises. Maybe we are dulled by our routines, schedules and duties, so much so that the good news of a better world interferes with those things that have taken on tremendous importance to us. Like Jesus, Mary confronts us with a choice: to stay in our own little world and suffer the consequences, or be converted, believe in the good news of salvation and fulfillment, and get a healthy taste of "the real world!"

Reflection Questions:

- Are you living in "the real world"?
- Can you come nearer to God and manage not to be afraid?

Thursday, June 10, (#362)
Tenth Week in Ordinary Time

Matthew 5:20-26: *"Go first and be reconciled with your brother or sister, and then come and offer your gift."*

Meditation:

Mother Teresa of Calcutta said, "Give until it hurts," and Jesus seems to say "Forgive until it doesn't hurt anymore!" Forgiveness is a basic attitude, a calling, a vocation. Reconciliation is not simply a one-time occurrence. We cannot simply forgive and forget, as the saying goes. Forgiveness is like a surgeon's scalpel that reopens old wounds in order to clear out the infections of anger, bitterness and resentment. At the same time, forgiveness is a soothing ointment, liberally applied, to cleanse and heal old or new wounds. Jesus bids us to *"forgive seventy times seven times"* (Matthew 18:22). Forgive even though everyone does not request it. Forgive even though everyone does not deserve it. This gift Jesus offers as a key to heaven; our eternal happiness can begin now if we so choose.

THE OLDEST AND BEST KNOWN TITLE OF OUR LADY OF LA SALETTE is Reconciler of sinners. In her apparition she assures us that she *"prays without ceasing for us,"* thereby affirming that forgiveness – rather than an occasional act of kindness or isolated instance of bigheartedness – is a lifelong vocation for the Christian. *"And this is from God who reconciled us to himself in Christ, and has entrusted to us the ministry of reconciliation... God was in Christ not counting our trespasses against us"* (2 Corinthians 5:18-19).

Reflection Questions:

- Have you ever been the one to take the first step in bringing about reconciliation with a friend, a neighbor, a relative?
- Is there someone in your life you cannot bring yourself to forgive?

Friday, June 11 (#171B)
The Most Sacred Heart of Jesus

Note: Today you may wish to begin the First Day of the Novena to Our Lady of La Salette, in the appendix of this book.

John 19:31-37: *"...one of the soldiers pierced his side with a lance; and immediately there came out blood and water. This is the evidence of one who saw it.."*

Meditation:

Here, in John's gospel, the evangelist goes out of his way to make sure that we notice another "sign", when he gives the details that Jesus' side was pierced and blood and water flowed out. He sees this as no mere physical happening but a great "sign" or reminder from God. St. Ambrose was later to see this event as the Church being born from the wounded side of Christ. And in Apostolic times water and blood were often seen as reminders or "sings" of the sacraments of Baptism and the Eucharist. This event had a wealth of meaning for the members of the early church.

IN THE APPARITION OF MARY AT LA SALETTE, we also see "signs" of a great teaching from God. Mary's attitude of welcome and sensitivity to the two startled children standing before her teaches us about how welcoming and understanding Jesus is. His heart burns with love for his people. Mary's response to Maximin – about the happening at the field of Coin and the decaying wheat – is gentle and personally responsive. She sincerely loves these two children and more than once urges them to make her message known to all her people.

Some Reflection Questions:

- How responsive are we to those around us in need?
- Do we think first of ourselves or rather of those who need our help?

Saturday, June 12, (#573)
The Immaculate Heart of Mary

Luke 2:41-51: *"His mother stored up all these things in her heart."*

Meditation:

There are many profound lessons in this gospel passage for young and old, married or single, parents or childless. Just one piece of wisdom is that we all need to be open to learning more each and every day. Even in the Holy Family of Nazareth, the parents of Jesus were not perfect or all-knowing. They needed to appreciate that their Son indeed had a very special calling. Their obvious and reasonable upset was justified on the one hand but also needed to be tempered with a deepened appreciation of who their Son was and what he was called to do. This event was just one example of how loving and accepting these parents needed to be as they did their best to surround their Son with love as he grew up. In a sense, as all parents realize at one time or another, parents truly need to "grow up" along with their children. That Mary did by *"(storing) up all these things in her heart."* We should do the same, whether we are parents or not. God has much more to teach us

AT LA SALETTE, Mary came to bring the message of her Son to *"her people."* Her words and actions give us much to ponder. *Her invitation* to *"Come near, (and) do not fear"* should calm our hearts no matter what our concerns. Her warnings could initially seem severe but certainly came from a loving and compassionate heart. She needed to get our absolute attention. *Her promises* were to encourage "her children" not to lose hope but instead be faithful to our vocation as baptized followers of her Son. *Her mission* was one that every follower of her Son should be willing to do – to be an evangelizer and *"make her message known".*

Reflection Questions:

- How well have you "pondered in your heart" the message and mission of Mary at La Salette? Have you allowed her words to touch and renew your faith in her Son?
- When have you shared her powerful message with others?

Sunday, June 13 (#092)
Eleventh Sunday in Ordinary Time

(Ezechiel 17:22-24; 2 Corinthians 5: 6-10; Mark 4:26-34)

Meditation: *Looking at how God makes things grow*

Christ told stories. It is worth remembering to note that all the thick theology books are based on them. Going back to these gospel stories called parables is the best way to learn about the Lord...

It is like a mustard seed, ... it grows and becomes the largest of all garden plants

The story of the Mustard Seed pictures what was known then as the "smallest of all the seeds," but "becomes the largest of plants" by the very power of God.

Growth in plants and in humans is surely God's most powerful sign of love. Not only does God create people but provides for their development. This means constant presence and care, just as the loving presence of parents is vital for the proper growth of children. Growth in humans is nothing less than the visible presence of a loving God in our lives...

Each one of us enjoys that same caring presence. If we can thank God for growing gardens we certainly can be grateful to the God who constantly chooses to grow within each person. This is the story of God's loving affair with humans. It is our story, one that should be slipped into wallets and hung on walls.

At La Salette, we hear both about dying and yielding a great harvest. First, Mary speaks about the harvest of wheat being ruined, disintegrating into dust and adds that the harvest is going to *"...continue to spoil, and by Christmas this year there will be none left... The walnuts will become worm-eaten; the grapes will rot."*

Second, Mary pleads for us, her children, to follow the path of her Son, Jesus, by allow ourselves to be converted. With the exaggeration of a prophet, she states that *"If (her wayward children) are converted, rocks and stones will turn into heaps of wheat, and potatoes will be self-sown in the fields..."*; that is, great blessings will follow.

Like the mustard seed mentioned in the gospel and Ezechiel's trees which God helps to grow strong and tall, we "shall bear fruit even in old age; vigorous and sturdy (we) shall be" if we allow God to show us the way. (Written by Frs. Normand Theroux, M.S. and Ron Gagne, M.S.)

Monday, June 14, (#365)
Eleventh Week in Ordinary Time

Matthew 5:38-42: *"Offer no resistance to (the wicked)."*

Meditation:

The word "injury" calls up all sorts of mental images, from a cut on a finger to injuries sustained in a serious accident. Wouldn't a person want to offer resistance to injury? Isn't that the normal thing to do? It is the pain and suffering that come with injuries that people shun? This goes to the core of our being. Jesus, however, did not shun injury or suffering. He embraced it for the good of all. The inconvenience and bother of reaching out and attending to a fellow human being in need draws us out of ourselves.

Earning a modest living as a farmer in the mountain villages around La Salette was an ungrateful task. It was very hard work with precious little to show for it. Mary urges these poor people to return to the practice of their faith, promising them newfound closeness to God, consolation and hope.

Reflection Questions:

- How can the injury you embrace and the suffering associated with it bring you closer to God?
- In what way can embracing injury and its attendant suffering bring you closer to others?

Tuesday, June 15, (#366)
Eleventh Week in Ordinary Time

Matthew 5:43-48: *"… be perfect, just as your heavenly Father is perfect."*

Meditation:

We may think that Jesus' call to "perfection" in today's gospel is almost impossible. How can we be as perfect as our heavenly Father is perfect? The command that Jesus gives us is a continuous action. It is something that we continually work toward. Our human nature is always in need of conversion and healing. Jesus offers us healing that can bring us closer and closer to our goal of perfection. We are not saints, but we are striving for the wholeness that only Jesus can give.

At La Salette Mary sought to encourage Maximin and Melanie and us to seek wholeness. This can be found in her Son alone. When we pray for our enemies, we are working toward that wholeness. Running in circles is certainly not the answer; changing the subject is not the answer; neither is blaming others. Unless we change our hearts, wholeness will elude us. And how do we change our hearts? By praying. Prayer can change our hearts.

Reflection Questions:

- What area of reconciliation do you need to work on in your life?
- Is there any healing that you need to attempt – perhaps with an estranged family member, coworker and friend?

Wednesday, June 16, (#367)
Eleventh Week in Ordinary Time

Matthew 6:1-6,16-18: *"Be careful not to parade your uprightness in public to attract attention."*

Meditation:

We are probably very familiar with our gospel today. As part of its annual instruction on the proper observance of Lent, the church proclaims this gospel on Ash Wednesday. Jesus tells us it is not the exterior action that matters most but the innermost intention of the person performing the act of fasting, penitence, or prayer. Our heavenly Father not only sees our actions but the intentions and motives behind them.

MARY AT LA SALETTE grieved that the people of the day at times only practiced their faith to mock religion. Their hearts and souls were not really in it. They spoke Jesus' name not in prayer but in swearing when they were angry or upset. By keeping inward their sentiments of adoration, love and trust from their worship, it was only a grudging and reluctant service they offered to their Maker.

Reflection Questions:

• When doing a good deed for someone, or giving to a charity, or participating at Mass, are you doing so with a truly sincere intention or are you performing the action with an ulterior motive in mind – perhaps your own gain?
• Who are you called to serve in your life? Your family, friends, neighbors, or co-workers?

Thursday, June 17, (#368)
Eleventh Week in Ordinary Time

Mark 8:27-33: *"Who do people say that I am?"*

Meditation:

Jesus was a human being. As such he must have been curious about What was being said about him. We spare no effort in putting our best foot forward so as to impress others favorably. In the defining moment this classic scene at Caesarea Philippi recalls, Jesus puts the crucial question to his disciples: "And you, who do you say that I am?" In the depths of his frustration with their slowness to understand, Jesus thrills to hear the long-awaited word: "You are the Messiah!" We have here a first confession of Christian faith, of faith in Jesus as our loving God's Only-begotten, come to save us. Amid the many questions our life, its changing circumstances and our relationships constantly raise, we must ask life's ultimate questions: Where do I come from? What is my final destination? A kind of vague understanding and ambivalent commitment simply will not do here.

"**MARY'S MATERNITY** in the order of grace continues uninterruptedly from the con-sent she gave at the Annunciation and sustained without wavering beneath the cross until the final fulfillment of all the elect. By her maternal charity she cares for the brothers and sisters of her Son, who journey still amid dangers and difficulties until they reach their blessed homeland" (Vatican Council II, *Constitution on the Church*, no. 62). As her appearance at La Salette reminds us, Mary's solicitous love for us has, in God's providence, added to that of intercession the role of prophetic intervention: "I am here to tell you great news."

Reflection Questions:

- Who was Jesus Christ to you five years ago?
- Who do you say that Jesus Christ is today?

Friday, June 18, (#369)
Eleventh Week in Ordinary Time

Matthew 6:19-23: *"Where your treasure is, there your heart is also."*

For Your Reflection:

How often we have heard this phrase! But do we really understand its meaning? It means keeping material things in their proper place and spiritual things at the center of our concerns and lives. The material treasures we store up bring us a fleeting satisfaction and enjoyment. It is usually in the striving for the material treasure that we find the most pleasure. Once we have obtained it, we become bored and seek yet another treasure. Spiritual treasures, at the center of our lives, serve to anchor us. They bring us serenity and stability amid the distractions and annoyances of everyday living.

THE DISTRACTIONS AND EVILS OF CONTEMPORARY SOCIETY can lead us to dejection and disheartenment. They can cause us to lose our inner peace and serenity. Mary encouraged Melanie and Maximin to become well-anchored in prayer, so that the enticements of the world would not blind them to the true and lasting values. Prayer and spiritual realities at the heart of our lives can give us welcome light and hope.

Reflection Questions:

- Have you heard Our Lady of La Salette's call to cultivate your inner life?
- Do you really see spiritual goods – such as love, prayer, gratitude and the like – as the most valuable "possessions" in your own life?

Saturday, June 19 (#370)
Eleventh Week in Ordinary Time

Matthew 6:24-34: *"Do not worry about tomorrow..."*

For Your Reflection:

The AA (Alcoholics Anonymous) program is centered on two days of the week that one should not worry about: yesterday and tomorrow. One is already over – its hopes and joys, its gains and failures are gone. Tomorrow is not yet here – neither are the joys or disappointments it can bring. In today's gospel Jesus gives us a similar message: "Which of you by worrying can add a moment to your life span?" Jesus tells us to remain anchored in the present moment. That is the only place where we can seek God's will for us and endeavor to carry it out. Attempting to do God's will today should be all that we are concerned about.

"**COME NEAR, MY CHILDREN, DON'T BE AFRAID.**" These were the opening words of Mary at La Salette to Maximin and Melanie. Once these children's fear and worry had vanished, they were able to be present to that graced moment in their lives. Mary as an ambassador for her Son urges us to be fully present to the graced moments in our own lives.

Reflection Questions:

- Have you allowed your anxiety and fear to be dispelled so that you can hear God's word more clearly?
- What might God's will be for you today?

Sunday, June 20 (#095)
Twelfth Sunday in Ordinary Time

(Job 38: 1, 8-11; 2 Corinthian 5:14-17; Mark 4:35-41)

Meditation: *"Why are you so frightened? Have you still no faith?"*

Christ stilling the tempest by Currier & Ives

The storms on the "sea of Tiberias" are legendary. ... Peter and his companions were experienced boatmen, accustomed to the changing moods of their lake. If they were afraid, then there was reason to fear. Waves were rolling into the boat and as the darkness closed in, the fishermen felt the terror of death as water rose inside the small craft.

What follows is typical in the gospel of Mark who is noted for reporting words and deeds in their original state. No embellishments. This is only chapter four in the first gospel ever written and Mark's disciples still do not have the awe and the respect characteristic of Matthew and Luke. Only here could the words of the disciples be reported with brazen candor: "Teacher, do you not care that we are perishing?" Incredibly, Christ was sleeping through the havoc of wind and rain.

God, completely comfortable in his own creation had chosen to sleep. We can see the disciples, struggling to stay on their feet in the swaying fishing boat and drenched in fear, accuse the Master of not caring for them: "do you not care...? ...

The miracle that ensued was an epiphany, a manifestation of God on earth. The scene recalls Genesis when God gathered the waters of the earth together and called them seas. This was clearly a display of power. It was also proof of the presence of God in the midst of terror and confusion.

The inspiration we might draw from this storm story is that God is actively present in life. God is not only the God of incense and worship and quiet pleading but the God of turmoil and hurricanes. God is not only powerful; God cares powerfully.

AT LA SALETTE, MARY'S OPENING WORDS WERE: *"Come closer, my children; don't be afraid. I am here to tell you great news."* Fear is powerful but faith is stronger. Later Mary, as a concerned prophet, reminds her children about the habits of faith that many have forgotten or discounted as unnecessary; namely, daily prayer, weekly Eucharist, reverence for the Name of her Son, and Lenten faith-practices – all significant ways to keep the fire of faith burning in their heart. Yet she also has one final request: *"Well, my children you will make this (message of great news) known to all my people."* These are words both to remember and act upon. (Written by Frs. Normand Theroux, M.S. and Ron Gagne, M.S.)

Monday, June 21, (#371)
Twelfth Week in Ordinary Time

Matthew 7:1-5: *"... the standard you use will be the standard used for you."*

Meditation:

How often we like to think our way of seeing or doing things is the right way. Others are wrong. We like to make ourselves superior to others because this boosts our own ego. In the Christian way of life things are quite different. The way for us to avoid judgment, Jesus tells us, is not to judge others. We find this mandate very difficult because seeing the faults in our brothers and sisters is easier than seeing them in ourselves. An unknown author once wrote: "There is so much good in the worst of us, and so much bad in the best of us, that it ill behooves any of us, to find fault with the rest of us."

AT LA SALETTE Mary, whose entire life was devoted to the person and mission of Christ, speaks to the two children about conversion, conversion to the person and mission of her Son. Those who follow him share their Lord's mind and do his deeds. They look upon others with understanding and show them compassion.

Reflection Questions:

- What plank in my eye is now obstructing my view of certain other people?
- What plank in my eye is blocking my vision of my mission in Christ?

Tuesday, June 22, (#372)
Twelfth Week in Ordinary Time

Matthew 7:6,12-14: *"So always treat others as you would like them to treat you."*

Meditation:

Often, we may try to live by two separate standards: the way we like to be treated and the way we treat others. There is usually a great difference between the two. Jesus tells his disciples to be calculating and discerning. What is worthwhile should not be wasted on lesser opportunities or with the reckless. The road that leads to perdition is indeed enticing and inviting. It can easily attract. But it inevitably leads to a dry and arid wasteland. The road to what is life-giving is often difficult and presents many obstacles. However when we invest our best talents and gifts in this effort, the outcome is life-giving for ourselves and for others as well.

MARY CHOSE TO LEAVE A MEMORIAL of her visit to La Salette. The spring that sprang forth following her visit to that privileged site, and which has not ceased flowing since the day of the apparition, remains a sign and symbol of all that is life-giving, of all that sustains life. The life Mary refers to is eternal life in her Son. Following him in faithful discipleship is the road that leads to abundant and full life.

Reflection Questions:

- What gifts and talents has God given you as a special means to eternal life?
- Are you aware of double standards in yourself when you relate to others?

Wednesday, June 23 (#373)
Twelfth Week in Ordinary Time

Matthew 7:15-20: *"...you will be able to tell them by their fruits."*

For Your Reflection:

Jesus gives us a warning: "Be vigilant where the behavior and actions of others are concerned." Again, if we are discerning, we will recognize the goodness and genuineness of people by their behavior, by what they do. Jesus used the ordinary experiences familiar to the people of his day to illustrate his teachings, comparing the kingdom of God with nature and agricultural realities. A healthy plant or tree, for example, will yield healthy fruit. The essence of goodness within the plant or tree manifests itself in the fruit it bears. Decay, too, is telltale.

SO TOO DID MARY AT LA SALETTE graphically call the attention of Melanie and Maximin to spoiled wheat, worm-eaten walnuts and rotted grapes, reflections in nature of what was happening in their day, in the lives of the people around them. The evils of today's society: crime, drugs, and murder are indicators that the core of our society is in need of conversion and healing.

Reflection Questions:

- What good fruits do you recognize in your life that help in the building of the Kingdom of God?
- How much care and prayer do you bring to the choices and decisions you are called upon to make?

Thursday, June 24, (#587)
The Nativity of St. John the Baptist

Luke 1: 57-66,80: *"All their neighbors were filled with awe and the whole affair was talked about throughout the hill country of Judaea."*

Meditation:

In the lives of most people, there are certain moments that family members and neighbors will never forget. Perhaps it is the successful outcome of a medically difficult birth. Or it may be someone surviving an accident which could easily have been resulted in a fatal outcome. Or perhaps it is an simple as a birth of a child or the celebration of a wedding. Special moments can affect people for the rest of their lives! The situation around the birth of John the Baptist was accompanied by several such events. One was that Elizabeth in her older years would have conceived at all! Another was the naming of her newborn son being affirmed by Zechariah and, of course, Zachariah's being able to speak once more. And lastly, due to all these special events that led up to his birth, his friends and family had reason to wonder: "What will this child turn out to be?" As we already know, *"the child grew up and his spirit grew strong."* His was a very special life and vocation, to *"prepare the way"* for the Savior.

AT LA SALETTE another very special event happened: Our Lady appeared, bringing a message and giving "her people" a mission: **"You will make this message known to all my people."** Although many years have passed since that special Saturday morning on the top of a mountain in the Alps of Southeastern France, the effects of that event still ring through those beautiful mountains and ring forth for the entire world to hear: Mary's Son wants us to follow him closely and faithfully, praying, celebrating and living the message of her Son.

Reflection Questions:

- What words of Mary (or her Son) do you need to reflect on? What area of your life needs a spiritual boost or strengthening?
- Whom should you share the La Salette message with in the near future?

Friday, June 25, (#375)
Twelfth Week in Ordinary Time

Matthew 8:1-4: *"Lord, if you are willing, you can cleanse me."*

Meditation:

Jesus is the divine physician and he does want to heal us. Like the leper and so many others in the gospels that Jesus cured, there was one prerequisite: they recognized that Jesus could do it. They put faith in his power rather than in their own. They appealed to his compassion and gentleness. Jesus wants us to be healed of our anger, our pride, our self-centeredness that often keep us from seeing his will and that of the Father for us. Trying to let go of these personality defects allows the healing power of the Lord to enter and penetrate to the core of our inmost self.

IN HER EXERCISE OF PROPHETIC MINISTRY Mary at La Salette diagnoses her people's spiritual illness and prescribes a remedy. Her entire message, through strategic repetition, calls attention to this medicine: *"As for you, you pay no heed... You paid no heed."* Our moral condition can be cured, she tells us, if we resolve to be alert, attentive, vigilant, watchful in the future and if we learn to pay attention to what is really important, to eternally important matters.

Reflection Questions:

- Is the act of seeking healing a sign of strength or of weakness?
- If you say to the Lord, *"Lord, if you are willing, you can cleanse me."* and Jesus should respond, "Do you will to take the prescribed medicine", how would you reply?

Saturday, June 26, (#376)
Twelfth Week in Ordinary Time

Matthew 8:5-17: *"In truth I tell you, in no one in Israel have I found faith as great as this."*

Meditation:

Jesus came not only for his own – the house of Israel –but for all people. A centurion, a Roman pagan interceded with him to cure one of his servants. The centurion recognized the greatness of Jesus. And recognizing the authority Jesus had, he did not feel it necessary that he enter his house – perhaps to spare Jesus the ritual impurity attached to his entering the house of a Gentile. He has faith and trust in Jesus' words. This is enough for him. Jesus responds with high commendation and praise. He has never seen as much faith in all of Israel. The basis of it all was the centurion's unwavering trust that Jesus could and would do this.

WE WOULD NOT BE OFF THE MARK to say that Mary shed tears at La Salette over her people's lack of faith and loss of trust. In the unfolding of today's gospel story these very traits draw Jesus' commendation and praise: *"It shall be done because you trusted."* Our faith and trust, themselves gifts of God, open the compassion and power of Christ to us.

Reflection Questions:

- Do I believe that the Lord's word can work powerfully in my personal life?
- Am I confident that the Lord will show me his compassion?

Sunday, June 27 (#098)
Thirteenth Sunday in Ordinary Time
(Wisdom 1:13-15 & 2:23-24; 2 Corinthians 8:7-15; Mark 5:21-43)

The Book of Wisdom acknowledges death as an unhappy fact of life. Our Lady of La Salette tearfully acknowledges the death of children in the arms of those who hold them. We, too, understand instinctively that this is not how things were supposed to be.

In today's Gospel two persons in dire need approach Jesus. Jairus desperately wants his daughter to live. The woman in the crowd has been sick for twelve years and wants

Jesus raises the daughter of Jairus

to live a normal life. They come to Jesus because they believe in his power to heal.

But their immediate reaction after each of the two miracles is not what we would expect. The woman tries to disappear into the crowd, but then feels obliged to come to Jesus "in fear and trembling" to tell him "the whole truth," as if she feels guilty. Later, when Jesus raises the 12-year-old girl, her parents and the few disciples present are "utterly astounded," as though they had not really believed it possible.

Does this mean their faith was insincere? By no means. It was real, but perhaps they were also "hoping against hope" (cf. Roman 4:18), like Abraham, the model of faith. This is why Jesus encouraged Jairus: "Do not be afraid; just have faith."

When the Beautiful Lady enumerated the ills afflicting her people, she wept also over their response to their sufferings. Far from turning to God in faith, they abandoned hope, speaking blasphemies when they should have been saying prayers.

Mary's tears reflect the words from Wisdom, "God did not make death, nor does he rejoice in the destruction of the living." We find the same in Ezekiel 33:11, "I take no pleasure in the death of the wicked, but rather that they turn from their ways and live." She wanted her people to understand that "God's anger lasts but a moment; a lifetime, his good will," as we read in today's Psalm.

When we are open to experiencing God's good will, especially in hard times, we can live again, and join the Psalmist (and the sick woman, and Jairus) in singing, "You changed my mourning into dancing; O Lord, my God, forever will I give you thanks."

Monday, June 28 (#377)
Thirteenth Week in Ordinary Time

Matthew 8:18-22: *"Follow me."*

For Your Reflection:

Multiple choice test... On the surface it would seem easy to follow Jesus. Anyone who counts himself or herself a true believer would readily and gladly do whatever Jesus might ask if he came down and spoke his request directly. But he doesn't do that. Instead he invites us in today's world to discern among multiple possible actions what we must accomplish to follow him faithfully. For guidance as we make our choices we look to prayer, our own inner light, and especially the input of our sisters and brothers in the faith.

THE CHILDREN OF LA SALETTE WERE GIVEN A MISSION – to make Mary's message of reconciliation known. On that first day, no doubt, the mission was glowingly clear for them. Each day afterward they had to decide over and over again to be true to her mission. Many times they were offered excruciatingly difficult choices – to betray their calling or even face the threat of death or imprisonment. The first miracle of La Salette was the apparition itself. The second was the fidelity with which the children followed their calling.

Reflection Questions:

- Do you understand your own calling with great clarity?
- If not, are you reaching out to others for help in discerning what it could be?

Tuesday, June 29, (#591)
Sts. Peter and Paul, Apostles

Matthew 16:13-19: *"But you,"* he said, *"who do you say I am?"*

Meditation:

In speaking of the new evangelization, the Church is reminding us that we must stand on our own two feet and be able to respond to Jesus' question posed in the gospel for today: *"But you,"* he said, *"who do you say I am?"* Nobody else can answer that for us. We must have reflected deeply on this subject and sought to answer it for ourselves. We must have taken seriously our Baptismal call to follow Christ personally, daily, faithfully.

OUR LADY OF LA SALETTE brought us a message that is truly one of evangelization – for ourselves and for the other members of the Church. Since the essence of the Church which Saints Peter and Paul helped establish is evangelization – that is, supporting in ourselves a lively faith and reaching out to others to help them to live their Baptismal commitment – Our Lady could bring no other message except the message of her loving Son. She mentioned many helps to faith when she commented on daily prayer, the Eucharist, reverence for God's name, the use of Lenten faith habits and sharing her message with "all her people."

Reflection Questions:

- How well have you listened to Mary's words at La Salette?
- Have you examined your life to see how you are doing with regard to daily prayer, the Eucharist, reverence for God's name, the use of Lenten faith habits and sharing her message with "all her people"?

Wednesday, June 30, (#379)
Thirteenth Week in Ordinary Time

Matthew 8:28-34: *"They implored him to leave the neighborhood."*

Meditation:

Thanks for the help, Jesus. Now, please leave. Demons are for real. Jesus, the great prophet, came among his people to deliver them from the demons that were plaguing them. And those demons, like demons of all times, kept the people shackled. In doing his Father's work, Jesus came forward to purify, to cleanse, to set free. And the latter is well exemplified in this gospel passage. In return for all the good things that he did, he got the usual prophet's reward. He was, rather unceremoniously, asked to leave!

AT LA SALETTE Mary came to speak to us about the demons of the era. She was the great prophet speaking in her Son's name, targeting the evils attendant upon a dying, if not entirely dead, faith in far too many. She invited us to follow in her Son's footsteps and in hers too. To be prophets, denouncing, not only with our words, but especially by our actions; casting out the evils of addiction, corruption, materialism, poverty, racism, and violence. Being aware all the while that like Jesus, and Mary at La Salette, our reward may be simply to be asked to leave. Actually, it may even be the true litmus test of our success. Not a happy thought!

- What demon is choking my own spiritual growth these days?
- What prophetic words are welling up in my heart these days and are waiting to be uttered by me?

Thursday, July 1, (#380)
Thirteenth Week in Ordinary Time

Matthew 9:1-8: *"A feeling of awe came over the crowd."*

Meditation:

The people were simply awestruck. That would have blown us away too. This paralytic was healed not only of his infirmity, but also, and more importantly, he was forgiven his sins. There was universal applause from the crowd for the healing... but concerning his act of forgiving sins, some scribes mumbled, calling this blasphemy. Jesus, in effect, was making himself the equal of God. That was certainly too much to accept.

OUR LADY AT LA SALETTE talked about humanity's sins (read: yours and mine). Our sins are to be forgiven if we but ask. That is a miracle in itself, but in addition, she promised that *"rocks and stones will turn into mounds of wheat."* In the Sacrament of Reconciliation (and certain other sacramental moments) we are cleansed and made whole. And when we get in touch with the deepest part of ourselves, we are in touch with that deep-down, hidden part that touches God and is touched by God. In those rare but gifted moments of great spiritual insight, we cannot but be in awe of the wondrous work the Almighty does in us. Those graced moments fill us with the deepest feelings of awe and wonder.

Reflection Questions:

- How open are you to experiencing (and giving thanks for) those graced moments described above?
- At any time in your life have you been deeply awed by God's work in you, perhaps even to the point of tears?

Friday, July 2 (#381)
Thirteenth Week in Ordinary Time

Matthew 9:9-13: *"And indeed I came to call not the upright, but sinners."*

Meditation:

Jesus didn't come mostly for the upright, but especially for sinners. If ever there were words in Scripture that are both shocking and comforting, they are the ones cited above. First, the virtuous need some help and support. But realistically, since they are already doing so well, they weren't Jesus' prime target audience. Second, it is a great comfort that Jesus does in fact seek out sinners. It should be comforting that we can look forward to getting serious help in our efforts toward goodness, for Jesus says we are number one in his book. How about that!

AT LA SALETTE, VERY MUCH IN HER SON'S MODE, Our Lady came to seek out sinners, just as Jesus so generously offers help and forgiveness to his more needy people. She speaks powerfully about her suffering and prays for all who are far from being virtuous. Many people may have thought that the church was the exclusive home of only the holy and Eucharist was our reward for good behavior. However a more accurate view is that Eucharist is also food and drink for the wayfarers, the ever-needy people who sometimes falter along the way. Indeed the Church includes both saints and sinners.

Some Reflection Questions:

- Are you thankful that the Church welcomes both saints and sinners?
- Whom do you know who is a very strong person of faith?

Saturday, July 3, (#593)
St. Thomas, Apostle

Gospel: John 20:24-29: *"Thomas replied, 'My Lord and my God!'"*

Meditation:

Our lifetime is probably filled with more ordinary days that extraordinary ones. We usually move from day to day – on some days enjoying life, and on other more challenging days, trying just to survive them. In all our days, however, Jesus and his grace are there to assist us in our every need. In our gospel for today we hear about a challenging time in the life of the apostle, Thomas, when he was confronted with the other disciples who said, *"We have seen the Lord,"* to which he responded with his words explaining that he must see for himself, and only then will he choose to believe what they said to him. Only later does he respond with his truer, faith-filled self by saying, *"My Lord and my God!"*

MARY AT LA SALETTE tries to help the initially fearful children with her tender and inviting words, *"Come near, my children, do not be afraid."* For these two children, this was anything but an ordinary Saturday morning. After all, they were being gifted with a visit from the Mother of God! However after that most special event, there were many other more challenging days to follow, where their faith and patience were to be duly tested, even by fellow Churchmen. Yet they consistently responded with their truest faith-filled selves and remained faithful to Mary's message and mission.

Reflection Questions:

• When have you been challenged or tested in your life, and you felt God's grace (perhaps through the support of a friend) helping you through it?
• When have you seen how God helped a person in need?

Sunday, July 4 (#101)
Fourteenth Sunday In Ordinary Time

(Ezekiel 2:2-5; 2 Corinthians 12:7-10; Mark 6:1-6a)

Meditation: *Strength in Weakness*

We often experience our tears as a sign of weakness or vulnerability. We struggle against them, we hide them if we can. In many cultures, it is extremely rare for adults to cry in front of other persons, and only the most intense grief or pain can cause them to do so.

At La Salette, the Blessed Virgin showed herself in tears. Far from demonstrating weakness, however, they are one of the strengths of the Apparition, an important part of its appeal.

When we are in the presence of someone crying, most often we want to find a way to comfort or console. But Mary said, "However much you pray, however much you do, you will never be able to recompense the pains I have taken for you." Before such words we feel powerless ourselves.

St. Paul, however, encourages us when he writes, "When I am weak, then I am strong." In the notion of weakness he includes "insults, hardships, persecutions, and constraints," such as Jesus experienced even in his visit home and Ezekiel

Jesus teaching in the Temple **from Standard Bible Story Readers, Book Five (1928)**

was told he could expect to encounter as a prophet.

It is in this context that St. Paul quotes the Lord's words to him: "My grace is sufficient for you,

for power is made perfect in weakness." In other words, the source of our strength does not, cannot lie in ourselves.

When the Beautiful Lady calls us to conversion, she highlights prayer and the Mass because these are the best ways to obtain from the Lord the strength that can come only from him—strength to make necessary changes in our lives, to accept the hardships or rejection they may entail. If we rely on our own efforts, we will fail.

The hardest part for us is giving up. I don't mean abandoning hope but acknowledging how powerless we are. This is painful. It may even lead to tears.

In the confessional at La Salette Shrines we often encounter penitents who weep as they confess their struggles with sin. They apologize for their tears, but one of our priests has learned to say to them, "This is La Salette. Tears are welcome here."

Monday, July 5, (#383)
Fourteenth Week in Ordinary Time

Matthew 9:18-26: *"She touched the fringe of his cloak."*

Meditation:

Pay attention. These two miracles offer us great insight as to Jesus the man. An important religious official came to see him imploring that Jesus do something about his daughter. She had just died, yet the man stated his first belief that she was not beyond Jesus' power to save. Jesus and his disciples were on their way to another mission of mercy. Jesus certainly was single-minded, but not so focused that he could not sense power leaving him as a person touched his cloak in a confident bid for healing. What amazing presence to people Jesus had even in times of personal stress!

Mary at La Salette tells us that God has not lost that desire to be present to us in all the moments of our lives. Although taken up with the providential guidance and maintenance of the ongoing miracle of creation – an expanding universe whose size is beyond calculation, this same God notices a father and child discussing spoiled wheat in the corner of a remote field. Mary communicates this concern for Maximin's father and his anxiety about being able to provide for his family. God (and Mary) truly care for the "little ones" of this world. That is most comforting.

Reflection Questions:

• When have you felt anxious about a person or event in the circle of your family or friends?
• When has God (perhaps through the assistance of a friend or family member) helped you through an anxious time or challenging event? How have you expressed your thankfulness to them for their help or their love?

Tuesday, July 6, (#384)
Fourteenth Week in Ordinary Time

Matthew 9:32-38: *"They were... like sheep without a shepherd."*

Meditation:

Jesus is looking for a few good men (and women). Jesus had a special love for the poor. Surely most of those who followed him were such. Life for them undoubtedly was one of harassment by the rich and powerful and of burnout from the constant struggle just to survive. Jesus felt very sorry for them. He saw how great their need was and realized that he as a person could not meet them all. And how he wished that more people were available to give him a hand. He himself was in great demand as he went about curing and healing, listening and sustaining, encouraging and challenging.

THE TEARS OF OUR LADY OF LA SALETTE speak of an endless love for her people. She saw the crowds of a Europe at the threshold of the industrial age. She could not help but see how harassed and dejected they were. It is true they were sinners and yet, as once was said, they were more sinned against than sinning. Mary, like Jesus, in his name, took pity on them. Her tears spoke most eloquently and she missioned two new young disciples, Melanie and Maximin, to spread the message of God's concern for her often harassed and dejected people.

Reflection Questions:

• Today's communications revolution makes us immediately aware of the evils being perpetrated against the innocent around the world. How do you do your part to help those most in need?
• At times, do you use "limited resources or personal obligations" as an excuse for your inaction?

Wednesday, July 7, (#385)
Fourteenth Week in Ordinary Time

Matthew 10:1-7: *"Do not make your way to gentile territory ... go instead to the lost sheep of the House of Israel."*

Meditation:

Scripture contradicting itself? Reading the above passage brings to mind a number of contradictions found in Scripture. In this case Jesus prohibits his disciples from going to evangelize people outside the Jewish faith. And yet toward the end of this same Gospel according to Matthew he tells us to "go and make disciples of all nations" (Matthew 28:19). Well, which is it? Both, actually. Some are called to be missionaries in faraway lands. Others are called to stay put and work among and with their own. In God's eyes, disciples are making disciples in both instances.

MARY AT LA SALETTE speaks especially to those who are of the faith, in need of conversion or a change of heart – of metanoia, to use the fancy word. Is she against preaching the gospel message in distant lands? Of course not! She simply makes it clear that those sheep within the fold are in need of continuous conversion. And the La Salette Missionaries have historically expended a great deal of their energies staffing shrines, spiritual life centers, as well as preaching parish missions in that very same spirit.

Reflection Questions:

• St. Therese of Lisieux was designated Patroness of the Missions, despite the fact that she never stepped out of her cloister. Have you ever met missionaries who serve in foreign lands, perhaps even some La Salette Missionaries?
• Have you personally exercised your call to evangelize (from your Baptism) by reaching out to inactive Catholics in your own circle of friends or acquaintances?

Thursday, July 8, (#386)
Fourteenth Week in Ordinary Time

Matthew 10:7-15: *"Provide yourselves with no gold nor silver, not even with coppers for your purses."*

Meditation:

We are called to travel light. Perhaps some of the image of Jesus on which we were fed as youngsters was a bit saccharine, syrupy. Jesus seemed anything but a forceful leader. Very different from the picture we get in listening to his words in the gospel for today. In staccato fashion he tells us what disciples should and should not do in carrying out their mission: *"Cure the sick, raise the dead, cleanse those suffering from virulent skin-diseases, drive out devils."* And for good measure, *"give without charge."* Then just in case we have failed to notice how exacting and demanding a taskmaster he is, he bids us leave on our apostolic journeys with nothing in support, except other people's willingness to share with us. His demands are quite radical. Norman Vincent Peale's classic work on how to win friends and influence people was obviously not on his reading list.

WE NOW TURN TO MARY in her apparition at La Salette. The message that she entrusted to Melanie and Maximin was a commissioning that went beyond belief. Not only were they lacking gold, silver, or copper to fulfill their journey, they were also bereft of basic human qualifications, such as charisma, education, an outgoing personality or being articulate – to say nothing of prayerfulness, theological grounding, or pastoral know-how. They had to get out there and "tell everyone" what their Beautiful Lady had told them "to make known."

Reflection Questions:

• As odd as it may seems, are you aware that it is precisely because of what you lack, and not what you have, that makes it possible for God to work through you?
• Do you ever get fooled by a messenger's high-class appearance, bearing, and considerable credentials which influence your acceptance of their message or can you see "to the heart"?

Friday, July 9, (#387)
Fourteenth Week in Ordinary Time

Matthew 10:16-23: *"I am sending you out as sheep among wolves."*

Meditation:

From Jesus, we don't hear the most compelling slogan for a recruitment poster for his followers. He doesn't offer people to "be all they can be." He doesn't entice them by promising them an endless stream of benefits that grow with the passing of the years. No – quite the contrary. He offers persecution (if the job is done right). And then he says that we will be guaranteed protection from death. Of course, he is not referring to physical death. If we should get in harm's way in his service we may even die. But he does promise that under questioning you will be given by the Spirit what you should say. He promises that we will escape death only in the sense that we are promised a final resurrection. Can it be surprising that so few choose to follow him in any radical way?

AGAIN WE FOCUS ON THE CHILDREN OF LA SALETTE, on the message they had to impart, their lack of human, material or spiritual resources, on the opposition with which they frequently met. If the apparition at La Salette is miraculous, the faithfulness of the witnesses in spreading the message comes in a close second in terms of the miraculous. Undaunted, they went out in true gospel fashion, *"as sheep among wolves"*. They were offered bribes, ridiculed, and even threatened. Secular and church officials subjected them to grueling and seemingly interminable interrogations. Though humanly unprepared for the task, they were given what to say under very difficult questioning. Amazing!

Reflection Questions:

- Do you rejoice that the Lord has decided to foil the crafty and the clever and reveal the mysteries of the kingdom to the humble?
- Whom do you know who are seen by the world as less than impressive but whom you feel are actually filled with the wisdom of God? What attitude should this divine partiality toward the lowly inspire in you?

Saturday, July 10, (#388)
Fourteenth Week in Ordinary Time

Matthew 10:24-33: *"So if anyone declares himself for me in the presence of human beings, I will declare myself for him in the presence of my Father in heaven."*

Meditation:

All hands on deck! This is a call to witnessing. As Catholics many of us are not very good at it. We weren't trained for it as children. Probably it was not part of our religious upbringing. Religion for us was pretty much a private affair, except of course for those who are supposed to be doing it professionally: religious brothers, sisters, deacons, and priests. However the vast majority of us are simply satisfied to approach the Sacraments as spectators, and give a minimum in the collection. And in our consumerist society, finding a church that "feeds us" amounts to saying: a church that says what we want to hear, and will not challenge us beyond our comfort zone. All Jehovah's Witnesses, all Mormons, among others, are expected to witness. Witnessing is an integral part of living their faith. Most of us are just not aware of our call to evangelize which comes from our Baptism.

AT LA SALETTE Mary, Mother of the Church, the first and most eminent of all Christians, does precisely what "witnessing to the faith" calls for. She tells us about the privileged place her Son holds in her own life. She shows what her Son means to her. She proclaims this for all the world to hear. At La Salette she not only does witness to her Son and his Gospel message, she is the prophet who speaks his words to us in his name, indicating how deeply she has absorbed him and his Word. She witnesses boldly, straightforwardly, and without equivocation. She also responds to her children with untold compassion, understanding and love.

Reflection Questions:

• When was the last time you fearlessly let you faith convictions become known when the circumstances demanded it?
• In social or work-related settings, how often have you expressed your Christian beliefs and values when the need arose?

Sunday, July 11 (#104)
Fifteenth Sunday in Ordinary Time

Note: Today you may wish to begin the First Day of the Novena to Our Lady of La Salette, in the appendix of this book.

(Amos 7:12-15; Ephesians 1:3-14; Mark 6:7-13)

Meditation: *Chosen*

Today's reading from Ephesians is used also for December 8, the Feast of the Immaculate Conception. Mary was chosen "before the foundation of the world, to be holy and without blemish before him." So were we.

The prophet Amos, a nobody, was chosen. "I was a shepherd and a dresser of sycamores. The Lord took me from following the flock, and said to me, Go, prophesy to my people Israel." The Twelve, chosen by Jesus in Mark 3, are now sent out on mission.

As we have often seen, Mélanie and Maximin, young shepherds, were chosen in 1846 for a mission which they carried out to the best of their ability. In 1855, exactly nine years after the Apparition, the Bishop of Grenoble declared, "The mission of the shepherds is ended, that of the Church is beginning."

The seed of that new beginning was planted in 1852, when the previous Bishop founded the Missionaries of Our Lady of La Salette, a group of diocesan priests, handpicked to serve the pilgrims on the Holy Mountain, and to preach parish missions throughout his diocese. Six years later, the Missionaries became a religious congregation, which eventually included laymen also, La Salette Brothers.

Portrait of Saint Mark by
James Tissot (1836-1902)

In 1872 a woman from Marseille, Henriette Deluy-Fabry, founded the Reparation Sisters of Our Lady of La Salette. They worked with the Missionaries in their ministry to the pilgrims at the Shrine. In 1930, Fr. Crozet, Superior General of the Missionaries, founded the Missionary Sisters of Our Lady of La Salette, to join in the work of the foreign missions. Much later, in 1997, the Messenger Sisters of Our Lady of La Salette were founded in Angola. These three congregations are now one: The Sisters of Our Lady of La Salette.

Over the years, more and more lay persons have also been chosen by the Beautiful Lady. Depending on their country, they are known as La Salette Associates, La Salette Family, La Salette Fraternity, La Salette Laity, etc. called to serve the La Salette cause of reconciliation in a wide variety of ways. They have their own identity, but also work alongside the Missionaries and the Sisters.

So many La Salette ways to be chosen! What a gift!

Monday, July 12, (#389)
Fifteenth Week in Ordinary Time

Matthew 10:34 to 11:1: *"Anyone who welcomes a prophet because he is a prophet will have a prophet's reward."*

Meditation:

Prophets are those who, having experienced conversion themselves, carry that message of our need for conversion to the people of God. Maximin Giraud, the younger of the two cowherds to witness the apparition at La Salette, did not have a happy home life. His mother died when he was young and his stepmother mistreated him. His father, a wheelwright by trade, spent much of his time in the village tavern. Shortly after the apparition, when Maximin was repeating the story, Mr. Giraud interrupted him. The little boy protested, "But, Father, that is not all; let me tell you what concerns you. The Beautiful Lady also spoke about you." His father was aghast as Maximin repeated the incident of the field at Coin. As a consequence of their discussion, Mr. Giraud assisted at Mass daily until his death three years later.

ONE OF THE MANY GRACES OF LA SALETTE is that of conversion. The Beautiful Lady undoubtedly appeared as a prophet at La Salette; she, whose life was formed by bearing the Word of God, proclaimed that word faithfully to the people of God. Her simple words and loving gestures touched the heart of the two children and have done so for many thousands of pilgrims who have followed in their steps to the site of the apparition on the Holy Mountain in France.

Reflection Questions:

• What do you hear in the message of La Salette that speaks to you personally?
• What conversion is needed by you; what part of your life needs to be changed? Have you brought the message of conversion to others whom you know?

Tuesday, July 13 (#390)
Fifteenth Week in Ordinary Time

Matthew 11:20-24: *"You shall go down to the realm of death!"*

Meditation:

There is only one means of transit from this life to the next, and none of us gets out of this world alive! We are all destined to die. And we believe that the passage from death to life involves some sort of judgment. Looking at our own lives, we are quick to realize that we have sinned and that our love is genuine but imperfect. Moreover we realize that the way we choose to live in this life helps to determine the way we will experience eternal life. So we continue to throw ourselves upon the mercy of God, trusting that God knows us better than we know ourselves.

IT WAS OUT OF LOVE FOR US THAT GOD SENT THE BEAUTIFUL LADY TO LA SALETTE to call all people away from sin. The "great news" the Beautiful Lady came to proclaim is that of God's forgiveness. There is no such thing as an unforgivable sin, or else God's call is in vain. Instead, the Beautiful Lady draws us to God with a wonderful picture of what forgiveness effects: "If they are converted, the stones and rocks will change into mounds of wheat, and the potatoes will be self-sown in the land."

Some Reflection Questions:

- Are you willing to accept God's gift of forgiveness?
- Do you recognize that your latent desire to "do it your own way" is actually a temptation to refuse to live your life God's way?

Wednesday, July 14, (#391)
Fifteenth Week in Ordinary Time

Matthew 11:25-27: *"I bless you, Father, Lord of heaven and of earth, for hiding these things from the learned and the clever and revealing them to little children."*

Meditation:

God respects the dignity of every human person. God loves every human person. Thanks be to God, that love does not depend on our intelligence or goodness, age or strength. We are literally expected to "do the best we can with what we have." God wants us to strive for perfection, knowing full well that we aren't and never will be *"perfect as my heavenly Father is perfect"* (Matthew 5: 48).

AS WE REFLECT ON THE LA SALETTE APPARITION, there is something that genuinely alarms us; namely, the character of Maximin and Melanie, the witnesses of the apparition. They were uneducated: neither spoke formal French neither could read or write. The boy was a regular chatterbox and a constant fidget. The girl was moody, stubborn, sulky, withdrawn, and was known to have a temper. Yet it was to these two that the Beautiful Lady was sent to convey her message of great news. We may judge the witnesses of the apparition to be of less-than-sterling character but that is not judging by God's standards. God could only look upon Maximin and Melanie the way he looks upon us all: with deep love and acceptance of us as we are – with our faults and our good qualities.

Reflection Questions:

• Do you treat every person with the God-given dignity that is due them? Do you sometimes allow externals to prevent you from seeing others (or yourself) as God does?

• Who is a person who accepts you as you are – in other words, like God does? Have you thanked God for them lately?

Thursday, July 15, (#392)
Fifteenth Week in Ordinary Time

Matthew 11:28-30: *"Come to me, all you who labor and are overburdened, and I will give your rest."*

Meditation:

This Gospel passage, proclaimed at today's Eucharist, is also read during the celebration of the Sacrament of the Anointing of the Sick. When we are beset by illness, whether of mind or body, the Church reminds us of this invitation of Jesus to come to him and be refreshed. Even when we are not sick, the world has a way of wearing us down. Sometimes life seems quite overwhelming. The good news is that we are not alone! God is always with us to help lift our burdens and brings us the peace that only God can give.

At La Salette the Blessed Virgin in her words and actions reminded us that we are not alone. No matter how far people felt separated from God, she reminded them that they simply needed to turn away from those things that separate us from God. This is always the case. Jesus said, *"Come to me..."* The Blessed Mother said, *"Come near, my children..."* Every time we notice the weight of the world on our shoulders, God seems to send someone to call us back. God loves us that much!

Reflection Questions:

- Do you pause to listen to the voice or inner yearning which is calling you back to God? Have you become so busy that you forget to pray?
- Do you take the time regularly to thank God for his unending invitation to draw closer to him?

Friday, July 16, (#393)
Fifteenth Week in Ordinary Time

Matthew 12:1-8: *"For the Son of Man is master of the Sabbath."*

Meditation:

The rules and practices of our faith are important. They help form our identity as a people; they help guide us along the way. They put us in touch with deeper truths about our life with God. In the Old Testament, special attention is given to the Sabbath because of its place in the scheme of creation and the focus on God's activity above all else. In the New Testament, special attention is given to the first day of the week as the day on which Jesus rose from the dead and those known as Christians met to break bread in memory of him. But even the regular practice of our faith and its rituals can sometimes become empty of their original meaning. We need to remind ourselves of the deeper meaning of what we do and celebrate. Jesus is doing exactly that for his hearers in today's gospel.

AT LA SALETTE, Mary came to remind us of the religious practices that were being neglected, especially noting that people chose to work on Sundays, rather than participate in the Mass, the Eucharistic Celebration. But Mary's point could not simply have been to fill the churches. Her people had forgotten God and the primacy of the call to love God, our neighbor and ourselves. She simply listed some elements of our faith that her people needed to once again pay attention to, as followers of her Son. One such valuable habit was participating in weekly Eucharist. This "Sabbath habit" was central to who they were and what they regularly needed in order to live a life of love and service as Jesus has shown them.

Reflection Questions:

- Are you aware of the deeper truths behind the religious practices that are a part of your Christian life?
- How can or should you make the Sabbath holy?

Saturday, July 17, (#394)
Fifteenth Week in Ordinary Time

Matthew 12:14-21: *"In (my servant whom I have chosen) the nations will put their hope."*

Meditation:

This passage from Matthew's Gospel reminds us how greatly the name of Jesus came to be prized. In the Acts of the Apostles, we see that converts to the New Way (Christianity) are baptized in Jesus' name; people are healed in Jesus' name; his name is the way to salvation. In Philippians 2:9-11, Saint Paul quotes an early hymn that states that God is glorified in giving Jesus the *"name which is above all other names, so that all beings ... should bends the knee at the name of Jesus."*

IT IS WITH THIS BIBLICAL BACKGROUND that we can appreciate the importance of Mary's complaint at La Salette about misusing the name of her Son. *"Those who drive the carts cannot swear without introducing the name of my Son!"* How easy it can be to allow her Son's name to be irreverently included in our crude exclamations. How trivial we make this holy name, using it for precisely the opposite purpose for which it was revealed to us. Yet how quickly we get upset when someone trivializes our name or that of our family. We readily take this as a personal insult. It is so easy to use Jesus' name irreverently without thinking. Hopefully our efforts at disciplining our own speech is one way to respond to Mary's tearful pleas at La Salette.

Reflection Questions:

- Do you give the name of the Lord Jesus the respect it truly deserves?
- Also do you readily go out of your way to give compliments to those around you who deserve a "thank you"?

Sunday, July 18 (#107)
Sixteenth Sunday in Ordinary Time

(Jer. 23:1-6; Ephesians 2:13-18; Mark 6:30-34)

Meditation: *Moved with Pity*

The Miracle of the Loaves and Fishes by James Tissot (1836–1902)

The word "shepherd" in Church usage refers to priests, and Jeremiah's "Woe to the shepherds" text may well make us think of the scandals continuing to rock the Church. But in the Old Testament, it was the rulers who were called shepherds, and it is they whom Jeremiah condemns.

God promises his sheep that he will "appoint shepherds for them who will shepherd them," and give them a king "who will reign and govern wisely." We can easily see this prophecy fulfilled in Jesus, whose "heart was moved with pity for the crowd."

Many centuries later, a Beautiful Lady's heart was moved with pity for her people. And, like Jesus, she "taught them many things."

St. Paul writes, "In Christ Jesus you who once were far off have become near by the blood of Christ." Our Lady of La Salette sorrowfully reverses this saying in her message. Her people, who once had become near, were now far off from her Son.

Simply by speaking of her Son, who "is our peace," she "preached peace" as he did. Just as St. Paul cannot seem to find enough ways to say how Jesus brought reconciliation to Jewish and Gentile Christians alike, so Mary finds abundant ways to describe how her people need that reconciliation. She also shows how they might encounter it, namely by honoring the Lord's Name, respecting the Lord's Day, turning to him in prayer, participating in the Eucharist.

All of these, and more, are expressions of the trust expressed in today's Psalm. The God who spreads a table before us is the same God who saw Maximin's anxious father give him a piece of bread. This is the compassionate God whose goodness and kindness follow us all the days of our life.

Instead of suffering famine, those who respond to Mary's message shall not want. Instead of being like sheep without a shepherd, they will walk in right paths, their souls will be refreshed, they will fear no evil. This is not a dream. It is a prophetic vision.

Pity is not just a feeling. It leads to action. Jesus taught the people looking to him for hope. Mary came to renew that hope. Look around you. Whom do you pity? How will you act?

Monday, July 19, (#395)
Sixteenth Week in Ordinary Time

Matthew 12:38-42: *"On Judgment Day the men of Nineveh will appear against this generation and they will be its condemnation."*

Meditation:

In the time of Jonah, the nation of Assyria, whose capital was Nineveh, was the most powerful nation in the world. The Assyrians had invented the chariot and were able to conquer their neighbors. They were without equal. The story of the conversion of Nineveh is, then, a great and important one. That such a mighty people heard and took to heart the word of God shows what power that word has. They knew that all their achievements were worth nothing if they had strayed from God. No wonder Jesus invokes them as judges to condemn those who don't recognize the revelation of God in their midst.

THE VIRGIN OF LA SALETTE is reminiscent of Jonah. She comes into the midst of a people indifferent to God's presence among them, indifferent to the truth of the Gospel. She calls them (and us) to repentance and conversion. God never gives up on us but uses every means to call us back. In God's eyes, none of us is a lost cause. He considers us worth *"the pains"* Our Blessed Mother has taken on our behalf.

Reflection Questions:

• Just as the Ninevites repented, are we willing to (or need to) repent? What needs forgiving in your life?

• Do you listen to homilies at Mass with your full attention? At Mass do you wait for God to speak to you through the words or prayers of the priest or deacon?

Tuesday, July 20, (#396)
Sixteenth Week in Ordinary Time

Matthew 12:46-50: *"Anyone who does the will of my Father in heaven is my brother and sister and mother."*

Meditation:

The most sublime and profound title bestowed upon the Virgin Mary is certainly the "Mother of God." The Word was made flesh and made his dwelling among us, taking his human nature from his mother in her womb. It is indeed a great honor. But Jesus is not speaking about mere biological connections when he refers to his "brother and sister and mother." Jesus is speaking about the "kinship" or connection that is based on discipleship

MARY IS CONSIDERED BY MANY BELIEVERS as the first disciple of Jesus. Her response of "fiat" to the angel at her Annunciation was the official beginning of her discipleship. We also recall her fidelity at the foot of the Cross, when most of the disciples fled in fear. At La Salette, she comes again as the faithful disciple. Where the others have forgotten, she has remembered how her Son has brought salvation and how his name continues to save. Our Tearful Mother, the first disciple, is calling us back to the ways and message of her Son. She can speak with genuine pride about him since she has been faithful to him from his cradle to his grave and beyond. We should listen well to her words, her gestures and her mission given to us all.

Reflection Questions:

• As true disciples and sisters and brothers of Jesus from our Baptism, how do you share your faith with others?
• Do you look like and sound like his disciple? What have you sacrificed in order to remain faithful to her Son, Jesus, your Brother?

Wednesday, July 21 (#397)
Sixteenth Week in Ordinary Time

Matthew 13:1-9: *"Anyone who has ears should listen!"*

For Your Reflection:

In the parable of the sower, Jesus addresses different reactions to the word of God. Not all the seed fell on fertile soil. One question this raises is whether we allow our own faith to bear fruit in our lives. Or is the faith we profess somehow cut off from the lives we lead? Is Sunday so separate from the rest of the week that it has no bearing on how we act? By its very nature, our faith should be all-encompassing. Buried in the innermost recesses of our hearts, it has the ability to affect every aspect of our lives. Not allowing it to do so assures that we will produce no fruit, no good works, no legacy of love in our lives.

AT LA SALETTE THE BLESSED VIRGIN COMES TO NOURISH THE SEEDS OF OUR FAITH. It is as if she is saying that it's never too late: there is still time for the seed to fall on fertile ground and bear much fruit. When we hear the promise of stones being turned into wheat, does the picture of that happening in fields and on mountain slopes move us? Or is it more of a miracle to know that our stony hearts, our rock-hard minds, can yet yield a harvest for ourselves and others – even a hundredfold!

Reflection Questions:

- Do you consider your daily choices and actions as necessarily flowing from the faith you profess?
- What part of the parable of the seeds matches your own life at this time?
- What concrete action can you take today to express your own faith and trust in God's love and mercy?

Thursday, July 22, (#603)
St. Mary Magdalene

John 20: 1-2,11-18: *"So Mary of Magdala told the disciples, 'I have seen the Lord,' and that he had said these things to her."*

Meditation:

The word "witness" in the bible does not mean being passively present to an event; rather it has an active connotation, an obligation to share what we have witnessed. Such is the case of Mary of Magdala in the gospel of John. After she met the person whom she thought was the gardener at the tomb of Jesus, and once the risen Jesus had revealed himself to her, she couldn't contain her excitement and wanted to embrace Jesus with love, she quickly returned to the disciples with the news that she had seen the Lord! She is a wonderful example to us of what it means to spread the "gospel", that is, the "good news." Mary of Magdala was a dedicated and quite genuine evangelizer.

AT LA SALETTE, Our Lady told the two witnesses of her apparition, Melanie and Maximin, to do what Mary of Magdala had done so well, *"make the message known"* to all her people. This task of witnessing or making the message known is now passed onto us who have also heard her words and hopefully taken them to heart. We are the contemporary "Mary Magdalenes, Melanies and Maximins" who are urged to share what we have witnessed – that God's love and forgiveness are alive and well and ready for the taking.

Reflection Questions:

- Do you remember who told you first about the message of La Salette?
- In turn, with whom have you shared the message of La Salette?

Friday, July 23, (#399)
Sixteenth Week in Ordinary Time

Matthew 13:18-23: *"the seed sown in rich soil is someone who hears the word and understands it; this is the one who yields a harvest..."*

Meditation:

God's grace knows no bounds. It is able to accomplish amazing things. I think of the difference between Peter and Judas. Both apostles betrayed Jesus. In fact, an argument can be made that Peter's betrayal is worse – a three-fold denial of knowing Jesus. However, Peter trusted in Jesus' forgiveness; Judas despaired over what he had done. Neither is so different in many ways from us. Trusting in forgiveness is what allowed Peter to produce a hundredfold.

ON SATURDAY, SEPTEMBER 19, 1846 – a specific day in a specific year – the Blessed Virgin Mary came to La Salette to remind us of the specificity of God's forgiveness. In the midst of the people's indifference to God's presence among them, their indifference to the power of Jesus' name, nevertheless forgiveness was promised. If only they would listen, if only they would heed. If only they would be converted: the result would be wheat in abundance, potatoes self-sown. Ah, even the hundredfold will be specific to our lives!

Reflection Questions:

- Are you willing to accept God's forgiveness in the specific events of your own life?
- Do you understand that this will allow you to lead a fruitful life, dedicated to loving and serving others?

Saturday, July 24 (#400)
Sixteenth Week in Ordinary Time

Matthew 13:24-30: *"But he said, 'No, because when you weed out the darnel you might pull up the wheat with it.'"*

For Your Reflection:

It is the sower of the seed that will not allow the weeds to be uprooted. He is afraid of damaging, and thereby losing good plants. We also wonder whether the sower is hoping that the weeds will turn into good plants. After all, if we identify with the harvest, how do we know whether we are weed or wheat? The conclusion of the story of our life remains yet untold. God is slow to condemn us; we are given every chance to change our lives. God will employ any means to win us back. The fate of the weeds is postponed.

THE WEEPING MOTHER WAS SENT TO LA SALETTE TO REMIND US of the salvation already won for us in Christ, her Son but how easily we forget. However God uses every means to remind us. Perhaps God was hoping that Mary's words would turn the weeds into good plants. After all, if he can turn rocks into wheat, why not weeds into good plants! And if Mary's words can't make it happen, maybe her abundant tears will. God uses every means possible to turn our hearts and minds back to God.

Reflection Questions:

- When have you seen how Christ can turn people's lives back to God?
- Has there been a point in your life when God helped you in some unexpected or wonderful way?

Sunday, July 25 (#110)
Seventeenth Sunday in Ordinary Time

(2 Kings 4:42-44; Eph 4:1-6; John 6:1-15)

Meditation: *A Worthy Life*

"At this sight the poor children were struck with fear and dared not move forward. But the Lady reached out her hands to them and said kindly, 'Come, my children, and get your lunch and don't be afraid to eat it. I am Mary your mother.'"

Wait a minute! you think. That's not right! The Beautiful Lady never said that.

Correct. This is from an account sent February 19, 1847—five months after the Apparition—to the pastor of Corps, Fr. Mélin, for verification. It is obviously based on hearsay, and contains many other mistakes. I first read it about 30 years ago and was fascinated.

What made me remember it now is the feeding of multitudes in our first reading and in the Gospel. Food figures largely in Mary's message, but not right at the beginning.

Depiction of Jesus Feeding the Multitude by Julius Schnorr von Carolsfeld (1794–1872)

In the coming weeks, John's Gospel will make the connection between the multiplication of loaves and fish, on the one hand, and faith on the other. Our Lady of La Salette does the same.

Our second reading has the powerful saying of St. Paul about "one Lord, one faith, one baptism;

one God and Father of all." He urges the Christians of Ephesus to "live in a manner worthy of the call you have received."

This ideal is not always achieved, however. That is what prompted the Blessed Virgin to intervene. She describes ways in which the way of life of her people is far from worthy of their Christian call.

Fr. Marcel Schlewer, M.S., often points out an "unworthy" behavior that Mary did not mention, but which aggravated the famine of which she did speak. As wheat was becoming scarce, those who had it were refusing to sell it, preferring to speculate on the prospect of rising prices. Riots ensued, adding political chaos to the hardships to be endured.

It would be wonderful if, like Jesus or Elisha, we could miraculously feed the multitudes. However, if we think of ourselves as the loaves and fishes, maybe we can. Living a life worthy of our call, we can place ourselves in the Lord's hands, and who knows the good he can then multiply through us?

Monday, July 26, (#401)
Seventeenth Week in Ordinary Time

Matthew 13:31-35: *"The mustard seed ... is the smallest of all seeds, but when it has grown it is the biggest of shrubs and becomes a tree, so that the birds of the air come and shelter in its branches."*

Meditation:

Our consumer society puts emphasis on having, possessing, consuming. "More is better" is the unspoken motto. There is little room in our commercial world for the message of Julian of Norwich that "spirituality is about sub-traction." It is not easy to appreciate that "less is more." It is not an easy choice to be without when abundance is possible and encouraged. Today's Gospel invites us to consider this counter cultural perspective. Jesus' metaphor invites us to see beyond the mere externals, to recognize the potency hidden within the simple, within the ordinary, within the moments of life that are not sensational.

THE INTERVENTION OF MARY AT LA SALETTE is an example of this. Hidden away in the Alps, on a lonely barren hillside, some cows for company and two poor, illiterate peasant children for witnesses is indeed a wasteland scene. Yet it is here that Mary's presence emerges. It is in this unworldly scene that the simple words spoken offer life, encourage abundance and hold promise for future generations.

Reflection Questions:

- Are you ready each day to accept and recognize the surprises of grace that life's simplest moments may hold for you?
- What are some little events which have been true gifts to you, whether it be within your family, your circle of friends, or your parish community?

Tuesday, July 27, (#402)
Seventeenth Week in Ordinary Time

Matthew 13:36-43: *"Then, leaving the crowds, he went to the house; and his disciples came to him and said, 'Explain to us the parable about the darnel in the field.'"*

Meditation:

Life is filled with opportunities for communication. Each day brings moments for us to experience the richness and complexity of the universe, of our fellow human beings and of our own hearts. Listening to each of these "communications" may be very challenging in a world filled with constantly distracting influences. At times it is not easy to understand either others or ourselves. Often understanding demands exceptional attention. Jesus is aware that the disciples do not fully grasp his message, his parable. He takes them to a quiet place and creates an opportunity to listen to their questions and speak directly to them. With loving care he takes the time to explain further the underlying meaning of his parable. After all, his disciples have become truly significant people in his life and mission.

At La Salette, Mary, thankfully attentive to the non-verbal communication of the two children, becomes aware that their understanding of her words is limited. She then begins to speak in the local patois or dialect. She reaches out to communicate in a way that respects the needs of her listeners. She honors clear communication as central to this relationship that she is establishing with these two peasant adolescents. She takes the necessary time to be sure that there is some understanding of the message that she shares with them.

Reflection Questions:

• What is the quality of your communication with the significant people in your life? Are you attentive to the words, questions, gestures and non-verbal messages that are given to you?

• Are you patient and flexible in your efforts to respond to people's questions and concerns?

Wednesday, July 28, (#403)
Seventeenth Week in Ordinary Time

Matthew 13:44-46: *"...the kingdom of Heaven is like a merchant looking for fine pearls; when he finds one of great value he goes and sells everything he owns and buys it."*

Meditation:

We live in a world of abundance. The abundance, however, is not equally distributed. Some people experience abundance as clutter, overwhelming their lives. Others experience abundant needs. We are all merchants in the marketplace of material goods. All that we humanly need to be comfortable may be available to us, yet we may not be at peace. The desire for more may leave us living in an unsatisfied manner. Today's scripture invites us to look at the choices we make and to examine our priorities.

MARY INVITED THE TWO CHILDREN to consider what was important in their lives. Although they lived in a harsh peasant world, their daily lives were filled with simple but profound choices. Did they understand the importance of each choice? Were they able to pay attention to the God who loved them? Did they appreciate the actions of their parents?

Reflection Questions:

• In what way is your life cluttered? Are you able to pay attention to what is truly important and central? Are "first things first" for you in your life?
• How does your faith rank in importance in your daily life? What about prayer and worship?

Thursday, July 29, (#404)
Seventeenth Week in Ordinary Time

Matthew 13:47-53: *"Again, the kingdom of Heaven is like a dragnet that is cast in the sea and brings in a haul of all kinds of fish. When it is full, the fishermen bring it ashore; then, sitting down, they collect the good ones in baskets and throw away those that are no use."*

Meditation:

Each day brings opportunities to choose. Usually, we attend first to our survival needs. Then, other demands and expectations for the use of our time enter the fabric of our days. What choices will I make for quality relationships, for responsible work, for acting with integrity within the community of human beings where I find myself this day? How clear are my intentions? Am I able to sort out that which strangles and limits creativity, responsiveness to the good, holy and sacred? Jesus invites, by way of parable, his disciples to daily be attentive to their choices.

AT LA SALETTE, Mary calls attention to Maximin's experience of dried wheat in the fields. Starkly, she notes the difference between that which gives life and nourishment and what is unable to sustain life. In this, she invites her young hearers to be attentive to the choices they make. "Choose life that you and your descendants may live" (Deut 30:19).

Reflection Questions:

• Life offers us a plethora of choices. Can you be attentive today to sorting through the options?
• Do you continually ask yourself: Is this a life-giving choice?

Friday, July 30, (#405)
Seventeenth Week in Ordinary Time

Matthew 13:54-58: *"A prophet is despised only in his own country and in his own house."*

Meditation:

Jesus is in the midst of men and women who consider themselves learned – be it from their studies or from their experience of human nature. They are quick to judge, analyze, speculate and evaluate. Perhaps an overbearing self-confidence fills their hearts and being. The head may control the feelings of the heart. It is then difficult to believe their eyes. It is difficult to trust their hearts. It is uncomfortable to hear others' words of wisdom. The consequence: wisdom present in their midst goes unrecognized and unacknowledged.

Mary arrives at La Salette to choose the simple, unlettered, peasant children. Her appearance, words and gestures and her choice of witnesses have nothing in common with what the world considers sensational. Simple dress, humble shepherds, an unadorned grassy knoll and clear commonsense scripture words create the scene of her intervention in human history. She is able to recognize what so often our prejudiced eyes are unable to see – the sacred in the midst of the ordinary.

Reflection Questions:

• What is the attitude you bring towards the down and out or estranged in your society – the poor, the unkempt, the street people, the less than civil people in your midst?

• When will you spontaneously give a handout to a poor person without counting the cost?

Saturday, July 31, (#406)
Seventeenth Week in Ordinary Time

Matthew 14:1-12: *"Prompted by her mother…"*

Meditation:

This Gospel may be an opportunity for us to reflect on the influence our own mothers and other significant people have had in our lives. Herodias suggested to her daughter that she ask for the head of John the Baptist on a dish. Salome, perhaps not yet her own person or out of filial devotion, obliges. An evil act is initiated. Herod does not have the will power to follow his own inner instincts. He succumbs. A chain reaction begins, unstopped because neither Herodias nor Herod is able to break the chain of negative influence.

At La Salette, Mary acknowledges the love and compassion that her Son bears for humankind. She acknowledges the pain of her Son who sees the faithless living of those who call themselves Christian. She has always urged disciples to "do what he tells you." Here, as mother, she seeks to prompt and influence these two shepherds. She invites them to pray more attentively, She encourages them to be attentive to the gestures of their parents. She urges them to make the message known. The task she gives to the children is simple: within their sphere of influence, their small world, they are to be in communion with God and announce what has happened to them.

Reflection Questions:

- Are you conscious of your opportunities today to influence others?
- Is it possible for you to seize these moments, to initiate positive thinking and action among those with whom you will come in contact?

Sunday, August 1 (#113)
Eighteenth Sunday in Ordinary Time

(Exodus 16:2-15; Ephesians. 4:17-24; John 6:24-35)

Meditation: *Futility of Mind*

St. Paul writes that the Gentiles live "in the futility of their minds." His audience, the Christians of Ephesus, used to live this way but ought not to do so any more. He does not explain the term in detail but associates it with the "corruption of evil desires."

Evil desires are expressed in the first reading: "Would that we had died at the Lord's hand in the land of Egypt, as we sat by our flesh-pots and ate our fill of bread!" There's nothing wrong with hungry

221

people wanting food, but in this case the evil resides in their lack of trust, in their accusing Moses of making the whole community die of famine, in their ingratitude.

God had rescued them, with strong hand and outstretched arm, from their oppressors, and yet they failed to place their trust in him. Nonetheless, he saved them once again. But in the very next chapter of Exodus, the people fell back into the futility of their minds, complaining that Moses brought them out of Egypt only to have them die of thirst.

As one listens to the discourse of Our Lady of La Salette, one senses that she is addressing a similar situation. Her people have fallen into a kind of futility of mind, blaming God for their troubles. As St. Paul says in another place (Romans 1:21), "Although they knew God they did not accord him glory as God or give him thanks. Instead, they became vain in their reasoning, and their senseless minds were darkened."

In the Gospel, Jesus sees the vain thinking of those who had witnessed the miracle of the loaves and fishes. It was not out of faith that they were looking for him, but because they desired to be fed again. He tells them to work for food that endures for eternal life. The 'work' in this case is faith: believing in the one sent by God. He then goes on to proclaim himself the bread of life.

In the coming weeks we will have occasion to reflect on this more deeply. For the moment, let us rest with the importance of the 'work' of faith.

At La Salette, Mary speaks much of religious practice, not because it constitutes faith, but because its absence shows a lack of faith. Without this vital relationship with the Lord, even religion can be little more than futility of mind.

Monday, August 2, (#407)
Eighteenth Week in Ordinary Time

Matthew 14:13-21: *"They collected the scraps left over, twelve baskets full."*

Meditation:

Jesus goes with his disciples to a secluded place and reflects with them on the death of John the Baptist. They take time in prayer. When the crowd finally finds them, they immediately begin ministering to these needy people, and also wonder how all these people could find something to eat. When they bring the problem to Jesus, he first says: *"There is no need for them to go: give them something to eat yourselves."* The disciples are startled at Jesus' response that they simply provide food for the crowd themselves. Yet Jesus then provides food for all present. Then the gospel simply states that twelve baskets of food were left over. The sign for all who would look and listen was that God provide us with more than we need in life.

MARY, THE QUEEN OF HEAVEN, was described by the children simply as the "Beautiful Lady". Her approachability and compassionate presence were obvious to the two initially scared children. Her sincere interest in the plight of Maximin's father was a touching gesture indeed. She even attended to those who were not standing in front of her! The fears of Maximin's father was important to Mary and she felt that she needed to respond to it. Just as her Son responded to the hungry "cast of thousands," Mary was similarly concerned about the fate of those parents who had the responsibility to feed their family.

Reflection Questions:

- How aware are you of those in your own neighborhood or city which have little or no food each day?
- Have you ever donated to or participated in serving food to the hungry? If not, why not volunteer to do so?

Tuesday, August 3, (#408 alt)
Eighteenth Week in Ordinary Time

Matthew 15:1-2,10-14: *"(Jesus) called the people to him and said, 'What goes into the mouth does not make anyone unclean; it is what comes out of the mouth that makes someone unclean.'"*

Meditation:

Jesus invites his listeners to be attentive to the sentiments and values of their hearts. He wants to be clear in his teaching. The core values that influence how a person lives, makes decisions and acts are the very values with which Jesus invites us to be concerned. We are not to be distracted by the superficial, the external, the secondary. Jesus challenges us to be clearly focused on what is re-ally important in our lives.

At La Salette, Mary raises the question of language. Sacred language is being used carelessly, betraying an underlying attitude of disrespect. Speech is one way to express the sentiments of the heart It is a distinct way to reveal who we are, what is important to us and how we shape our lives. Attentive to our speech, we may become more attentive to the core values that govern our lives, motivate as and influence the way we live.

Reflection Questions:

• Do I consider that what comes spontaneously to my mouth may help me to reflect on the values I have adopted?
• How attentive am I to the way that I express myself? Am I aware that my words are a mirror of my soul?

Wednesday, August 4, (#409)
Eighteenth Week in Ordinary Time

Matthew 15:21-28: *"the (Canaanite) woman had come up and was bowing low before him. 'Lord,' she said, 'help me.' He replied, 'It is not fair to take the children's food and throw it to little dogs.' She retorted, 'Ah yes, Lord; but even little dogs eat the scraps that fall from their masters' table.'"*

Meditation:

It is a humble, peasant, gentile woman who challenges Jesus to extend his compassion beyond the house of Israel, beyond the boundaries of family and tribal clan with whom Jesus had become initially identified. Jesus boldly responds to someone, who might be considered an outcast in the eyes of his society, with compassion and love and healing.

Is it possible to imagine that Mary could have chosen others to be the witnesses at La Salette? In the eyes and opinions of the residents of the hamlets located around La Salette, the response would be a resounding yes. The credibility of the witnesses challenges the credibility of the message. The fact is that these two illiterate, unknown and little appreciated adolescents were chosen and entrusted with a profound message and a daunting mission. The good news is certainly not restricted to the well to do or to any exclusive club founded on ethnic origin, skin color or cultural tradition. It is addressed to all people.

Reflection Questions:

• If this day you encounter someone different from yourself – whether unemployed, homeless, speaking a language other than your own, with a different skin color, what attitude will guide your words and deeds?

• Will you share the good news of God's love by your presence?

Thursday, August 5 (#410)
Eighteenth Week in Ordinary Time

Matthew 16:13-23: *"But (Jesus) turned and said to Peter, 'Get behind me, Satan! You are an obstacle in my path, because you are thinking not as God thinks but as human beings do."*

For Your Reflection:

What a challenge! To think as God thinks and not in the terms of human perspective and vision. Paul urges us "to put on the mind of Christ." Jesus lets it be known that following him will challenge us to look at life in a new way. There is no such thing as "cheap grace." This is a Savior willing to pay the price himself first. This is a Savior willing to love us first. And as beloved sons and daughters, we are called to follow in his footsteps, to understand the transitory nature of human life in this world and to share in paying the price of humankind's redemption.

AT LA SALETTE, MARY CLEARLY STATES that a business-as-usual or a lax attitude toward the sacred is unacceptable behavior for the disciples of Jesus. Whether it is one's language, prayer, attendance at Mass or respect for Lenten regulations, these matters are serious because they reflect what is in the heart. Mary's communion with her Son is so profound that she longs for each of "her people" to share that intimacy with the Holy One. Our words and deeds are valued not because of a prevailing fad or custom but because of their intrinsic worth and merit.

Reflection Questions:

- What control do the opinions of others have upon the decisions you may make this day?
- Do you listen most attentively to the prompting of your heart or the whispers of your friends?

Friday, August 6, (#614)
The Transfiguration of the Lord

Luke 9:28b-36: *"(Peter) did not know what he was saying."*

Meditation:

The event of the Transfiguration was certainly a spectacular event and it is quite understandable that Peter got caught up in the glory of the moment as he suggested that they make three shelters for Jesus and the two extraordinary guests. Jesus dismissed the idea but did not scold Peter. As we know, Peter had a lot to learn and Jesus was patiently preparing his disciples for his Passion and Resurrection. He taught them by who he was, what he said and what they themselves experienced of his stories and acts of love.

MARY AT LA SALETTE is also a wonderful, patient teacher, a Weeping Mother whose loving concern shows through her every word, gesture and tear. The two children, although they had no idea who she really was, were completely taken in by her radiant presence and listened well to this woman in tears. Their dialogue was geared directly to the two children and her concern that they understand was of paramount importance to Mary. After her initial prophet words of warning, she spoke directly to the minds and hearts of her simple, poor cowherds.

Reflection Questions:

- How patient and understanding are you to those around you, young and old alike?
- Do you take the time to be present and listen well or do you think that you are the expert and everyone should listen to you for

your pearls of wisdom?

Saturday, August 7, (#412)
Eighteenth Week in Ordinary Time

Matthew 17:14-20: *"If your faith is the size of a mustard seed... nothing will be impossible for you."*

Meditation:

Life is filled with unpredictable events. It is filled with joys and tragedies. A human life usually knows praise and undeserved hurt. Life brings with it many hopes and aspirations as well as disappointments. The disciple is one who often responds with prayer to these various moments of life. We rejoice when events seem to go our way and we anguish when our expectations are unfulfilled. We hope that our prayer will be met with answers that respond to our desires. Jesus suggests a richer, more complex and profound faith. We are invited to bring who we are in prayer and entrust that to our God. Such prayer will give us a new appreciation of God's presence and lead us to new ways of living, loving and being healed.

MARY HELPS MAXIMIN recall the spoiled wheat that he and his father saw at the field of Coin. She connects the breakdown of human relationships and the rupture of our relationship with God to the agricultural disaster of spoiled wheat, rotted potatoes and worm-eaten walnuts. She suggests that when our hearts have turned to our God then *"rocks and stones will turn into heaps of wheat and the potatoes will be self-sown in the fields."* Once true faith burns within our hearts, life takes on another perspective. Our human relationships will know wholeness when we are in a right relationship with God. Inner strength will sustain us. We will have an inner force to face the future with hope.

Reflection Questions:

•Are you able to acknowledge a desire for God's strength to sustain, empower and guide you this day?
•Do you have the courage to hear God's call for you in the desired as well as in the unwelcome experiences of each day?

Sunday, August 8 (#116)
Nineteenth Sunday in Ordinary Time

(1 Kings 12:4-8; Eph. 4:30—5:2; John 6:41-51)

Meditation: *Food for the Journey*

"I am the living bread that came down from heaven. Whoever eats this bread will live forever."

John 6:51

The Sacrament of the Anointing of the Sick used to be called Extreme Unction. Today, Catholics understand that the sacrament is in view of healing, not death. There are, however, certain rites to be observed when death is imminent.

Among these is Viaticum. The Latin word originally meant provisions (money, food, etc.) for a journey. In the Church, it refers to Holy Communion brought to a dying person. The Catechism of the Catholic Church describes it in these terms: "Communion in the body and blood of Christ, received at this moment of 'passing over' to the Father, has a particular significance and importance. It is the seed of eternal life and the power of resurrection, according to the words of the Lord: 'He who eats my flesh and drinks my blood has eternal life, and I will raise him up at the last day.'"

When Elijah was discouraged and wanted to die, God provided food for his journey, to strengthen him and help him continue his prophetic mission.

The message of Our Lady of La Salette was addressed to "her people" who, among other things, paid little importance to the Eucharist. Not only had the Church in general suffered from the persecutions of the French Revolution, but even before that, anticlericalism had entered deeply into French culture as a result of the Age of Enlightenment.

In that context, "Taste and see how good the Lord is" would find little resonance. "Only a few elderly women" took it seriously, it seems.

And yet, there is something about the Beautiful Lady and her message that has touched even the most hardened hearts. Maximin's father, originally hostile to the Apparition, came to understand God's love, and afterward went to Mass every day. His conversion was due to an episode in his life which involved bread, and of which Mary had reminded Maximin.

St. Paul writes: "Do not grieve the Holy Spirit of God, with which you were sealed for the day of redemption." Yes, the practice of faith has always faced challenges, but it is especially difficult in secular cultures.

So, we all need Christ's food for the journey. It's not just for the dying; it strengthens all of us to go on.

Monday, August 9 (#413)
Nineteenth Week in Ordinary Time

Matthew 17:22-27: *"...a great sadness came over them."*

For Your Reflection:

We live in a society that seems to operate on stress. It seems like no matter where we look or in whatever work we are engaged, stress is part of our everyday life. Many books are written on how to deal with our tensions and how to learn to relax. But so often we forget that the best way to deal with our stress was given to us by Jesus. He often told his disciples to come to a deserted place where they could pray. Jesus himself did this many times throughout his ministry.

MARY AT LA SALETTE understood the stress that people were dealing with at that time with their wheat spoiling, the grapes and the walnuts rotting, children dying in the arms of those who held them. But she also reminds us how to deal with stressful situations. "Do you pray well, my children?" She invites us to recreate ourselves by going to the source of life — her Son, Jesus Christ. Mary wants us to understand that through prayer we become united with her Son who gives us true rest. "Come to me all you who are overburdened and I will give you rest," he says.

Reflection Questions:

- How do you deal with stress?
- Is your prayer life a cause of stress or is it life-giving?

Tuesday, August 10, (#618)
St. Lawrence, Deacon and Martyr

John 12: 24-26: *"Anyone who loves his life loses it; anyone who hates his life in this world will keep it for eternal life."*

Meditation:

Jesus spent his three years of public ministry on earth teaching by word and example. His was a fully integrated life. Jesus life and "day job" were intimately united in his mission, given to him by the Father. He was called to do the Father's will in all things. His was a basically simple message: God loves you; therefore share that love with others. Yet there are seeming contradictions in his message as evidence in the "sayings" Jesus used in the gospel for today: *"Anyone who loves his life loses it; anyone who hates his life in this world will keep it for eternal life."* These are not conundrums given to us to confuse us but rather truths that seem contradictory but are actually visions of life that we must appreciate, absorb and live. On this feast of St. Lawrence, we remember the absolute dedication of Lawrence who, in the most difficult circumstances, remains true to the vision and message of Jesus.

ON THE MOUNTAIN OF LA SALETTE, Mary mentioned – in the most prophetic language and in the most simple of words – that Jesus wants us to follow him each and every day. We are to strengthen and increase our faith by feeding it with God's Word and Sacrament and by doing those things that will keep our faith alive; that is, daily prayer, regular Sunday Eucharist, Lenten habits of faith and making the message of Jesus (and Mary) known. This is our basic Baptismal call, our mission in this life. If we do this, then, we will lose our life in order to save it; we will keep our life eternally if we "hate (or look beyond)" our life in this world.

Reflection Questions:

- When have you said or done things of which the Lord would be proud?

• In what ways have you lived out the vision of Jesus words: "Anyone who loves his life loses it"?

Wednesday, August 11, (#415)
Nineteenth Week in Ordinary Time

Note: Today you may wish to begin the First Day of the Novena to Our Lady of La Salette, in the appendix of this book.

Matthew 18:15-20: *"For where two or three meet in my name, I am there among them."*

Meditation:

The Church is the People of God who have been gathered by the Holy Spirit to make Christ alive in today's world. God gathers in the young and the old, the lost and forsaken, the proud and the strong. He gathers all his people so that they may be light for the world today. He calls his people together so that they may become witnesses to his love and mercy to a world that is divided by war, hatred, racism and religious intolerance. We, as God's people, are asked to carry on Christ's mission of reconciling God and God's people. In order for us to accomplish our mission of being Christ's light in the world, we need to have hearts that are true and a willingness to allow God to fashion our lives in holiness. We should be joyful in answering God's call to gather together.

MARY COMES TO LA SALETTE to remind us of the need and purpose of answering God's call for us to gather as his people. "In the summer none go to Mass but a few somewhat aged women. And in winter, when they do not know what to do, they go to Mass only to mock at religion." People were refusing and still refuse to answer God's invitation to come together to form his people. Mary wanted to remind us of how life-giving it is to gather around the Table of the Lord. It is there that we find strength to go forth and live the vocation to which God has called us. Mary asks us to become a Church that celebrates and prays.

Reflection Questions:

• How important is Mass in your spiritual life?

• Do you believe that God is calling you to gather to form God's community?

Thursday, August 12, (#416)
Nineteenth Week in Ordinary Time

Matthew 18:21 to 19:1: *"Lord, how often must I forgive my brother if he wrongs me? As often as seven times?"*

Meditation:

To forgive is not easy. It is difficult in two ways. We find it hard at times to ask for forgiveness because we do not want to be reminded that we do things that need to be forgiven. It is often embarrassing to admit that we did something wrong. Sometimes pride will also get in the way of our seeing the need to be forgiven. And there are times when we justify what we have done and so do not see the need to ask for forgiveness. On the other hand it is also difficult to forgive people, especially if they have hurt us deeply or if they seem to continuously hurt us. Peter's question seems very logical to us: How many times should I forgive someone who sins against me'? There are times when we find it hard to forgive because we believe an injustice has been done to us and we want the offender to pay the price. If we do not like the person who is asking for forgiveness, we tend not to be very merciful. But why should we forgive or ask for forgiveness? Jesus teaches that forgiveness is an integral part of our spiritual life. We find the strength to forgive because God has forgiven us so much. When we receive forgiveness it helps us grow as persons.

THE LA SALETTE EVENT reminds us that we are in need of forgiveness. Mary mentions the way that we have chosen not to be in union with her Son. The result of all this is various hardships, even death. The Beautiful Lady reminds us that this does not have to be the case. *"If they are converted, the stones and rocks will become mounds of wheat, and the potatoes will be self-sown in the fields."* By admitting our need for forgiveness and reconciliation, we open ourselves to the peace and joy that God's forgiveness and mercy bring us.

Reflection Questions:

• How forgiving are you?
• Do you see the act of forgiving as something that is life giving?

Friday, August 13, (#417)
Nineteenth Week in Ordinary Time

Matthew 19:3-12: *"Let anyone accept this (teaching) who can."*

Meditation:

If we are to be true followers of Christ we must be open to the whole Gospel message. We cannot pick and choose what we think is important and disregard the rest. To accept a teaching requires openness to someone else's point of view. We must be good listeners so that we can focus on what is being presented to us. The Pharisees were not open to Christ and his teaching because they were too absorbed in their own point of view and were thus unaccepting of what Christ was presenting. To accept Christ's teaching means that we must put it into practice in our lives. It must become a part of who we are. It is not enough to say that we believe what Christ teaches, but it is necessary to witness to that teaching by living it in our lives.

THE WEEPING MOTHER AT LA SALETTE reminds us that many times we fall short of being a listener or follower of Christ. *"If I would not have my Son abandon you, I am compelled to pray to him without ceasing; and as for you, you take no heed of it."* Mary underscores the importance of listening to the Word of God in our lives. We are asked to take heed of what is being proclaimed to us, to share that Word with others, and to allow that Word to live in our own hearts. We may choose to be deaf at times, but it is hard to be blind to the tears of a mother who loves us and her Son so deeply.

Reflection Questions:

- How open are you to the Word of God?
- How do you live the Word of God in your daily life?

Saturday, August 14 (#418)
Nineteenth Week in Ordinary Time

Matthew 19:13-15: *"Let the little children alone, and do not stop them from coming to me; for it is to such as these that the kingdom of Heaven belongs."*

For Your Reflection:

The Gospels portray Jesus as being a very approachable person. He had a way of making people feel at ease and was able to make people feel very welcomed. Jesus not only treated children that way but anyone with whom he came in contact. He wanted nothing to hinder people from being touched by the presence of God made human. Everyone was able to approach him, even the dreaded and hated Roman Centurion. Jesus gives us a very good example of how we should be open to our brothers and sisters with whom we come in contact every day. It is through our openness to the presence of Jesus in our brothers and sisters that we become more aware of the kingdom of God growing in our midst.

"**COME NEAR, MY CHILDREN, DO NOT BE AFRAID.**" These were the first words spoken by Mary at La Salette. It was more than an invitation. Mary was letting us know that she too was approachable just like her Son. She wants to be with us and encourages us to spend some time with her and her Son in prayer. Mary's first concern for Maximin and Melanie was to remove their startled reaction at seeing the bright light, "as though the sun had fallen there in the ravine." One of the charisms of La Salette is hospitality. We are asked to follow the example of Mary in inviting the poor, the marginalized of society, the refugees, the sinners, and the unwanted to "come near" in order that they may experience God's love and mercy.

Reflection Questions:

- How open are you to other people?
- Do you allow people to approach you?

Sunday, August 15, (#622)
The Assumption
of the Blessed Virgin Mary

Luke 1:39-56: *"My soul proclaims the greatness of the Lord... because he has looked upon the humiliation of his servant... the Almighty has done great things for me. Holy is his name, and his faithful love extends age after age..."*

Meditation:

Erasmus, priest, great teacher and theologian once said "Humility is

234

truth." Further expounding on the saying, St. Vincent de Paul added: "Humility is nothing but truth, and pride is nothing but lying." There is a basic worth in being humble, in knowing yourself so well that you need no external façade to hide who you really are. Mary seemed to be a truly humble person. The words of her *Magnificat* seem to say as much. *"My soul proclaims the greatness of the Lord ...because he has looked upon the humiliation of his servant... the Almighty has done great things for me. Holy is his name, and his faithful love extends age after age..."* Her words belied her

Assumption of the Virgin by **Bartolomé Esteban Murillo (1617–1682)**

inner attitude: I thank God for all that God has done for me. I have simply followed God's will and God has blessed me abundantly. On this Feast of Mary's Assumption, isn't it most fitting that she "was taken up body and soul into heavenly glory" (*Catechism of the Catholic Church*, #966), so sinless was she.

MARY AT LA SALETTE shows who she truly is in her attitude of compassion, graciousness and patience. She welcomes the children and dispels their fear. She changes her dialect when she realizes that the children have trouble understanding her. Her connection to their families and their plight (concerning food for the winter) is so touching and tender. She is truly the humble Mother of the Church, caring for us and praying for us "without ceasing."

Reflection Questions:

- How honest and forthright are you in expressing your thankfulness to God and others for what they have done for you?
- Who for you is a truly humble person in your family and acquaintances?

Monday, August 16, (#419)
Twentieth Week in Ordinary Time

Matthew 19:16-22: *"Master, what good deed must I do to possess eternal life?"*

Meditation:

There are some who think that following the commandments are enough to gain everlasting life. But this life is gift from God. Jesus said, *"I came that you may have life and have it to its fullness."* In order to possess this life we must do more than follow commandments. We must give of ourselves to God. Like the rich young man, we are asked to get rid of anything that prevents us from being in union with God. This act of "selling your possessions" will give us the freedom to follow Jesus who is the source of everlasting life. What Jesus asked of the people of his time and what he asks of us today is that we trust him and love him with our whole heart and soul. If we firmly believe in Christ, then we should have little difficulty in following his commandments.

THE MESSAGE OF LA SALETTE IS A CALL TO CONVERSION – a change of heart. We are asked to look at things through the eyes of God. It is not enough for us just to follow rules. Mary is asking us to change our lives in order to give more of ourselves to her Son. This tearful mother implores us to return to her Son so that we might have life. She gives us a choice: we can choose to remain in our sin and thus experience death, or we can choose life by following her Son. Like her Son, Jesus, Mary came to the mountain of La Salette in order that we might have life. Let us choose this life and follow Jesus by always growing in our love for him.

Reflection Questions:

- Do you choose to follow Jesus and thus choose life?
- How open are you to an ongoing conversion?

Tuesday, August 17, (#420)
Twentieth Week in Ordinary Time

Matthew 19:23-30: *"Who can be saved, then?"*

Meditation:

The disciples put a very interesting question to Jesus. They seemed to think that a person could be able to do something that would help them to be saved. Jesus answer is that, by and of ourselves, we will find it impossible to be saved; but for God all things are possible. It is when we are willing to open ourselves to the salvific power of Christ that we realize that our salvation is a gift from him. It is Jesus himself who saves and there is nothing we can do for our salvation unless we are united with him. Christ offers this salvation to all people. We have the choice to cooperate with him in working out our personal salvation and that of the world. When we choose to unite ourselves with Christ, it is then that we accomplish the most good.

MARY CAME TO LA SALETTE to ask us to return to her Son because he is the source of our salvation. She points out to us that when we tried to accomplish things on our own, we did not succeed too well. Only if we are converted will we experience the new life. It is in this conversion that we discover the presence of God in our lives and in that of others. It is in our union with her Son through prayer and in following his way of life that we are able to realize that we are a People saved by Christ.

Reflection Questions:

• Are you aware of the presence of Christ working in you?
• How are you an ambassador of Christ's reconciliation in today's world?

Wednesday, August 18, (#421)
Twentieth Week in Ordinary Time

Matthew 20:1-16a: *"Why should you be envious because I am generous?"*

Meditation:

The workmen in the parable seem to have a legitimate complaint against the owner of the vineyard. After all, they worked all day long and received the same pay as the man who only worked for an hour. But that was the agreed wage. The owner has a right to do with his money as he pleases. And so if he chooses to be generous to one person, why should the other man complain? Jealousy and envy are often caused by a preconceived idea of an injustice or unfairness being done to us. If someone else has been blessed this way, then I should be blessed that way also. By looking at others' blessings, we can sometimes overlook God's graciousness. And, in reality, God has blessed us all with different gifts and talents.

MARY'S MESSAGE AT LA SALETTE attempts to take us from our own little world to an awareness of a world that has hunger, injustice, the death of children and alienation from God. Mary challenges us to use the gifts and talents with which God has blessed us to change this world. When we become aware of the suffering around us, how can we be envious of others? How can we not be generous and share the blessings we have received in our lives? Mary's tears are an indicator of not only her own suffering but of the suffering of our brothers and sisters as well. It is our own generosity that can help to dry these tears.

Reflection Questions:
- Are you grateful for the blessings that God gives you?
- How generous are you with your time and talent?

Thursday, August 19, (#422) Twentieth Week in Ordinary Time

Matthew 22:1-14: *"For many are invited but not all are chosen."*

Meditation:

God's invitation to the kingdom is extended to everyone. God does not choose the elect. They are those people who decide to accept the invitation to build the kingdom of God. It is not enough to say that I believe in God, but we must put our faith into action. Jesus said that not everyone who says, *"Lord, Lord"* will enter the kingdom of God. But the one who does the will of God will enter hoe us to be an active participant in the kingdom of God we must seek to do the will of God and not our will. Each and every one who decides to be a part of the kingdom must use the talents and gifts God has given them to help build up the kingdom of God on earth. Through our lives we must witness to the presence of God's kingdom among us. Let our prayer be, *"Your kingdom come. Your will be done."*

THE INVITATION to be part of the kingdom is offered again at La Salette. The invitation is to draw near to Jesus and his mother, Mary. Mary, as taught by the Second Vatican Council, is the model of the Church and she teaches us how we are to build the kingdom of God. Her appearance on the Holy Mountain gives witness to her concern for her children. She intercedes for us *"without ceasing"* so that we may willingly accept her Son's invitation to the kingdom. She hands on the work of reconciliation to us, *"Well, my children, you will make this known to all my people."* What a beautiful invitation for us to participate actively in the building of the kingdom of God.

Reflection Questions:

• What gifts and talents has God given you to use in the building of his kingdom?
• How do you use them?

Friday, August 20, (#423) Twentieth Week in Ordinary Time

Matthew 22:34-40: *"Master, which is the greatest commandment of the Law?"*

Meditation:

What a question to ask if you are trying to trip someone up! It is a good question to ask if you are looking for an argument. But Jesus gives the only answer that leaves no room for argument, *"You shall love the Lord your God with your whole heart, with your whole soul, and with all your mind ... You shall love your neighbor as yourself."* To this very day, this response of Jesus is the basis of our religion and our faith. If we can truly live these two commandments then we will be fulfilling the law and the prophets as well. Jesus, in his own life, demonstrated how we should live these commandments. At the Last Supper he told us to love one other as he has loved us. We have much to learn from the way that Jesus loves us. Once we can accept his love in our lives, it becomes easier for us to love others.

MARY'S SOLICITUDE FOR HER PEOPLE when she appeared at La Salette is a wonderful example of how she loves us. She came pleading for us to return to her Son so that we may again open our hearts to the love that Christ has for us. She also encourages us to grow in our love for her Son. We are asked to turn away from sin, to be converted and to experience the life found in being in union with Christ. Her love for her people remains operative today. We invoke her as Our Lady of La Salette, Reconciler of sinners and she, without ceasing, continues to intercede for us.

Reflection Questions:

• How do you express for your commitment to the first commandment (to love the Lord your God)?
• How do you act on and live out the second commandment (love your neighbor as yourself)?

Saturday, August 21, (#424)
Twentieth Week in Ordinary Time
(The Queenship of Mary)

Matthew 23:1-12: *"Anyone who raises himself up will be humbled, and anyone who humbles himself will be raised up."*

Meditation:

We don't hear much about humility these days. Maybe it is because there seems to be a negative connotation connected with the word. A humble person is often seen as someone who has no backbone and lets other people walk over him. Humility is sometimes seen as degrading who we are. But the true meaning of humility is quite the opposite. To be a humble person requires that we accept ourselves as we are and like who we are. It means that we stop pretending to be someone we are not. We stop wishing to become someone cannot become. Humility demands a lot of honesty from us. Jesus had difficulty with the Scribes and Pharisees because they were presenting themselves as other than they really were. They were hypocrites. What Jesus is asking of us is to see ourselves as he sees us. That is true humility.

AT LA SALETTE Mary does not come looking for a place of honor but rather she comes to lead us to her Son. She is dressed as a working homemaker of the day — a woman who is desperately trying to keep her family together. She knows and understands that her Son is the source of our salvation and the fullness of our life. She understands that her role is to serve us by showing the way that leads to her Son. Mary encourages us to be true to the calling that we have received from God. She shows that we are badly mistaken in thinking that we do not need God. It is Mary's humility that gives her the place of exaltation as Queen of Heaven, *"If my people..."*

Reflection Questions:

- How do you live out these two commandments in your life?
- Do you accept yourself for who you are? Or would you rather pretend to be someone you are not?

Sunday, August 22 (#122)
Twenty-First Sunday in Ordinary Time
(Joshua 24:1-18; Eph. 5:21-32; John 6:60-69)

Meditation: *Whom shall we Serve?*

When Joshua challenged the people to decide which gods they would serve, they answered, "We will serve the Lord." That generation did their best to be faithful to keep that pledge.

Jesus asked the Twelve: "Do you also want to leave?" Peter answered with a question of his own: "To whom shall we go?" His profession of faith, which followed immediately, did not prevent his later denial, but preserved him from despair

" ... as for me and my household, we will serve the Lord."

Joshua 24:15

241

and prepared him to devote his life to the Lord's service.

St. Paul also speaks of service. The word in our translation is "subordinate," which sound more like servitude than service. He says that reverence for Christ should make Christians "subordinate to one another," in other words willing to serve each other.

The question of choosing whom we shall serve finds a different expression on the lips of the Beautiful Lady of La Salette, in her use of the conditional "If my people refuse to submit" is equivalent to "will you submit or not?" or, to paraphrase Joshua, "decide to whom you will submit." Let's look at the alternatives.

The pursuit of pleasure, power or wealth is easily confused with the pursuit of happiness, and yet none of those good things can ensure we will be happy.

Knowledge, wisdom, and the arts have the power to uplift us. Practical skills can bring satisfaction, especially when placed at the service of others. But even here a certain self-sufficient, self-serving arrogance can creep in, undermining the good we do.

After Peter's question, "To whom shall we go?" we read, "You have the words of eternal life." This is more than a declaration, it is a commitment.

We must not assume that the Twelve understood Jesus' discourse on the Bread of Life, especially the part about eating his flesh and drinking his blood, any better than those other disciples who said, "This saying is hard; who can accept it?" and who no longer accompanied him.

And notice that Peter calls Jesus Master, a word indicating submission. That means Peter sees himself as both disciple and servant.

Mary's words at La Salette, even her hard sayings, call us to submit to him who has the words of eternal life.

Monday, August 23 (#425)
Twenty-First Week in Ordinary Time

Matthew 23:13-22: *"Alas for you, scribes and Pharisees, you hypocrites! You* *shut up the kingdom of Heaven in people's faces."*

For Your Reflection:

The verses in the gospel of today form the most terrible and most sustained denunciation in the New Testament. Here Jesus directs a series of Woes against the Scribes and Pharisees. Here we see the righteous anger that burns in the heart of love, a heart broken by the stubborn blindness of men. The word hypocrite occurs here again and again. It came to mean an actor in the worse sense of the term, "a pretender." A hypocrite is one who wears a mask to cover his or her true feelings, one who puts on an external show while inwardly their thoughts and feelings are quite different. To Jesus, the Scribes and Pharisees were men who were acting a part. He understood that their whole idea of religion consisted in outward and meticulous observance of the rules and regulations of the law but in their hearts, there was bitterness, envy, pride and arrogance. Jesus accused these men of being missionaries of evil. The abusive attitude of the Pharisees and Scribes was strongly criticized by Jesus. It is very clear that this list of indictments is not directed solely to Israel's leaders of generations past but is leveled at any false leadership in the Christian community of today.

"...AND AS TO YOU, YOU TAKE NO HEED OF IT." Even many years after the apparition at La Salette, blasphemy and hypocrisy still thrive in and around our homes and families. Many still do not believe in God. Many Catholics and Christians do not care to go to Mass or to pray. There is rejection of God and stubbornness everywhere. Many still abuse the name of God and scorn religion. We need to listen again to the message of the Blessed Mother and accept the challenge of bringing our society back to God and to his Son, Jesus,

Reflection Questions:

- Can you see any forms of blasphemy, hypocrisy or stubbornness in your life?
- How are you responding to Mary's call to conversion in your daily life?

Tuesday, August 24, (#629)
St. Bartholomew, Apostle

John 1:45-51: *"You are going to see greater things than that."*

Meditation:

Is this still the age of miracles? Indeed, if we belief that Jesus can do great things, we should only be pleasantly surprised when prayers are answered and hearts are changed and healings happen, people come back to the sacraments. But we shouldn't allow our faith to rely on such wonderful graces from God. We should be faithful in both the green wood and the dry (Luke 23: 31). Jesus invited us to step out in faith and not depend on miracles for us to continue believing. Our vision should be that of "Taking up our cross", not "sitting at the right or left hand of God." Dedication and self-sacrifice is our motto for living. St. Bartholomew was martyred but little else in known of him. But his giving of his life for the faith is a model we can certainly follow as we meet the gifts and challenges of believing in today's world and urging others to follow our example of faith.

OUR LADY OF LA SALETTE brings to her children a mission of reconciliation and evangelization. She speaks of the importance of coming back to faith in her Son as central to daily living (reconciliation). She also leaves the children and us a mandate to "make her message known." Her simple words summarized well the gospel message of her Son: "love God, neighbor and self; baptize all people in the name of the Father, and of the Son and of the Holy Spirit."

Reflection Questions:

- What wonderful works of God (miracles or graces) have you witnessed in your life (or that of others)?
- What do you do to keep your faith alive?

Wednesday, August 25, (#427)
Twenty-First Week in Ordinary Time

Matthew 23:27-32: *"You are like whitewashed tombs that look handsome on the outside, but inside are full of the bones of the dead and every kind of* *corruption."*

Meditation:

The central thrust of Jesus' indictment against the Scribes and Pharisees is that they lack discernment, love and good faith. Jesus continually tells us that true love for God and neighbor should always be the guideline in the application of the law. Jesus condemns the distance and disparity that separates one's actions from one's heart – the plastic mentality that allows one to distort external behavior from one's true motivations. Jesus is making a radical call for integrity and purity of heart. That call remains pertinent today.

MARY'S WORDS TO MAXIMIN AND MELANIE as well as her physical proximity to the children reflects her appreciation for humility and sincerity in our life. How important it is to be childlike in our attitudes! She is also very aware of the malice in people's hearts. Her call to conversion, to humility, to submission to her Son is needed in all generations.

Reflection Questions:

• When, how and why is your heart far from your words and actions?
• Who are good examples to you of people who live their faith well?

Thursday, August 26, (#428)
Twenty-First Week in Ordinary Time

Matthew 24:42-51: *"… you too must stand ready because the Son of man is coming at an hour you do not expect."*

Meditation:

We, the People of God, are responsible for the gift of life. We are called to make the best of it at each moment. There is no time to waste. We are reminded by Jesus to make good use of our treasure, time and talent in accor-dance with the golden rule and to be ready to render an account of our stewardship. Each hour of life here on earth is a gift from God and we could profitably see it as our last since no one of us is guaranteed the next. All of this is a call to fidelity and trustworthiness. An uncertain future holds no real terror if, as faithful and trustworthy servants, we care for our household with compassion, love and forgiveness.

Mary's message at La Salette is call to life, a call to make the best of life, with God's help. Mary was very much aware of the presence of evil in our world. At La Salette she points to the tragedies of infant mortality, famine and pestilence as a starting point on the road to conversion and reconciliation.

Reflection Questions:

- How can you show the Lord that you are trying to live for faith in the here and now?
- What have you done within your family or friends to encourage their life of faith or to strengthen their hope?

Friday, August 27, (#429)
Twenty-First Week in Ordinary Time

Matthew 25:1-13: *"So stay awake, because you do not know either the day or the hour."*

Meditation:

The parable of the ten virgins is found only in the Gospel according to Matthew. Its story of two very different types of wedding attendants is an allegory on the need for alertness during the indefinite period of time before the end. Lack of vigilance costs the foolish bridesmaids entrance to the wedding celebration. There is some evidence in Jewish writings of the day that "oil" was a symbol of good deeds. If Matthew intended that symbolism here, then he would have neatly blended the two dominant themes of this section. Five of the virgins are wise because they have filled their lives with good deeds, the product of the wise use of the gifts of God. The lives of the foolish are empty and thus they are "unknown" to the Bridegroom. This parable is a call to make good use of our talents, blessings and gifts. Jesus reminds us to make the best of our lives even in the ordinariness of our day-to-day activities.

Mary's call to do good and to be vigilant is very evident in her message at La Salette and in her life. Mary was always active in the service of others: for Jesus and Joseph, for the elderly Elizabeth, for the newlyweds at Cana. Mary was particularly active by her willing assent to events, to God's hand in her life. And Mary is still very active "spending her heaven doing good on earth."

Reflection Questions:

- Do you cherish the gift and the blessing of time given to you here on earth?
- Who has been a true blessing to you in your times of challenge or difficulty? Why not pray for them today.

Saturday, August 28 (#430)
Twenty-First Week in Ordinary Time

Matthew 25:14-30: *"Well done, good and trustworthy servant; you have shown you are trustworthy in small things; I will trust you with greater..."*

Meditation:

The parable of the talents continues the emphasis on the good use of time while shuttling back to the theme of fidelity. The good and faithful servants are those who are willing to risk their own security in using their gifts well. All are given generous gifts (even one talent is an enormous sum) but not all are willing to use them. The servant with the one talent lets fear smother his initiative and he must, therefore, stand accountable before his master. Fear had crippled the fate of the disciples in the boat in Mt. 8:26 and fear caused Peter to sink into the waves in 14:30-31. Here again, Matthew cites fear as the enemy of generous discipleship. Initiative and trustworthiness are very much expected from each one of us. In this parable of the talents, Jesus questions the stand of the Scribes' and Pharisees. Like the man with the one talent, they desired to keep things exactly as they were and for that they are condemned. It is not a person's talent that matters. What matters is how one makes use of it.

MARY RISKED HER OWN SECURITY in speaking her fiat, making it possible for the Incarnation to grace human history. Mary is a supreme model of responsible stewardship of her gifts and talents, of her life itself. This generosity permitted her to become the Mother of God and the Mother of all generations. Mary's call at La Salette to submission to the will of God is a call to risk our life for the sake of God's kingdom.

Reflection Questions:
- How is a person with fewer gifts able to avoid being jealous of the person with many?
- Who is a very gifted person whom you know personally?

Sunday, August 29 (#125)
Twenty-Second Sunday in Ordinary Time
(Deuteronomy 4:1-8; James 1:17-21; Mark 7: 1-8, 14-15, 21-23)

Meditation: *Walking Blamelessly*

After their return from exile around 539 BC, the Jewish people adopted an attitude of strict observance of the Law of Moses. They had learned their lesson. They began, we might say, to protect the Law by surrounding it with practices making it less likely one would break the law.

For example, if you do not want to take the name of the Lord in vain, you never pronounce his name at all. Problem solved. Our responsorial psalm takes largely a similar approach, focusing on what not to do in order to be blameless.

The discussion in today's Gospel revolves around a practice that we could summarize as "cleanliness is next to godliness." The commandments about "clean and unclean" were reinforced by the traditional ritual washings we see described. Jesus opposes giving traditions the same weight as the Law. He condemns not ritual but ritualism.

In her message at La Salette Our Lady focuses on commandments, not traditions: honoring the Lord's Name and observing the Sabbath rest are in the Ten Commandments; Lent and Sunday Mass are among the Commandments of the Church, based on very ancient Christian practice. This is not ritualism.

St. James writes, "Religion that is pure and undefiled before God and the Father is this: to care for orphans and widows in their affliction and to keep oneself unstained by the world." He adopts both a positive and a negative approach.

Blamelessness doesn't lie merely in "getting it right." It is a far cry from obsessive perfectionism.

The Eucharist, for example, is a celebration composed of many prescribed elements. It is a ritual. But if our participation is purely ritualistic, i.e., not accompanied by our mind and heart, its capacity to nourish our faith is seriously undermined.

Psalm 119, 9 asks, "How can the young keep his way without fault?" and answers, "Only by observing your words." In verse 16 the psalmist exclaims, "In your statutes I take delight; I will never forget your word."

Mary, who is utterly blameless, wept at La Salette, but one way we can dry her tears is to carry out God's commands in joy.

Monday, August 30, (#431)
Twenty-Second Week in Ordinary Time

Luke 4:16-30: *"He has sent me to proclaim liberty to captives, sight to the blind, to let the oppressed go free, to proclaim a year of favor from the Lord."*

Meditation:

Jesus' inaugural sermon in his hometown synagogue might be likened to the U.S. President's inauguration speech. In that speech the President defines his goals and conveys a vision of what he plans to accomplish during his tour years in office. Jesus preaches that the prophecies in Isaiah 61:1-2 and 58:6 are being fulfilled in his ministry. These prophecies define his goals. Although Jesus' ministry has a strong social component, it cannot be equated with mere social action. The liberty and freedom that Jesus brings is liberation from the oppression of sin. Like a new president's statement, Jesus' inaugural sermon meets with reaction. The four years of favor are for the entire nation's poor, captive, blind and oppressed. Jesus stresses the idea that God's mercy and favor extend beyond the borders of the hometown neighborhood, the chosen people. Salvation is for all those who believe. Our mission is not limited to a certain place or race. It has a universal dimension. Especially, it should reach out to the marginalized and oppressed of the world.

"**MAKE THIS KNOWN TO ALL MY PEOPLE.**" For Mary, the mission of reconciliation in Christ is directed to the whole human race. Mary is the mother for all nations. She pleads and prays without ceasing for all her children. She works tirelessly for us all. She wants to embrace all peoples in the reconciling love of her Son.

Reflection Questions:

• As a reconciler, how wide is the horizon of your vision and mission?
• Is there anyone who shares their life of faith with you from time to time? How often do you do that as well?

Tuesday, August 31, (#432)
Twenty-Second Week in Ordinary Time

Luke 4:31-37: *"He gives orders to unclean spirits with authority and power and they come out."*

Meditation:

Each of Jesus' miracles should be seen as a sign that the kingdom had come in his own person. According to the popular belief of the day, mental illness was attributable to possession by evil spirits. The coming of Jesus' kingdom means that these evil spirits no longer have any power in the human domain. Luke draws on the Old Testament image of God's kingdom – a rule where God's will establishes peace, health, justice and forgiveness, a rule that will reign supreme in the Incarnate Word himself. God's rule is present in the deeds and teaching of Jesus. He acts with the authority of God to overcome the evil spirit. In Jesus, we claim victory over all and any evil spirits that exist in this world.

MARY IS VERY MUCH AWARE of the evil existing on earth. She recognizes the evil of oppression and hunger, social injustice, environmental disaster, the lack of faith in God, the lack of a sense of sin and much more. Our Blessed Mother is very much concerned about these evil situations. The call of Mary at La Salette urges us to turn away from evil and to reconcile with God through her Son, Jesus.

Reflection Questions:

- Are you sincerely working at making God's rule alive and present today?
- When have you (or someone you know) experienced an event of reconciliation?

Wednesday, September 1, (#433) Twenty-Second Week in Ordinary Time

Luke 4:38-44: "... At sunset all those who had friends suffering from diseases of one kind or another brought them to him, and laying his hands on each he cured them."

Meditation:

Jesus was always ready to serve. Healing all kinds of illness and vanquishing all existing evil was the heart of his mission. Jesus had come to overcome the power of the devil and lead humankind towards the coming of the kingdom. Jesus is the Anointed One of the Father bringing peace, health, justice and new life on earth. Jesus has given that healing power to his apostles. In fact each one of us is given the power to heal to the extent that we believe and trust in Jesus, our master, and see him as the source of healing, justice and victory. In Jesus we find liberation from the sway of evil. In Jesus' ministry, the power of God undermines the power of evil that holds people captive.

MARY IS VERY MUCH AWARE of the evil in today's world. Actually her apparitions at La Salette, Lourdes and Fatima reveal her preoccupation with the spiritual blindness of her people. Her call to prayer and conversion is an appeal to use the power of Jesus in doing battle with the powers of evil.

Reflection Questions:

- How can you make God's presence and power real today?
- Are you aware of the challenges that will touch your life today?

Thursday, September 2, (#434)
Twenty-Second Week in Ordinary Time

Luke 5:1-11: *"Put out into deep water and lay out your nets for a catch."*

Meditation:

We see here a turning point in the career of Jesus. He leaves the synagogue and goes to the lakeside. Jesus went to places where people would listen to him. Fish and fishermen, fishing net and the shoreline are to become commonplace in the mission and ministry of Jesus. The call of Peter and his companions brings the focus of the Lord's ministry to the simple and ordinary folk. They in turn put much trust in this Nazarene. They observed him closely, asked their questions, followed his orders and advice and came to know the success of their new tide, *"fishers of men."* All those who are called to be his disciples and missionaries are likewise asked to risk their very selves for the sake of the Master. With Jesus around the catch is sure. Without the touch of the Master the mission is impossible. We are asked to evaluate the motives of our ministerial service. If it is rooted in our love for the Lord, energized by our trusting and risking in his name, then it will indeed bring forth fruit.

MARY WAS VERY MUCH AWARE of the mission of Jesus. From the time of her fiat response to the angel, she was never very far from his projects and concerns. She stood firm in her mission. She pleads at La Salette for the sake of her Son, Jesus. At Pentecost she rightfully assumes the focal point of the gathered apostles because she did everything for the sake of her Son and she trusted in him.

Reflection Questions:

- Whom do you know who has put out into the deep – that is, has taken chances in their life and succeeded well?
- When was the last time you did something nice "just for the love of it"?

Friday, September 3, (#435)
Twenty-Second Week in Ordinary Time

Luke 5:33-39: *"Surely you cannot make the bridegroom's attendants fast while the bridegroom is still with them?"*

Meditation:

Jesus was radically opposed to religion based on rules and the dutiful observance of them. He challenged this stand of the Scribes and Pharisees at every turn. They prided themselves on the strictest observance of the Law but Jesus could see that their hearts were far from the love of God. This pharisaic attitude still exists today. There seems to be in many religious people a passion for what is old. It is said that, in her wisdom and experience, nothing moves more slowly than the Church. However, the Good News proclaimed by Jesus was indeed news and the Pharisees could not adjust to this radically new approach of Jesus. This whole passage is Jesus' condemnation of the shut mind and a plea that people should not reject new ideas. We should never be afraid of adventurous thought. God is ever leading us into a deeper and wider appreciation of the truth in the power of the Holy Spirit. We should never be afraid of new methods in our approach to mission and ministry. In our own generation, Vatican II has given us new (not novel) approaches in understanding and living in the Church in the modem world. What might we expect from Vatican III?

MARY WAS A WOMAN who was aware of the situation, of the signs of the times. She fully supported the vision of Jesus. Mary was always open to the inspiration of the Holy Spirit. Her call at La Salette is a call to change, an opening to liberation, a call to new life in Jesus.

Reflection Questions:

- What is your attitude towards the changes in the community and the parish, in the mission and ministry?
- Are you open to change for the better?

Saturday, September 4, (#436)
Twenty-Second Week in Ordinary Time

Luke 6:1-5: *"The Son of man is master of the Sabbath."*

Meditation:

The Pharisees and leaders were really after Jesus. The opposition was emerging very strongly. The immediate charge against Jesus, they found, was that he violated the law of the Sabbath. The Jewish law states that on the Sabbath it is forbidden to reap, to thresh, to winnow and to prepare food. We see that technically the disciples had broken each of these. To us the whole thing seems fantastic; but we must remember that to a strict Pharisee this was deadly sin. Rules and regulations had been broken. For them this was a matter of life and death. This passage contains a great general truth. Jesus said to the Pharisees, "Have you not read what David did?" The answer was of course "yes." But they had never understood what it meant. It is possible to read Scripture meticulously, to know the Bible inside out from cover to cover, and yet miss its real meaning. They did not bring to the reading of their Scripture an open mind and a needy heart.

JESUS VERY CLEARLY EMPHASIZES the fact that his mission of doing good and saving life is more important than mere Sabbath observance. Mary comes at La Salette to teach and instruct, to beckon with tears and to cajole with maternal love that we open our minds to a new understanding of our Faith and let our hearts be touched and healed. Her entire life was dedicated to making the saving plan of God come true. She is still at work in manifold ways to bring humankind back to the love, mercy and salvation made available to us in and through Jesus Christ.

Reflection Questions:

• Why did the Pharisees "miss the forest for the trees"?
• Do you know any people who seem to get caught up in the little things of life (or maybe even you) and miss the important events?

Sunday, September 5, (#128)
Twenty-Third Sunday in Ordinary Time

(Isaiah 35:4-7; James 2:1-5; Mark 7:31-37)

Meditation: *Saved*

If you are familiar with Alcohol
ics Anonymous, you know that
the second step reads: We came
to believe that a Power greater
than ourselves could restore us
to sanity. This comes close to
what we read in Isaiah: "Be
strong, fear not! Here is your
God, he comes with vindication;
with divine recompense he
comes to save you."

*The Blind and Mute Man Possessed by
Devils* by James Tissot (1836–1902)

When we talk of salvation, often
we mean getting to heaven. That
is the ultimate goal, of course,
but between now and then, can
we not be saved? The answer is obvious: yes, we can.

Isaiah gives concrete illustrations of God's saving power: "Then will
the eyes of the blind be opened, the ears of the deaf be cleared; then
will the lame leap like a stag, then the tongue of the mute will sing."
The responsorial Psalm evokes the same theme. And the friends of
the deaf man were inspired by that same tradition of seeing salvation
in healing.

The Greek word for save, can be translated as heal, or make whole. It
implies preservation (in advance) or deliverance (after the fact) from
evil in any form. Thus, St. James's insistence on not showing partiality
within the Christian community is well within the prophetic proclamation of freedom from oppression.

The Apparition of Our Lady of La Salette stands squarely within this
tradition. We need to be saved not only from external evils, but from
our own sinfulness. We cannot do this alone, but Mary reminds us of

the great news that salvation is ours for the asking.

Evangelical Christians speak of accepting the Lord Jesus as our personal savior. The Beautiful Lady uses different language but calls us to that same reality. The purpose of her visitation is that we might (again in the words of AA) make a decision to turn our will and our lives over to the care of God.

Miraculous cures, in the Gospels especially, are a sign of the salvation Jesus offers. More wondrous, however, is the conversion of heart, such as has been experienced since 1846 by countless pilgrims to the Holy Mountain of La Salette.

Sin makes our lives unmanageable. The saving grace of reconciliation with God through Jesus Christ is our best hope, our only hope.

Monday, September 6, (#437)
Twenty-Third Week in Ordinary Time

Luke 6:6-11: *"Is it permitted on the Sabbath to do good, or to do evil; to save life, or to destroy it?"*

Meditation:

In today's Gospel, opposition to Jesus has become quite open. The Scribes and Pharisees are looking for something to use against him. Jesus might just as well have cured the man with the withered hand the next day; but he broke the Sabbath law to teach us something very important: namely, that it is always permitted to do good on the Sabbath. *"Is it lawful to do good on the Sabbath – or to do evil?"* This question must have struck home to his listeners: while Jesus was seeking to restore life, the scribes and Pharisees were doing all they could to destroy Jesus.

AT LA SALETTE, Mary wept because her children had gone astray and no longer sought to follow the ways of her Son. Her very presence on that mountain in the French Alps makes us realize that she always sought to carry out her Son's wishes. Mary knew what Jesus was about and she pleaded with her children to return to him. Her tears conveyed to Melanie and Maximin how serious her message was. Her gentle voice told them of her deep love for them.

- In moments of indecision, do you stop and ask, "What would Jesus do?"
- Do you seek to do good in every aspect of your life?

Tuesday, September 7, (#438)
Twenty-Third Week in Ordinary Time

Luke 6:12-19: *"Jesus went onto the mountain to pray; and he spent the whole night in prayer to God."*

Meditation:

Jesus was about to make a very important decision, one that would have consequences even to our day. He was about to choose twelve men to be his intimate followers. Much would be asked of them: to give up families and work, their personal desires and goals, to follow a man none of them fully understood. It would require a tremendous leap of faith. Before inviting them, Jesus spent the night in conversation with his Father. Together they would decide whom to invite.

AT LA SALETTE, MARY ASKED THE TWO CHILDREN if they prayed well. Immediately they responded, "Not very well, Madam." Mary must have smiled at their complete honesty. Perhaps that is why they were chosen. Mary then told them, "But you must pray well, my children." Mary knew the power of prayer. She knew how conversing with the Father gave her Son courage and strength in the darkest moments of his life. Mary knew there would be dark moments in the lives of Maximin and Melanie. There will be dark moments in our lives as well. Whether dark or light, prayer seeks to put us in touch with God at every moment.

Reflection Questions:

- "Do you pray well, my children?"
- When is it hardest for you to pray?

Wednesday, September 8, (#636)
The Nativity of the Blessed Virgin Mary

Matthew 1-16,18-23: *"... the Lord had spoken through the prophet (Isaiah): Look! the virgin is with child and will give birth to a son whom they will call Immanuel, a name which means 'God-is-with-us'."*

Meditation:

Pope St. John Paul II, in the introduction to the Vatican's 2001 *Directory on Popular Piety and the Liturgy: Principles and Guidelines*, explains that "Popular piety is an expression of faith which avails of certain cultural elements proper to a specific environment... Genuine forms of popular piety, expressed in a multitude of different ways, derives from the faith and, therefore, must be valued and promoted. Such authentic expressions of popular piety ... predispose the people for the celebration of the Sacred Mysteries."

Indeed, popular piety is seen as "a true treasure of the People of God" (*Directory*, #59). The Directory, in chapter five, discusses extensively "the veneration of the Holy Mother of God, which occupies a singular position both in the Liturgy and popular devotion."

AT LA SALETTE, Mary showed how much she loved her Son and how closely she expressed his wishes for us to follow him. On this celebration of the birth of Mary, we are reminded among other things that, as William Wordsworth wrote in 1822 in a sonnet entitled "The Virgin", Mary is "our tainted nature's solitary boast." She is Mother of Jesus and, as St. John the evangelist described about Jesus on the cross, he gave his mother to us all and she is indeed Mother of the Church.

Reflection Questions:

• What do we especially admire about Mary at La Salette?
• What is our favorite Marian prayer or devotion?

Thursday, September 9, (#440)
Twenty-Third Week in Ordinary Time

Luke 6:27-38: *" ... love your enemies and do good to them, and lend without* *any hope of return."*

Meditation:

In the early morning hours of June 7, 1998, in the small community of Jasper, Texas, three white men dragged a black man behind a truck for three miles down a dirt road to his death. The gruesome murder shocked the country and the world. The community of Jasper, white and black alike, was appalled that so horrible a crime could occur in their midst. The victim's family immediately called for forgiveness and peace. They wanted healing to begin. As active members in their church, they had often heard their minister preach the words of scripture that are quoted above. Were these words merely a fantasy of some beautiful world to come, or words that held promise for the present situation? This family showed the community, not by mere words but by their actions, just what it means to "love your enemies."

AT LA SALETTE, Mary spoke of children dying in the arms of their parents. There seems to be so much hatred and violence in our society. Mary's entire conversation with the two children was one of great compassion and love. Her very presence at La Salette told of her deep love for her children. She told them she was compelled to pray without ceasing on their behalf. How reassuring for us!

Reflection Questions:

• Do you love your enemies? Do you do good to those who hate you?
• When was the last time you prayed for anyone who maltreated you? Have you reflected on the fact that all these "enemies" are actually your brothers and sisters in Christ?

Friday, September 10, (#441)
Twenty-Third Week in Ordinary Time

Luke 6:39-42: *"Why do you observe the splinter in your brother's eye and never notice the great log in your own?"*

Meditation:

Jesus's message here seems blunt and unmistakable. We have no right to criticize since we are not free of faults. How quick we are to notice the faults of those around us. They seem so obvious. A poet once said, "There is so much bad in the best of us and so much good in the worst of us that it ill becomes any of us to find fault with the rest of us." These are surely good words to live by, for in the *Our Father* we ask God to forgive us our failings in the same way that we forgive the failings of others. We need to leave judgment to our heavenly Father, for he sees the complete picture while we often see only a small part of the reason behind another's actions.

AT LA SALETTE, Mary shed tears of sorrow. Melanie would later state, "She wept all the while she spoke to us." Our Blessed Mother told Melanie and Maximin, *"If my people do not obey, I shall be compelled to let go of the arm of my Son. It is so heavy that I can no longer restrain it."* It is our own lives she asks us to reflect on and not the faults of others.

Reflection Questions:

- Do you often judge others?
- How often do you criticize your neighbor while failing to see your own shortcomings?

Saturday, September 11, (#442) Twenty-Third Week in Ordinary Time

Note: Today you may wish to begin the First Day of the Novena to Our Lady of La Salette, in the appendix of this book.

Luke 6:43-49: *"Good people draw what is good from the store of goodness in their hearts; bad people draw what is bad from the store of badness. For the words of the mouth flow out of what fills the heart."*

Meditation:

We cannot be judged in any way but through our deeds. Our actions indeed speak louder than our words and leave impressions long after our words are forgotten.

On January 23, 1998, a fence which for 163 years divided graves in a city cemetery in Jasper, Texas, was taken down. The ministers in that town had often spoken of racial harmony, but when loved ones were buried, the blacks were always on one side of the fence and whites were on the other side. That fence made sure that even in death blacks and whites would be separated.

But on that chilly January morning, as members of the town gathered in prayer, that fence was torn down. Perhaps the tearing down of an old iron fence in a small cemetery seems insignificant in this country's battle with racism and segregation; but to the people of that community, it was an important symbol of good people producing goodness from the good in their hearts.

THE MESSAGE OF LA SALETTE was not merely for the people living in that small hamlet high in the French Alps. It was a message of God's deep love and Mary's great concern for all people in all places. Mary spoke of "a great famine coming," in which "people would pay for their sins through hunger." There seems to be such a hunger today for genuine equality in our society where all people, regardless of race or religion, have the same opportunities and the same freedoms. And that hunger seems to be of God.

Reflection Questions:

- By your actions, do you speak words of peace or of discord, of equality or of racism, of justice or of injustice?
- Which is "abundant" in your heart?

Sunday, September 12, (#131) Twenty-Fourth Sunday in Ordinary Time

(Isaiah 50:5-9; James 2:14-18; Mark 8:27-35)

Meditation: *Take up your Cross*

I have often wondered how the crowd took Jesus' saying that his disciples must 'take up their cross.' After long searches for this expression outside its five occurrences in the Gospels, I must conclude it does not exist elsewhere.

Christians understand those words in the light of the crucifixion of Christ. Suffering is part of every life; that is our share in his cross.

At La Salette Mary says, "How long a time I have suffered for you." In the context of the Apparition, this means the trouble she has taken to protect us from the consequences of sin. But in the *Memorare* to

The Prophecy of the Destruction of the Temple by **James Tissot** (1836–1902)

Our Lady of La Salette, we look farther back: "Remember the tears you shed for me on Calvary."

The sufferings of the Blessed Virgin were uniquely hers. We may say the same for all of us. Jesus is specific. Each disciple must take up his or her own cross.

Looking at the lives of saints, we find many examples. A few have literally shared the sufferings of the crucified Christ, through physical wounds in the hands and feet, or around their head. Besides the pain, they endured sometimes humiliation from those who considered them imposters.

Some were ridiculed or persecuted or killed for their faith. Others experienced periods of excruciating spiritual dryness. Or they deprived themselves of even the simplest pleasures in order to have some share in the Cross of Christ.

Still others, like Simon of Cyrene helping Jesus to carry his cross, gave themselves completely to the service of the sick, the homeless, the "brother or sister has nothing to wear and has no food for the day," as we read in the Letter of James.

Sometimes another person can be a cross. I am reminded of what Dorothy Day wrote about a troublesome resident at a Catholic Worker house: "He is our cross, specially sent by God, and so we cherish him."

The saying of Jesus about taking up our cross is so familiar that we may forget that is really is a hard saying. The Beautiful Lady, bearing the crucifix on her breast—on her heart—invites us to accept lovingly whatever uniquely personal cross we are called to take up as disciples of her Son.

Monday, September 13, (#443)
Twenty-Fourth Week in Ordinary Time

Luke 7:1-10: *"I tell you, not even in Israel have I found faith as great as this."*

For Your Reflection:

Some years ago some Jewish refugees in Mexico expressed a desire for German pastries. The pastries were not essential, but they would be a treat. Rev. Oswald Goiter, a missionary to Mexico, went through extra trouble and expense to obtain these pastries. "But why did you do that?" someone protested. "They don't even believe in Jesus." Rev. Goiter responded, "But I do!" We do what we do because of our faith, a special gift from God. We are called to be people of faith.

THE LA SALETTE MESSAGE IS A CALL TO BE FAITHFUL AND FAITH-FILLED. We are called to make the message known to the entire world. At all times we will need that special faith to carry out this message of La Salette.

Reflection Questions:

• Reflect on an example of where and how your faith has sustained you.
• Can you remember a time you performed an act of kindness because you are a Christian, regardless of the belief of the recipient?

Tuesday, September 14, (#638)
The Exaltation of the Holy Cross

John 3:13-17: *"God (so) loved the world: he gave his only Son..."*

Meditation:

Often while watching a baseball or football game on television, we may see some scripture passages on signs that people hold up for all to see. Many see these as acts of a religious fanatic but we may be missing something good if we do that. In fact, "John 3:16", an oftenused bible citation is certainly a central passage of the New Testament. In fact, no other verse in the scriptures summarizes God's relationship with humanity in such a succinct way. First, God loves us abundantly. Second, the unimaginable extent of God's love is that God sent his only Son to live, and die, and rise – all for love of us! Thirdly, anyone who does believe in Jesus will be saved – and will be welcomed into heaven "for ever and ever." All this comes from this one remarkably short verse and gives us a great revelation and immense hope. In other words, the cross of Jesus does save us.

MARY AT LA SALETTE wore a crucifix on her breast during the apparition. The children stated that, during the entire apparition, the crucifix gave off tremendous light which almost overpowered everything else. The light from the crucifix was so bright that it was even difficult to see Mary. This unique La Salette crucifix was not only the central focus of the apparition. It was also the summary of the purpose of our lives. People later commented on the possible meaning of the symbols of the hammer and pincers that "floated" under the right and left arms of the crucifix on which the living and moving body of Jesus could be seen! The hammer seems to be symbolic of our sins, which hammer the nails into Jesus' hands. The pincers can be seen as our good and loving acts which mercifully remove the nails from the Lord's bloody hands.

Reflection Questions:

- What words or actions of yours have put the nails into Jesus' hands?
- What good actions of yours have removed the nails from his holy hands?

Wednesday, September 15, (#639)
Our Lady of Sorrows

Luke 2: 33-35 (second option): *What the Old Man, Simeon, saw*

Meditation:

He was quite a man this "certain man" named Simeon. He as not only just, he was also pious, awaiting "the consolation of Israel and the Holy Spirit was upon him." He was so just and pious that the Holy Spirit had revealed something quite special to him: he would not die until he had seen the Messiah. The Holy Spirit, in fact, seems quite partial to Simeon. This is the only time Simeon is mentioned in the

New Testament and three times in this passage he is associated with the Holy Spirit.

The Holy Spirit was upon Simeon, that is, the Spirit of God had come from above as a free gift to rest on Simeon, and his presence, recognized and heeded, made Simeon just and pious. There is a great deal of light for you and me in these verses. The revelation to Simeon is not of his own composition; it comes from the Spirit and it is this Spirit who is speaking to me through this old man. He is telling me that the Child he is holding in his arms is, in fact, the Lord and Savior. ..

It is good to recall that the Holy Spirit that gave old Simeon the power to believe is the very same Spirit that allows us to believe that Christ is alive within us. It is this same Spirit that gives us the strength to hope and cope and to live in fidelity to the word of God in our lives...

And so it is that an old man believed and ..prophesied about the Christ before Christ himself could walk and talk. Simeon... may have appeared only once in the New Testament but it was quite a walk-on.

AT LA SALETTE, THE SPIRIT WAS AT WORK IN THE TWO UNSUSPECTING YOUNG WITNESSES. At first, Melanie said to Maximin: "...look at the pretty light over there!" Then they both approached the globe of light. He described: "At the beginning we saw nobody in that light. And then it lowered and we saw it part. And all of a sudden we saw a Lady in it. "We were both afraid", said Maximin, and Melanie dropped her walking stick in surprise. He assured Melanie, saying "Keep your stick, now! I hold onto mine and if she does us any harm, I'll give her a good whack!" But once Mary stood and welcomed them, their fear simply dissolved. They had a change of attitude, a change of heart.

The Spirit was now helping them listen to this Heavenly Messenger. And certainly, following the Apparition, their new ministry of "of making (Mary's) message known" they did with heartfelt sincerity, dedication and consistency. (Writers: Frs. Normand Theroux, M.S. and Ron Gagne, M.S.)

Reflection Questions:

• When have you been graced with the ability to deal with a sur-

prising or challenging situation?
• Can you remember a situation where God's grace was evidently present in your own life or that of others?

Thursday, September 16, (#446)
Twenty-Fourth Week in Ordinary Time

Luke 7:36-50: *"Jesus said, 'You are right.'"*

Meditation:

Whenever we go shopping, we can pick and choose. Those of us who are asked to give talks tend to pick our favorite topics for elaboration. The Lectionary (the book of readings for Mass) does not permit us to do selective shopping with God's word. Some days we are faced with concerns we might wish to avoid. Msgr. Andy Cusack of Seton Hall University gave the La Salette Missionaries a retreat many years ago. He left us with the suggestion, "We are invited not to judge others and not to belittle ourselves." Msgr. Cusack's test is this: for thirty days do not say anything negative about your neighbors. If you can do that, you will most likely not say anything negative about yourself either.

Mary's message at La Salette was a positive one. It was about returning to penance, prayer and zeal. Mary gently asked the children, *"Do you say your prayers well?"* There is no privilege to pick and choose. We are called to be missionaries – a people of penance, prayer and zeal. If we are such people, we will be people of right judgment.

Reflection Questions:

• Do you tend to have a negative judgment about other people?
• Why not try the "30 Day Test" outlined above.

Friday, September 17, (#447)
Twenty-Fourth Week in Ordinary Time

Luke 8:1-3: *"(Jesus) made his way through towns and villages preaching and proclaiming the good news of the kingdom of God."*

Meditation:

Brother Juniper once asked St. Francis, "Teach me to preach as eloquently as you. I am not good with words." Francis replied, "I will teach you to preach more eloquently than I. Meet me tomorrow morning." Brother Juniper dutifully met Francis early the next morning. To Juniper's surprise, they began walking. They walked through the marketplace, smiling at the laborers, the merchants, the children. They helped an old woman carry her wash up a set of stairs. They walked and walked. Finally, an exasperated Brother Juniper asked, "Francis, when will you teach me to preach?" Replied the Saint, "Why, we *are* preaching but sometimes we may even need words!"

IN TODAY'S GOSPEL, Jesus invites us to practice what we preach – and to preach what we practice. What did Mary preach at La Salette? Prayer, reconciliation, penance; come to the Lord's table; don't abuse Jesus' name. Mary's homily at La Salette was an "action parable" – a mother weeping over the sins of her children. Action parables are positive gestures without words. Often our actions shine forth better than our spoken words.

Reflection Questions:

• What do you "preach" by the way you live your daily life?
• Do you remember any words or phrases in a sermon or in the scripture that got your attention?

Saturday, September 18, (#448)
Twenty-Fourth Week in Ordinary Time

Luke 8:4-15: *"As for the (seed) in the rich soil, this is people... who... yield a harvest through their perseverance."*

Meditation:

The fact is, in Jesus's depictions of the Kingdom of God, a little goes a long way. A little yeast makes the whole dough rise; a little seed grows into a big tree; a few loaves feed thousands. If we catch onto this dynamic of the way things work with God, we understand the call to perseverance. The lack of signs of success often tempt us to give up. "What's the use? Look at the way the world is! Nothing changes; nothing does any good." But over and over Jesus calls his disciples to persevere. "It was never the big things," he seems to say.

"It was never what you were doing; but what God is doing. Hang in there; keep your eyes fixed on God."

MARY'S PROMISES AT LA SALETTE sound very much like the promise of seed on good ground: stones turned into heaps of wheat and potatoes self-sown in the fields. That sounds a lot like the "hundredfold." So I think, "Maybe submission isn't so different from perseverance." Perhaps we will hear the call to conversion and perseverance throughout our lives. Perhaps that's "all it takes" to be disciples of Jesus!

Some Reflection Questions:

- What helps you "hang in there" when things look dark or useless?
- Have you noticed how God uses small things to bring about great results?

Sunday, September 19, (#134)
Twenty-Fifth Sunday in Ordinary Time

(also the 175th Anniversary of the La Salette Apparition)

(Wisdom 2:12-20; James 3:16-4:3; Mark 9:30-37)

Meditation: *Wisdom from Above*

St. James writes: "The wisdom from above is first of all pure, then peaceable, gentle, compliant, full of mercy and good fruits, without inconstancy or insincerity." How aptly this description applies to the message of Our Lady of La Salette.

It is pure, coming from a heart full of unalloyed love and at the same time speaking the truth "without inconstancy or insincerity."

It is peaceable and gentle: "Come closer, my children, don't be afraid"—and compliant: "Don't you understand, my children? Let me find another way to say it."

It is full of mercy, not only in the words spoken and the tenderness shown to the children, but in the very fact of Mary's coming to us. When in 1851 the Bishop of Grenoble decided to erect a Shrine at La Salette and to found the Missionaries of Our Lady of La Salette, he intended that both would be "a perpetual remembrance, of Mary's merciful apparition."

And history has shown that it is full of good fruits, sometimes in the spectacular form of miraculous healings, more often in the privacy of the confessional. The shrine attracts pilgrims and volunteers from around the world. The La Salette Laity movement has seen ample growth in recent decades.

Christ blessing the children
**by Julius Schnorr von Carolsfeld
(1794–1872)**

Note also the wisdom saying of Jesus to his disciples, "If anyone wishes to be first, he shall be the last of all and the servant of all." Here we see yet another quality that we can attribute also to the Beautiful Lady.

The Queen of Heaven came to us in all simplicity, not to impose her authority but to serve her people by drawing them to be their best Christian selves and become once again a people of faith and fidelity.

A few weeks ago we read the words of Moses, encouraging the people to observe the law carefully, "for thus will you give evidence of your wisdom and intelligence to the nations, who will hear of all these statutes and say, 'This great nation is truly a wise and intelligent people.'" Mary at La Salette desires that her people be truly wise in the ways of God.

The more time we spend with her, the more we are enabled to absorb and live her wisdom from above.

Monday, September 20, (#449)
Twenty-Fifth Week in Ordinary Time

Luke 8:16-18: *"No one lights a lamp to cover it with a bowl or to put it under a bed. No, it is put on a lamp stand so that people may see the light when they come in."*

For Your Reflection:

In the "great commissioning" before his Ascension, Jesus told the disciples to "go forth, to teach and to baptize." In order to do that they had to be prepared and so do we. Jesus tells us that we are to be salt and light and leaven. We need the Lord's help in order to actualize that. "Apart from me you can do nothing." Our work is to reflect Christ, the "light of the world."

MARY AT LA SALETTE REMINDS US of our Christian duties. She deeply lamented the lack of enthusiasm for the Gospel that was so prevalent among her people. Prayer and worship are prerequisites for anyone, especially those involved in the Lord's work.

Reflection Questions:

• What type of light are you reflecting to others at this time in your life?
• Are you reflecting or deflecting the light of faith that was enkindled in you in Baptism?

Tuesday, September 21, (#643)
St. Matthew, Apostle and Evangelist

Matthew 9:9-13: *"I came to call not the upright, but sinners."*

Meditation:

Sometimes we have certain expectations even before we meet someone. If they are millionaires, we might expect a person with obviously expensive clothes, an aloof attitude and an inflated self-image. However some of the richest people in the world in reality dress quite casually and are very affable and approachable. The Pharisees had definite expectations about how Jesus would act, with whom he would relate and eat a meal, and so on. Today we hear Jesus pointing out to the Pharisees that their attitudes needed adjusting. They were looking at some people with their own eyes rather than that of God. Jesus saw people – who were judged by some as "unworthy and to be avoided" – as persons who needed his love and forgiveness, much like the sick who need a doctor. The truth was that Jesus "came to call not the upright but sinners."

MARY AT LA SALETTE came, like her Son, to call sinners back to repentance, forgiveness and reconciliation. She was concerned about all her children and their needs, but especially those who had lost their way and needed to be welcomed back into the fold of the Good Shepherd. Her gestures and words were those of a tearful Mother welcoming back her wayward children – and doesn't that include all of us in some way!

Reflection Questions:

- How welcoming are you to those who have fallen away from active faith?
- Do you criticize or look down on them or are you as welcoming and encouraging as Mary at La Salette?

Wednesday, September 22, (#451)
Twenty-Fifth Week in Ordinary Time

Luke 9:1-6: *"... (Jesus) sent them out to proclaim the kingdom of God and to heal."*

Meditation:

As Christians, our reference point regarding God is Christ. Valiant men and women who believed in the power and in the name of God's Son have handed down the Christian faith to us. The power of Christ's Resurrection has generated believers of every race and way of life. We should be thankful for all that God has done for us through these early missionaries of Word and Witness.

MARY AT LA SALETTE reminds us all of what God in his goodness has done for us. "How easily they forget" is a phrase that we often use for people who should know better. Mary's tears at La Salette are definite reminders of God's love and concern incarnate in the Mother of his Son. We too are asked to go forth and preach and teach as Jesus did. And like Mary we too are to remind others of God's goodness to ourselves.

Reflection Questions:

- Do you realize that the Church is basically missionary in nature? Do you support those who go too far away places to witness to the faith?
- How do you share your own faith with others?

Thursday, September 23, (#452)
Twenty-Fifth Week in Ordinary Time

Luke 9:7-9: *"So who is this (person) I hear such reports about?"*

Meditation:

Religion writers speak about a growing disinterest in "denomination-alism." That term basically refers to the many brands of Christianity. The problem these days is that increasing numbers of people don't really care what denomination they belong to. Many change from one to another with increasing frequency. Herod, in our Gospel passage today, is interested in Christ because he was unique and not like the others. A generic, "feel good" Christianity is not what Jesus came to announce.

OUR LADY OF LA SALETTE lamented indifference in religion and especially within the Catholic Church in regard to practices in prayer and worship. When we think of France in the 19th century we see a country where at least a majority of the people were baptized. But even then there were many "unchurched" and lapsed members. Coming to know, love and serve God is a genuine vocation.

Reflection Questions:

- How genuine is your commitment to the Catholic faith?
- Can you speak intelligently about it?

Friday, September 24, (#453)
Twenty-Fifth Week in Ordinary Time

Luke 9:18-22: *"'But you,' he said to them, 'who do you say I am?' It was Peter who spoke up. 'The Christ of God,' he said."*

Meditation:

Our lives as believers are a continuous "proclamation of faith." We are expected to witness to Christ whether "convenient or inconvenient." The profession of faith in Jesus as Messiah and Lord on Peter's lips is also our own. We are often challenged by the voices of this world to proclaim our faith. The martyrs do this eloquently. They are beacons of strength for us who can be so weak. Through the Holy

Spirit we are taught what to say and how we are to say it. Christ promises us that even our adversaries will not be able to refute us. Remember the most effective Christians are those who are committed to the cause of truth. The Church holds up for us great saints to give us an example of heroic virtue in the face of difficulties.

OUR LADY OF LA SALETTE spoke and wept about the way we miss living out our faith. She lamented our indifference to the life-giving sacraments of salvation. How sad indeed if we forget how to pray to the very Source and Center of our existence.

Reflection Questions:

• Who do you say that Jesus is? How do you show this in the way you live?
• From your life and actions, would anyone suspect that you are a Christians?

Saturday, September 25, (#454) Twenty-Fifth Week in Ordinary Time

Luke 9:43b-45: *"You must have these words constantly in mind: The Son of man is going to be delivered into the power of men."*

Meditation:

There is something innate in us, which wants to have everything go our way, according to our plans. Simon Peter, for one, had other plans for Christ. Jesus, we are told, "remonstrated" with him. In other words, he showed Simon that he was wrong about his perceived goals. The prophet Isaiah says: "'...for my thoughts are not your thoughts and your ways are not my ways', declares Yahweh. For the heavens are as high above earth as my ways are above your ways, my thoughts above your thoughts"* (Isaiah 55:8-9). God sees the big picture and His will is always for our continued growth and sanctity. We may not appreciate our own plans not being fulfilled but God's plans always seem to carry a blessing.

OUR LADY AT LA SALETTE asks us to go a different course. She asks that we be "converted." To leave our former way of life and to seek to live according to God's way is truly revolutionary. To pattern our life after Mary's is a good way to do this. Though Mary cried tears of grief for us at La Salette, they are poignant reminders of how serious and important it is to live according to God's plan.

Reflection Questions:
- Do you resist the Gospel call to repentance?
- How have you come to experience that your greatest good is not necessarily the one you want?

Sunday, September 26, (#137)
Twenty-Sixth Sunday in Ordinary Time
(Num. 11:25-29; James 5:1-6; Mark 9: 38-43, 45, 47-48)

Meditation: *A Collaborative Effort*

Jealousy has two forms. Either we resent not having what someone else has, or we are overly protective of what we do have. The latter case appears in both the first reading and the Gospel

Joshua, jealous for Moses' sake, wanted to stop Eldad and Medad from prophesying. John wanted to reserve to a select group, of which he was a member, the power to cast out demons. Neither Moses nor

Jesus takes that restrictive approach. The one says, "Would that all the people of the Lord were prophets! Would that the Lord might bestow his spirit on them all!" The other says, "Whoever is not against us is for us."

It is hard to imagine two New Testament writers more different than Paul and James. As forceful as Paul can sometimes be in chastising errant Christians, you will find in his letters nothing quite as ferocious as today's text from

Jesus heals boy possessed with demon from the book *The Very Rich Hours of the Duke of Berry*

James.

Is one more "for Christ," or more inspired, than the other? By no means. God is not held to account for the choices he makes in the distribution of his gifts.

We see the same thing at La Salette. Mary chose Mélanie and Maximin. We don't know why. She chose a place that was, and still is, not easily accessible. She said things that no one would have expected from the Mother of God. The choices were hers to make.

But it doesn't stop there. The Missionaries who were founded to spread her message and serve her pilgrims struggled to find their way and their place in the Church. They were not, and still are not, chosen for their perfections. The same may be safely said of La Salette Sisters, and La Salette Laity.

The preaching of the Gospel is a collaborative effort. In 1 Corinthians, Paul uses the analogy of the body for the Church, where each member needs all the others.

There is a Polish hymn for children with the words: "Tall ones, short ones, fat ones, thin ones—they can all be saints—just like me and just like you." We can expand the list to include every personality type, culture, level of education, and so on. Together we make up the whole Church, and it as Church that we are able, through the variety of our members, to be, in Christ, with no jealousy, all things to all people.

Monday, September 27, (#455) Twenty-Sixth Week in Ordinary Time

Luke 9:46-50: *"Anyone who welcomes this little child in my name welcomes me."*

Meditation:

Jesus had a great love for all people and especially for little ones. This famous scene often read at Baptismal celebrations shows Jesus welcoming the little children and telling the elders not to hinder them in their coming to Christ. As the Lord aligned himself with the lowly and the poor we are called to look upon all life as coming from God. In a world where many deny the very existence of God it takes much courage to proclaim his view of things. To welcome children is a great privilege. How important it is to transmit the faith to our youth!

MARY APPEARED AT LA SALETTE to two children. Of all possible messengers to communicate her words to the world, she chose unlikely candidates, poorly schooled and unconnected. Once again we see God's wisdom as very different from our own.

Reflection Questions:

- What is your attitude towards young people?
- Do you engage them in conversation and good example?

Tuesday, September 28, (#456) Twenty-Sixth Week in Ordinary Time

Luke 9:51-56: *"They went into a Samaritan village to make preparations for him, but the people would not receive him because he was making for Jerusalem."*

Meditation:

REJECTION IS ONE OF THE MOST PAINFUL HUMAN EXPERIENCES. This can happen in interpersonal relationships; it can happen when one is overlooked for promotion at work. We are told in the Scriptures that the Messiah would be rejected. We should all be appreciative of the fact that "by his stripes we are healed." Through the Lord's sufferings, his passion and death, we are redeemed. He suffered in his own innocent body for us! No greater love has anyone than one who "lays down his life for his friends."

MARY CRIED AT LA SALETTE because the Gospel of her Son was being rejected, in fact, by the way people lived. Indifference and apathy towards religion was the rule of the day. If Christ has laid down his life for us how can we continue to be so unloving toward God?

Some Reflection Questions:

- How does it make you feel when you are rejected in one way or another?
- Can you identify with Christ and his mother who also have seen their love and concern for us rejected?

Wednesday, September 29, (#647)
Sts. Michael, Gabriel
and Raphael, Archangels

John 1:47-51: *"Jesus replied (to Nathanael), 'In all truth I tell you, you will see heaven open and the angels of God ascending and descending over the Son of man.'"*

Meditation:

The word, *angel*, is derived from the Latin, *angelus*, meaning "messenger" and is indeed seen as a messenger of God. Our feast of the Archangels, Sts. Michael, Gabriel and Raphael, reminds us of God's protection of us, a mystical presence based on our belief that God oversees and guides us through the journey of life. In fact, many of us can point out people in our lives who, in one way or another, also do exactly that – watch over us lovingly.

In our gospel for this feast, we hear about Nathanael, who is described as "a genuine Israelite". The contemporary etymology of the name *Israel* was "one who sees God." He is promised a vision of heavenly things, and told that he will see "the angels of God ascending and descending over the Son of man."

At La Salette, Mary was sent to share her message with us. Yet we know that Mary could only be bringing the message of her Son, Jesus, and not her own. She had angelic qualities but was a very real human being who concern was expressed so touchingly in her gentle tears for her wayward and oftentimes ungrateful children. On this feast of the Archangels, we give thanks to God for watching over us on our journey back to the Father. We need to listen to the words of our Heavenly Messenger at La Salette and fulfill her mandate to make know her message of reconciliation to all her people, whenever the opportunity offers itself.

Reflection Questions:

- How has God protected you during your lifetime?
- Who has God placed in your life to watch over you?

Thursday, September 30, (#458)
Twenty-Sixth Week in Ordinary Time

Luke 10:1-12: *"But whenever you enter a town and they do not make you welcome, go out into its streets and say, 'We wipe off the very dust of your town that clings to our feet, and leave it with you.'"*

Meditation:

The work of evangelization is the work of the Church and all believers. To announce the Good News of Jesus Christ is the work entrusted to us. Where Christ has been preached well, the faith is firmly planted in the minds and hearts of the people. Conversely where Christ has not been presented well, the faith is weak. Receiving Christ is what our faith is all about. We receive Christ in both Word and Sacrament. In turn we are expected to give as a gift what we have so freely received.

THE REALITY OF CHURCH LIFE in Nineteenth Century France formed the context for Mary's apparition at La Salette. The indifference of the people to organized religion left much to be desired. The message of Mary's lament and challenge are relevant today as well. When Saint John Paul II went on one of his first trips to France, he asked, "France, eldest daughter of the Church, have you forgotten your baptismal vows?" That question could be addressed to many other nations and individuals as well.

Reflection Questions:

- Do you receive Christ into your heart on a daily basis?
- How do you or can you evangelize your family, your workplace or even your parish?

Friday, October 1, (#459)
Twenty-Sixth Week in Ordinary Time

Luke 10:13-16: *"Anyone who listens to you listens to me; anyone who rejects you rejects me, and those who reject me reject the one who sent me."*

Reflection:

OUR CONNECTION WITH GOD is called "religion". Its Latin root means "to tie or bind." We are "bound" to God by hearing the Word of God and keeping it. In a world of many voices we have chosen to follow Christ's voice. We do not always reflect that in our daily dealings with people. Remember the Jewish elder in the Old Testament who simply said, "As for me and my house, we will serve the Lord." That should also be our response in the midst of all that the world seems to be saying.

MARY APPEARED IN AN OUT-OF-THE-WAY PLACE AT LA SALETTE. It was more a home to wild flowers, breathtaking scenery, sheep and cattle, than a home to humans. It was there that the Mother of Christ engaged and challenged "her children" to listen to the voice of God. Mary's tears are a result of earthly voices distracting the "other worldly." One of the Psalms in the Bible says, "If today you hear His voice, harden not your hearts." God's voice is all around us. We need to learn to hear it and then listen to it.

Some Reflection Questions:

- How is the voice of the Lord not being heeded in your town or city?
- Can Christ be rejected even by "his own" within the fold?

Saturday, October 2, (#650)
The Holy Guardian Angels

Matthew 18:1-5,10: "... *unless you change and become like little children you will never enter the kingdom of Heaven.*"

Meditation:

There is an undeniable quality in infants. They instantly catch people's attention; they make even the sternest adult smile; they perhaps bring us back to the innocence and purity of life. New parents do not hesitate to sacrifice much for their newborns, including sleep deprivation, doing almost anything for their children. They will literally give their life to protect them. In the bible, God's care and protective presence is expressed well in the Old Testament when an angel visits Abraham just before he sacrifices his firstborn son, Isaac (Genesis 22:11 ff.) and an angel appears to Moses in the burning bush (Exodus 3:2). In the New Testament, Zechariah is told by the angel, Gabriel, that his wife of advanced years will bear a son (Luke 1:13). Gabriel also visits Mary to announce that she will become the mother of the *"Son of the Most High"* (Luke 1:31). We as Catholics believe in God's protection being expressed in each person's guardian angel, someone who protects and guides them.

It is absolutely remarkable that Mary chose, in particular, Maximin and Melanie to be the sole witnesses of the apparition. Certainly if we were to choose two children to be the bearers of Mary's message of "good news" for all her people to hear, it probably would not have been these two uncatechized, unchurched "Catholics in name only". Yet in the wisdom of God, their quiet Saturday morning on a mountaintop in the French Alps was anything but ordinary. Yet, in looking back at their actual experiences following this heavenly event, these children certainly responded with the directness and intelligence that wouldn't be expected of the most astute adult. It can be stated that they were being led through their most challenging interrogations and tests by the hand of God, by the presence of their Guardian Angels. They were heatedly questioned, bribed, cajoled and derided, yet they remarkably stood their ground, and never departed from the truth of the initial central points of Mary's message.

Reflection Questions:

- When have you felt the presence of God leading you, guiding you through some very challenging situations?
- Have you heard of similar situations in the life of others?
- Have you thanked God lately for God's ever-present protection?

Sunday, October 3, (#140)
Twenty-Seventh Sunday in Ordinary Time
(Gen. 2:18-24; Hebrews 2:9-11; Mark 10:2-16)

Meditation: *Questions*

Long before Moses, God said: "It is not good for the man to be alone." And so, he crowned the work of his creation with what poet John Milton called "heaven's last, best gift," woman.

Long after Moses, some Pharisees asked Jesus a question about di-

vorce, to which they already knew
the answer. He then posed a question of his own, to which he already
knew the answer. Then he looked
beyond the Law to the gift, and
gave a response that was far from
legalistic: "What God has joined
together, no human being must
separate."

The questions of the Beautiful Lady
of La Salette follow this pattern.
When she asked the children if they
said their prayers, she surely knew
they seldom prayed. They answered
no when she asked if they had ever

Jesus blessing little children
from The story of the Bible
from Genesis to Revelation

seen blighted wheat, but she herself reminded Maximin that indeed
he had.

Some of the earliest accounts of the La Salette event put the questions at the beginning, or rephrase elements of the message in question form. One version, from September 29, 1846, just ten days after
the Apparition, attributes various questions to the Blessed Virgin:
Don't you have enough to eat? Is there much wheat this year? Do you
[Maximin] remember when your father took you to the market? Do
you hear people blaspheming the Holy Name? Do you serve God and
say your morning and evening prayers?

It also seems that Maximin, barely 11 years old and an inquisitive
child himself, was struck by the Lady's questions, and would sometimes start with those when he was interrogated about the event.

Jesus often asked questions not only of his adversaries but also of
his disciples. At La Salette, however, we do not find the adversarial
context of today's Gospel story. Mary's purpose was, ever so gently,
to teach the children, and us, humbly and gratefully to acknowledge
God's presence in our life.

La Salette continues to question us, not only in the direct question
about our prayer but, in many subtle ways, about the depth and sincerity and the concrete living out of our Christian commitment.

281

All this goes well beyond legal concerns, looking beyond the law to the gift. What gift?

Monday, October 4, (#461)
Twenty-Seventh Week in Ordinary Time

Luke 10:25-37: *"Master, what must I do to inherit eternal life?"*

Meditation:

Our questions can have many meanings. Sometimes we question (challenge) authority or we question (doubt) another's sincerity or we question (inquire about) a motive. Sometimes a question is a test and really an effort to confuse the other, as the lawyer was attempting to do to Jesus here. And sometimes a question is really a statement, like Jesus's, *"Which of these three was the real neighbor?"* Jesus is saying that true Life is found in loving, and not in accumulating money or knowledge or by observing religious or social regulations. Indeed, prostitutes and tax collectors are among the first to enter the Kingdom. Why? Because they can love by squandering precious ointment or by giving back four-fold what they have stolen. Many of the rest of us just talk about love by asking many questions.

"Do you say your prayers well, my children?" A question from Mary at La Salette. Another question, *"Have you ever seen spoilt wheat?"* It's obvious that Mary is not looking for information here. She is trying to direct our attention to the fact that the Everlasting is aware of our life here and now and that Everlasting Life invigorates our earthly existence through prayer. Sharing in the Eucharist, keeping holy the Lord's Day, respecting the name of the Lord, observing the practices of Lent, saying at least an *Our Father* and a *Hail Mary* – these can all be an opportunity to pause and reflect, thereby becoming an invitation to do the loving thing.

Reflection Questions:

- Do you ask your "life questions" to the Lord?
- How can you live as a Christian disciple today?

Tuesday, October 5, (#462)
Twenty-Seventh Week in Ordinary Time

Luke 10:38-42: *"Mary ... sat down at the Lord's feet and listened to him speaking."*

We believe that doing the loving thing is the real ticket that gains admission to the Kingdom of God. Martha and Mary have gained Gospel fame over the centuries because they have helped distinguish between active and contemplative prayer, between the apostolic and contemplative consecrated lifestyles, or they have highlighted the legitimacy of different temperaments serving the Lord.

However, the real contrast here is not between activity and inactivity. Both Martha and Mary are doing something. One is busy about the matters of meal preparation and hospitality while the other is busy about the activity of listening and hospitality. And Jesus said that Mary has chosen the better portion. Why? This same Lord said elsewhere that whoever listens to the word of God and keeps it is true mother, brother and sister. Mary is very active in listening to her Lord. She is learning from him. She is doing heart-to-heart hospitality. She is seated at the feet of the Lord learning what "doing the loving thing" might mean for her.

WE KNOW THAT MARY, the mother of the Lord, listened well. She kept the word of her prayer and the word of her experience and *"pondered them in her heart"*. At La Salette, she continues to ponder as she listens to God and listens to the struggles and the suffering of her children. The result is tears and pleading, *"How long a time do I suffer for you... and as to you, you take no heed of it... I am compelled to pray to him without ceasing."* Yes, Mary is "doing the loving thing" for us and, like Martha's sister in the Gospel story, she has a direct connection to the heart of the Lord.

Reflection Questions:

- What are some of the ways that you listen to the word of God?
- What proportion of a typical day do you spend listening to God? What proportion do you spend in "doing things" for him?

Wednesday, October 6, (#463)
Twenty-Seventh Week in Ordinary Time

Luke 11:1-4: *"When Jesus had finished, one of his disciples said, 'Lord, teach us to pray.'"*

Meditation:

I wish I knew which disciple made this request of the Lord. That disciple was obviously close enough to Jesus to observe him at this very special activity. There must have been something attractive and compelling in observing Jesus in prayer. This disciple was moved to want the same thing. This disciple wanted the same peace, courage, strength, conviction, and clarity of vision and mission displayed by Jesus. This disciple was quite sure those gifts were granted in prayer. So, this disciple asks, *"Lord, teach us to pray."* In response, we were given the Lord's Prayer – an inexhaustible, life-long way to approach God in prayer. This disciple should be honored by all generations as the Patron Saint of Prayer.

"AH, MY CHILDREN, *you must be sure to (say your prayers) well, evening and morning, even if you say only an Our Father and a Hail Mary."* With this very simple and doable request, our Blessed Mother is giving us a formula for peace that will last a lifetime: God is our Father; his Name and Will are supreme; he is involved in our earthly lives (daily bread); a relationship with him means both giving and receiving forgiveness; and our faith assures our ultimate triumph over any adversity. In saying the *Hail, Mary*, we are taking literally Mary's words at La Salette. *"I am compelled to pray to (my Son) without ceasing."* Yes, she will be supporting us in that prayer at the two most important times of our lives – now, and at the hour of our death.

Reflection Questions:

• Where is your "certain place" to pray?
• Standing with Melanie and Maximin, let yourself hear the question, "Do you say your prayers well, my children?"

Thursday, October 7, (#464)
Twenty-Seventh Week in Ordinary Time

Luke 11:5-13: *"If you then, evil as you are, know how to give your children what is good, how much more will the heavenly Father give the Holy Spirit to those who ask him!"*

Meditation:

Our First World parents indulge their children in the excesses of consumerism such as have never before been seen. Yet we quickly see that such "good things" in themselves do not assure happiness. Certainly the "good things" of food, drink, clothing and shelter are necessary, but not worth the loss of our souls (Luke 12:18-19). For the Rich Man, they became the source of condemnation because he would not share with Lazarus at his door (Luke 16:25). However, we do know of loving and conscientious parents who would willingly sacrifice themselves to assure that their children have the necessities of life. "How much more" will the heavenly Father give? Luke says that he will give the Holy Spirit who assures intimacy with God as Father, a knowledge of his Will, and a desire to see a flourishing of his Kingdom. This Holy Spirit is given to those who ask, seek and knock. This same Holy Spirit is our eternal life.

LIKE MOST OF US, Maximin's father was a good person and a sinner. In the face of famine and deprivation, he would give his son his last piece of bread. Most probably he would have gone on to curse God and the famine when it came. But something happened. His scatter-brained son said that the Beautiful Lady mentioned him. The "farm at Coin" incident spoke of God's presence to a seemingly insignificant expression of fatherly love. This changed Mr. Giraud's life. He was given the Holy Spirit of conversion. He went to confession, went to Mass, and received Holy Communion for the first time in years. He was to do so every day for the rest of his life.

Reflection Questions:

•When and how have you asked for the Holy Spirit?
•How might you do so today?

Friday, October 8, (#465)
Twenty-Seventh Week in Ordinary Time

Luke 11:15-26: *"Anyone who is not with me is against me; and anyone who does not gather in with me throws away."*

Meditation:

Jesus declares himself to be the stronger one, the finger of God who casts out devils, the one in whose Sacred Heart the reign of God is found; and he rejects Beelzebul or any other source of spiritual or material power. And he asks us to choose. It's the choice of discipleship, a choice wherein we hear the words of Saint Paul, *"All things are yours... and you are Christ's and Christ is God's"* (1 Corinthians 3: 21-23). The vast sweep of vision contained in this verse reflects a direct line of order, a sense of possession and ownership that says our true meaning and purpose in life is in Jesus Christ, and no devil, no power for evil, can destroy the unity of that relationship. Vatican II would say it this way: "Jesus Christ is the goal of human history, the focal point of the longings of history and of civilization, the center of the human race, the joy of every heart, and the answer to all its yearnings" [*Gaudium et Spes*, 45].

"**IF MY PEOPLE WILL NOT SUBMIT**" begins Our Lady's plea at La Salette, urging us to seek the Lord while he may be found – in all places, at all times, and in all seasons. We certainly will find him in keeping holy the Lord's Day, in reverencing his Holy Name, and in sharing devoutly in the sacramental life of the Church. And we certainly find him in our sensitive and dutiful citizenship among the People of God, where famine, disease and the abuse of children scream for our attention and our efforts to build social and political structures that are just and equitable for all.

Reflection Questions:

- What problems do you find particularly vexing and challenging in your life of service to God and God's people? What can you do about them?
- Think of someone you know who needs God's help. Can you pray that God may help them today?

Saturday, October 9, (#466)
Twenty-Seventh Week in Ordinary Time

Luke 11:27-28: *"More blessed still are those who hear the word of God and keep it!"*

Meditation:

The quality of our discipleship needs constant attention. Parents are told at the baptism of their child that their word and example are essential for that baby to grow and "bring the dignity" of the new creation, symbolized by the white garment "unstained into the everlasting life of heaven." Similarly, they are given a lighted candle with these words: "Parents, this light is entrusted to you to be kept burning brightly." And so it is that many conscientious and loving parents embark on the grandest of vocations: to make their child's heart a most worthy and fertile receptacle for the seed of God's word. Those of us who have been blessed with such faith-filled parents can exclaim with the woman in today's Gospel passage, *"Blessed is the womb... !"*

But the burden of responsibility one day is passed on to another. Each of us reaches the point where we must discern for ourselves. Blessed as we have been with a Christian upbringing, we must see ourselves as a new creation, clothed in Christ. It is ultimately the daily routine of faithful obedience and the challenge of doing God's word today that deepens the light of Christ shining in our lives.

"FOR HOW LONG A TIME DO I SUFFER FOR YOU." Mary is all too aware that the white garments of our Baptism have been soiled and our candles are often flickering. Thus, her tears flow. She knows that we have the capacity to give love and to receive love. She has seen us do it before. This is the "submission" to which she calls us. She has not given up on us. In fact, the purpose of her visit is to remind us that hearing the word of God and keeping it begins with honoring the Name of God and the Lord's Day. She can't do it for us, but she can remind us of what to do. And she prays for us without ceasing.

Reflection Questions:

• Do you tend to be smug in your religious pedigree, rather than

perform the acts proper to discipleship?
•What will hearing the word of God and keeping it mean for you concretely today?

Sunday, October 10, (#143)
Twenty-Eighth Sunday in Ordinary Time

(Wisdom 7:7-11; Hebrews 4:12-13; Mark 10:17-30)

Meditation: *Accounting*

The Letter to the Hebrews reminds us: "Everything is naked and exposed to the eyes of him to whom we must render an account." Yes, we know there will be a time of judgment, just as we know we will die some day, but we prefer not to dwell on these things.

In finance, accounting includes a report on income and expenses. But how is that report to be evaluated? By comparing it to the budget. That is the criterion for determining fiscal health.

Our brief text from Hebrews sums up the "budget" with the expression, "the word of God." We will be judged by our lived response to God's word.

Our Lady of La Salette points to the "budget" by her allusions to the commandments, which most Christians think of as the first criteria for the account we must render to God. Most of us memorized them as children; I still remember a sung version I learned in elementary school in the 1950's!

Needle's Eye by **Edwin W. Rice (1881)**

But the word of God is much more than the Ten Commandments. Wisdom is preached as the ultimate goal in much of the Old Testament, the highest expression of God's word, the best teacher in God's ways. Her praises are sung in our first reading.

In the New Testament, the criteria for our account are too numerous to count. The sermon on the Mount comes immediately to mind, especially the beatitudes. Today's Gospel teaches about the danger of being overly attached to material wealth.

Solomon states: "I pleaded, and the spirit of wisdom came to me." In 1 Kings 3: 11-12, God congratulates him for not asking for long life, riches, etc., but for discernment to know what is right. So God gives him what he asked for.

Underlying all these texts is a desire to know God's will so as to carry it out. It was the lack of this desire that our Mother Mary observed among her people, and she came to La Salette in the hope of opening their ears to God's word, their eyes to God's work, and their hearts to God's will.

Only in this way can we commit ourselves to living a Christian life and be ready to plan our "budget" in view of the final accounting.

Monday, October 11, (#467)
Twenty-Eighth Week in Ordinary Time

Note: Today you may wish to begin the First Day of the Novena to Our Lady of La Salette, in the appendix of this book.

Luke 11:29-32: *"For just as Jonah became a sign to the people of Nineveh ... , so will the Son of man be a sign to this generation."*

Meditation:

The Ninevites heard the preaching of Jonah and saw something of God. They believed! The queen of the South heard about the wisdom of Solomon and saw something of God. She believed! Our present generation is given Jesus, the Son of Man. Do we believe? We are told, *"Philip, he who sees me sees the Father"* (John 14:9). We ask, *"Lord, when did we see you, give you to drink, care for you?"* We are told, *"Each time you did it to the least of my brothers and sisters, you did it to me"* (Matthew 25:40). The words quoted from today's Gospel were spoken by Jesus on his way to Jerusalem. Later, he would weep at the sight of the Holy City, because the people did not believe, and his efforts to keep those he loved from destroying themselves went for naught. *"When*

Jesus had come near, and when he saw the city, he wept over it. 'Would that even today,' he said, 'you recognized the things that would give you peace! But, as it is, they are hidden from your eyes ... because you did not recognize the day when God visited you'" (Luke 19:41-44).

"**COME NEAR, MY CHILDREN.** *Do not be afraid. I am here to tell you Great News.*" Mary, at La Salette, in true discipleship, continues the mission of Jesus. She weeps over our callousness and insensitivity to the things of God. She weeps with powerlessness in preventing the disasters and calamities that our greed and blindness will bring upon us. Yet, she speaks *Shalom (Peace).* She is visiting in the name of God. She is doing her Son's work. She speaks in his name, "*If my people will not submit... Six days have I given you to labor, the seventh I have kept for myself; and they will not give it to me.*" The Great News that Mary announces is the glorious, brilliant cross of her Son next to her heart. In paschal power, Christ will save us, not abandon us.

Reflection Questions:

• It is said that the blind and the deaf do not know what they are missing. What can we say of those who are spiritually blind and deaf?
• Do you know someone struggling with their faith or other challenges. Why not pray for them today?

Tuesday, October 12, (#468)
Twenty-Eighth Week in Ordinary Time

Luke 11:37-41: *"Give alms from what you have and, look, everything will be clean for you."*

Meditation:

Writing a check can give us a new lease on life. Almsgiving, when it originates within us – close to our hearts – is an act of faith and religion that connects us ever more closely to God. Why? Because it springs from an awareness of the other – outside ourselves – who has less than we: the poor, whom we are called to serve in imitation of Jesus. Almsgiving happens only when we can open hands and hearts and part with the money and material goods to which by nature we tend to cling. Now that's miraculous!

THE BEAUTIFUL LADY OF LA SALETTE seems to offer another route to God. Honor God's name, keep his day holy, live your sacramental and prayer life devoutly and you will see *the stones and rocks become mounds of wheat and the potatoes... self-sown in the fields.*" Then the poor, the sick and dying, and the hungry will be served. But almsgiving achieves the same end. Serve the poor with your heart, share with those who have nothing, and you will be honoring God and blessing his life-giving name. *"The commandment we have heard from him is this: those who love God must love their brothers and sisters also"* (1 John 4:21).

Reflection Questions:

- What causes or needs successfully prompt your almsgiving?
- When was the last time you gave alms to the poor?

Wednesday, October 13, (#469) Twenty-Eighth Week in Ordinary Time

Luke 11:42-46: *"Alas for you Pharisees! ... Alas for you lawyers as well!"*

Meditation:

"Stop it! Cut it out! Think about what you're doing!" This is what "woe!" means. Jesus is objecting to the neglect of central commands – the heart and meaning of the Law – while the details and externals are being lifted high on the public altar of observance. The term "pharisaic" comes from these verses in Luke. It refers to those who wash their outsides but not their insides, who tithe even a tenth of their garden herbs, but neglect justice, who love praise and attention and who load people down with burdensome religious demands. We act in that way when our service or worship comes from a desire to be seen rather than from a pure heart and out of love for others. People may sometimes be fooled, but God isn't. Our discipleship must be sincere. By bringing our inner life under God's control, our outer life will naturally reflect him.

"IN THE WINTER, WHEN THEY DO NOT KNOW WHAT TO DO, *they go to Mass only to mock at religion.*" This is Mary's way of saying, "Stop it!" Have we lost touch so much with the heart and meaning of Eucharist that our very presence at Mass can be construed as mockery at religion? Yet, that can indeed be what is happening if our presence in church is for show or based on externals or if our charity is limited to what we put in the collection basket. Only two persons can answer that question: God and ourselves. We know what discipleship calls us to be: salt, light, leaven. That is the purpose and meaning of our religion and its practices.

Reflection Questions:

- How and why is the Lord asking you to "Stop it!" today?
- How do you express righteous indignation in your ministry, work or relationships?

Thursday, October 14, (#470)
Twenty-Eighth Week in Ordinary Time

Luke 11:47-54: *"And that is why the Wisdom of God said, 'I will send them prophets and apostles; some they will slaughter and persecute.'"*

Meditation:

God sends prophets as mouthpieces into human history to touch our hearts, to shape our thinking, to help us to see the evil of the day, to call us back. Prophets never have an easy time of it. The eternal truth of the gifts of life and grace does not change, while the reality of sin, which separates us from God, has many guises. The mission of the prophet is to call the Word of God to bear upon sin in any age. Prophet and people share a dynamic relationship. Some scribes and lawyers in Jesus's audience prefer a religion of their own making. They prefer to control their people by the manipulations of tenets and regulations that make God's truth hard to understand and practice. Jesus presents himself here as more than just a human prophet. He is the very Word of God and is directly revealing God's message. They reject both him and the message.

MARY COMES AS A PROPHET at La Salette. The first sight of her reveals a woman dressed in the garb of the day, seated, weeping, her face in her hands. Her words of greeting, *"Come near, my children. Do not be afraid. I am here to tell you great news,"* melt any fear in the children and remove any defensiveness in us as we listen. Mary wants to talk to us and *with* us. She engages in dialogue, asks questions, chides gently. As a prophet, she speaks for God with the message that he knows about our life and struggles and that he is closer to us than we realize. It is a message we need to hear.

Reflection Questions:

- How are you called to be a prophet? How are you called to speak up or speak out in various situations?
- Have you (or anyone you know) ever been persecuted for being a prophet?

Friday, October 15, (#471)
Twenty-Eighth Week in Ordinary Time

Luke 12:1-7: *"To you, my friends, I say: Do not be afraid."*

Meditation:

Today's gospel passage says "a crowd of thousands had gathered, so dense that they were treading on one another." It's easy to imagine that pushing, tugging mob pressing on Jesus as his inspiration for talking about the number of hairs on one's head and flocks of sparrows. In the midst of that scene, Jesus speaks consoling words, *"I say to you who are my friends..."* This is the only time in the synoptic gospels that Jesus uses the term "friends" to address his disciples. He is obviously very adept at identifying his disciples. This Jesus who can identify his friends in the midst of a pressing crowd is talking about his Father, who knows each and every sparrow and excels at counting every hair on our heads. All the more reason to trust that he knows our hearts.

"Have you ever seen wheat that is spoiled, my children?" Hair, sparrows, grains of wheat – nothing, apparently, escapes the providential care of God and his Mother. Maximin was shocked by the detail of recollection; even more, his heart, that of his father, and those of all believers of the apparition, are awestruck by God's interest and involvement in even the most insignificant events of our lives. Jesus and Mary both tell us, "Do not be afraid." After this display of providential awareness, we feel that there is nowhere else that we would rather be than standing within that globe of light with our Mother, Mary.

- How and when do I experience fear in my life?
- Does my faith help me deal with my fears?

Saturday, October 16, (#472)
Twenty-Eighth Week in Ordinary Time

Luke 12:8-12: *"Everyone who says a word against the Son of man will be forgiven, but no one who blasphemes against the Holy Spirit will be forgiven."*

Meditation:

This sentence has worried many sincere and conscientious Christians, but it does not need to. Jesus is simply saying that any sin, any sin we can think of in our experience, the experience of others, or even our wildest imaginings, can be forgiven by God if that sin is brought to God. The "unforgivable sin" is a deliberate and ongoing rejection of the Holy Spirit's work and even of God himself. More than just a rejection of Christian preaching or the gospel, this sin is the persistent and obstinate opposition to God himself. A person who has committed this sin has shut himself or herself off from God so thoroughly that he or she is unaware of any sin at all. Jesus is not trying to scare us here nor to inflict doubt into sensitive souls.

BESIDES HER TEARS AND HER PLEAS, the chains Mary wore at La Salette point to the fact that God is not the undisputed Master of the Universe. If God were, we could rightly blame him for the evil around us. No, there is one thing that God cannot do – forgive someone who does not know enough to ask for forgiveness. Mary points to our abuse of her Son's holy name and his holy day as the *"two things which make the arm of my Son so heavy."* But she and her Son cannot infringe on our human freedom and responsibility in responding to God's overtures to loving intimacy with him. *"If they are converted...,"* Mary says. If...

Reflection Questions:

- Where do you find an absence of the sense of God among God's people? What forces have caused this alienation?

• Who do you know who feels alienated from God? Pray for them.

Sunday, October 17, (#146)
Twenty-Ninth Sunday in Ordinary Time

(Isaiah 53:10-11; Heb. 4:14-16; Mark 10:35-45)

Meditation: *Christian Ambition*

Imagine the disappointment of James and John! After they declared their readiness to drink from the same cup and share the same baptism as Jesus, and were assured by Jesus that they would indeed do so, their ambitious request was then denied.

Call of the Sons of Zebedee
by Marco Basaiti (1470–1530)

Ambition is not evil in itself, but it lends itself to selfishness. That is why St. Paul, in 1 Corinthians, when he urges the Christians to strive for the greater gifts, immediately goes on to tell them, with many examples, that the greatest of all the gifts is love.

Maybe this is why Our Lady of La Salette chooses as witnesses simple children who would be less likely to understand the nature of the gift they have received and so less inclined to indulge in vainglory.

Our ambition should be to do our very best in God's service and leave the judgment of our efforts up to him. Mary's visit to La Salette was a sort of "evaluation" of her people. They had come up short. They were far from ambitious for the things of God, and she wanted them to understand the danger they were putting themselves in.

At the same time, she did not wish to discourage them. Her message bids us, in the words of our reading from Hebrews, to "confidently approach the throne of grace to receive mercy and to find grace for timely help."

Jesus teaches his apostles that they must not claim any personal merit in their call. Yes, they have received authority from him, but it is to be exercised in service. Any good they are able to accomplish is no achievement of their own but is God's work.

Whatever hardships we endure are in imitation of our Lord, who came "not to be served but to serve and to give his life as a ransom for many," who, as God's servant, "was tested in every way, yet without sin," and "through his suffering shall justify many."

Psalm 116 contains the lovely verse, "How can I repay the Lord for all the great good done for me?" The next time you stand before a crucifix, remember what the Lord Jesus has done for you. Compare that to what you have done for him. Then answer the Psalmist's question. Be ambitious!

Monday, October 18, (#661) St. Luke, Evangelist

Luke 10:1-9: *"... send laborers to do his harvesting."*

Meditation:

It is amazing but true that none of the four gospels were signed. Later the Church and scholars attributed an author to each, but the writers literally wrote the gospels for the glory of God and not for their own notoriety. Their vocation from Christ was to be his follower. When they were chosen, they were sent "to do (Christ's) harvesting", to bring the good news to all nations, to gather more followers, to spread his message of love, forgiveness and peace. Four of his followers were chosen to write what we today call "gospels (good news)". From what we can gather from his writings (the gospel of Luke and the Acts of the Apostles), Luke was a doctor and friend of Theophilus and of Paul of Tarsus.

AT LA SALETTE, MARY CHOSE THE TWO CHILDREN, MAXIMIN AND MELANIE, TO BECOME DISCIPLES OF HER MESSAGE, sharing it with all who would listen. They were very successful and completed their mission. Then this mission was handed on to the Missionaries of Our Lady of La Salette and, eventually, to all who hear her message. The fact that Mary did not hand her message to Church hierarchy or local dignitaries but to these two poor children and that they were most successful is a testament to the trust Mary places in us who have heard her message. We are all called to be evangelizers of her message, and "doers" of her mission of faith and reconciliation.

Some Reflection Questions:

- From whom did you first hear the message of La Salette?
- Have you ever told the story of La Salette to another? If not, perhaps you should.

Tuesday, October 19, (#474)
Twenty-Ninth Week in Ordinary Time

Luke 12:35-38: *"Blessed those servants whom the master finds awake when he comes."*

Meditation:

Luke scatters his beatitudes like gold dust throughout his gospel. Now he raises readiness and preparation to the level of bliss. He associates "blessed" with the master and servants and his sentence echoes like an Hallelujah chorus. When you prepare for someone's arrival, that person is already present in the preparation. What Jesus seeks is the readiness of a loving presence. The passage concerns the large issues of life and death, bliss and eternal blame. Still, what is involved here is the simple preparedness of serving Jesus in daily responsibilities, caring for the needs of others and hands-on service of those around us.

Standing ready at the door for the Master's arrival means standing ready to change another's sadness into joy. It means a quick greeting, or an enduring presence to another's grief. It means being resolutely silent while listening to another's anguish with ears and heart. Christ points to constancy and consistency, both marks of holiness: but this is not the holiness of Christmas and Easter and peak, solemn moments in our lives. He is pointing to his coming *"in the second and third watch"* where he will find his servant working in the anonymity of the night. Then come words that make the spirit soar, *"Blessed are those servants,"* promising eternal gladness, when the servant will sit down at table and the Master will serve.

OUR LADY'S APRON receives frequent mention in most comments on La Salette. On her, it's more than a decoration or a complement to her dress. At the Annunciation she had told the angel, *"I am the handmaid of the Lord. May it be done to me according to your word."* She is the mother of the Suffering Servant of Yahweh. And she is a watchful servant, always ready to intercede for the people she has been given to serve: *"How long a time I have suffered for you! If my Son will not abandon you, I am obliged to entreat him without ceasing."* The light the children saw on the mountain may have disappeared from view, but she is ever there on that peak, waiting, suffering and weeping on her long watch.

Reflection Question:

- What is the quality of your watching, of your readiness to serve, of your waiting for the Lord?
- What has happened to you recently in which you learned something new about yourself, God or others around you?

Wednesday, October 20, (#475)
Twenty-Ninth Week in Ordinary Time

Luke 12:39-48: *"Blessed that servant if his master's arrival finds him doing exactly that."*

Meditation:

One would think that the Creator of heaven and earth, as well as of all humankind, might know better than to demand fidelity from those he calls to serve. Doesn't he have the whole history of Israel before him? Doesn't he know that the temptation to slip into the easy way out is endemic and almost irresistible to the human biped? He should know, too, that when the master disappears for the longest while, the second in command would snatch up his perks? There must be something precious in this phenomenon of fidelity for God to demand it so completely.

Ultimately, fidelity bespeaks respect for the other, and respect is the first law of love. Fidelity to God, according to this passage also implies fidelity to neighbor: the servants suffer when the one in charge is unfaithful to the Master. This is not a new law; it has always been so, "God neglected" means "people forgotten", or battered and killed. The final statement of this passage: *"Much will be required of the person entrusted with much..."* is arguably the most ignored sentence in the New Testament. People bless the Lord for their gifts but often forget the people for whom these gifts were granted. It is all part of being faithful.

MARY IS ONE OF THOSE to whom much, very much, was given. At La Salette she reminds her people of that very gift which made her pleasing to God. *"If my people will not submit..."* The cornerstone of Mary's spirituality was a sacred obsession with the will of God. At the Annunciation, her response to God's requests has an "of course" ring to it: *"You see before you the Lord's servant, let it happen to me as you have said"* (Luke 1:38). Elizabeth's pregnancy comes as a sign, indeed a summons to Mary, to be by her cousin's side. She goes "in haste." In the gospel of John, at the miracle of Cana, she urges Jesus to perform the miracle, but finally leaves it all to him: *"Do whatever he tells you,"* she advises the servers.

Reflection Questions:

- How has Mary's all-encompassing words, *"Do whatever he tells you,"* been a factor in your life? Do you respond to anyone like that?
- Who is someone who would do *anything* for you? How about giving thanks to God for that wonderful person!

Thursday, October 21, (#476)
Twenty-Ninth Week in Ordinary Time

Luke 12:49-53: *"I have come to bring fire to the earth, and how I wish it were blazing already!"*

Meditation:

The kingdom of God is always spoken of in terms of peace and reconciliation: but that is the kingdom achieved. Meanwhile, there is the question of commitment to Jesus in faith in the Sacrament of Baptism with its promises of life lived concretely in ongoing change and renewal. All this is a bit much for the gravitational pulls of greed and self-interest, with all the forces of consumerism thrown in. There is need for more power in our lives. *"I have come to bring fire to the earth, and how I wish it were blazing already"* says Jesus. This fire could well be the fire of the Holy Spirit, a fire much needed in the soul to live a life of commitment, prayer and self-giving mandated by life in Christ. John the Baptist spoke about *"someone is coming, who is more powerful than me; ... he will baptize you with the Holy Spirit and fire." (Luke 3:16).*

Early in the Acts of the Apostles, when all were gathered in one place, *"there appeared to them tongues as of fire; these separated and came to rest on the head of each of them."* (Acts 2:3). The burden of Christ may be light, but it might also be long lasting, and its light weight comes from the love of him who imposes the burden. The trumpet announcing rescue and deliverance is heard only at the coming of the fires of the Spirit, which makes all tasks and all commitments possible. That Spirit is called the Power, the Advocate, the Fire, the Spirit of truth. In many people's lives that Fire makes all the difference.

THE FIRST THING the children saw of the apparition of La Salette was the light. Then, slowly they discerned the figure of a woman seated within the oval of brightness. It was a light like no other they had seen on earth, a light from heaven, the light of the Resurrection and the fires of Pentecost. The Lady herself was wholly light yet with the appearance of humanity. She came to remind us that the fire of the Resurrection and Pentecost is still with us today to strengthen us for the journey.

Reflection Questions:

• You love the ideal of self-giving excellence in serving Christ. Are you taking the means given to you by Jesus to bring it to reality in your life?
• When have you needed to "read the riot act" (say something seriously) to someone who was acting badly? How did you feel? How did they react to your words of correction?

Friday, October 22, (#477)
Twenty-Ninth Week in Ordinary Time

Luke 12:54-59: *"How is it you do not know how to interpret these times?"*

Meditation:

We won't be judged by the past we have not lived or by the future we have not seen. "The present time" here alludes to the actual presence of Christ, his words and his life. If people are able to foretell the weather, to pontificate about events, and paint the future, they can surely note what Jesus is doing and saying in this "present time," or this kairos. Whatever we think and write concerning our life revolves around one question: is Christ alive or dead? Of course, we say he is alive, which is another word for present among us, as present now as he was when he was asking this famous question two thousand years ago.

This "present time" means a crucial time for me. Practically, it means wide awake awareness of Christ in the world and in my own life, present in prayer, in self-giving, in personal change and conversion, in awareness of others. It means avoiding the idea that this is only a "we" situation, a general, impersonal "present time" situation, not really an "I" or "me" issue or a "here and now" condition. All this may seem severe and unbending but, then again, so is love when the beloved asks, "Do you love me?" The answer has to be "yes," which is the same as choosing between black and white. No one would like to hear a "maybe I love you" here.

OUR LADY'S TEARS TELL US that there is suffering and affection in heaven because there is caring for us there. The Lady says, *"How long have I suffered for you! If my Son is not to cast you off, I am obliged to entreat him without ceasing."* She doesn't say the words "I love you," but she underscores what love always does for the beloved: suffer to preserve the love. La Salette is a *kairos* moment, a time-right now, to decide to be reconciled, to "turn around" in conversion, and to begin in this moment. We must respond to the Beautiful Lady's caring tears and suffering. It is time for us to give a caring response.

Reflection Questions:

- This is your own "present time." How will you respond to the calls of Christ and of Our Lady to "come near?"
- When an opportunity to help someone in need occurs, what is your usual response? Do you act like Jesus would do?

Saturday, October 23, (#478)
Twenty-Ninth Week in Ordinary Time

Luke 13:1-9: *"Sir, ...leave it one more year and give me time to dig round it and manure it."*

Meditation:

A judgment often pronounced on evildoers is that "God will get them for this." We associate God more with punishment than with any measure of leniency. No matter how often Christ may describe himself and the Father as kind and merciful, "filled with everlasting love," as the Psalms endlessly proclaim, still we remember the Christ of the Last Judgment more often than the image of the Good Shepherd. The message in this section is that a sinner should be given more time to put his life together, to repent, as much as a year – a rather undetermined length of time. Maybe Luke remembers what he wrote in an earlier chapter when, quoting Isaiah, Christ spoke of "a year of the Lord's favor," a year of reconciliation and healing.

One of the delights of life is the phenomenon of starting over, beginning anew, turning a new leaf. This poor tree was given a year to flower again and produce fruit. God's compassion goes further than mere leniency; it extends to coming to the aid of the tree, to "dig around it," and "put manure on it." The first five verses clearly say that God is not responsible for the evil in the world, and that he is more responsible for sustenance and restoration than for the destruction of peoples' lives and possessions often attributed to him. One might say about that famous fig tree what Augustine said about original sin: a "happy fault" that should have aroused such forbearance.

THE APPARITION OF LA SALETTE of and by itself is an act of leniency. Even if the Lady had done and said nothing but appear in tears, people would have understood the meaning of her action, that Heaven was steeped in sadness at the sight of what humans do to one another. The gardener of Luke's gospel intercedes for the fig tree and pleads for more time for renewal and repentance, and so does the Lady with her tears. She makes no mention of a year but pointedly reminds her people that "Forever have I suffered for you! If my Son is not to cast you off, I am obliged to entreat him without ceasing."

Reflection Question:

• With the occasion of the Millennium or of a Holy Year in mind, "a year of favor from the Lord," have you given those around you more time to put their lives together, to change, rather than condemning them and dismissing them without further ado?

Sunday, October 24, (#149)
Thirtieth Sunday in Ordinary Time

(Jeremiah 31:7-9; Heb. 5:1-6; Mark 10:46-52)

Meditation: *I Will Bring Them Back*

Healing of the Blind Man
by Carl Bloch (1834–1890)

We have no trouble connecting La Salette with images used in today's responsorial Psalm: "Although they go forth weeping, carrying the seed to be sown, they shall come back rejoicing, carrying their sheaves"— tears (Mary's and her people's) over blighted crops, followed by a promise of abundant harvests.

The context of the Psalm, as also of the first reading, is a vision of God's people returning from exile. This is God's doing. No one is excluded.

The context of La Salette is similar. Christians were living in exile from their own faith. In hard times they had only themselves to count on, and they had proven inadequate to the task. Through the Beautiful Lady, God was offering to bring them back.

The people of Israel were in exile some seventy years. They had ample time to reflect seriously on their apostasy and that of their ancestors. When they were finally allowed to return to their homeland, they were resolved to be faithful to God and worship him alone. They were ready to submit.

At La Salette, Mary says, "I warned you last year with the potatoes. You paid no heed." Like Israel of old, her people failed to understand what was coming. They, too, were in danger of being abandoned. Jesus had been, in the words of the Letter to the Hebrews, "able to deal patiently with the ignorant and erring," but now the time had come when his Mother was "obliged to plead with him constantly."

She spoke of submission, not of a slavish sort, but born of trust. Take the Blind Bartimaeus, for example. He knows he has no special claim on Jesus' attention; he says nothing to those who try to silence him, but continues to cry, "Son of David, have pity on me." Standing before Jesus, he calls him Master.

All of this bespeaks a rightly submissive spirit. He is powerless to change his situation, but believes that Jesus can lead him out of darkness into light.

Our Lady reminds us that we can be brought back from whatever darkness or slavery or exile we may be experiencing. What is required on our part is to recognize our need, and to turn to the Lord with unwavering hope. Then our tongue will be filled with rejoicing.

Monday, October 25, (#479)
Thirtieth Week in Ordinary Time

Luke 13:10-17: " ... *she was bent double and quite unable to stand upright.*"

Meditation:

Luke may have been describing the physical condition of this poor woman's ailment -- but Jesus saw the spiritual malady as well. This woman was carrying, not only her own burdens of life, but the burdens of family who saw her as "just another mouth to feed." She carried the burdens of her society and culture and saw her affliction as a punishment from God for her sins and the sins of her ancestors. The woman was an outcast – stooped and burdened from so many crosses that were not meant for her to carry. Jesus lifted these burdens from her shoulder, *"Woman, you are freed from your disability,"* and he laid on her the one cross that was meant just for her alone. Indeed her one cross was a burden that was easy and a yoke that was light! She is now quite capable of standing erect of walking uprightly with dignity before her God.

MARY ALSO APPEARED badly stooped – a telling symbol of how we see ourselves before God! She appears burdened and imprisoned by chains – our chains of guilt, anxiety, anger and resentment. But she stands up! And in her standing, she appears as the "Beautiful Lady" in all her splendor and light – another wonderful symbol of how God wants us to appear before him. She wears the roses of our dignity. The cross of our salvation shines brightly. It is a symbol of our own cross that is meant just for us to carry. This cross is indeed a burden, but that yoke is easy, that burden is light. That cross is very light: the light of the world, the light of our salvation.

Reflection Questions:

• What are the burdens that make you "quite incapable of standing erect'?" How many years have you been "stooped over" carrying the burdens of anger, resentment, another's guilt? What would happen if you dared lay down those burdens right now'?

• What is your own special cross that God alone has given you to carry?

Tuesday, October 26, (#480)
Thirtieth Week in Ordinary Time

Luke 13:18-21: *"What is the kingdom of God like? What shall I compare it with? It is like..."*

Meditation:

Jesus uses many images to explain what heaven and God are like. Heaven is like a mustard seed or yeast mixed with bread. God is like a shepherd who searches for lost sheep, or a woman searching for a lost coin. Above all, heaven is like a Father yearning for his lost children – a God who comes running to welcome and embrace the one who abandoned him long ago. No mention of a stern, harsh Judge! Not one mention of the demanding Master who "gives us what we really deserve"! Rather there is a lot of rejoicing, gladness and joy over one sinner who dares *"turn away from sin"* and *"believe in the Good News!"*

These stories are about giving up what little we have and receiving much, much more than we give.

At La Salette, Mary also gives us little images of what heaven is like. Heaven is like *"rocks and stones"* turning into *"heaps of wheat."* Heaven is like *"potatoes being self-sown in the fields."* Our God is like a father giving bread to his child. If only we can change our ways! If only we can be converted! Heaven is like a Mother yearning for her children not to run away, but to *"come closer"* and *"not be afraid."* Like Jesus, Mary assures us that, if we repent, there will be *"much joy and rejoicing in heaven."*

Reflection Question:

• Using images from your own life, complete this sentence: "Heaven is like..."
• When did you intensely feel the love of God – in what place did this happen; what people were with you?

Wednesday, October 27, (#481) Thirtieth Week in Ordinary Time

Luke 13:22-30: *"Try your hardest to enter by the narrow door."*

For Your Reflection:

This gospel reminds me of a house that some good friends of mine own. It has a beautiful front door that opens into a brick wall! Years ago, when the house was being constructed, the builders made a mistake and built a wall where the main entrance was supposed to be. But the woman and her husband said to leave it that way. They could use the extra space that would have been taken up by the doorway. Besides, they said, nobody will ever use the front door anyway, beautiful as it is. All their children, friends and family will be using the back door – that's the door that is important! Only those who don't know them – sales people, business people, strangers – will try the front door. And will they be in for a surprise!

Maybe that's why Mary at La Salette was dressed like "one of the folks" of that time. A simple peasant dress, a bonnet, an apron. Her demeanor and attitude tell us that God doesn't want us coming to heaven with pretenses of importance. Nor does God want us to be strangers. We are not worthy of the front door of the kingdom of God! That's only for people with "false fronts." But if we can become God's children, sisters and brothers of Jesus, then we have free access to the back door. Come as you are and enjoy. No need to "dress up." Just bring your own, unique, special gifts and enjoy the potluck, heavenly feast of the kingdom of God.

Reflection Questions:

- What door in your house is used most often?
- When was the last time you felt "at home" with a friend or relative? What does it feel like to be "a guest?"
- Do you have friends or relatives with whom you can simply come and "be yourself?" If you went to heaven today, would you describe yourself as "a stranger?" "a guest" or just "one of the folks"?

Thursday, October 28, (#666) Sts. Simon and Jude, Apostles

Luke 6:12-16: *"(Jesus) summoned his disciples and picked out twelve of them; he called them 'apostles…'"*

Meditation:

Although we may be Catholics from birth, often people get confused about some basic notions of faith. For example, the word "disciple" refers to a "learner" or "follower", of which there were many. The word "apostle" refers to one who is "sent out" of which an initial twelve were named, as in the gospel for today. Simon was called the Zealot because he was a member of a group of Zealots who refused to recognize any foreign power over Palestine. Jude was an actual cousin of Jesus. A tradition states that the two Apostles went to evangelize Armenia and Persia, and that they suffered martyrdom in the city of Suanir in the year 47AD.

MARY AT LA SALETTE also chose people to spread her message: at first, Maximin and Melanie, who shared Mary's message and thereby brought countless pilgrims to the apparition site. And as with Jesus, these initial two children, in turn, caused many others to become "evangelizers" and spread her message. It is simply remarkable that Mary's message is still being spread from person to person, across the face of the earth. At La Salette "her" message was, in fact, the message of her Son, Jesus. She called for daily prayer, making holy the Lord's Day, an active Lenten season and other practices of faith, and reverence for the Name of the Lord. These are some of the basics of our Catholic faith.

Reflection Questions:

- How well do you pray and share your faith with others? Do you encourage others to be active followers of Jesus?
- When was the last time you supported others in their faith?

Friday, October 29, (#483)
Thirtieth Week in Ordinary Time

Luke 14:1-6: *"Is it against the law to cure someone on the Sabbath, or not?"*

Meditation:

Isn't it amazing how a day of rest can turn into a day of guilt? We can become so preoccupied with the legalisms of observing the law that our very observances become a burden and trial to ourselves and to those around us. And, when we become obsessive about the minutiae of the law, we tend to become watchful of the shortcomings of others, rather than our own. The Pharisees observed Jesus closely, trying to "catch him in the act" of breaking the Sabbath law. The Sabbath day was made for us, Jesus would say. We were not made for the Sabbath. When observing the law becomes such an overbearing task, the law needs to be looked at and, possibly, revised. Sometimes we need to get back to simple basics of prayer and rest in order to appreciate fully the benefits of a day of rest.

"I GAVE YOU SIX DAYS TO WORK," says Our Lady speaking on behalf of her Son, *"I kept the seventh for myself, and they will not give it to me."* Perhaps the "they" is not so much the working poor, but the people in power who impose upon the poor so much that they cannot rest on Sunday. Maybe "they" are the employers who hire the young people of today all weekend long, part-time, for a minimum wage. so that there is no time to rest and to be with family. When the standards of our society and culture become burdensome and over-tasking, those standards need to be critiqued and revised so that our Sunday may once again be a "day of rest." Mary is telling us to get back to basics and to take back what belongs to us in the first place.

Reflection Questions:

- Is Sunday a day of rest for you? Or is it simply just another working day?
- Does work keep you away from your loved ones? Do you use your work as an escape from other problems? How can you reclaim Sunday as your day of rest?

Saturday, October 30, (#484)
Thirtieth Week in Ordinary Time

Luke 14:1,7-11: *"My friend, move up higher."*

Meditation:

There is an airline company that prides itself on its "first class" service. When one plans a trip with that airline, one is pleasantly surprised to find that the whole airplane is first class – wide, comfortable, leather seats, champagne, a menu with several choices of nice hot meals served with real napkins and china. Everyone is equal on that plane. Everyone is seen as valuable and served with grace, dignity and respect. I suppose that the folks who expect better treatment than the rest would be a little disappointed at first, while those expecting the minimum would be amazed at the quality of service. That's what Jesus means when he talks about the heavenly banquet. There are no "head tables" in heaven. Everyone is treated equally as a son and daughter of God. Everything is "first class" in heaven. Those who expect better treatment than the rest will be sorely disappointed; those who think they are unworthy of heaven will be amazed at how their dignity is restored and enhanced in God's heavenly kingdom.

MARY CAME TO LA SALETTE to speak to the poorest of the poor – children from broken homes who did not expect better than their lot in life– to remind them that they, as well as all of God's children, are first class citizens in the kingdom of heaven. We are all pearls of great price in the eyes of God, pearls that are not to be tossed to the indignity of bias, prejudice, self-righteousness or belittlement. In God's sight there are no First World or Third World countries. As God secs the world, so should we see each other! Good News, indeed, Good

News worth tell-ing to all God's people!

Reflection Questions:

- What "class" does the world seem to put you in? What "class" do you put yourself in?
- What sort of treatment would you expect if you were in heaven today? Or, do you think that you're not worthy of heaven? Why or why not?

Sunday, October 31 (#152)
Thirty-First Sunday in Ordinary Time

(Deut. 6:2-6; Heb. 7:23-28; Mark 12:28b-34)

Meditation: *The Lord our God*

The Israelites, in Egypt and in Canaan, were surrounded by peoples that worshiped many gods. Moses and the prophets often had to remind them that they had one God only, the Lord.

In Christianity, there is one Savior, Jesus, in whom "all the fullness was pleased to dwell, and through him to reconcile all things for him, making peace by the blood of his cross" (Col. 1:19-20). So, why do we call Our Lady of La Salette Reconciler of Sinners?

She did not take this title to herself. It was given to her by the faithful. They were not theologians, nor were they heretics. They understood, as we do, that Mary is a reconciler by association with the One Reconciler. On the one hand she pleads with him constantly on our behalf; on the other she comes to draw us to him, bearing the supreme symbol of reconciliation on her breast, her crucified Son who, as the Letter to the Hebrews declares, "is always able to save those who approach God through him, since he lives forever to make intercession for them."

The Beautiful Lady ultimately invites us to make our own the words of the Psalmist: "I love you, O Lord, my strength, O Lord, my rock, my fortress, my deliverer, my God, my rock of refuge, my shield, the horn of my salvation, my stronghold!"

Notice in particular the use of the word 'rock.' It is often used as a metaphor for God as the firm foundation of our faith. Jesus used it at the end of the Sermon on the Mount to describe his teaching (Mt 7:24).

Notice also the insistence on the pronoun 'my.' God is not just strength, rock, fortress, etc., in some abstract way, but he is claimed in a personal way. In a similar manner, we call God 'our' Father, and Jesus 'our' Lord and, yes, the Blessed Virgin 'our' Lady.

The same insistence is seen in the 'first of all the Commandments,' cited in the Gospel and in Deuteronomy. "You shall love the Lord your God with all your heart, with all your soul, with all your mind, and with all your strength." Faith is not pure theology, or academic knowledge of Scripture. Unless the faith becomes our faith, my faith, yours too, the most important element is missing.

Monday, Nov 1, (#667)
Feast of All Saints

[not a Holy Day of Obligation this year]

(Revelation 7:2-14; 1 John 3:1-3; Matthew 5:1-12)

Meditation: *Blessed*

A great many of the people who lived in the region around La Salette in 1846 were poor, but they did not feel blessed. Quite to the contrary, as Mary pointed out: *"When you found the potatoes spoiled, you swore, and threw in my Son's name."*

Still, the message of the Beautiful Lady has a lot in common with the Beatitudes. It is addressed to "the meek" in the persons of Maximin and Melanie. In its invitation to reconciliation it calls for *peacemakers.* *"They who hunger and thirst for uprightness,"* can see in Mary's allusions to prayer and Eucharist the need for a right relationship with God. Those who *"mourn"* the loss of children dying *"in the arms of the persons who hold them"* will be *"comforted"* by the image of the Weeping Mother.

Our Lord's Sermon on the Mount is foundational for Christian life. It is a source of both challenge and encouragement. The Beatitudes in particular are, as the rest of the Sermon makes clear, a sort of rule of life. The unnamed multitude of saints whom we celebrate today lived by that rule.

OUR LADY'S MESSAGE on another mountain serves as echo and reminder of our Lord's Sermon. The crucifix she wears reminds us also of his sacrifice offered out of love for us all. The hope she offers is not focused only on our ultimate salvation in the company of the saints, but also on our capacity to respond to his love as they did, even now—a response that St. John describes in these terms: *"Whoever treasures this hope of him purifies himself, to be as pure as he is."*

The Blessed Virgin, like St. John, wants to open our eyes to *"see what great love the Father has lavished on us by letting us be called God's children."* If all who glory in the name of Christian could take those words to heart, how eagerly we would respond to the message of La

Salette. How humbly we would accept Mary's criticisms and warnings. How sincerely we would submit to her Son. How greatly we would "*rejoice and be glad*," even in times of hardship. How deeply we would renew our life of prayer. And as a result, how "*blessed*" we would be!

Tuesday, November 2, (#668)
Feast of All Souls

John 6:37-40: "*It is my Father's will that whoever sees the Son and believes in him should have eternal life, and that I should raise that person up on the last day.*"

Meditation:

One of the central truths of the Catholic faith is that if we believe in Jesus and follow his way during our lifetime, we need not worry about the afterlife. Jesus promises that we will be raised up (to heaven) on the last day. It's as simple and as profound that that! There are times in our life which can be very challenging and, as Anthony Padovano writes, "we may feel more the dust of the earth than the breath of God." But we must choose to move on in hope. When we lose a loved one in death, we can certainly grieve at the loss but, with the passing of time, some of this grief will pass and we will, in a sense, rise with our loved one in the hope of their and our resurrection.

AT LA SALETTE, our Blessed Mother wept for our sins. The question may occur: "If Mary is in heaven and beholds the face of God, how can she visit us in tears?" Fr. Normand Theroux explains: "Without doubt those in heaven neither suffer nor weep… However the Virgin wept at La Salette not because she was sad but because she wanted to emphasize by her tears the alarming scope of her message as the Mother of the Lord. '*If my people will not submit, I will be forced to let go of the arm of my Son.*' She cried because she was speaking to human beings who need some signs. On earth, tears are the ultimate sign of sorrow. In addition, Mary's tears express her deep sadness at not being able to protect her people from coming misfortunes, although her capacity to suffer has passed." As we grieve for our loved ones, we know that Jesus' Holy Mother is concerned for us and prays always for our salvation and that of our loved ones. Let us take comfort in this truth of our faith.

Reflection Questions:

- Do you know of someone who is still grieving at the loss of a loved one? Why not say a prayer for them or go out of your way to comfort them by word or deed?
- When have you wept at the loss of a loved one? What memories of that person do you still treasure and why?

Wednesday, November 3, (#487)
Thirty-First Week in Ordinary Time

Luke 14:25-33: *"No one who does not carry his cross and come after me can be my disciple."*

Meditation:

In this passage, people now crowd around Jesus, perhaps to hear his exciting words, to see his miracles or to find out if he is the Messiah they seek. Maybe they want to share his glorious journey or insure their place at his side in the kingdom. For whatever reason, they are there. Jesus cuts to the quick. What it means to follow him is made perfectly clear. Nothing less than deliberate and total commitment to his cause is required, not a half-hearted "picking and choosing" of some of its demands.

MARY AT LA SALETTE came as the truly dedicated and committed follower of her Son. The cross she wore was no mere decoration but the visible reminder of the many swords that had pierced her heart as she journeyed with Jesus to Calvary and beyond. Her cross bespeaks her many pains that make reconciliation a reality.

Reflection Questions:

- Will you take up the cause of reconciliation, knowing it can and will "cost" you?
- Will you bring that message of mercy to all situations that need it, or do you "pick and choose" only the easier ones?

Thursday, November 4, (#488)
Thirty-First Week in Ordinary Time

Luke 15:1-10: *"This man welcomes sinners and eats with them."*

Meditation:

Jesus reminds his listeners that the God he proclaims is one who is always on the side of the lost, the stray, and the prodigal. He will not rest until they are safely home and in the divine embrace. While this does not sit well with those who have another view of who is inside or outside of God's care, Jesus courageously tries to broaden their horizons – even at the cost of being rejected.

AT LA SALETTE, Mary also comes to a people who have lost their vision of God and yet refused to admit it. For her the lost and the stray were not only those who were despised and outcast, but also those who by their words and deeds had made them so. Even these were important to God, but in ways their hearts had not yet come to understand. For the power of their acceptance, their ability to reach out to others in love and care she knew could make the miracle of God's healing possible. This message could have been rejected, but her maternal care for even those who did not know they were lost, began a most unique and ongoing homecoming.

Reflection Questions:

• Do you believe that God's love is partial or impartial?
• Do you believe that there are some people who are outside of God's love and mercy? Do your attitudes and actions betray that belief?

Friday, November 5, (#489)
Thirty-First Week in Ordinary Time

Luke 16:1-8: *"For the children of this world are more astute in dealing with their own kind than are the children of light."*

Meditation:

Jesus' story of the dishonest steward becomes clearer in the light of the practice of stewards, who represent their masters, often engaging

315

in the practice of usury. Their greed made them tack on extra fees to an original loan to be repaid that they would then skim off as the top of the debt. Having been caught, the steward "converts," goes back to the debtors and has them rewrite the debt to the original, minus the "hidden" commission. The master applauds the ingenuity in light of his personal situation. This is Jesus' way of calling people to a prudent use of material goods in the light of imminent crisis.

THE MESSAGE OF LA SALETTE is just such a wake-up call. Mary reminds the people of God of the imminent crisis that has resulted from their unwise stewardship of the gifts of life provided by their gracious God. The misuse of God's Name and Day, the irreverence towards people and the unwillingness to use more faithfully the time God gave them. She reminded them that the crisis could be averted through a turning back to God in their lives, to again use their lives as instruments of justice, healing and peace.

Reflection Questions:

- Are you using well the "goods" of the earth, the gifts of life and the talents with which God has entrusted you?
- How can you enter into that process of conversion that will make you more prudent "children of the light?"

Saturday, November 6, (#490)
Thirty-First Week in Ordinary Time

Luke 16:9-15: *"And if you are not trustworthy with what is not yours, who will give you what is your very own?"*

Meditation:

Jesus calls the people of his time to order their lives in such a way that the of God will always be the goal. If dishonest people can order their lives and dealings in a way that wins them friends and gets them what they want, should not honest people think of divine life and adapt their lives to obtaining it. Victory comes from the wise and honest use of the graces God gives to his faithful. Our lives are filled with opportunities to test our character as believers. The goals we set will guide us and determine the outcome. These goals cannot be compromised without leading to a divided heart.

At La Salette, Mary echoes Christ by calling us back to God's plans for us and the world, to seeing each other and our daily efforts through God's eyes. We must use the resources God has placed in our care to foster the healing, forgiveness and reconciliation which are the hallmarks of God's Kingdom. There are consequences both here and hereafter if we do not.

Reflection Questions:

- How are we, as persons, communities and nations, using our giftedness, our creativity, and the resources of our hearts and the fruits of our labors for the good of God's people?
- In the opportunities set before us that can test our character, is our allegiance to the God of Life or to "other gods?"

Sunday, November 7, (#155)
Thirty-Second Sunday in Ordinary Time
(1 Kings 17:10-16; Heb. 9:24-28; Mark 12:38-44)

Meditation: *Sacrifice*

The life of a widow was hard. 1 Timothy 5 offers a series of precepts for the care of widows; Exodus 22:21 reads, "You shall not wrong any widow or orphan."

The poor widow of today's Gospel, like many people of her day, was probably paid daily for whatever work she could find. But, instead of putting aside what little she could, she chose on this occasion to put all she had, a pittance compared to what others gave, into the temple treasury.

If she had not done so, her contribution would never have been missed. And yet it is famous, because it was noticed, praised by Jesus himself. He did not draw a moral, and so we are free to draw our own. At the very least it means that whatever we do out of a generous faith has meaning for God.

In our second reading we read that Jesus, by his sacrifice, took away the sins of many. Had it not been for the resurrection, his sacrifice on the cross might have gone unnoticed by history. Unfortunately, over time, in many parts of the Christian world, its importance came to be taken for granted, if not forgotten.

In 1846, she who had stood at the foot of the cross came to a mountain in France. Two innocent children were given a message to remind their people—her people—how far they had strayed, how little they understood the worth of what was accomplished for them by her Son, who was "offered once to take away the sins of many, [and] will appear a second time, not to take away sin but to bring salvation to those who eagerly await him."

Recently I read one of the great Christian classics, John Bunyan's The Pilgrim's Progress. A pilgrim named Christiana, on learning of Jesus' sacrifice and the forgiveness it brings, exclaims:

> "Methinks it makes my heart bleed to think that he should bleed for me. O thou loving One! O thou blessed One! Thou deservest to have me; Thou hast bought me. Thou deservest to have me all; Thou hast paid for me ten thousand times more than I am worth."

Indeed, we can never truly repay the price paid for us. Our first response may be regret, but then comes gratitude, and then the desire to give what we can in return, no matter how great, no matter how small.

Monday, November 8, (#491)
Thirty-Second Week in Ordinary Time

Luke 17:1-6: *"If your brother does something wrong, rebuke him and, if he is sorry, forgive him."*

Meditation:

In this passage, Jesus is addressing those he is calling to positions of leadership in his mission. A good leader is to be both courageous and compassionate in setting in motion the process of reconciliation. Sin and alienation are seen as facts of life, but so are both the need and the opportunities for offering the gift of forgiveness. The number "7" points out the importance of such unlimited love. The mission needs and seeks a constant growth in the faith which inspires and nourishes the life of a reconciler.

AT LA SALETTE, MARY CALLS THE ENTIRE PEOPLE OF GOD to be leaders in the work of reconciliation. In their conversion of heart they can confidently turn to the God who forgives 70 times 7 times and always trust in divine mercy. They in turn can call others, caught in the inevitability of human sin, to seek that forgiveness. They – through prayer, the Eucharist and works of repairing shattered lives – can grow in faith and be instruments of unlimited, prodigal mercy.

Reflection Questions:

- In what ways do you need to grow in your faith as a reconciler?
- In the arithmetic of forgiveness, do you conserve or liberate the power of God's mercy for others?

Tuesday, November 9, (#671)
Dedication of the Basilica of
St. John Lateran

John 2:13-22: *"Making a whip out of cord, (Jesus) drove all (the money changers) out of the Temple."*

Meditation:

With rapidly changing cultural customs, it's at times difficult to keep current or remain politically correct. For example, when someone says that they are going to see their doctor, do we presume that it is a man they are speaking about? Yet there are certain actions that are never allowed, such as one spouse beating another or someone using excessive force with another. In today's gospel, according to Jewish custom, Jesus went up with the entire population of the kingdom of Judah to the Jerusalem temple for the Passover, the seven-day holiday of the Feast of Unleavened Bread. In this passage, as the Jerome Biblical Commentary mentions, this incident emphasizes Jesus' opposition to the "sacrificial system of Judaism (which) made "a marketplace" of the Temple," his Father's house (1968 edition, Prentice-Hall Publishers, Bruce Vawter, paragraph 65:16).

OUR BLESSED LADY'S TEARFUL WORDS to the two children about *"How long a time I have suffered for you... As for you, you pay no heed..."* and I gave you six days to work... and no one will give it to me..." express her tearful upset with our thoughtless response to God's pleadings. She is rightfully upset with her children. Her compassionate words directed to the two children about her concerns for their faith and their bodily welfare express her desire and hopes for her wayward people. They have neglected her Son's commandment to "keep holy the Sabbath" entering the temple of God, their parish church, for worship. She even mentions that *"in the winter, when (people) don't know what to do, they go to Mass just to make fun of religion."* This too defiles God's temple.

Reflection Questions:

- There are many ways to honor the "temple of God", your parish church. Do you worship in it regularly, support the needs of your parish community, participate in parish ministries, and reach out to the needy?
- Are you a good example to others in your family by the way you worship – your regular participation, your generosity to the parish community and its members?

Wednesday, November 10, (#493)
Thirty-Second Week in Ordinary Time

Luke 17:11-19: *"Finding himself cured, one of them turned back praising God at the top of his voice..."*

Meditation:

In the context of this story of healing, remember that the Samaritans and Israelites were enemies. Common need creates unusual associations of people. Here both were in need of the healing touch of God. Both wanted to share the status of the clean so that their alienation and loneliness would end. The miracle of Christ created that possibility, but the result was that the "ungrateful nine" found this to be just another ordinary gift of God while the Samaritan foreigner realized that this was an invitation to a personal commitment to God. God's love was to be recognized as all encompassing.

Mary came at La Salette to announce the same "good news" of the abundance of God's saving love reaching out to the hurting, lost and alienated of all times, ages, nations and peoples. It is truly the profound tale of Salvation History in the "short story" of the Apparition. Yet, we are reminded that we have made that great story seem mundane by our forgetfulness; we have muted its power by our ingratitude. Over the years the few who are truly touched by the reconciling hand of God remind the rest of us to return often and gratefully to the source of all healing and hope.

Reflection Questions:

• In your ministry as a reconciler, do you come back gratefully in prayer and praise to the source of the healing?
• Do you treat the act of reconciling as just "another" gift of God or do you stand in awe of its powerful promise of new life?

Thursday, November 11, (#494) Thirty-Second Week in Ordinary Time

Note: Today you may wish to begin the First Day of the Novena to Our Lady of La Salette, in the appendix of this book.

Luke 17:20-25: *"For look, the kingdom of God is among you."*

Meditation:

Jesus is forever teaching his disciples and his listeners about the true meaning of the coming of the Messiah. Who will he be? How will we know him? What will his reign resemble? When will it arrive? Jesus taught, patiently but firmly, that the Messiah was not the revolutionary, political liberator his nation sought. The "revolution" was to be one of hearts mending, attitudes changing, lives turning around. This Kingdom's reign was to be already seen in his tolerance, love and forgiveness, in his welcoming of outcasts and sinners. And such a vision was a challenge to those with other, more fixed ideas.

Mary's Apparition at La Salette came in a time and place in history when thoughts of political "revolutions" still filled people's minds and hearts. Who would lead the nation to true peace? What type of government could allow such poverty and injustice to continue? Mary's message was a challenge to people to look first within themselves in order to recreate their hearts, turn their lives around, convert their relationships with God, self, others, the earth so that new ways of being and living would take shape from the inside out. This would truly be a revolution based on the power of the reconciling reign of God.

Reflection Questions:

- Do you look for answers to the great questions of peace and justice today by first examining your own heart, attitudes and actions?
- What role do you play as a reconciler in shaping the conscience of your institutions so that they may fashion instruments of peace rather than weapons of war?

Friday, November 12, (#495) Thirty-Second Week in Ordinary Time

Luke 17:26-37: *"Anyone who tries to preserve his life will lose it; and anyone who loses it will keep it safe."*

Meditation:

This statement of Jesus comes as he seeks to call people to be prepared for the reign of God coming in all its power in their midst. Those who were unprepared in the past times of Noah and Lot squandered their energy in activity that had no orientation to heaven and even resulted in disaster for them and for the earth. Such times and pursuits are not only past memories for us. They stand as present reminders of our need to pursue the work of the Savior – the journey of self-surrender which leads to the cross, and glory and communion beyond.

MARY CAME TO LA SALETTE to call us to a new period of preparation that, if taken seriously, would usher in a "new springtime" for the earth and the people whom God has invited to care for it. The signs of the Kingdom coming would be seen in renewed relationships and reconciled lives and families. People would "lose" themselves in the healing service of a loving God and "save" their lives in passionate stewardship. Following the way Mary indicates for conversion, becomes a committed following of "The Way" that leads from death to life.

Reflection Questions:

• Does your seeking to "preserve" your way of living betray an unwillingness to enter the paschal mystery? Do your pursuits have a hint of heaven about them?

• In what ways do you "lose" yourself in service to the Kingdom of peace, reconciliation and justice?

Saturday, November 13, (#496)
Thirty-Second Week in Ordinary Time

Luke 18:1-8: *"Then (Jesus) told them a parable about the need to pray continually and never lose heart."*

Meditation:

Jesus taught his disciples to pray for the coming of the kingdom. He also taught them that this prayer must be an ongoing, vital and courageous part of their daily lives. Wherever and whenever justice is threatened or the poor, defenseless, vulnerable and powerless suffer, we must pray and work so that those who can make things right will open their ears and hearts to the cries that summon them "in the middle of the night." Our faithful prayer to the God who will not abandon those who cry out in their deepest need, to the God who cannot condone injustice will be heard if we do not despair. Hearts will change, conversion will happen and the work of our good and just God will prevail.

At La Salette, Mary recalled us to that sacred conversation with the God of life and hope that we call prayer. She urged us to explore again its most personal and public forms for their potential to heal and bring life. She reminded us to sanctify time and our daily routine by those moments of grace. She proclaimed again the promise that those who "pray well" can help "make well," by God's grace, what is ill, hurting and suffering.

Reflection Questions:

• Do you take the time to "pray well" as a vital part of your ministry of reconciliation? Or is your inability to pray a sign that you are "losing heart?"

Sunday, November 14, (#158)
Thirty-Third Sunday in Ordinary Time

(Daniel 12:1-3; Heb. 10:11-18; Mark 13:24-32)

Meditation: *Like the Stars*

... people will see the Son of Man coming in clouds with great power and glory.
Mark 13:26

Would you like to be a star? The prophet Daniel tells us how: "Those who lead the many to justice shall be like the stars forever."

Of course, if we are to lead others to justice, we need to be on that path ourselves. Can we find it on our own? No. The act of trust expressed in the responsorial psalm is our hope, too: "You will show me the path to life."

This reminds me of the Consecration to Our Lady of La Salette. The prayer concludes by asking her "to enlighten my understanding, to direct my steps, to console me by your maternal protection, so that exempt from all error, sheltered from every danger of sin, strengthened against my enemies, I may, with ardor and invincible courage, walk in the paths traced out for me by you and your Son."

Mary's purpose in coming to La Salette is beautifully summed up in this prayer. Many pilgrims to the Holy Mountain express the same thought through the symbolic gesture of literally following the path taken by the Beautiful Lady from where the children first saw her to where she stood and spoke to them, and then to where she wound her way up the steep hillside to the spot where she rose in the air and disappeared from sight.

Like drinking the water of the miraculous fountain, this prayerful physical movement is a commitment to living by the light of La Salette, which simply reflects light of the Gospel.

Looking at today's Gospel, one might be inclined to compare the apocalyptic description of the end time to the prophetic warnings of Our Lady of La Salette. That is not incorrect, but we must extend the comparison further. The hope Mary offers—not only of future abundance but also of her watchful care—is in keeping with Jesus' promise that he will "send out the angels and gather his elect from the four winds."

Being his elect does not mean we are perfect. If we ever are perfect it will be the Lord's doing, "for by one offering he has made perfect forever those who are being consecrated."

The same God who made the stars in the heavens, can make stars on earth. We call them saints.

Monday, November 15, (#497)
Thirty-Third Week in Ordinary Time

Luke 18:35-43: " … *(the blind man) only shouted all the louder, 'Son of David, have pity on me.'"*

Meditation:

It may be that there is a slim line between hope and desperation. This gospel passage gives us a story of risk. The blind man takes a risk in asking what the commotion is all about: he may have been ignored.

He takes a risk in calling Jesus' name: he could be quieted. (Indeed, he was!) He risked calling out a second time: he could have called forth a sterner rebuke. He risked answering Jesus' question: he could have been refused. He risked wanting to see, not knowing what his eyes would behold.

The main character in any gospel story, of course, is Jesus; but we can lose track of that when presented with such a compelling secondary character, especially if the character portrays something of issue in our own lives. If we keep our attention on Jesus, however, we find God's answer to our desperation and our risking. Jesus asks that the man be brought forward; he asks him what he can do for him; he grants the request. Could it be that Jesus is asking us to come closer? That he waits to hear what we want from him? That he continues to grant such requests? Have we called out to see?

LA SALETTE SUGGESTS that such may still be the case. The Beautiful Lady, in inviting the children closer, echoes all the Biblical passages that issue a similar invitation. God always seems to be inviting us closer. Our Lady's discourse and the choice she offers for conversion ask us to be in touch with what we really want from this life. The stories of the people who flock to the site of the Apparition, stories of conversion and healing and forgiveness, tell us that God had not been deaf to the prayers of his people. Can we dare believe that God hears us still?

Reflection Questions:

•What is the deepest desire of your heart? What do you want Jesus to do for you? Have you risked formulating that desire in your prayer?
•When you ask for some favor from God, do you first thank God for all that God has given you?

Tuesday, November 16, (#498)
Thirty-Third Week in Ordinary Time

Luke 19:1-10: *"The Son of man has come to seek out and save what was lost."*

Meditation:

The words of Jesus to Zacchaeus recall so many of Jesus' remarks and teachings in other places. The parables in Luke 15 readily come to mind: the shepherd who leaves the ninety-nine sheep to go in search of the stray; the woman who diligently sweeps her house until she finds her lost money; the father who is found to be anxiously awaiting the return of his prodigal son. And yet this response to Zacchaeus seems somehow out of place. The full story makes it seem as if it were Zacchaeus' initiative that brought him into Jesus' sight. After all, he heard that Jesus was passing by; he sought for a way to see him; he ran ahead and climbed a tree. And yet Jesus says that he has been in search of the lost, and has found such a one here. And this is great news. Maybe Jesus is suggesting that God is always taking the initiative no matter what it looks like. All our efforts to seek God end in our realizing that God has been seeking us all along.

WHEN WE TURN OUR ATTENTION TO LA SALETTE – or to Marian apparitions in general – there is an underlying question that often goes ignored. Beyond the questions of what happened and what was said, there is the question of why this would happen in the first place. What is God doing in these graced events? The answer to that question seems so obvious at La Salette. It is obvious in Mary calling us her children; it's obvious in the way Maximin's father was convinced when he heard the story of his own experience at Corps on the lips of the Beautiful Lady. God has shown us once again that the lost continue to be God's concern. The words that Jesus spoke to Zacchaeus could very easily have been Mary's at La Salette: *"I have come to search out and save what was lost."* "Because I love you; because my Son gave his life for you; because you are precious in God's sight." **"Make this known to all my people."**

Reflection Questions:

• Does the suggestion that God always takes the initiative ring true in your experience?
• Are there parts of your life that even now feel "lost" or "strayed?" Might God be seeking these out for God's forgiveness? How might you be called to share in the reconciliation ministry of Jesus?

Wednesday, November 17, (#499)
Thirty-Third Week in Ordinary Time

Luke 19:11-28: *"Take the (gold coin) from him and give it to the man who has ten (gold) coins."*

Meditation:

Jesus will borrow from all avenues of human experience in order to make the points in his stories. That is probably just another way of showing that all of experience is revelatory of God. In this parable there are elements of economics and politics with which the people of the time no doubt readily identified. But what is the point of this story about a dangerous and ruthless king? It appears to be one of those parables of contrast Luke is fond of recounting. *"If a friend would get up at midnight, won't your heavenly Father be quicker to answer?" "If you know how to give good things to your children, won't your heavenly Father give the Holy Spirit?" "If an unjust judge will give justice to an aggrieved widow, won't your heavenly Father give justice to his children who cry to him?"* Here we might paraphrase: *"If a ruthless ruler rewards faithfulness in the investing of time and property, won't God's reward be even greater?"*

IN REFLECTING UPON THE DISCOURSE AT LA SALETTE, we also find an economic and political aspect. The poverty that besets the people is reflected in their choices of working overtime. Their lives are consumed with worry about future harvests: will there be enough? Mary's words echo those of the Gospel: "If you are faithful, the harvest will be plentiful. You who choose to ignore God's invitation to life will find that there is nothing left." The invitation is to life, whether in the Gospel, at La Salette, in our prayer, or in our coming together as Church.

Reflection Questions:

• Have you experienced God's bounty as a result of conversion or faithfulness?
• Do you recognize the call to conversion as the invitation of a loving God?

Thursday, November 18, (#500)
Thirty-Third Week in Ordinary Time

Luke 19:41-44: *"If you too had only recognized on this day the way to peace! But in fact it is hidden from your eyes!"*

Meditation:

Jesus speaks the above line as he weeps over Jerusalem. And even though the words can seem like a final judgment, phrased as it is in the conditional past, that never seems to be the way it is with God. That's what upset Jonah, for example, when he preached God's judgment upon Nineveh, only to find that when the population repented in sackcloth and ashes, God "repented" of the destruction planned. So, too, with the people Moses was leading out of Egypt. When God looked upon their desertion and their worship of the molten calf, his judgment to Moses was that he was going to destroy all of them. Moses' intervention swayed God once again to repent. One has the distinct impression that Jesus in tears would still relent of the judgment against the rulers of the age, if even now they would recognize the path to peace being offered in the person of Jesus.

MARY'S WORDS AT LA SALETTE are similar and are also spoken in tears. *"If only* my people recognized how much I suffer for them! *If only* they recognized the power in the name of my Son! *If only* they would come again to church, to the banquet spread before them! *If only* they would be converted! *If only...*" The possibility exists that we might even now recognize the offer being made with tears, and return to the God who loves us. That possibility is never taken from us.

Reflection Questions:

•What could possibly be an obstacle to your knowing the path to peace or recognizing God present in your daily life?
•Are there times when you think God's offer of love has been revoked? What would convince you to keep your hope alive?

Friday, November 19, (#501)
Thirty-Third Week in Ordinary Time

Luke 19:45-48: *"... the whole people hung on his words."*

Meditation:

Well, maybe not the entire populace; after all, this Gospel says that the chief priests and scribes and leaders of the people were looking for a way to destroy Jesus. But you get the picture: a charismatic speaker, one whose message was eagerly received, one whose message captured the people's imagination, fired their hope. This is someone to reckon with, someone not to be ignored. And yet that was somehow not enough. How do people move from captivating words to a change of heart? What could God do to move that process along? And the answer God presents is Jesus on the Cross. It's God asking, "Can you ignore this? Is this convincing enough for you? What more can I do?"

WHAT MORE INDEED! And yet the event at La Salette is God trying to get our attention. "Look, I send the Mother of my Son in tears!" At La Salette the children also hung on Mary's words. Her discourse demanded attention. But the children recounted that their attention was drawn to the crucifix the Beautiful Lady wore on her breast. The light seemed to radiate from that point and the corpus seemed so life-like. Whatever the message God sends, whatever the promise, whatever the invitation, it has to be heard against the backdrop of the Cross. This shows how serious God is about wanting us, about loving us, about saving us.

Reflection Questions:

- Do you find the Cross compelling in your own life of faith, your own devotional practices?
- How has your understanding of the place of the Cross, at the center of Christian faith, changed over the years?

Saturday, November 20, (#502)
Thirty-Third Week in Ordinary Time
The Presentation of the Blessed Virgin Mary

Luke 20:27-40: *"Now he is God, not of the dead, but of the living; for to him everyone is alive."*

Meditation:

Jesus' detractors could not have argued with the first part of his conclusion. That God is the God of the living is clear in the Old Testament. Isaiah 38:18-19, for example, says that it is not the dead who praise God, but the living. There are a number of Psalms that sing of praising God *"in the land of the living."* God is the one who confers life, calls to life, and through the Prophet asks the people to "choose life." Life is what God is all about, so it is not strange to see that Jesus would identify himself with that orientation.

In John's Gospel, Jesus declares that he is *"the resurrection and the life,"* and that he has come that we *"may have life and have it to the full."* But the second part of Jesus' argument poses a problem. To assert that *"all are alive in him"* suggest an inclusiveness in God that does not characterize the leaders of the people – at least as they are portrayed in the Gospel. It was Jesus' inclusivity that got him in trouble with the authorities: he *"ate with sinners,"* was seen in the company of "outcasts," invited a tax collector to be his disciple, told the lowly they were blessed. What he was saying is that God's love is extended to everyone. All need to have the good news preached to them. In God's eyes, everyone matters – *"all are alive in him."*

MARY'S MESSAGE AT LA SALETTE is just as inclusive. Her tears are for the cart drivers who take the name of her Son in vain, for those who never go to church and those who go only to mock religion, for those who hold the dying children in their arms, and for those who will suffer because of famine. Mary's maternal concern reaches out to all her children. All are to be the recipients of the message of hope that she entrusts to Maximin and Melanie – themselves counted as little in the eyes of the world, but of infinite value in God's eyes. *"Make this known to all my people,"* says the Beautiful Lady. All need to know they matter; all are alive for God.

Reflection Questions:

• Do you believe that you matter in the eyes of God? Did you always believe this? What changed your mind?

• Are there people (or groups of people) you "naturally" consider cut off from God's love and God's offer of salvation or forgiveness? Where does this come from? Is it in accord with the view of the Gospel?

Sunday, November 21, (#161)
Feast of Christ the King

(Daniel 7:13-14; Revelation 1:5-8; John 18:33b-37)

Meditation: *A Holy House*

Christ in front of Pilate by **Mihály Munkácsy (1844–1900)**

"Holiness befits your house, O Lord, for length of days," declares the psalmist. This statement of fact is also a commitment to preserve the holiness of God's house, especially if we take 'house' in the sense of 'household.'

This calls for integrity, the striving to be what we know we are meant to be as Christians. In Revelation Jesus is called "the faithful witness," and that is how we see him before Pilate. He declares: "For this I was born and for this I came into the world, to testify to the truth." A true disciple of Christ does the same.

When Our Lady told Mélanie and Maximin to make her message known to "all my people," they became faithful witnesses. No one was excluded; the children went, as it were, to many nooks and crannies, and spoke to all who would listen.

The truth to which they witnessed was specific, limited to what they had seen and heard in the hills above the village of La Salette: ruined crops, the people's infidelity, lack of respect for the things of God, as well as the all-important fact that conversion is always possible. The light of faith can enter through the tiniest opening of the heart or mind.

In Daniel's vision, "The one like a Son of man received dominion, glory, and kingship; all peoples, nations, and languages serve him. His dominion is an everlasting dominion."

Mary uses the image of the Arm of her Son as an expression of his dominion, but other parts of her message echo Revelation's words about Jesus, "who loves us and has freed us from our sins by his blood, who has made us into a kingdom, priests for his God and Father." He is Alpha and Omega, beginning and end, seeking out in every time and place those who belong to the truth and hear his voice.

Accepting his dominion is an act of submission—not groveling, but in genuine humility, seeking the remedy to the ills we have brought upon ourselves. He is eager to bless us with peace and make us holy.

The Beautiful Lady seeks to draw us more completely into the household of God, so that her people can become ever more truly God's holy People. For holiness befits his house for length of days.

Monday, November 22, (#503)
Thirty-Fourth Week in Ordinary Time

Luke 21:1-4: *"I tell you truly, this poor widow has put in more than any of them."*

Meditation:

I recall as a child hearing this "poor widow" praised for her generosity and held up as a model for us. "Don't give from your excess; give from what you need to live on." This would be an expression of our trust in God. Indeed there are some who continue to preach this "ideal" of trust: give away what you need and God will provide. But none of this is contained in this Gospel story found only in Mark and Luke. Luke especially critiques the rich in his Gospel; the rich too easily exploit the poor, too easily ignore the word of God. We might do well, then, to suspect an issue of justice is being raised in this story. "Widows and orphans" were two groups to be treated with care, respect, and justice in Israel. The sustaining relationships in their lives – those of husband and father respectively – had been taken away. It was incumbent on the community to support those so bereft. This widow should not have been expected to support the temple treasury, and yet gives the little she has – maybe in appreciation that she is cared for by the community. And Jesus, who says she has given so much, is judging as God judges: the little given is recognized as the gift of a generous heart.

THERE IS A SOCIO-ECONOMIC CRITIQUE inherent in La Salette as well. It may not be most obvious, but it is there. Our Lady's tears are for those who have been cut off from the church, those who no longer recognize her Son living among them. But often those working on Sunday were not doing so because they enjoyed it; they had no choice if they were to eke out a living. Landlords and tax collectors expected to be paid and didn't care what that meant for the people subjected to them. But conversion has amazing ramifications – *a humble, contrite heart, O God, you will not spurn.*" (Psalm 51) Yes, God loves generous hearts; but conversion is also needed on the part of society. The workers should not be enslaved; all human life is worthwhile; the Sabbath recalls our dignity and our relatedness. We are converted as we relearn those lessons together.

Reflection Questions:

• Do you act out of the belief that the community dimension of salvation is important? Where do you most feel or experience that dimension?
• How do you stand up for and speak out for the dignity of the lowly, those whose voices often go unheard?

Tuesday, November 23, (#504)
Thirty-Fourth Week in Ordinary Time

Luke 21:5-11: *"And when you hear of wars and revolutions, do not be terrified."*

Meditation:

There are many "background" themes in the Bible, themes to which we may not pay immediate attention as we focus on the dominant themes of God's love, forgiveness, salvation. One of these important background themes is that of the presence of fear and anxiety and the calming reassurance that these lose power in the face of faith in the presence of a loving God. Jesus had earlier declared that his disciples should not be anxious about what to eat and what to wear. God would provide those things (Luke 12: 22-32). Tomorrow's Gospel passage suggests the disciples should not worry about what to say when dragged before the magistrates. What is necessary for their defense will be provided.

And so today the words *"do not be terrified"* about wars and insurrections are meant to comfort. Even more, they are meant to focus the hearers: "Don't be sidetracked," Jesus might be saying. "If your fears and anxieties get the better of you, you will not be focused on my words, on the truth of my teachings, on the presence of the Spirit among you." Jesus never said we would not feel fear or anxiety. It is simply that every time we do feel those things, we should hear him saying to his disciples (and to us), "Don't be afraid; don't be anxious."

IT IS ALSO COMFORTING that at La Salette our Weeping Mother bid the children not to be afraid. But more than comforting, it is also focusing. Putting aside their fears, the children are able to hear clearly the message they are meant to retell. It is likely that through all the times ahead when they were questioned, put through examinations and accusations, they took courage and strength from Our Lady's words, *"Do not be afraid."* Our own lives are filled with fears and anxieties, trivial or sublime, about ourselves or those we love. On a larger scale, we live in a world of war and violence. "Where is God in all this?" we may ask. God is present in the midst of it, saying, "Don't be anxious or perturbed, otherwise you may miss the words and ways of peace I am even now speaking."

Reflection Questions:

- Are you aware of the things, the situations that stir up fears and anxieties in you?
- How has focusing on God's words (in Scripture, in Eucharist) or God's presence (in the Spirit, in the love of your friends) helped you make it through those anxious times?

Wednesday, November 24, (#505)
Thirty-Fourth Week in Ordinary Time

Luke 21:12-19: *"You will be handed over to the synagogues and to imprisonment... for the sake of my name."*

Meditation:

Throughout the New Testament it is evident that Jesus' name is special and important. Reflected back into the infancy narratives, the very story of the Annunciation, the name is given: *"Look! You are to conceive in your womb and bear a son, and you must name him Jesus"* (Luke 1:31). It is this name that has power to heal: *"In the name of Jesus Christ the Nazarene, walk!"* (Acts 3:6). It has the power to save: *"Only in him is there salvation; for of all the names in the world given to men, this is the only one by which we can be saved."* (Acts 4:11-12). But that name also brings Jesus' disciples into conflict. This is the other side of the story, one not to be forgotten or denied. The choice for Jesus means standing beside him even when that incurs the loss of relationships and reputation. *"Your perseverance will win you your lives."* (Luke 21:19).

AT LA SALETTE, Mary reminded us that we had forgotten the power of the name of her Son. Instead, that name became a convenient "throw-in" when swearing. It no longer remained the source of healing, the source of salvation, the name that demanded a decision for discipleship. In calling her people to salvation, Mary was calling them to remember their own identity as disciples. Yes, that road is a rocky one. But it is the remembering of our identity as loved and blessed and saved that is at stake here. Only this sacred memory gives us the power to see those rocks on the road changed into *"heaps of wheat."*

Reflection Questions:

•Have you ever experienced rejection because of your own deci-sion for Jesus? Or has fear of rejection kept you from acknowledg-ing your own joy and blessedness in being a Christian? What did either of those experiences feel like?

•At what times have you known beyond a doubt that Jesus' name was a source of power in your life?

Thursday, November 25, (#506)
Thirty-Fourth Week in Ordinary Time

Luke 21:20-28: *"Alas for those with child, or with babies at the breast, when those days come!"*

Meditation:

The image of a nursing mother is a revered one in Scripture. It describes the tender love that exists between God and Israel; and should a mother forget the child in her arms (which cannot be imag-ined!), even then would God remember Israel, says Isaiah. *" ... like a little child in its mother's arms, like a little child, so I keep myself"* (Psalm 131:2). *"Blessed the womb that bore you and the breasts that fed you,"* shouts a woman from the crowd when Jesus had finished preaching (Luke 11: 27).

This symbol of life, of tender love, of goodness, then, becomes a source of great mourning when not fulfilled. When the world is a place of darkness, to have brought children into it is a great sorrow. When Jesus meets the sorrowing women on the way to Golgotha, he says, *" ... do not weep for me; weep rather for yourselves and for your chil-dren. For look, the days are surely coming when people will say, 'Blessed are those who are barren, the wombs that have never borne children, the breasts that have never suckled!'"* (Luke 23:28-29).

AMONG THE LIST OF DIRE SITUATIONS named by Our Lady at La Salette, the most difficult to hear is that of infants dying in the arms of those who hold them. This is made all the more terrible when spoken by our Weeping Mother, one who knows the sorrow of the loss of a child. There is no greater anguish than that experienced by a mother who says, "I wish I had never given birth!" And so this becomes an

337

appropriate metaphor for existence in a world that has lost all meaning. It is only through the eyes of the converted that the ugliness and sin of the world can be redeemed at all. It is only in the hearts of the converted that there is enough space, enough courage, to hold grief and death until it become transformed by the Spirit of God residing there. That is why Our Lady begs us in tears to remember her Son and to submit our lives to him.

Reflection Questions:

• Have you ever felt that the world had become "too crazy" to endure? That your life had lost all meaning? What assured you that such was not the case? Do images of childbearing and nursing speak of God's tender love today?

• Are there other, more compelling images for you or for us? What might they be?

Friday, November 26, (#507)
Thirty-Fourth Week in Ordinary Time

Luke 21:29-33: *"Sky and earth will pass away, but my words will never pass away."*

Meditation:

When writing to his friend, Timothy, Paul is in prison. He says he is wearing chains for preaching the Gospel, the very Gospel he is urging Timothy to preach fearlessly. *"I have to put up with suffering, even to being chained like a criminal. But God's message cannot be chained up."* (2 Timothy 2:9)! This is an image with roots in the Old Testament, where God declares through the prophet Isaiah, *"the word that goes from my mouth ... will not return to me unfulfilled or before having carried out my good pleasure and having achieved what it was sent to do."* (Isaiah 55:11). Our faith always calls us to discern that which is lasting, to note what is of value in a world where so much is transient and unimportant. It is listening (with the ears of our hearts) to the Word of God that allows this discernment to take place, recognizing that Word as incapable of being chained, recognizing that Word as always fruitful.

THAT MESSAGE OF SOMETHING LASTING at the heart of the world could be proclaimed from the mountains of France over 1,800 years after Jesus' death; that the words of the Gospel are still proclaimed among a people of faith today gives testimony to its lasting character. Even more amazing is when we recognize this Word in places we didn't expect – on the streets, at work, from our children, on the lips of the outcast – when we thought it was "only in church" or in the passages of Scripture. If that message could be heard (and proclaimed!) by two children who counted little in the eyes of the world on the barren slopes of the French Alps, then maybe that Word can be at work in our world today – maybe even in our own hearts and kept alive on own lips.

Reflection Questions:

• Where are the "normal" places you go to be nourished by the Word of God? How do you count on the Word being fruitful?
• Have you ever been surprised by hearing God's Word in places or from people where you never expected to hear it or recognize it?

Saturday, November 27, (#508)
Thirty-Fourth Week in Ordinary Time

Luke 21:34-36: *"Stay awake, praying at all times …"*

Meditation:

These are the last words Jesus speaks in the Gospel of Luke prior to the account of the Last Supper and his Passion and Death. They are words that have been spoken before as Jesus recounted parables of vigilance. They are words taken up especially by Paul as he writes to various communities of Christians. Watch and pray. Perhaps these are the hallmarks of the Christian life, interwoven in the way we live out each day. We are alert for the signs of God's presence; we pray daily for God's coming. Our praying helps keep us vigilant; our vigilance shows us what to bring into our prayer. Once we have recognized our call to redemption in Jesus; once we have given our lives over to Christ in Baptism, this may be – surprisingly – the best description of what to do "until Jesus, comes again:" watch and pray.

OUR BLESSED MOTHER doesn't give us a very different message at La

Salette. She calls us, through the message given to the children, to notice our own behavior as well as what goes on in the world. It's as if, being alert to God's presence in the world, we would never have forgotten the name of her Son, never have wanted to separate ourselves from the community that gathers to remember Jesus at Eucharist. Moreover, the poignant story Mary tells of Maximin and his father at the farm in Coin, suggests that God is ever alert to what happens in our lives. If we were as alert, we would notice God's loving gaze upon all that transpires. Maybe this is why Mary tells the children that prayer is so important: it's the activity that will help us notice that loving presence of God in our lives. Watch — and pray. Pray — and notice.

Reflection Questions:

• *"Do you pray well, my children?"* How well do I pray?
• Are there things I am becoming aware of that keep me from being watchful, alert to the presence or action of God's Spirit in my life?

Sunday, November 28, (#003)
First Sunday of Advent

(Jeremiah 33:14-16; 1 Thess. 3:12-4:2; Luke 21:25-28, 34-36)

Meditation: *Be Vigilant at All Times*

Vigilance is like attention or observation but adds an element of persistence and urgency. When we are vigilant, we are careful not to allow something to escape our notice. We are anxious to see what is coming, whether bad, so as to avoid it, or good, so as to embrace it.

Beginning twenty verses before today's text, Jesus predicts various dire events, emphasizing the hardships they will cause. After all that he adds: "When these signs begin to happen, stand erect and raise your heads because your redemption is at hand."

This turns our expectation on its head. Can the bad be the harbinger of good? Can famine and the other troubles mentioned by Mary at La Salette, for example, actually lead to hope? The answer is yes, if we are vigilant enough to see not only the events, but their meaning.

The Vale of Tears by **Gustave Doré (1832–1883)**

The people around La Salette were vigilant, to be sure, but the signs they observed concerned the weather and its effects on their agriculture. They knew that famine was coming. But Our Lady points out that they had failed to understand the 'warning,' a year earlier, in a blight on the potatoes. "Instead, when you found the potatoes spoiled, you swore, and threw in my Son's name."

The Day of the Lord can inspire hope or fear, depending on our attitude. In our reading from Jeremiah (a prophet of doom if ever there was one) we find "those days" to be all hope and joy. In 1 Thessalonians, St. Paul comments at length on it: "You yourselves know very well that the day of the Lord will come like a thief at night… Therefore, let us not sleep as the rest do, but let us stay alert and sober" (1 Thess. 5:2,6).

In our second reading, St. Paul exhorts the Thessalonians, who are conducting themselves to please God, to "do so even more."

This too is a form of vigilance. The more intense our relationship with the Lord is, the more we will see what he intends. La Salette points us in that direction. So does the Church in this Advent season. We cannot fail to recognize Christmas when it comes, but we must not miss its deepest meaning.

Monday, November 29, (#175)
First Week of Advent

Matthew 8:5-11: *"...just give the word and my servant will be cured."*

Meditation:

Mother Teresa of Calcutta was asked in a television interview why she worked among the poorest of the poor. Her answer was simple and straightforward: "Because Jesus asked us to do it." There is no other reason to act, except for our faith in the person of Jesus.

"If you had faith the size of a mustard seed, you would be able to say to this mountain, 'Move from here to there,' and it would move" (Matt 17:20). This simple statement, "just say the word," is evidence of the father's faith. Strengthened by his desire to see his servant get better, he expresses not doubt but only true belief in the person of Jesus. "Jesus asked us to do it!" This is all we need do in order to act according to the Father's will. By retelling countless saving acts he performed in our midst, the Advent season helps strengthen our faith in preparation for the Savior's coming anew.

IN MARY'S MESSAGE at La Salette we find this simple statement: "Rocks and stones will be changed into mounds of wheat and potatoes will be self-sown in the fields." Is this difficult to believe? "Just do it" and it shall come to pass. Mary seems not to favor a middle-of-the-road position either. With her it is all or nothing. The disciple must believe with undivided heart. "One cannot serve both God and money" (Matt 6:24b). Coming to believe with an undivided heart is possibly the greatest journey of all. It leads to the greatest gift of all, the freedom of the children of God.

Reflection Questions:
- Is your heart divided?
- What do you really care about?

Tuesday, November 30, (#684)
St. Andrew, Apostle

Matthew 4:18-22: *"(Jesus) said to them, 'Come after me and I will make you fishers of people.' And at once they left their nets and followed him."*

Meditation:

Would that we were as instantly responsive to Jesus as the disciples in the gospel. In both Matthew and Luke, the point of this story is that the four disciples actually followed Jesus despite the fact that they did not know him. Perhaps a deeper point might be that, in the realm of faith, we can – and at time are urged to – "make a leap of faith", doing what would probably look quite reckless or thoughtless by those who insist on clear "reasoned decisions" from mature and responsible adults. When we look at the wider vision of what Jesus is doing – choosing specific men to become leaders in his church – perhaps we can sense a "joyful, inspired response" in this gospel event.

AT LA SALETTE, Mary chooses two unschooled children to be her messengers. They too respond quite spontaneously to her invitation to *"Come near"* and eventually to *"make (her) message know to all (her) people."* Certainly Mary is truly being led by the Holy Spirit in her mysterious choice of Maximin and Melanie. Yet surprisingly – and, it might be said, miraculously – they are true to their task until the end of their days. At times we are a bit too cautious in matters of faith. When our pastor asks from the pulpit or elsewhere for assistance with this or that project, if we feel a mysterious urge to respond instantly, perhaps we should step out and take a chance, like in the instance with the disciples of old, that it might be God's spirit calling us to serve in some unexpected way.

Reflection Questions:

• Has there been an instance where you instantly felt an inner calling to step forth to help in a special situation and did so willingly?
• Whom do you know who often responds with generosity to help others in their need?

Wednesday, December 1, (#177)
First Week of Advent

Matthew 15:29-37: *"I do not want to send them off hungry..."*

Meditation:

In these words of Jesus we detect the very heartbeat of the Father: *"Look at the birds in the sky; they do not sow or reap"* (Matthew 6:26). That the Father cares for his creation is an often-repeated theme of Scripture. Are we not of great importance? Yet how difficult it is to trust! Have we not been conditioned and trained for self-sufficiency? The rugged individualism rampant in our culture has its roots in the human nature we share. In an environment such as this, the trust Scripture calls for is indeed foreign. We put forth every reason possible in support of our position – the theory of the self-made person, the spirit of the pioneer, the myth that success is of one's own making. Few are willing to place their trust in a God who cares; most relate to a God who judges. This is a consequence of a rather significant shift: matters have slipped from God's hands into our own. The saying, *"I do not want to send them off hungry,"* would have us know that God cares for all his children and make us ask, "Could that also mean me?"

MARY'S OPENING WORDS AT LA SALETTE, *"If my people..."* are meant to convince us that she comes to us out of love and concern. She cannot remain distant from her people. We were formally entrusted to her care by the crucified Christ: *"Woman, this is your son"* (John 19:26). That her tears flowed during the entire apparition tells us how concerned this maternal love of hers really is. In this way she resembles and imitates her Son in the pity he felt for the hungry. She is not aloof; she does not stand apart, nor is she disengaged. Mary's is a bold love; it moves her into action. The apparition at La Salette is but one among her many loving gestures. Can anyone find here anything but the heartfelt appeal of a mother's solicitude?

Reflection Questions:

- Do you trust the caring love of God?
- How do you put this trust into practice?

Thursday, December 2, (#178)
First Week of Advent

Matthew 7:21,24-27: *"Everyone who listens to these words of mine and acts on them will be like a sensible man who built his house on rock."*

Meditation:

The 14-year-old newspaper carrier blushed with embarrassment at the attention given him by the media. After noticing strange circumstances at a customer's residence, he had done no more than what he believed was the right thing to do. The elderly man had suffered a stroke and had been lying on his kitchen floor unable to move for some time. Because he had called for help, the teenager was credited with saving the man's life. Actions bring life into clear focus. Furthermore, putting Jesus' words into practice quickens the blessing of God's Spirit within us. Jesus showed us the way by living his life as the Father designed every human life to be lived, in deep trust and with loving submission to its Creator. And so his actions and deeds were grace-filled.

THE BEAUTIFUL LADY OF LA SALETTE calls us to action. There is order in creation, she reminds us, and we must respect such order: *"And they will not give it to me ... "* Though we "will never be able to repay the pains she has taken for us," it is quite evident that the La Salette Event calls for a response. Her tears must not leave us unmoved. We are her people; her visit is designed to challenge us. Through it she begs us to find a better way of serving her Son. It is no less than a call to conversion: "Open your eyes to reality," the gracious Lady seems to be telling us. "Advent time is here. Prepare to welcome the Lord of your life!"

Reflection Questions:

- Can you list a few way that show you are living the gospel message?
- Do you know someone who is obviously living the gospel message?

Friday, December 3, (#179)
First Week of Advent

Matthew 9:27-31: *"Do you believe I can do this?"*

Meditation:

We learn from Scripture that while visiting his own town, Jesus could work no miracle there. The townspeople knew him too well as the son of Mary and Joseph, and as a result would put no faith in him (Matthew 13:58). His inquiry then, *"Do you believe I can do this?"* is not a mere rhetorical question, but one that is probing for trusting hearts, channels open to grace. Jesus seems to confirm this interpretation when he tells the blind men, "'According to your faith, let it be done to you.'" Life itself is gift. We should expect that each enhancement of life will be a gift as well. All things come to us as a blessing from God. Trust in God's goodness must mark each of our days. Jesus seems to be emphasizing this very fact by asking, *"Do you believe I can do this?"*

THE STORY OF THE APPARITION reveals a similar call. Mary prods Maximin's memory concerning spoiled wheat, recalling a walk back home to Corps with his father some time before. His dad had said to him, *"Here, my child, eat some bread while we still have it this year, because I don't know who will eat any next year if the wheat keeps up like this."* This very personal information startles the boy and jogs his memory. It further tells us that no human adventure eludes God's awareness. In visiting with us at La Salette, Mary attempts to reach that hidden core of goodness which is found in each and every one of us. Is this not a call to greater openness and deeper trust?

Reflection Questions:

- What is your part in God's creation?
- Do you trust that you can make a difference?

Saturday, December 4, (#180)
First Week of Advent

Matthew 9:35 and 10:1,5a,6-8: *"And as you go, proclaim that..."*

Meditation:

Quite popular is the following passage from the prophet Isaiah, *"How beautiful on the mountains are the feet of the messenger announcing peace, of the messenger of good news"* (Isaiah 52:7). Going about announcing that *"the kingdom of heaven is at hand"* (Matthew 10:7b) was Jesus' mission. It is also the mission of the disciples as they go through life. There is good news to be told. *"No one light a lamp and then put it under a tub; they put it on the lampstand where it shines for everyone in the house"* (Matthew 5:15). Making this announcement is part and parcel of the call to be a Christian. The gift is so great that it must be brought to the attention of all. The true blessing of the word is the life it bestows, a life it abundantly blesses with peace and joy, with hope and fulfillment. *"I have told you this so that my own joy may be in you and your joy be complete"* (John 15:11).

"Well, my children, *you will make this known to all my people.*" Our Lady's closing words are similar. Since she said this twice, her commission also carries a note of urgency. Little Maximin was the first to share the exciting news of the visit from the Beautiful Lady with childlike excitement. Melanie was called away from her chores in the stable and asked whether she too had seen a lovely Lady. Without hesitation she confirmed the truth of her companion's report. The news spread like wildfire. After all, the episode included a number of startling aspects: the cowherds repeated the message the Lady had delivered in French, a language they were barely familiar with; questioned separately, the two witnesses related essentially the same rather detailed story; they would also subsequently remain steadfast in the testimony over a long period of time and under sometimes grueling questioning. The message is clearly good – and even great – news. The efforts we expend to spread this gift should be proportionate to our appreciation of its value.

Reflection Questions:

- Are you ready to share the tremendous blessing of your faith?
- What first step in this direction might you take today?

Sunday, December 5, (#006)
Second Sunday of Advent

(Baruch 5:1-9; Philippians 1:4-11; Luke 3:1-6)

Meditation: *Remembered by God*

Saint John the Baptist

At the end of her Apparition, Our Lady of La Salette rose above the children, as Maximin tried to seize one of the roses around her feet. She seemed to look at the only point on the horizon where one could see beyond the surrounding mountains.

What made me think of this is a sentence in our first reading: "Stand upon the heights; look to the east and see your children gathered from the east and the west at the word of the Holy One, rejoicing that they are remembered by God."

I will not claim that Mary was thinking precisely of this text from Baruch but, still, the match is nearly perfect. It was surely just such a vision and hope that inspired her to grace us with her presence.

And there is more. Devoted as we are to the Beautiful Lady, our hearts are attuned to the themes of mourning, glory, peace, worship, mercy and justice, all of which are found in the same reading.

What moves me most powerfully is the image of Jerusalem's children returning to her, "rejoicing that they are remembered by God." A similar thought is expressed in Psalm 136:23, "The Lord remembered us in our low estate, for his mercy endures forever."

A very famous passage from Isaiah 49 says the same, but from a negative perspective. "But Zion said, 'The Lord has forsaken me; my

348

Lord has forgotten me.' Can a mother forget her infant, be without tenderness for the child of her womb? Even should she forget, I will never forget you."

St. Paul writes to the Philippians, "God is my witness, how I long for all of you with the affection of Christ Jesus." He not only longs to be with them, but he desires every spiritual good for them. The encounter with God is the goal.

John the Baptist was the fulfillment of Isaiah's prophecy, sent to prepare God's people for just such an encounter. Mary at La Salette carries on the same tradition.

To facilitate the encounter, we need to remove any obstacle that might prevent or even delay it. If we can rejoice that God has remembered us, perhaps then we will never forget him.

Monday December 6, (#181)
Second Week of Advent

Luke 5:17-26: *"What are these thoughts you have in your hearts?"*

Meditation:

What lies in the heart distinguishes people one from another. One person will be capable of heroic sacrifice; another will be crassly self-serving. One will be happy and radiate enthusiasm; another will wrestle with doubt and court despair. Let us recall the fate his brothers visited upon Joseph because their hearts were jealous of the love their father lavished on this son (see Genesis 37). What is the difference between Cain and Abel? Is it not a decision reached in the recesses of the heart? The fully transparent heart is entirely of one mind, and the commandment of love requires us to be of undivided mind, the mind of God. It follows then that the heart of the Christian must be of Christ's mind, fully given over to the Father: *"My food is to do the will of the one who sent me ... "* (John 4:34). The thoughts of a heart divided will prove divisive and thereby contribute to the disintegration and destruction of life. *"Anyone who is not with me is against me,"* Jesus cautions, *"and anyone who does not gather in with me throws away"* (Matthew 12:30).

Mary's words at La Salette are a heartfelt plea for the people's return to their God, a single-minded and unyielding call for submission to his will in crucial areas of their religious practice: Sunday rest and worship, reverence for the Lord's holy name, fidelity to the church's precept of abstinence. The decision to make "a mockery of religion," she is at some pains to emphasize, can have rather adverse consequences: *"I warned you last year with the potatoes. You paid no heed."* Though we rarely carry the thought that far, our abuse, rather than proper use, of God's creation is a rebellious proposition – a perilous declaration of independence.

Reflection Questions:

- What lies in your heart? Dare you sound its depths in light of this day's gospel passage?
- How are you doing God's will for you today?

Tuesday, December 7, (#182)
Second Week of Advent

Matthew 18:12-14: *"...it is never the will of your Father in heaven that one of these little ones should be lost."*

Meditation:

The Father's plan is fully revealed in Jesus. "[Jesus] went around all of Galilee, teaching in their synagogues, proclaiming the gospel of the kingdom, and curing every disease and illness among the people" (Matt 4:23). Because of Jesus' coming into our world, gifts of harmony and wholeness have been bestowed upon us. After being away from the church for a number of years, a woman approached the Sacrament of Reconciliation. Her life's journey had reached a graced and defining turning point. A marriage gone bad, acts of unfaithfulness, a divorce, years of alcohol abuse, and a successful 12-step rehabilitation program preceded it. She had carried within herself a deep feeling that, during her rebellious years, God had never withheld his fatherly care from her. Countless stories confirm this truth about the Father's exquisite care and concern. His plan is fully operative in the lives of all who turn to him in sincere repentance.

Mary at La Salette paints a vivid word picture of creation's original wholeness as only conversion can restore it: "If they are converted, rocks and stones will be changed into heaps of wheat." This thorough renewal of creation fully reveals the Father's plan. To everything there is a place and a purpose in God's plan. Any distancing from this plan by the human stewards of creation results in disruption of right order. Away from the Lord, we display a spirit of independence rather than communion, a spirit of arrogance rather than reverence. It is this grave concern that the tearful mother of the Lord voices at the very outset of her address: "If my people will not submit..."

Reflection Questions:

- Where do you fit in the Father's plan?
- Do you lend your heart, mind and voice to creation that it might give your Creator fitting worship?

Wednesday, December 8, (#689) The Immaculate Conception

[Holy Day of Obligation]

Luke 1:26-38: "... for nothing is impossible to God."

Meditation:

It seems that God does not shy away from what we would consider impossible. As Jeremiah proclaims: *"Ah, Lord (God), you made the heavens and the earth by your great power and outstretched arm. To you nothing is impossible"* (Jeremiah 32:17). Even Job, struggling from the depths of utter loss professes: *"I know that you are all-powerful: what you conceive, you can perform"* (Job 42:2). In the New Testament the Matthean Jesus assures his weak-willed disciples: *"If your faith is the size of a mustard seed you will say to this mountain, 'Move from here to there,' and it will move; nothing will be impossible for you"* (Matthew 17:20). Again Jesus was explaining to his disciples how attachment to riches can prevent people from giving their lives to God. In response to his disciple's fearful question, *"Who can be saved, then?"*, Jesus simply states: *"By human resources, ... this is impossible; for God everything is possible"* (Matthew 19:25-26). All in all, God will provide for God's creatures. In the gospel for today, the words uttered by the angel to Mary were perhaps God's most marvelous impossibility: *"You are to conceive in your womb and bear a son, and you must name him Jesus"* (Luke 1:31). Motherhood and giving birth to a Son – the Son of God – this is an impossibly wonderful gift to give us, God's people!

AT LA SALETTE Mary concludes her visit by giving a seemingly impossible task to these two unschooled children: *"You will make this message known to all my people."* Yet by the grace of God they held true to her challenging task and did make her message known. The "impossible" was accomplished. Now it is our turn – all we who have heard her tearful and challenging message – to take up this seemingly impossible task and be evangelizers of her message, which is essentially the gospel message of her Son.

Reflection Questions:

• How did you first learn about the La Salette message?

• With whom have you shared it? If not, why not?

Thursday, December 9, (#184)
Second Week of Advent

Matthew 11:11-15: *"... he, if you will believe me, is the Elijah who was to return."*

Meditation:

We all need to grow in understanding and knowledge. Understanding is not given all at once. In his Gospel Luke offers a precious note on Jesus' own personal development: *"And Jesus increased in wisdom, in stature, and in favor with God and with people"* (Luke 2:52). Matthew's Gospel shows Jesus wondering about our readiness to give Scripture and everyday events a new interpretation: *"And if you had understood the meaning of the words: Mercy is what pleases me, not sacrifice ..."* The mystery of life is gradual in its unfolding. As life goes on we should expect our insights to reflect the experience of our accumulating years and more mature understanding. As one searches the Scriptures one's knowledge of God's loving ways deepen. For their original audience the words of Jesus in today's gospel will have cast John the Baptist in an entirely new light and role, that of forerunner to the

Messiah: *"he, if you will believe me, is the Elijah who was to return."*

MARY PREPARES THE CHILDREN to receive her message: *"Come near, my children; don't be afraid."* Her gentle words and the reassuring tone in which she spoke them dispel all their fears and apprehensions. She then takes a few steps toward them. They run to her and later reported on the great ease and joy with which they conversed with their Beautiful Lady. We too must in our own lives open the way before deeper spiritual truth and insight. We are to open our hearts to the caring and concerned words she spoke at La Salette, and give serious consideration to the change or conversion they inevitably call for. She challenges us to open our lives to the coming of her Son into the world.

Reflection Questions:

- Do you place obstacles in the path of the Lord?
- Are you patient with the steps of your spiritual journey?

Friday, December 10, (#185) Second Week Of Advent

Matthew 11:16-19: *"What comparison can I use to describe this breed?"*

Meditation:

No one likes to be told his or her "truth." Yet to know the error of one's ways is *essential* to spiritual growth. Such is the case also for the times in which we live. Every generation must evaluate its life and times, honestly assess its areas of potential growth and seriously devise means toward that growth. Jesus calls attention to the basic duplicity of the human heart. There is no integrity in the ways of people. Their views vary with the tides, their positions sway to suit the powers that be. It is our responsibility to come to grips with the ways of our own age and help it benefit from the liberating gift of God's word, that is a *"two-edged sword: it can seek out the place where soul is divided from spirit, or joints from marrow ... "* (Hebrews 4:12). This period of Christmas preparation offers a timely opportunity to evaluate the age in which we live and to speak to it by our very life the truth of God's word.

How specifically Mary at La Salette describes the spiritual climate of the times in which she appeared: *"I gave you six days to work; I have kept the seventh for myself and they will not give it to me. This is what makes the arm of my Son so heavy. And then, those who drive the carts cannot swear without bringing in my Son's name. These are the two things that make the arm of my Son so heavy."* We sense that the state of mid nineteenth-century European Christians had been carefully examined, that their spiritual health had been found wanting. Illness called for treatment. Appropriate and effective treatment required an accurate diagnosis. The Mother of Jesus pinpoints "the two things" most in need of her people's attention. If she were to return and underscore "two things" most in need of change in our own day and in our own land, what might they be?

Reflection Questions:

- How well do I know myself?
- How well do I know my "era" and surroundings?

Saturday, December 11, (#186) Second Week of Advent

Note: Today you may wish to begin the First Day of the Novena to Our Lady of La Salette, in the appendix of this book.

Matthew 17:9a,10-13: *"Then the disciples understood..."*

Meditation:

A number of realizations come to us thanks to the gift of God's word: the realization that we have been chosen by God; the realization that God first loved us into being; the realization that Jesus is the Son of God; the realization that he came into the world for the specific purpose of having us share his life. This realization opens up before the believer a whole new approach to life. "I had no idea. I didn't realize." Such words are among the saddest words in any language. As the late Anthony De Mello, in his book entitled, Awakening, wished people to acknowledge: most of us are asleep. We are sleepwalkers on a grand scale! We get up, we go to work, we get married, we raise a family, we read the newspaper, we go to church, we hear the word of God proclaimed. We are up and around. But how alert and awake are we? Advent issues a major wake-up call each year. It challenges us to arouse our awareness, to wake up to the true gift of life, the gift of the Kingdom in our midst, the ongoing gift of Christmas.

THE LA SALETTE APPARITION TOOK PLACE IN 1846, ON SEPTEMBER 19TH. "I am here," she matter-of-factly announces. A timeless presence. "I am here to tell you great news." A timeless call to heed a timely message. The Word incarnate is in our midst, the new Adam of a new human race. He has come to restore God's good creation to its original state. He has come to refurbish God's image in our hearts. "If the harvest is ruined it is only on account of yourselves," Mary tells us. She would have us realize that the fruits the earth bears are intimately linked with the fruits the human heart bears. She would make us aware that earth and fields, crops and harvests are submissive to hearts submissive to the Creator of all.

Reflection Questions:

- Are you fully aware of the ongoing grace of your baptism?
- How fruitful is your faith in good words and deeds?

Sunday, December 12, (#009)
Third Sunday of Advent

(Zephaniah 3:14-18; Philippians 4:4-7; Luke 3:10-18)

Meditation: *Unafraid*

In some respects, the most important words spoken by the Beautiful Lady of La Salette were the first: *"Come closer, children, don't be afraid."* Without these, the rest of her message would never have been heard.

We love such assurances, because we need them. They abound in today's Scriptures. Zephaniah: "Fear not... be not discouraged." St. Paul: "Have no anxiety at all." And our responsorial psalm, which is not from the Book of Psalms but from Isaiah 12: "I am confident and unafraid."

In the Gospel John the Baptist encourages his listeners to be generous in sharing, to avoid greed, to be honest, to be satisfied with what they have. These are excellent ways to reduce stress and anxiety in life.

But then comes the shock. The Baptist adopts a more ominous tone

The Sermon of St. John the Baptist by
Bernardo Strozzi (1581–1644)

in preaching about the one who is to come after him. "His winnowing fan is in his hand to clear his threshing floor and to gather the wheat into his barn, but the chaff he will burn with unquenchable fire."

Luke then concludes, "Exhorting them in many other ways, he [John] preached good news to the people." The Good News is not always pleasant news.

Any public speaker knows that you need to find diverse ways to reach people. The more diverse the audience—adults, teens and children, various cultures or levels of education, etc.—the more difficult that task is. There needs to be something for everyone.

The Blessed Virgin understood this. First she had to establish that she is on our side (*"Don't be afraid... How long a time I have suffered for you..."*), and then she was free to say other things her people needed to hear. Some would respond more to her warnings, others to her promises, others again to her tears, or her concern for their well-being.

We often point out that Mary's *"great news"* is like the "Good News," not only in its content but even its style. Both can be demanding, even harsh to certain ears. Both confront us with choices.

None of this means we need to live in fear. Whether the call comes to us from the Scriptures or from La Salette, we can be confident and unafraid.

Monday, December 13, (#187)
Third Week of Advent

Matthew 21.23-27: *"What authority have you?"*

356

Meditation:

Hearing this hostile question should come as no surprise. For at one time or other we ourselves probably asked it of people who were offering us guidance or support; that is, parents or teachers. It probably came from anger, rebellion or from lack of self-esteem. But upon reflection, we usually can come to the realization that it is not a valid question. Rather we find ourselves coping with a totally different issue – we simply don't agree or don't want to be told. Jesus, understood that the chief priests and elders had a totally different agenda. So he refused to get involved in this no-win situation. When such challenges are offered to us, we are given an opportunity to deepen our own convictions. Will we allow ourselves to justify our positions or simply go on proclaiming them from the heart? And thus allow that to be the authority!

AT LA SALETTE THE TWO VISIONARIES were faced with the same question. "By what authority are you recounting this story?" asked the police investigators. The children simply responded: "Mary's words to us were, 'Make this known to all my people.'" That was the children's authority. They didn't need to be crafty; they just needed to be honest and fulfill Mary's wishes.

Reflection Questions:

•Do you feel mandated to proclaim or witness in Jesus' name?
•If you challenge someone's authority, are you clear about your motivation?

Tuesday, December 14, (#188)
Third Week of Advent

Matthew 21:28-32: *"What do you think of this case?"*

Meditation:

In today's gospel Jesus continues with this parable to pursue the issue of sincerity and authority. Who does better, the one who agrees to do so but does not act, or the one who protests but after reflection comes around? When do most of us churchgoers fit into this scheme of things? Do we too quickly commit ourselves? Upon realizing the cost do we simply procrastinate, hoping it will all go away? Or do we hesitate, and wrestle with the pros and cons before committing ourselves? Jesus is likely to be more impressed with us if we don't rush in. Commitment was such an essential element in his life that he treasured - follow through.

AT LA SALETTE the two visionaries stayed committed to all they had seen and all they had heard. Conviction was the key element which allowed them to resist bribes and even threats. In no way were they to be coerced into negating the events that took place on the mountainside.

Reflection Questions:

- What does it take to convince me?
- At what cost am I willing to remain committed?

Wednesday, December 15, (#189)
Third Week of Advent

Luke 7:18b-23: *"John, summoning two of his disciples, sent them to the Lord to ask, 'Are you the one who is to come, or are we to expect someone else?'"*

Meditation:

Delivered by his disciples, John's question to Jesus reflects different possible expectations of Jesus' mission. Is John doubting who Jesus really is? Is John disappointed because Jesus is not turning out to be the kind of Messiah he had been expecting; that is, not enough of a freeing reformer? Or is John totally unaware of the healings, the liberation, the return to life, the restoration of sight to the blind, the cure of the lame, the cleansing of lepers? Jesus in Luke 4:17-23 had clearly stated what his mission was to be. In fact, he was rejected for it by his own townspeople.

Do our expectations at times do us in? We tend to narrow or to exaggerate what we think should be. People missioned around us have no choice but to measure up to it. Unfortunately, we can totally miss out on the witness the Lord is asking of them. Jesus reminds John, or is it a slight reprimand, that his zeal has blinded him to the Kingdom that is already blossoming before him! We need to change our premises:

It's the Lord's call. It's his mission. Let's always allow ourselves the space to be surprised!

AT LA SALETTE THE VISIONARIES must have been taken aback at the various hostile reactions to Mary's apparition. Why wouldn't people rejoice? On the contrary many were disturbed because the event could raise havoc with their plan to secularize society. So they never wanted to hear about the healings, about the radios' changes in the hearts of people who came to the Holy Mountain. They wanted to control the situation by wishing it away, by ridiculing it or even by threatening those who believed.

Reflection Questions:

• How many situations have I refused to see and hear about simply because they did not measure up to my expectations?
• Do I allow myself the gift of being surprised?

Thursday, December 16, (#190) Third Week of Advent

Luke 7:24-30: *"Prepare the way of the Lord."*

Meditation:

The call to dream dreams is the call of all Christians. Because we dream of being with Jesus in eternity, we embark daily on the project of living the day fully. Faith carries us into a future of dreams to be fulfilled. We all have in our personal stories of actions that helped us sacrifice for fhb sake of our tomorrows. We plant trees at times knowing full well we will never see them bearing fruit. We make decisions that can assure our children better lives even though we will not personally witness the wisdom of these choices. To be forerunner, to be prophet, to be messenger is a vocation we are called to embrace. It calls us to trust Jesus as Script-writer, it reinforces our mission to "prepare the way of the Lord" not only in our personal lives but also in the lives of others.

The children of La Salette possibly never imagined what their mission would one day produce. They only knew in their hearts that they were called to prepare the way of the Lord. From that conviction no one was to deter them. Mary's parting words: "Make this known to all my people" were deeply embedded in their young hearts!!

Reflection Questions:

- How do I do as a sower?
- Do I easily trust Jesus as Script-writer?

Friday, December 17, (#193)
Third Week of Advent

Matthew 1:1-17: *The family record of Jesus Christ*

Meditation:

Because it is as important as it is off-putting, the late Scripture scholar, Father Raymond E. Brown, conducted a somewhat solitary campaign to make today's gospel passage a major Advent topic. If we were asked to tell the basic story of Christ to someone who knows nothing about Christianity, where would we begin? Surely not where St. Matthew does. His listing of Jesus' ancestors contains some of Israel's most prominent names, those of patriarchs and kings; it also includes a number of unknown and unexpected entries. It teaches that God did not hesitate to enlist schemers as well as noble folks, outsiders as well as insiders, the lowly as well as the mighty. The first fruit of the Incarnation is that we should be God's children, that Christ should be born in us. The all-inclusive lineage of Jesus assures us that God can bring Him to birth in our hearts, their waning good and evil impulses notwithstanding.

THOUGH SHE REPROVES OUR INDIFFERENCE and our straying, Mary at La Salette nonetheless addresses us in our essential dignity as a holy nation, a people of God's own choosing, though a people of saints and sinners. *"If my people are converted,"* she promises, *"rocks and stones will be changed into mounds of wheat"* Her words bring to mind the picture Jesus painted in the parable of God's field: wheat and stones ... side by side.

Reflection Questions:

- How literally do I take the statement that Christ is to be born in me?
- What might that mean in practical terms?

Saturday, December 18, (#194)
Third Week of Advent

Matthew 1:18-24: *"Look! the virgin is with child and will give birth to a son whom they will call Immanuel, a name which means 'God-is-with-us.'"*

Meditation:

The name Jesus means "God is with us". A holy name, it expresses God's saving intention ever-present and at work in the world. It describes the mission and the ministry of Jesus: to set people free from the bondage of sin and fear. This great redemptive act, reflected in Jesus' name, is what the Advent season is preparing us for: the birth in our midst of the One who saves.

LITTLE WONDER THAT MARY SHOWS SUCH CONCERN at La Salette for the name of her Son. She deplores our taking the Lord's name in vain, because such irreverence both demeans and dismisses the very purpose of God. The name Jesus sums up all God's loving overtures to humanity; it tells us repeatedly that God desires to relate intimately with each one of us. What is at stake here is nothing less than acceptance of God's gift of salvation in Jesus. Nothing less than intimate friendship with Jesus.

Reflection Questions:
- "What's in a name?" when that name is Jesus?
- What does a careless, unthinking use of his name say about my relationship to Jesus?

Sunday, December 19, (#012)
Fourth Sunday of Advent

(Micah 5:1-4; Hebrews 10:5-10; Luke 1:39-45)

Meditation: *Visit*

Mary had received great news, two things. First that she was to be the mother of the Messiah. Second, that Elizabeth, an elderly relative, was six months pregnant! Her response was to go, indeed, to hurry to Elizabeth's home to help her. She who had called herself the handmaid of the Lord, eager to do his will, placed herself also at the service of her kinswoman.

When Mary arrived, her greeting was great news to Elizabeth's ears, literally a revelation, as she suddenly understood Mary's place in God's plan and called her "mother of my Lord."

At the birth of Elizabeth's son John, his father Zechariah rejoices that God has "visited" his people, a typically poetic biblical expression to say that God has intervened in his people's life and history.

Angels visited shepherds with "good news of great joy," the shepherds visited the Holy Family in the stable, later the Magi, guided by Micah's prophecy, also found him.

The Visitation
by James Tissot (1836–1902)

Through missionaries especially, the Church "visits" many peoples, bringing the great news that we call the Good News of Jesus Christ.

Our Lady of La Salette is often called a "heavenly Visitor." She "visited her people," bringing what she called "great news." The news was not just for the two children to whom she appeared, since she told them—twice—to make this known to all her people.

The children did indeed make it known. Then, in 1852, just six years after the Apparition, the Bishop of Grenoble founded the Missionaries of Our Lady of La Salette for the same purpose, and in 1855 his successor stated clearly that the Church had taken up the mission originally entrusted to the children.

"The Church" means both the Bishops who have the first responsibility to see that the authentic Good News is passed on from one generation to the next, and the Christian faithful who share how both the Gospel and, in the case of the Beautiful Lady, the great news of La Salette, have touched their lives with peace.

Micah says of the Messiah: "He shall be peace." Our world sorely needs that Visitor still.

Monday, December 20, (#196)
Fourth Week of Advent

Luke 1:26-38: *"Mary said to the angel, 'But how can this come about...?'"*

Meditation:

In announcing his marvels to us and in eliciting our misting response, God seems to place major emphasis on the "what" and always skim over the "how". Though she might have kept a prudent silence, Mary responded to the news that the angel had brought with the words, "How can this be?" She does not doubt the event, but wonders how it shall come about. She is not asking whether it will happen, whether God can make it happen, but how. Her faith and her question are not at odds. Informed by the angel's evocative yet very mysterious reply, she acquiesces freely and fully.

NOT SURPRISINGLY, AT LA SALETTE MARY PUTS QUESTIONS to Melanie and Maximin: "Do you say your prayers well, my children?... Have you never seen wheat gone bad?" In each instance a faith dialogue is opened. Questions and answers give shape to a conversation that plumbs unseen depths, the depths of God and those of the believer. Questions and answers underscore the need to communicate with God in regular moments of prayer, the value of viewing the happenings of our everyday life and the events of history in the light of faith.

Some Reflection Questions:

- What feelings come over you when you struggle with the "hows" of God's action in your life?
- What in the message of Our Lady at La Salette is best suited to your own day?

Tuesday, December 21, (#197)
Fourth Week of Advent

Luke 1:39-45: *"Mary set out at that time and went as quickly as she could into the hill country to a town in Judah. She went into Zechariah's house and greeted Elizabeth."*

Meditation:

Mary had just heard the incredible news of her own pregnancy yet her first thoughts are for her elderly kinswoman Elizabeth, now with child as well, It is this remarkable ability to focus first on the needs of others rather than her own that Mary will pass on to her child. Learning from the self-forgetfulness of his mother, Jesus, who first surrendered his divinity in order to share in our humanity, will learn to pour out his very life in opening the gift of life and sharing it with all.

MARY'S CARING FOR OTHERS IS EVIDENT at La Salette, as she shares with us there a twofold concern: God's grief at the sight of human sinfulness and humanity's sinful squandering of opportunity. Prayer gives roots to faith. Faith blossoms into love. Love in turn bears fruit in selfless service. Mary's journey to the Judean hill country and her coming to the mountains of southeastern France offer striking examples of timely assistance. Errands of mercy in time of need.

Reflection Questions:

- How deeply convinced am I that as a Christian I am to love, not in word, but in deed?
- How will I put my love for God in action today?

Wednesday, December 22, (#198)
Fourth Week of Advent

Luke 1:46-56: *"(God's) faithful love extends age after age."*

Meditation:

The Dominican theologian, Edward Schillebeeckx, has aptly called Our Lady's canticle "A Toast to God." The core of her *Magnificat* contrasts the drastically different fates of the humble, the lowly, the hungry and the haughty, the proud, the rich. It is, essentially, a hymn of praise for the liberation a God ever mindful of his mercy is bringing about. On the doorstep of her kinswoman's house, his Mother proclaims her unborn Child to be the absolute and definitive manifestation of God's ageless mercy. Because human history can be rather resistant to God's loving purpose, believers in Christ never cease to proclaim that "God's mercy is from age to age."

MARY'S VISIT TO LA SALETTE should be seen as part of that ongoing outpouring of mercy. We need not be content with the ripples radiating from events in the remote past. The Advent of God's mercy takes place in our own time. New life and moral rebirth are gifts being offered to us today as surely as they were being offered to their world through Elizabeth and Mary.

Reflection Questions:

• What are some of the signs of God's mercy in my life?
• What new insight into the La Salette apparition and its relevance for these times have I gained?

Thursday, December 23, (#199)
Fourth Week of Advent

Luke 1:57-66: *"All their neighbors were filled with awe and the whole affair was talked about throughout the hill country of Judaea."*

Meditation:

Events of special significance we tend to tell and retell. In each retelling, different details are highlighted and take on new significance. Such repeated telling breathes fresh life into these happenings and can bring to light insights and meanings that may have previously gone unnoticed. The birth and naming of John the Baptizer, prelude to those of Jesus himself, were such events in that hill country neighborhood. Generations of Christians have tirelessly told and retold the circumstances surrounding these mysteries, pondered them in their hearts and claimed their spiritual fruitfulness.

NEWS OF WHAT MAXIMIN AND MELANIE saw and heard that memorable day in September of 1846 spread rapidly through mountain villages and was greeted with utter amazement. People who had felt abandoned learned that they were anything but forsaken by the God whose "mercy is from age to age" Their difficulties were part of the larger problems the world was grappling with at the dawn of the industrial age. These difficulties, however, were not going unnoticed by heaven. Early reflection on Mary's message made it clear that it restates the gospel challenge to discern the signs of the times, signs of this particular time and particular day.

Reflection Questions:

- How do you make sense of what takes place in the world around you?
- Where do you seek God's concrete will for the times we are now living?

Friday, December 24, (#200) Fourth Week of Advent

Luke 1:67-79: "... because of the faithful love of our God ... the rising Sun has come from on high to visit us."

Meditation:

On the threshold of the Nativity, we hear a closing Advent hymn of praise that the promises God made to Abraham and to David will soon come true. We meditate today on a poetic prelude to the dawning of our Dayspring. The One whose coming we await once more will enflesh "the bowels of God's compassion." Jesus comes to make known the inmost depths of God, to translate the mystery of God into terms we can grasp, into a reality that will grasp us. God's love for us in Christ is not a cool, detached Platonic benevolence but manifests itself as a visceral love, a love felt in the pit of the stomach, a lump in the throat, a welling up of tears.

THE MOTHER OF JESUS REMINDS US at La Salette that, if she knew the unspeakable joy of giving this world its Hope and Light, she also experienced an unspeakable depth of pain and sorrow. On the day of her apparition, two innocent cowherds witnessed an astonishing anguish, an anguish only an overflow of maternal tears could convey, an anguish they surely could not fathom.

Reflection Questions:

• "The hopes and fears of all the years" will meet in Bethlehem this night. Do I have a dream for our entire world?

• This Christmas Eve, do I dare bid the "heart-felt kindness of God" make its home in my heart?

Saturday, December 25 (#015_01)
The Nativity of the Lord

Luke 2: 15-20 (Mass at dawn): *"And the shepherds went back glorifying and praising God for all they had heard and seen, just as they had been told."*

The *Nativity* painting by Lorenzo Lotto (1480-1556)

Silent night, holy night! It was approaching midnight on Christmas eve, 1870. The Franco-Prussian war was raging. On a battlefield in France that evening, one young Frenchman suddenly decided to stand up in his trench. As the sounds of battle raged around him, his sonorous voice could be heard, singing a Christmas carol in French – *O Holy Night*. As his clear voice pierced the din, the noise surprisingly lessened and lessened, until all that could be heard was the sound of his melodic young voice wafting across the trenches for all to hear.

No sooner had he concluded his song when a young German soldier then stood up and began the Christmas carol, *Silent Night*, in his own native German. All paused, all listened. The night was truly "silent and holy." All were being treated to the soothing Christmas songs of the two young strangers, so-called enemies. All was silent through the night until dawn, when the battle raged once more. But none who were there would ever really be the same! Silent night, holy night!

On the Feast of the Nativity we celebrate the fact of Jesus' birth, when he was first introduced to his people, the unsuspecting shepherds, accompanied by the message of the angel: *"Do not be afraid. Look, I bring you news of great joy, a joy to be shared by the whole people."*

SIMILARLY, MARY CAME TO A REMOTE MOUNTAINTOP near the hamlet of La Salette on Saturday, September 19, to speak to the two unschooled children, Maximin and Melanie - her people. Her first words were similar to that of the angel on that first Christmas: "Come closer, my children; don't be afraid. I am here to tell you great news." Her message touched the hearts of these simple children; their fear dissolved and they drew closer to listen to the Beautiful Lady.

As we know, hers was a special message of love and mercy, an invitation to conversion and reconciliation. On this marvelous Christmas Day, let us join in singing those moving hymns, *Silent Night* and *O Holy Night*, reminding us that we are loved, we are family and that we need to "Come closer" to Jesus, Mary's Son with the hope and joy that only God can give.

Reflection Questions:

- When you sing Christmas carols, what comes to mind from your past Christmases?
- What has been the best gift you have received from anyone?

Sunday, December 26, (#017C)
The Holy Family

(1 Samuel 1:20-28; 1 John 3:1-2, 21-24; Luke 2:41-52)

Meditation: *La Salette Family*

Hannah had made a deal with the Lord. If he gave her a son, she would give her son back to the Lord. And so she did. He would minister in the Lord's house. In becoming a member of Eli's household, he entered what we might call the Temple family.

In the Scriptures, house and family and similar words are often used and translated interchangeably. Today I would like to reflect on the La Salette family.

Unlike natural human families, we have not grown up together. On the contrary, we live in different worlds: country, language, culture. There are many things that divide us. What unites us, however, first and foremost, is our love for a Beautiful Lady. We take her words to heart, we try to live by them, we do our part to make them known.

Jesus in the temple, talking with the doctors taken from The story of the Bible from Genesis to Revelation

Then there is a 'La Salette culture,' which is filtered through our local cultures. For many, it is summed up as Reconciliation; for others, the Weeping Mother, or the invitation to 'come closer,' or the challenge to recompense the pains she has taken for us.

Everywhere events, political and otherwise, raise concerns that touch the La Salette heart. For example, who of us can fail to be aware of famine and the death of children, of which Mary spoke, and which is still a reality in many parts of the world. Such things evoke a La

Salette response in us, tears first, perhaps, but also a desire to reach out to those who suffer.

Here we can read again the words of St. John: "We should believe in the name of God's Son, Jesus Christ, and love one another just as he commanded us." Mary at La Salette leads us to a renewed faith, which in turn, especially through the sacraments, nourishes our love of neighbor.

At the end of the Gospel, we are told that Mary "kept all these things in her heart." Her coming to La Salette was, precisely, a matter of the heart. Without love, her presence and her message make no sense.

The boy Jesus said, "I must be in my Father's house." Members of the La Salette Family who go to the Holy Mountain for the first time, often have the experience of being home. Why not? After all, they are in their Mother's house.

Monday, December 27, (#697)
St. John, Apostle and Evangelist

John 20:1a,2-8: *"He saw and he believed."*

Meditation:

This was not a simple case of "seeing is believing." Rather, St. John saw only an empty tomb that day. The absence of the Lord's body could have meant that "they have taken the Lord and we don't know where they have laid him." Presented with the facts, however, John made a choice. He chose the option that Jesus had arisen as he said. This brings the gift of faith into perspective.

What we do with faith and the knowledge it brings to us is a matter of choosing one option over another. The virtue of faith makes it possible for us to trust in the Lord's word and to choose the options which correspond to the truth of that word. Some schools of thought which influence us tend to equate observation with proof. Sadly, however, the meaning of the proof is often predetermined. Thus, some would always tend to deny the things we cannot see. Faith makes it possible for us to see the things we Christians must not deny.

THE MOCKING OF RELIGION WHICH OUR LADY SPOKE ABOUT does not necessarily mean a blatant lack of religion, though it often is. Failure to honor and worship God as we should is characterized by callousness toward the saints and the things which are especially consecrated to God. It can also be marked by insensitivity toward another's piety and devotion. The presence of Our Lady inclined the children toward deeper faith.

Some Reflection Questions:

- Have you attempted to help others grow in faith in legitimate ways?
- Or have you taunted them by mocking their faith at times?

Tuesday, December 28, (#698) Holy Innocents,

Matthew 2:13-18: *"Then were fulfilled the words spoken through the prophet Jeremiah: A voice is heard in Ramah, lamenting and weeping bitterly: it is Rachel weeping for her children, refusing to be comforted because they are no more."*

Meditation:

Innocent children were put to death by Herod so that he might not have to face a rival to his kingship. All the male children two years and under were killed with the intent of eliminating Jesus. These children became victims to the totalitarian exercise of power which places the State before the inherent dignity of the person. They had no defense. Today, the failure to respect innocent life, the crimes of abortion and euthanasia, are the results of policies and attitudes which over time place the "cult of having" above the basic rights of persons.

OUR LADY'S PREDICTION that children would be seized with trembling and die in the arms of those who hold them, stands as a warning of the consequences of sin. The weakest always suffer most. Our Lady calls even the most hard-hearted to repentance with her tears. The voice of the Beautiful Lady of La Salette is heard, she is weeping for all her children.

Reflection Questions:

- Who has the power of Herod today in our society?
- Have I acted responsibly in fulfilling my civic duties in order to create a more just society where all Mary's children, human embryos, the unborn, the disabled, the elderly, and the dying will he protected from the violence which would deprive them of the fundamental right to life?

Wednesday, December 29, (#202)
Fifth Day Within the Octave of Christmas

Luke 2:22-35: *"My eyes have seen your salvation, which you have made ready in the sight of the peoples."*

Meditation:

When Simeon took Jesus in his arms and blessed God, he proclaimed the universal scope of Jesus' saving work. He came that all may have life and have it to the fullest. Yet, the message must still be proclaimed in every corner of the world, and effectively in every aspect of culture from the arts to the realm of technology. Each Christian has a role to play in the evangelization of culture, in his or her circle of friends, work, and entertainment. No place or culture, no aspect of human existence is to be ignored in the proclamation of the Good News of salvation in Christ.

OUR LADY'S MARCHING ORDERS could not be clearer: *"Make this known to all my people."* We have seen the salvation that the Lord has prepared. We have heard the message of La Salette which speaks to us of God's great mercy. What was first proclaimed to the children as a way to avoid human tragedy still stands as a model for action. *"If they are converted,"* she indicates, justice will be restored. But justice, in order to reach its perfection, begins and ends as the work of God, who first justifies us and then perfects us by his love. A call to the heart for conversion opens up the way for the saving grace of God. "I come to bring you great news."

Reflection Questions:

- Do I believe that the merciful apparition at La Salette has the power of the gospel to transform the world and so help bring light to all peoples?

•Have I helped the sinful to repent by announcing to them the great mercy of God with the enthusiasm and love of Mary?

Thursday, December 30, (#203)
Sixth Day Within the Octave of Christmas

Luke 2:36-40: *"(Anna, the prophetess) never left the Temple, serving God night and day with fasting and prayer."*

Meditation:

The sacred authors present to us the reality of sin's threefold structure – the lust of the flesh, the lust of the eyes, and the pride of life (I John 2:16). In his temptation in the desert, Jesus overcame this structure of sin which ruled the world from the time of Adam and Eve. He showed us the means of overcoming sin in our own lives by the traditional practices of prayer, fasting and almsgiving. It was just this kind of devotion that made Anna's heart burn with love for Jesus.

AT LA SALETTE OUR LADY EXPRESSES her many concerns about worship, the proper use of food in the season of Lent, and prayer. In so doing she recalls the example that Jesus has already established for us in overcoming temptation. Freedom from sin is nurtured by the proper discipline of mind, the body, and the senses, by talking with God and the saints, and by the works of mercy. Such things set our hearts free, like Mary's and Anna's, to grow in love for Jesus and for all those for whom he gave his life.

Reflection Questions:

•Are prayer, fasting and almsgiving in imitation of Jesus regular practices in my life?
•How can I further develop these practices in order that I may rejoice over the work of the Messiah?

Friday, December 31, (#204)
Seventh Day Within the Octave of Christmas

John 1:1-18: *"... from his fullness we have, all of us, received – one gift replacing another."*

Meditation:

There are two principles that God provides us with as means to goodness. One is the law and the other is grace. John tells us that grace and truth came through Jesus Christ. The New Law of the Gospel has as its primary element the grace of the Holy Spirit. In baptism, we receive this grace which recreates us to new life, joining each of us individually to the Risen Jesus. This is the gift that keeps on giving. For throughout our lives the Holy Spirit perfects our spiritual capacities with his gifts, purifying and elevating all of our dispositions, leading us on to greater goodness.

Our Lady helps us to understand, however, that these gifts may be rejected. As she indicates, we can refuse these graces and reject – even the grace of salvation itself. The submission of which she speaks has as its most fundamental characteristic the humility required to receive the grace and gifts of the Holy Spirit by acknowledging our need of them. Conversion follows. Prayer, the Sacraments, the Scriptures, and the Magisterium of the Church all assist us in our spiritual and moral growth. A sincere appreciation of these elements of the Evangelical Law of Christ enhances the life of grace. Saying, *"If they are converted,"* Our Lady promises a consequent abundance of food. This material abundance becomes the sign of the spiritual bounty, grace in place of grace, available to each believer.

Reflection Questions:

- In what ways does my daily living reflect thankfulness and praise for the gift of new life which I received through the Holy Spirit?
- Are there signs of the spiritual bounty which I have been promised? For what special blessings in your life should you give thanks to God?

Appendix:

La Salette Novena for the 175th Anniversary
of the La Salette Apparition (1846-2021)
Province of Mary, Mother of the Americas

MARY, WAY OF PEACE AND HOPE FOR ALL CULTURES

175 years of Mercy

1846 2021

First Day: The Holy Mountain

Scripture says: "[Jesus] made the disciples get into the boat and go on ahead to the other side while he sent the crowds away. After sending the crowds away he went up into the hills by himself to pray. When evening came, he was there alone" (Matthew 14:22-23).

Reflection: Behind the slope of this Holy Mountain, isolated from the outside world below, the site of the Apparition reminds us of the special encounter between the Beautiful Lady and the two unsuspecting children, Maximin and Melanie.

The Dialogue:

In our imagination, as we sit on the rock overlooking this ravine, we ask the Beautiful Lady why she has chosen this place – so isolated from the world below.

And Mary says: "The world has become accustomed to our busy cities and noisy streets, to a certain spirit of restlessness. The working day has become all-important and everything else seems to fade from view. In my visit so long ago in this very place, I wanted to speak to my people, expressing the desire and hope of my Son for these some-times-lost souls. I have chosen this timeless mountain vantage-point to remind my people that they are called by their baptism to love God more than anything else in this passing world. I spoke of the importance of prayer and the Eucharist and the advantage of the habits of faith to nourish and strengthen their life.

"As we sit together on this mountaintop, my hope is that you receive a renewed perspective on your daily life. I pray unceasingly that, through the grace and example of my Son, you may appreciate your ongoing need to 'come to the mountain and pray'. And hopefully you can return to your daily life renewed by a clearer vision and a stronger determination to follow the ways and message of my loving Son."

Our Response:

Our Anniversary prayer:

Mary, Mother of Reconciliation, in this time of celebration we rejoice that: *The Father* asked you to carry out his plan of salvation; *The Son* chose you to be his Mother and his First Disciple; *The Holy Spirit* fashioned you into his living temple, our sister in faith.

At La Salette, with abundant tears of mercy, you spoke to the two poor children in their own language and urged us to share your message of peace and hope with needy people of every culture and nation. Pray for us to your loving Son that we may draw all your people closer to him. Amen.

[Mention intention]

Pray: *the Lord's Prayer and the Hail Mary.*

Invocation: Our Lady of La Salette, Reconciler of sinners,
pray without ceasing for us who have recourse to you.

Reflection Questions for today:

• What is a peak-experience in your life where you were touched by the grace of God?
• What is very important in your daily life and what has eventually become less important?

Second Day: The Unsuspecting Shepherds

Scripture: "I am the good shepherd: the good shepherd lays down his life for his sheep... And there are other sheep I have that are not of this fold, and I must lead these too. They too will listen to my voice, and there will be only one flock, one shepherd" (John 10:11,16).

Reflection: Melanie had been tending the cows for more than six months on the mountainside near La Salette. On Monday, the 14th of September 1846, Pierre Selme, the farmer, went down to Corps. He wanted to ask Mr. Giraud if Maximin could take the place of his hired man who was sick.

The Dialogue:

In our imagination, we ask the Beautiful Lady: "Why do you often speak to shepherds when you visit your people?"

And Mary says: "Those who watch over herds of animals learn to become attentive, to have patience and to become skilled in the ways of the creatures that they guard. Everyone needs time to reflect in silence. Without some quiet time, there is a danger of losing yourself in a multitude of projects, interests and wants. I would like everyone to take the time to reflect and find peace in solitude.

"Time and time again, people who come here soon discover that they are lost, like the sheep mentioned in the gospels. My Son follows them into the wilderness of their lives, into the thorns and thistles of their difficulties and challenges. He finds them, frees them and then holds them close to himself. As reconcilers, you are to be my Son's

377

hands and feet in search of the lost and forsaken. But first, you yourself must be reconciled."

Our Response:

Our Anniversary prayer:

Mary, Mother of Reconciliation, in this time of celebration we rejoice that: The Father asked you to carry out his plan of salvation; The Son chose you to be his Mother and his First Disciple; The Holy Spirit fashioned you into his living temple, our sister in faith.

At La Salette, with abundant tears of mercy, you spoke to the two poor children in their own language and urged us to share your message of peace and hope with needy people of every culture and nation. Pray for us to your loving Son that we may draw all your people closer to him. Amen.

[Mention intention]

Pray: *the Lord's Prayer and the Hail Mary.*

Invocation: Our Lady of La Salette, Reconciler of sinners, pray without ceasing for us who have recourse to you.

Reflection Questions for today:

• When have you found yourself lost and someone else lifted you up?
• When have you "shepherded" other people, helping them in their need?

Third Day: The Fire of God's Love

Scripture: "Moses was looking after the flock of his father-in-law Jethro... [and...] he came to Horeb, the mountain of God... The angel of [the Lord] appeared to him in a flame blazing from the middle of a bush. Moses looked; there was the bush blazing, but the bush was not being burnt up. Moses said, 'I must go across and see this strange sight, and why the bush is not being burnt up.' ...[The Lord] then said, 'I have indeed seen the misery of my people in Egypt. I have heard them crying for help... And I have come down to rescue them...'"

(Exodus 3:1-3,7-8a).

Reflection: The children's first impression at the time of the apparition was that a ball of fire that had fallen into the ravine. They were afraid until, out of this brilliant sphere, a figure appeared and spoke to them.

The Dialogue:

In our imagination, we ask the Beautiful Lady: "Why did you come, seated within this globe of fire that frightened the two children so much?"

And Mary says: "Fire has tremendous power. Scripture often speaks of it – from the burning bush to the tongues of fire at Pentecost. It is a symbol of passion but does not necessarily destroy anything, just as the fire did not consume the bush on Mount Horeb.

"Just before I went back to heaven, the two children noticed that the grass was gently swaying in the breeze, moving under my feet, unharmed. The world is imbued with the presence of God and lives in harmony with it. The fine Fire of God's love wishes to animate and give everyone a deep enthusiastic love for God. Allow yourself to be seized by the fire of God's love, so evident during my visit at La Salette. Share it unhesitatingly – in everything you do."

Our Response:

Our Anniversary prayer:

> **Mary, Mother of Reconciliation,** in this time of celebration we rejoice that: The Father asked you to carry out his plan of salvation; The Son chose you to be his Mother and his First Disciple; The Holy Spirit fashioned you into his living temple, our sister in faith.
>
> **At La Salette,** with abundant tears of mercy, you spoke to the two poor children in their own language and urged us to share your message of peace and hope with needy people of every culture and nation. Pray for us to your loving Son that we may draw all your people closer to him. Amen.

[Mention intention]

Pray: *the Lord's Prayer and the Hail Mary.*

Invocation: Our Lady of La Salette, Reconciler of sinners,
pray without ceasing for us who have recourse to you.

Reflection Questions for today:

- In what event in your life have you felt the intense fire of God's love?
- Who is a person whom you could describe as afire with God's love?

Fourth Day: The Two Young Children

Scripture: "People even brought babies to him, for him to touch them; but when the disciples saw this they scolded them. But Jesus called the children to him and said, 'Let the little children come to me, and do not stop them; for it is to such as these that the kingdom of God belongs. In truth I tell you, anyone who does not welcome the kingdom of God like a little child will never enter it'" (Luke 18:15-17).

Reflection: The Beautiful Lady at La Salette speaks to the children. These children, neglected by their families, are important to her. She addressed her words to us through these two children.

The Dialogue:

In our imagination, we ask the Beautiful Lady about the place of children in our life of faith.

And Mary says: "It is always the children who suffer in the conflicts of the world. They are most often killed or maimed in war, victims when their parents separate or argue. Have you forgotten what it means to be a child? My Son, Jesus, said that we are to 'accept the kingdom of God like a child.'

"It is important to recover the childlikeness of your earlier years. Just as my Son guided Maximin and Melanie in their trials as they were subjected to intense questioning and yet remained faithful to my message at La Salette, you also can be strengthened with the purity and simplicity of a child to face the demands and responsibilities of your adult faith-life to build my Son's kingdom on this earth. You will also be able to hear more easily what they are saying. In this way, you allow them to enter into our world and the world will change."

Our Response:

Our Anniversary prayer:

Mary, Mother of Reconciliation, in this time of celebration we rejoice that: The Father asked you to carry out his plan of salvation; The Son chose you to be his Mother and his First Disciple; The Holy Spirit fashioned you into his living temple, our sister in faith.

At La Salette, with abundant tears of mercy, you spoke to the two poor children in their own language and urged us to share your message of peace and hope with needy people of every culture and nation. Pray for us to your loving Son that we may draw all your people closer to him. **Amen.**

[Mention intention]

Pray: *the Lord's Prayer* and the *Hail Mary.*

Invocation: Our Lady of La Salette, Reconciler of sinners,

pray without ceasing for us who have recourse to you.

Reflection Questions for today:

- When have you been touched by the words or actions of a child?
- What habits strengthen your life of faith – a special way of praying, certain practices of a Liturgical season, certain ministry groups in your parish or shrine, etc.?

Fifth Day: Our Blessed Mother

Scripture: "Can a woman forget her baby at the breast, feel no pity for the child she has borne? Even if these were to forget, I shall not forget you" (Isaiah 49:15).

Reflection: At first, the two children at La Salette thought they had met a mother who ran away from her abusive children in order to cry alone in the solitude of the mountain.

The Dialogue:

In our imagination, we ask the Beautiful Lady: "What does it mean for us to have a mother and to be a mother?"

And Mary says: "Your own mother may have answered this question already. Children mean more to a mother than anything else in the world. A mother is the center of the family. She is the 'knot' that holds the threads of a fabric together. No matter where or who her children may be, she carries them in her heart.

"Mothers begin by giving life and then instinctively protecting the life to which they gave birth. At La Salette, I came in tears to remind you that I am often in anguish for your sometimes-poor response to the words and invitations of my Son. His loving examples of prayer, forgiving, healing and other good works are events to be appreciated and done by you in his Name.

"You lift your hearts in prayer to me as 'Reconciler of Sinners' and that is who I am. My Son's call to a lifelong ministry of reconciliation should be the center of your life as his disciple. Hopefully my compassionate words and actions at La Salette will also encourage you to do 'motherly' acts of kindness and generosity, mercy and love without counting the cost, just as I have done for you unceasingly."

Our Response:

Our Anniversary prayer:

Mary, Mother of Reconciliation, in this time of celebration we rejoice that: The Father asked you to carry out his plan of salvation; The Son chose you to be his Mother and his First Disciple; The Holy Spirit fashioned you into his living temple, our sister in faith.

At La Salette, with abundant tears of mercy, you spoke to the two poor children in their own language and urged us to share your message of peace and hope with needy people of every culture and nation. Pray for us to your loving Son that we may draw all your people closer to him. **Amen.**

[Mention intention]

Pray: *the Lord's Prayer* and the *Hail Mary*.

Invocation: Our Lady of La Salette, Reconciler of sinners,
pray without ceasing for us who have recourse to you.

Reflection Questions for today:

- What are the qualities in a mother (yours or another's) which attract you?
- When have you been called to take on "motherly duties" (as a life-giver, consoler, protector or forgiver)?

Sixth Day: The Power of Listening

Scripture: "Then [the LORD said], 'Go out and stand on the mountain before [the LORD].' For at that moment [the LORD] was going by. A mighty hurricane split the mountains and shattered the rocks before [the LORD]. But [the LORD] was not in the hurricane. And after the hurricane, an earthquake. But [the LORD] was not in the earthquake. And after the earthquake, fire. But [the LORD] was not in the fire. And after the fire, a light murmuring sound. And when Elijah heard this, he covered his face with his cloak and went out and stood at the entrance of the cave" (1 Kings 19:11-13a).

Reflection: When the children spoke about their meeting with the Beautiful Lady, they said: "We didn't think about anything, we simply were there, ... we were listening and absorbing her words as if it were music."

The Dialogue:

In our imagination, we asked the Beautiful Lady: "Did the two children respond well to your presence and listen attentively to your message?"

And Mary says: "Did you notice how the two children were 'simply there', drinking in my words? They were in tune with the prophetic words I was drawn to share. Some were severe words of warning, yet they were honest and direct. As your mother, I was speaking my message directly to the heart of the two children and to your heart as well.

"It was also important to me to respond to each child personally. When I realized that the two children were having difficulty understanding my initial words, I changed into the local patois for their sake. Also my questioning of Maximin concerning the event at the field of Coin was a gentle reminder of his father's deep fear of not being able to feed his family. This was a troubling expression from his anxious father and I ensured that Maximin appreciated his father's concern."

Our Response:

Our Anniversary prayer:

Mary, Mother of Reconciliation, in this time of celebration we rejoice that: The Father asked you to carry out his plan of salvation; The Son chose you to be his Mother and his First Disciple; The Holy Spirit fashioned you into his living temple, our sister in faith.

At La Salette, with abundant tears of mercy, you spoke to the two poor children in their own language and urged us to share your message of peace and hope with needy people of every culture and nation. Pray for us to your loving Son that we may draw all your people closer to him. **Amen.**

[Mention intention]

Pray: *the Lord's Prayer* and the *Hail Mary*.

Invocation: Our Lady of La Salette, Reconciler of sinners,
pray without ceasing for us who have recourse to you.

Reflection Questions for today:

• Who has listened well to you in your lifetime?
• Which people have gotten your full and rapt attention when they spoke to you?

Seventh Day: Her Heartfelt Words

Scripture: "After hearing Jesus' words about the bread from heaven, many of his followers said, 'This is intolerable language. How could anyone accept it?' Jesus was aware that his followers were complaining about it and said, 'Does this disturb you? What if you should see the Son of man ascend to where he was before? It is the spirit that gives life, the flesh has nothing to offer. The words I have spoken to you are spirit and they are life" (John 6:60-63).

Reflection: The children were so intent on the Beautiful Lady's words that they had the distinct impression that she spoke to them for a very long time.

The Dialogue:

In our imagination, we asked the Beautiful Lady: "What brought you to share your words in this remote place to these untutored children?"

And Mary says: "As I urged the two children to come closer, they did so without hesitation. They were a very attentive audience – open and receptive to me. They seemed to drink in my every word. In their presence, I could speak from the heart. I chose to begin with austere and foreboding predictions. The words came spontaneously.

"Words have a way of finding their own path when the heart is filled with pain and concern, with the need to admonish as well as to counsel. These may be words that sometimes disturb but they are also words that are full of promise and blessings. My message was one which could catch the attention of even the hardest heart. I do believe that they also heard my merciful and tender concern for all the parts of their lives, including the possible ruin of food staples such as potatoes, grapes and walnuts. These words of mine demanded a response – not only of the mind but also of the heart."

Our Response:

Our Anniversary prayer:

Mary, Mother of Reconciliation, in this time of celebration we rejoice that: The Father asked you to carry out his plan of salvation; The Son chose you to be his Mother and his First Disciple; The Holy Spirit fashioned you into his living temple, our sister in faith.

At La Salette, with abundant tears of mercy, you spoke to the two poor children in their own language and urged us to share your message of peace and hope with needy people of every culture and nation. Pray for us to your loving Son that we may draw all your people closer to him. **Amen.**

[Mention intention]

Pray: *the Lord's Prayer* and the *Hail Mary.*

Invocation: Our Lady of La Salette, Reconciler of sinners,
pray without ceasing for us who have recourse to you.

Reflection Questions for today:

- What topic of Mary's message at La Salette gets your attention?
- How does Mary express her direct concern for the children?

Eighth Day: Her Abundant Tears

Scripture: "As [Jesus] drew near and came in sight of the city [of Jerusalem] he shed tears over it and said, 'If you too had only recognized on this day the way to peace! But in fact it is hidden from your eyes!'" (Luke 19:41-42).

Reflection: "The Beautiful Lady cried all during the time she was speaking to us. I saw the tears running down her cheeks. They fell down... they fell down..." What was so remarkable about the tears is that they fell to the level of her feet and there, became pearls of light and just melted away.

The Dialogue:

In our imagination, we asked the Beautiful Lady: "Why did you allow yourself to shed these constant tears?"

And Mary says: "We as human beings need to weep in order to express our deep-seated feelings. It just may be that we are brought to tears when we are finally overcome by a powerful overflowing of our painful emotions. Just as my own Son wept over Jerusalem, so too I wept unceasingly for my wayward children on the Mountain of La Salette.

"Of course, sorrow and its tears can soften the hardest of hearts.

When I allow others to feel my concerns as my tears flow, I allow others to suffer with me. Maximin and Melanie instantly sensed my sincerity and were touched not only by my words but also by my abundant tears.

"In another sense, I brought two messages for the world: one in my words and another in my tears. In your daily life, be aware of others who are hurting and often brought to tears. They are sharing a precious part of themselves and you must respond promptly and lovingly."

Our Response:

Our Anniversary prayer:

Mary, Mother of Reconciliation, in this time of celebration we rejoice that: The Father asked you to carry out his plan of salvation; The Son chose you to be his Mother and his First Disciple; The Holy Spirit fashioned you into his living temple, our sister in faith.

At La Salette, with abundant tears of mercy, you spoke to the two poor children in their own language and urged us to share your message of peace and hope with needy people of every culture and nation. Pray for us to your loving Son that we may draw all your people closer to him. **Amen.**

[Mention intention]

Pray: *the Lord's Prayer* and the *Hail Mary*.

Invocation: Our Lady of La Salette, Reconciler of sinners,

   pray without ceasing for us who have recourse to you.

Reflection Questions for today:

• When have the tears of another affected you deeply?
• When was there a time when you expressed yourself through tears?

Ninth Day: Our Spring of Life

Scripture: "...no one who drinks the water that I shall give will ever be thirsty again: the water that I shall give will become a spring of water within, welling up for eternal life" (John 4:14).

Reflection: On the morning of Monday, September 21, 1846, Melanie discovered a spring of water at the spot where the Virgin appeared to them. Once there was another spring located there, named "Little Spring", but it had stopped flowing a long time ago.

The Dialogue:

In our imagination, we asked the Beautiful Lady the meaning of the abundant spring of water arising at her feet on the Holy Mountain of La Salette.

And Mary says: "Water can teach us much. Where water flows, it brings life. It gives itself to all who need it. Water is often good and generous. It knows how to moisten and give life to the ground. It is courageous – it flows around rocks that wish to block its flowing current. It is good-natured – its gentle force is at work, day and night, to eliminate all obstacles. It is persevering – all these qualities we should emulate.

"During my visit at La Salette, I used many symbols to remind my children about the basics of faith: light to emphasize the crucifix on my breast, the instrument of our salvation; chains to express the challenge of living a life of faith; roses to express the beauty and joy of following my Son; and finally the hammer and pincers on the crucifix, expressing the two choices we have in life – maintaining unforgiven sinful habits (nailing the nails in my Son's hands and feet) or maintaining a Christ-like life (mercifully removing the nails from my Son's hands and feet). All this we learn from the flowing spring and the other symbols of my visit to La Salette."

Our Response:

Our Anniversary prayer:

Mary, Mother of Reconciliation, in this time of celebration we rejoice that: The Father asked you to carry out his plan of salvation; The Son chose you to be his Mother and his First Disciple; The Holy Spirit fashioned you into his living temple, our sister in faith.

At La Salette, with abundant tears of mercy, you spoke to the two poor children in their own language and urged us to share your message of peace and hope with needy people of every culture and nation. Pray for us to your loving Son that we may draw all your people closer to him. **Amen.**

[Mention intention]

Pray: *the Lord's Prayer* and the *Hail Mary*.

Invocation: Our Lady of La Salette, Reconciler of sinners, pray without ceasing for us who have recourse to you.

Reflection Questions for today:

- In your life, what is a "spring" that has given you the strength to move on?
- What place that you have visited has given you a sense of beauty or peace?

Acknowledgements: The Swiss Province of the La Salette Missionaries originally wrote this Novena for the 150th Anniversary of the La Salette Apparition. This was recently edited and expanded for the 175th anniversary by Fr. Ron Gagne, M.S. Sources of these La Salette materials are available on: www.lasalette.org ... La Salette Library... La Salette Masses.

La Salette Prayers

Memorare to Our Lady of La Salette

Remember, Our Lady of La Salette, true Mother of Sorrows, the tears you shed for us on Calvary. Remember also the care you have taken to keep us faithful to Christ, your Son. Having done so much for your children, you will not now abandon us. Comforted by this consoling thought, we come to you pleading, despite our infidelities and ingratitude.

Virgin of Reconciliation, do not reject our prayers, but intercede for us, obtain for us the grace to love Jesus above all else. May we console you by a holy life and so come to share the eternal life Christ gained by his cross. Amen.

Dedication to Our Lady of La Salette

Most holy Mother, Our Lady of La Salette, who for love of me shed such bitter tears in your merciful apparition, look down with kindness upon me, as I consecrate myself to you without reserve. From this day, my glory shall be to know that I am your child. May I so live as to dry your tears and console your afflicted heart.

Beloved Mother, to you and to your blessed charge and sacred keeping and into the bosom of your mercy, for this day and for every day, and for the hour of my death I commend myself, body and soul, every hope and every joy, every trouble and every sorrow, my life and my life's end.

O dearest Mother, enlighten my understanding, direct my steps, console me by your maternal protection, so that exempt from all error, sheltered from every danger of sin, I may, with ardor and invincible courage, walk in the paths traced out for me by you and your Son. Amen.

La Salette Invocation

Our Lady of La Salette, reconciler of sinners,
pray without ceasing for us who have recourse to you.

Made in USA - North Chelmsford, MA
1211624_9781946956668
12.09.2020 1613